THE YEARS BETWEEN

1939-44

Cecil Beaton's Diaries
Volume Two

THE YEARS BETWEEN

1939-44

Published by Sapere Books.

20 Windermere Drive, Leeds, England, LS17 7UZ,
United Kingdom

saperebooks.com

ISBN: 978-1-912546-23-7

TO THE MEMORY OF REX WHISTLER

Foreword to the New Edition

I welcome the republication of the six volumes of Cecil Beaton's diaries, which so delighted readers between 1961 and 1978. I don't know if Cecil himself re-read every word of his manuscript diaries when selecting entries, but I suspect he probably did over a period of time. Some of the handwritten diaries were marked with the bits he wanted transcribed and when it came to the extracts about Greta Garbo, some of the pages were sellotaped closed. Even today, in the library of St John's College, Cambridge, some of the original diaries are closed from public examination, though to be honest, most of the contents are now out in the open.

The only other person who has read all the manuscript diaries is me. It took me a long time to get through them, partly because his handwriting was so hard to read. I found that if I read one book a day, I had not done enough. If I did two in a day, then I ended up with a splitting headache! This in no way deflected from the enormous enjoyment in reading them.

Altogether there are 145 original manuscript diaries dating from Cecil going up to Cambridge in 1922 until he suffered a serious stroke in 1974. A few fragments of an earlier Harrow diary survive, and there is a final volume between 1978 and 1980, written in his left hand. 56 of these cover his time at Cambridge, some of which appear in *The Wandering Years* (1961). 22 books cover the war years, and were used for *The Years Between* (1965), and nine books record his *My Fair Lady* experiences, some of which appear in *The Restless Years* (1976) and were the basis for *Cecil Beaton's Fair Lady* (1964). These six volumes probably represent about ten per cent of what Cecil Beaton actually wrote.

The diaries attracted a great deal of attention when first published. James Pope-Hennessy wrote of Cecil's 'thirst for self-revelation', adding that the unpublished volumes were surely 'the chronicle of our age'. Referring to Cecil's diaries, and those of Eddy Sackville-West, he also commented: 'We could not be hoisted to posterity on two spikier spikes.'

I have to tell the reader that these volumes were not always quite the same as the originals. Some extracts were rewritten with hindsight, some entries kaleidoscoped and so forth. Certain extracts in these six volumes were slightly retouched in places, in order that Cecil could present his world to the reader exactly as he wished it presented. And none the worse for that.

Hugo Vickers

January 2018

Part I: Ashcombe, 1939-40

September 1939, Ashcombe, Tollard Royal, Wiltshire

I feel frustrated and ashamed. This war, as far as I can see, is something specifically designed to show up my inadequacy in every possible capacity. I am too incompetent to enlist as a private in the army. It's doubtful if I'd be much good at camouflage — in any case my repeated requests to join have been met with, 'You'll be called if you're wanted.' What else can I do? I have tried all sorts of voluntary jobs in the neighbourhood, helping Edith Olivier organize food control, and the distribution of trainloads of refugee children from Whitechapel. I failed in a first aid examination after attending a course given by a humorous and kindly doctor in Salisbury. Now I start as night telephonist at the ARP centre in Wilton.

September 18th

Our squad is on duty from eleven at night until 8 a.m. On arrival at ugly, Victorian-Gothic, Fugglestone House, we study maps of the vicinity and check our individual tasks. But we all express the hope, for more reasons than one, that there will be no air raid tonight. We have been only rather vaguely briefed in our duties; at the sign of an alarm I am bound to get hopelessly entangled with all the various wires and plugs at the switchboard. Mr Lush, the Town Clerk, is here in case we need help, and Mr Keating, a retired civil servant, is our rather quavering lead. We are an odd assortment and I fear not of marked efficiency, all tweed clad, and country folk (except myself), with rugs, top boots and thermoses of cocoa and Bovril. There are two gentlemen farmers from nice grey stone houses in the neighbourhood, and a grey, hatchet-faced, older woman with a balloon-cheeked debutante daughter. Lady Pembroke, her face drained white, has come across from the big house in grey flannels and heavy overcoat, accompanied by Smith, the Pembroke butler, lobster-coloured, deep-voiced and with perhaps enough ballast to keep our whole group afloat. During the watch he sits quietly, imbibing a crackling pipe and blinking in front of him. When, at early dawn, the switchboard gives us a false alarm, Smith, although dozing at the time, is the first to be on the spot.

Grouped together in this room, reinforced against blast with stanchions of rough wood and sand-bags and curtained with the heaviest felt, we gradually settle down to read, the women to sew; each has a turn to be on a truckle bed for an hour's sleep. It is a boring, dispiriting job, and it is difficult to find volunteers to fill it. We are resigned to be together for the duration of the war; a pretty grim prospect.

I lie listening to the others talking. They have the friendly easy personalities that you find only in the countryside. Full of human sympathy, they have a stolid sense of the humorous. They know how to be serious too, and when discussing politics are not ashamed of a cliché.

After midnight the radio is silent, but for the whispering sounds it gives out, like those of a peat fire.

Another hour to go. As I sit on the window-sill watching the others staring at mental pictures of war deprivations, cold, and general cheerlessness, my esteem for them is very high. It hurts almost as much to muse upon pain as to endure it. These civilians are suffering the anticipation of wounds to those they love the most. How gallant they are! Yet in the early grey dawn how much older and greyer they appear. Even the pullet-like debutante has grown overnight to maturity, and Captain

Myddelton has become like an actor who, in the last act, puts on a grey wig and must appear thin in his clothes and walk with a stiff gait. Dear old Mr Keating, wrapped in a fishing coat, is suddenly a little Methuselah.

Noises of heavy boots and whistling come from the rooms above. Down the carpetless stairs the fire brigade and first aid squad return to duty. The first night of the watch is over.

December 3rd

It is just three months since that Sunday morning when, at 11:15, here, in this small sitting-room, the radio told us that we were at war with Germany. Slow tears trickled down my mother's cheeks on to the needlework rug she was making: every time I look again at those pictures I was pasting into an album I hear again Mr Chamberlain's pewter-grey voice.

The radio became the focal point of all our days. Each bulletin brought more news than we had known in a decade. Yet the catastrophe we braced ourselves to face did not happen; a quiet stalemate was achieved on the Western front and the undramatic weeks of waiting were perhaps the dreariest of all our lives — a numbing continuation of anxiety and boredom. Like states of ill health we fortunately forget the mental anxieties through which we pass. By degrees we've accustomed ourselves to the fact that we are at war and try to go on leading our own ordinary existences as best we can.

Blackout material is now tacked to the orange and yellow striped curtains, one of the wall-lights flickered on the blink and then went out. Since Graham, the manservant, got a job in the Air Ministry, and with Mrs Graham, her cat in her arms, has bidden us farewell, there is no one to mend it. The front door bell is also broken.

We try to get used to restrictions, shortages and irritations, but it is being a long, hard winter.

March 1940

To amuse the troops on the Plain, as well as keep up our own spirits, some friends and neighbours organized a pantomime. Success greeted *Heil, Cinderella*, but not before much suffering. To control and keep together a troupe of amateur actors is to weave each night a Penelope's web. Unlike professionals, who are seldom prevented from appearing, some of our company were always laid low with unexpected diseases or overwhelmed by accident.

This has been the coldest winter in living memory. Snow fell on the day of our dress rehearsal, and for weeks thereafter we might have been in Alaska. While understudies were thrown on stage, the missing principal would be floundering in a snowdrift or, having slipped on the ice, being bound in a plaster cast. Yet somehow a troupe was put together and went by omnibus to strange moonlit camps on icebound Salisbury Plain whence Blenheim bombers in the middle of the night were flying off to Kiel and Cuxhaven. The enlisted men paid sixpence for their tickets, and they liked our show.

Sometimes we would arrive to find the familiar theatrical clothes nailed up in readiness in a wooden outhouse, and our scenery hoisted to a canteen stage not much larger than a Punch and Judy's. The excitement of the theatre keeps one warm under ordinary conditions; but to exchange one's thick woollen clothes, in a below zero Nissen hut, for cotton motley was as great an effort as to plunge into an ice bath. Small wonder that, the prevalent flu epidemic apart, most of us were struck low with every throat and chest malady. At each performance some new piece of bad news greeted us,

'Margaret's[1] off tonight.' 'Maggie Hyde's[2] feeling terrible.' 'David's[3] ricked his back.' However, undeterred, we planned an elaborate tour. We went to south coast towns, through ice and snow and at last reached our goal in London — to hand over quite a large sum to the 'Cigarettes for the Troops' fund.

The rush of the pantomime is over. It has been our lives for nearly four months, bringing an evening's respite from boredom to a great number of troops, and more jealousy among the performers than is ever known in the professional theatre. But now the scenery is folded into crates, the clothes packed away in baskets — to lose their life for ever; if they are ever opened again they will have become old theatrical rags — never to resume that life they had during their brief span.

It is always a sad moment when a communal effort, even as small as this, is suddenly over. But once the decision was made to close the play I had no regrets. For at last I have some work that purports to be of 'national importance'! The Ministry of Information has given me an interesting variety of photographic jobs; some are intended to encourage blood donors or to lure women volunteers into the services. Others show shipbuilding and the making of munitions or aircraft. My camera has brought me into contact with the war leaders and members of the Cabinet, for I have been entrusted with their 'official portraits'. Some of these visits are pretty awe-inspiring, others are merely footling, but it is a good opportunity to break new ground and illustrate 'England at war' from many points of view.

---

[1] Our Prince Charming.
[2] Our red-headed pianist.
[3] Our Buttons.

EDITH OLIVIER, MAYOR OF WILTON

Have been photographing the tanks and army training on Salisbury Plain — a valid excuse for staying at Ashcombe and wheedling an extra gallon or two of petrol. As a result I have been running into Wilton almost every day.

On Saturday afternoon Edith Olivier, the popinjay Mayor of Wilton, in Her Worship's robes, complete with entourage, was the magnet for me and my camera. The scene staged in the front court of Wilton House was of traditional fantasy — which is almost the same as perfect taste — and the spectacle was splendidly unaccustomed in these khaki days.

No half measures for Madame Mayor: she was clad in black and scarlet, complete with tricorn and buckled pumps, and contrived to combine, at the same time, the appearance of a Hogarthian lawyer and a blackbird. Her attendants were top-hatted, one carried the Charles II mace, and the Beadle, in scarlet stockings, although grown wizened and grey, still looked like a child. In the course of ten minutes Edith postured in a hundred ways as she processed at the head of her retinue. Her staccato movements were accentuated by her pointed nose and long pointed toes.

The tweed-clad Pembroke family came out from the 'big house' to enjoy the scene. This encouraged further the histrionic performance of the Mayor who strutted like a peacock — a peacock doing a goose-step — and many another balletic gyration to the huge amusement of her audience. The Pembrokes sniggered, snorted, dug each other in the ribs, bent double, then roared with laughter. Suddenly, as the dark ink sky opened itself in a violent downpour, to the accompaniment of a thunderclap, they all disappeared.

The storm in no way fussed Madame Mayor, who continued to dominate her little group of attendants under the vaulted arches and stone columns of the porter's lodge. The sunshine returned and the photograph sitting came to a jubilant finale.

Later, as I watched dear Edith walking over the green lawns towards her chalet in the park, I realized how easy it is to take for granted someone who towers above the usual run of humanity. And Edith does just that. She is a woman in whom a taste for the fantastic in life and the arts are combined somehow together with a deeply religious sense and practical goodness. At the age of sixty she is the inspiring and stimulating companion of many young people: Rex Whistler is the person she worships most in the world, and he relies upon her friendship and devotion above all others. But her friends consist of a strange heterogenous company — actors, bishops, archaeologists and professors. Her passionate interests range from tapestry to prison reform, to organizing a concert, to birdwatching or a study of the stars.

As Edith tripped so jauntily across the lawns gesticulating and discoursing with enormous gusto and intensity to a relation (who was felicitously wearing a plum-coloured dress to complement the Mayor's scarlet cape), she somehow seemed even to reduce to smaller proportions the great, but transient, earls and countesses painted by Van Dyck in the near-by double-cube room.

The diary she writes throughout the long nights, and into which she pours her heart, is a testimony to her vitality and indefatigable enthusiasm for life.

PETER WATSON

In the absence of telephone and telegram the art of letter writing is again practised. The war has made correspondents of us all. The old postman lumbered over the Downs past Wingreen[4] and brought a tidy packet of letters. One envelope was written in familiar handwriting: 'Tell me if you come to London. It is too long since we have seen one another.' The war had brought my elusive, enigmatic and charming friend, Peter Watson, back from France where he has been living for three years: the only pleasant news since the declaration.

We went out together, and our evening was a long voyage of re-discovery. Peter has changed a lot. The skin is stretched tight over his cheekbones, his hair is untidy, and the elegant tweeds he used to wear with such ambient grace are replaced by 'off the peg' Macintosh and round-toed shoes. He is no longer a 'play boy'. The days of big cars are over for him: 'I now dislike all forms of speed.' He is tired of most things that rich people buy. He bicycles to and from his work as a clerk in a first aid station: he leads a very poor life in comparison to former days. It has impressed me to discover, by degrees, that from a rather negative character he has become an authority on his own. Having been a dilettante he is now a real critic. He relies less on his charm and sex appeal. He is never bored, for he has a relish for imbibing new things every day. He has read much with intensity and concentration, and his knowledge is now substantial. But others can educate themselves — it is Peter's instinctive taste and sensibility that, to me, make him unique.

---

[4] A pre-Druid burial ground, a near-by landmark to be seen silhouetted on the Downs.

Our relationship, too, has changed: he is now the leader in the direction of the arts, whereas he used to be my pupil. When I showed him his first Matisse he said it meant nothing to him; now he has outstripped me in knowledge and appreciation. Of course I put up a pretence at holding my own, and on this evening-out expressed strong views on subjects about which I really know little, even contradicting him violently about paintings, music and people on which he has become expert.

But my pretence was very palpable and must have made the evening difficult for him. It is sad when such a friendship as we had grows apart, and a one-sided attempt is made to get back to former intimacy.

Peter seemed thoroughly disillusioned by the French and his Parisian circle, but he harbours no resentment against their being such fair-weather friends. Apropos people's ages, he said the year meant nothing to him: he had no idea, for instance, how old I was. 'And you?' I asked. 'How old are you?' He was thirty-one that day. We walked back to Peter's hotel where he fumbled for his words. 'Well, good-bye — nice din.' But when I said, 'Well, I'm glad you're back home,' he snarled, 'Well — err-yess-er.' The moon was full, and London looked unlike itself with the barrage balloons above like silver spawn.

Part II: London and New York, 1940

WAR LET LOOSE

May 11th, 8 Pelham Place, London[5]

It was a particularly idyllic early evening. Cyril Connolly paid a visit. London was looking defiantly beautiful, its parks with their blue vistas of Watteauesque trees — so different from the trees that grow in the country — and its gardens behind the railing a mass of lilac and blossoming trees. As Cyril was about to leave, we stood at the front door enjoying the opalescent evening light. The sun made the barrage balloons very bright gold, and the Gothic towers of the Victoria and Albert Museum at the end of the road and the peach blossom trees in the Williams's[6] garden opposite were seen in an apricot haze. We remarked on the paradox of the scene. Nothing here was indicative of the turmoil in the world today, a turmoil created by one gangster. We could feel the peace and repose of the evening so forcibly that it was almost tangible, or something that one could eat.

I dined with Loelia Westminster. After six months she had thrown aside the dust covers and re-opened her drawing-room. To celebrate this great event she gave a party. We all felt the dinner to be so excellent that we wanted to keep the menu in an album, as an archaeological specimen showing that this was the meal that we, in England, were fortunate enough to enjoy

---

[5]This new house in Pelham Place was discovered by my mother, and we made a home together there when my work for the Ministry of Information made it necessary for me to spend most of my time in London.
[6] Emlyn Williams, actor, author.

even after six months of war effort. Perhaps it would be the last of its sort. Anyhow, while we could, we would be as gay as possible. We went out to night clubs and danced all night. When we came back to our beds Germany had invaded Holland, Belgium and Luxembourg. Hell had broken loose.

May 14th

The intensity of feeling during the past few days has been like a knife being turned without cease in one's stomach. Events have moved so fast: the debate on the Norwegian campaign has overthrown Mr Chamberlain: changes come so suddenly and decisively that one becomes almost immune to shock — the new order accepted immediately as if it had existed for ever.

The news from the front is almost completely disastrous: Belgium is managing to hold out a little, but Holland, undermined by treachery, has been vanquished in four days. The fifth column were only in the nick of time prevented from capturing Queen Wilhelmina, who rushed to the microphone and implored, 'Do not trust your best friend!' These new methods of war are devastating; a handful of parachutists can create havoc. The news gets worse every day. At every setback we suffer the Italians menace us more.

WEEK-END AT MOTTISFONT

Whitsun 1940

For the Whitsun week-end I went to the Gilbert Russells at Mottisfont. Overnight the war had developed into something almost too alarming to contemplate. Today's machinery used for slaughter makes barbarism seem something innocent in comparison. It was a strange feeling staying in this luxuriously ordered house, so far and yet so near, to all the terrors that had broken loose. Duff Cooper was to have been there, but having just been made Minister of Information in Churchill's Government, we were without his company, though continuously receiving pieces of news of him through Diana.[7] Things were bad, things were worse than bad. The Queen of Holland had fled her country.

The holiday was peaceful in exterior, turbulent internally. The trout streams gushed with silver ripples, the gowans at the river banks were lush, the meadow-sweet, or Queen Anne lace, so finely grown that it might have been cultivated, the pink and white may trees weighed heavily with blossom. It was all so sylvan that one's heart became the heavier that at this very moment, the most rewarding time of the year, Hitler should have so successfully ordered fire and destruction. Maud Russell visited the local people about housing more refugee children. Doria Haig-Scott knitted, Freddie and Violet Cripps fished trout, Diana went full blast ahead at all hours of the day, always with a plan, a visit to a bluebell wood with Conrad Russell as her companion, or reading aloud an article by Stalin. I sketched in the garden some of the queer tree-trunks at whose mossy roots primroses were growing.

Our host, Gilbert Russell, was a new pleasure to me. I had never known him well before, been rather shy of him, and wondered perhaps if he was not a bit of a crabby martinet. How wrong could I be? He is, in fact, a most amusing personality. I am told that now, as a man weakened by asthma, he is far from being in his former form when he could 'make strong men cry with laughter or groan at the cruelty of his wit'. His humour is dry and fanciful. To watch him listening, or to hear him tell a story, is to be in the presence of a great

---

[7] Lady Diana Cooper.

personality, and only a poet could say 'Dash' in such a way when the lemon slips from the cocktail tray. Even his way of reading the newspaper, or listening to the news, is individual. He showed me a slab of stone on which he had had a Latin testament inscribed, telling that Mottisfont had come back into his family after twenty-six generations. 'I like that sort of thing, it's romantic,' he said.

While pouring himself out a few drops of port (he is evidently not allowed more), he explained that his wife Maud, when she had first met him, had thought him such a shit that she wanted to hit him in the face. The idea of his wife saying such a thing is extremely comical as, of course, Maud is very elegant.

Once, when in *The Times* the death was announced of 'The Fox', or 'The Mackintosh', or some such Scot bearing a unique title, Gilbert (who is rich enough) fancied the idea of buying a title. He would, in fact, like to be called 'The Elemental', especially as elementals are supposed to give off a most frightful stink. It pleased him to think that whenever 'The Elemental and Mrs Russell' were announced there would be an overpowering skunklike stench.

I hope when peace is regained that I may meet Gilbert Russell again and find him in as good spirits as now, when, in spite of the bad news, he is determined that we could never lose the war.

LEAVING FOR NEW YORK

May 22nd

My military permit to go to the Maginot Line did not arrive at the Ministry of Information until the day of the German onslaught. I was disappointed that I could not now go to

France, but thankful to have escaped being taken prisoner in the *blitzkrieg*. Meanwhile a private offer of great commercial benefit to me had come: I had been approached to go for six weeks to America to take advertising photographs. I was loth to leave at such a time, but it would be perhaps the last opportunity to get even with my finances (which were in a bad way), and to come back with enough to pay my income tax and put more in the savings bank.

I half hoped that I would not be given permission to go. Indeed every sort of technical difficulty arose over my papers. For days messages were sent backwards and forwards to the Passport Office, to the place for birth certificates, and to the Board of Trade. Eventually, on the eve of the departure of my boat, the final permits came through, but with them the news that the Germans had broken through the Maginot Line. Incredible mistakes, 'which must be punished', had been made: bridges had not been blown up by retreating armies. New methods of mechanical attack were proving so surprisingly successful that suddenly, after six months of waiting, of careful preparation, we had all been taken by surprise.

Overnight the Germans were at our gates. Any day now their air attacks might begin, and the south of England could be shelled from the French Channel ports. My own private courage was badly bruised, and each person one spoke to was more depressing than the last. Diana was in complete despair. I asked her, 'Should I go to America after all?' She suggested I should seek Bobbety Cranborne's advice. 'He is wise, and doesn't know how to panic.' I telephoned throughout the evening but Lord Cranborne was out. Eventually I caught him at midnight as he was coming into his hallway. He was somewhat surprised to hear me ask whether or not I should leave early next morning. 'Well, the news is howwid (he does not pronounce his 'r's), but if you're only going to be away six weeks and can make a lot of money in that time, I should go, as by the time you come back the news will still be howwid.'

I was too utterly miserable and frightened to sleep except in a half-conscious nightmare. The night passed seeing a series of pictures of the chaos created by the attacks of 2,000 tanks, of houses with their façades bombed away, and tortures inflicted by the Nazis. These Breughelesque visions were mixed with the more personal disappointment that Peter had not, in answer to my call, rung me up to say good-bye. Happily, at about 3 o'clock in the morning, the telephone bell rang. I woke to talk very forlornly to Peter. He'd been out 'on the town', feeling rather cheerful in spite of the general news. I was relieved he telephoned.

Soon after dawn, I was impatient to be gone on my journey. The household was also about early. After alternative delays and panics I arrived at the station to find the platform deserted. By degrees, dark and depressed refugees arrived with their greasy pallor and bundles of thrown-together luggage. Most of them spoke German; all wore a desperate look in their eyes.

At last the train, due to take us to the north, departed after slow, jolting delays. My mother was tearful and was led away martially by Maud Nelson, my secretary. I felt weepy and old and useless. Life really was a beastly business, and perhaps it's only the impetus that one has worked up that keeps one going.

'Our backs are to the wall.' The headlines proclaimed the gravity of the hour and made the journey seem claustrophobic. They gave one an extra urge to be up and doing something, working in a factory, or running or shouting: certainly not just waiting and sitting in terror.

A huge businessman, slumped opposite me, was in a ghastly state of apprehension. He groaned, sighed, raised his eyes to heaven and tried to command sleep, but his tortured imagination prevented that, and he came to in a renewed frenzy.

After six hours we halted outside Liverpool, and from then on the day became one long queue: we stood for hours upon end. Fortunately I had only my books to hold, but many old men and women had heavy baggages to lug. The emigration officers were hard working enough, and had been on their job since dawn; no one could be blamed for the delays. It was war. It was inevitable that all our papers, books and bags should be searched. At last the boat!

THE VOYAGE OUT

SS Samaria

Never have I embarked upon a trip to New York with such a heavy heart. The thought of quitting England at this crucial time filled me with remorse. If only there were other means of getting out of my finance dilemma: yet I must thank my stars that I am still able to work in this way!

How different this trip to those of the old days when there were concerts, celebrities, dances, champagne, balloons. This is a load of German refugees making their escape from persecution, and a sprinkling of moth-eaten English people like myself, going out on business. I have a cupboard-size cabin but it is my own, and, if it is cold, this does not prevent me from sleeping for hours on end.

A boat drill on deck brought out a sorry-looking crowd. Mustering in excited clumps, all swelled with lifebelts under our chins, we had only one thought in our minds: the possibility of being torpedoed. One couple was rather hysterical, and laughed loud and explosively. A fat old lady was asking, 'Iss dis der vindoh we most get hout off?', and, nuzzling her lifebelt, she called it her 'papie'. Instructions were given. The boats would be lowered here. The bugle would call six times, gongs would ring. The sea looked cold and menacing — a forlorn prospect in case of shipwreck.

We carry our lifebelts with us wherever we are. Lying in bed, I can hear fog sirens and distant gunfire echoing against my mattress. One afternoon, near the north coast of Ireland, the gunfire was not distant: in fact, the noise was so portentous that it gave a slight idea of the magnitude of a battle at sea. An aeroplane was sighted and, as we watched its swift and ear-splitting approach, we felt the horror and hopelessness of what it must be to be bombed. Not that this was a German aeroplane, for the Allied circles of colour were a boon from heaven; but for the first time I felt the impotency of waiting for a bomb to drop without being able to retaliate, or even to escape.

DR LOEWI

SS Samaria

It is my daily delight, on board, to seek out, in the tourist section, Raimund's[8] sister and husband, the Zimmers. With them is their little, owl-like friend, Professor Loewi from Graz, who won the Nobel prize for discovering that the nervous system was dependent on chemical reaction. It is a revelation to hear the point of view of intelligent people, who were fighting against us in the First World War, discussing the present situation. One's childhood's ideas of war are so

---

[8] Raimund von Hofmannsthal, son of the poet, librettist.

covered with the horror of blood that even now it is hard to realize that a war can end because of an economic breakdown.

Strange, too, to hear these Germans and Austrians — and I am in no hesitation about their sincerity — in a state of anguish lest Germany should win. Raimund's mother is now ensconced in Oxford and having said, during the last war, that she wished she were on the other side, now finds being on the other side is not altogether agreeable. Zimmer, a man of intensity and torrentlike vitality, who works in Intelligence, says he knew after the first two months that Germany had lost the war. He is so robust and optimistic, so strong within his convictions that he makes me feel like a wriggling winkle. How can I be so paltry as to be put off by his farouche appearance? This man's intellectual range is enormous. He is brilliant when discussing anything from *Jane Eyre* to the 'Galician nobility' on board the ship. Figuratively, he gave me a slap on the back when I said I felt isolated and lost on the boat, having mislaid my personality and individuality. My ruminations in my cabin seem so pitiable and mawkish when in the fresh air of this man's vitality.

Professor Loewi was working with his assistants in his laboratory in Austria when news came that Hitler had arrived. 'Hitler? Where?' 'Here in Austria.' 'Our experiment must be finished. We must work hard. It can be finished in two hours.' The experiment was completed, the system plotted, but not before the guards were at the door. The old man was arrested. His immediate fear was not of death or torture, but of his experiment being lost to the world. He was allowed a postcard. The table of his discovery was written thereon and sent to the chief scientific magazine, and his name signed 'Prisoner'.

After two months he was released from prison, and now at the age of sixty-seven he is starting life again. He is not depressed. Although once rich, all his possessions have been confiscated, and he is now without a country. His ambitions are for humanity; he is sad for the world. I know nothing of science, theology, or philosophy, and yet was so stimulated that I was disgraced into making an effort to rise from my apathy. Here was an old man, a dandy by inclination and manner, sharing a cabin with three marines, yet working all day, translating his lectures from one foreign language to another. And here was I moping my heart out for a dead past...

We sat drinking beer. Loewi, with wrinkled lines on his face, talked of what, pray? Garbo! But in what a way he talked of her! He has no money for the cinema, but makes one exception each time there is a Garbo film: he considers that excitation of the brain in any field creates inspiration and that this stimulus, produced from however feeble an interest, is valuable. Why should Garbo appeal universally — to him, to me, to millions of others? He considers that she, as with certain lyric poetry, is the condensation, the concentration of the hidden, but ever present, sadness that is in all people.

For every grown-up person Garbo possesses, too, the sadness that is dormant in a child, when, robbed of its protective armour of courage against the world, it lies asleep.

The little Professor told us of a new experiment he was working on. It has always been thought that we sleep as a result of our day's work, but he is convinced that we sleep in proportion to the amount of life before us. Thus a baby, awake for two hours of bottle feeding, falls back into a tremendous daze for another twenty hours. Children need a great deal of sleep, but the older one becomes, the less sleep is needed. This old man now requires only five hours each night. He considers the fact that I need eight or nine is a healthy sign. When asked if sudden death caused by an accident counted, he waved his hands aside, 'Doesn't matter, doesn't matter at all!'

A few quotations: Certain tangents of the brain develop and grow stronger. A hand that becomes useless atrophies, so certain parts of our character and brain.

One must judge which of those paths in life one is most equipped to follow, and which to ignore safely.

The spiritual and aristocratic always have their hopes. Only superficial people are dependent on comforts, luxury. In the new world order the old Professor does not miss his former possessions.

Professor does not approve of practice of psychology for money. Story of performer at theatre who died of exhaustion from effort of concentrating in psychological act.

Churchill says the news for England is very grave and each day or hour becomes more critical. This from so great a fighter.

CHILDHOOD REMINISCENCES

SS Samaria

My powers of concentration seem to become more limited with the years. My deficiency shows itself most depressingly and vividly when I read anything but the frothiest of literature. By now I have developed almost a phobia about the printed word. I have every wish to read, but lately I find I shy at the sight of a long paragraph, and instinctively look at the end of an article before summoning up energy to compete with the whole. I can look at pictures and photographs by the hour, but a whole page article or a novel makes me wonder if my eyesight isn't being strained.

As a child, I never read. All the books young people enjoy as foundations to literature were unknown to me. At my day school we were given as a 'holiday task' enormous tomes like *Middlemarch*, but the effort needed to embark upon such a vast undertaking was never made by me. I skipped so much that I never even gathered what the book was remotely about. My brother Reggie knew better: he did not intend to waste a minute from his cricket practice: he did not even open George Eliot.

In my family no one ever read: apart from *Vanity Fair*, which he had devoured at least thirty times and which was always by his bedside, my father possessed few books. When he was slumped in an easy chair it was with *Whitakers' Almanack* or *The Economist*. One room was called the library, but there were never any books about the house: books were never discussed.

It was while at Harrow, when waiting for an underground Metropolitan train which was to take the sketching class back to school, that I was looking at an advertisement for the summer number of *Punch*. 'Copiously illustrated', it said. 'What is "copiously"?' I asked Jack Gold, my companion. 'Really, Cecil, you should open a book one day.' This reprimand from one of my most frivolous friends produced an effect.

There and then Harrison Ainsworth, Compton Mackenzie and the Brontës were devoured ravenously in my bed by the light of a candle placed in a biscuit tin. But when there was anyone else present in my room it was hard for me to concentrate. I remember Jack came one afternoon to lie and read in a wicker chair. His presence prevented me from paying attention to W. J. Locke, and after listening to the creak of the wicker and the flutter of his pages being turned, I became self-conscious and began to giggle. Even now it is hard for me to read while others are present, and impossible if they are talking to one another.

On this boat trip I have read most of the time. But my powers of concentration are dreadfully undisciplined: a name or sentence, on a page, can throw me off into vistas of day dreaming. So it happened, when reading E. M. Forster's *Howard's End*, I came across the description of Leonard's wife, the old tart who was down on her luck. In a flash I found myself remembering a scene that had made such an impression upon me as a small boy but which, during all these years, I had forgotten.

It was a Sunday evening one summer. My family had been on the river. It was when the river was still quite fashionable, and it gave me a tremendous thrill to be at Boulter's Lock or Marlow where actresses of the day were photographed in a punt or sitting at a table under Dorothy Perkins rambler roses on a sloping lawn. We had had a family picnic. Somehow our picnics were always rather a disappointment. I wanted to be 'smart'. The rest of the family had no thought of such a thing; they just wanted to be themselves and enjoy the day naturally. I pined to go to Phyllis Court, or the club at Henley where my spectacular Aunt Jessie had once taken me for strawberries and cream. My father, in particular, asked nothing more than an outing on the river that should cost as little as possible. So with rugs, macintoshes (just in case), and a luncheon basket, we set off in the punt, my father showing prowess with the pole. (He had been a great figure on the river in his youth.) The dank river-smell always had a certain mysteriousness to it, and the hamper contained the hard-boiled eggs which, with their green poison-looking yolks, were always an event. But the sandwiches were a comedown — obviously made from the remains of the Sunday family joint, grey bits of beef were placed between squares of gritty, white, crustless bread. Somehow we could never find the ideal place for our alfresco meal.

Invariably a few large drops of rain would presage a downfall. We would shelter beneath some inadequate twiggery. Soon, with soaked spirits and overcoats, my father punted us back to our starting-off post. Here we would wait impatiently the longed-for return of the chauffeur and the old Renault to take us, worn out, cold and exasperated, home.

It was while sitting, after the rainstorm, on the lawns of the 'boat hire' place that I remember seeing a wretched woman whom, now I have read *Howard's End*, I shall never again forget. She was waiting near us, in a bentwood chair on the lawn. She must have been quite elderly, for she had tired old dog eyes and knotty-veined legs and neck, though to a child anyone showing a crow's-foot or veined neck seems to be monumentally aged. But this lady wore finery that, in intention, was extremely youthful, and it had doubtless been brought out, from old forgotten boxes and attic parcels. She wore, without having ironed it, a dress of string-coloured lace, champagne shoes of cracked kid, and a battered picture hat jammed low over beef-tea dyed hair. She sat with a brandy and soda in her gnarled hand, and I knew from the way that my parents whispered about her that she was wicked — that, in fact, this travesty, dressed in the pretence of youthful coquetry, was the embodiment of vice.

The wretched old bird and a boy friend had been out for a day on the river. When they returned here, her friend had probably left her to go to the wash-room; at any rate he had failed to return. So she waited patiently: she had ordered a drink, and still he had not reappeared.

I remember daddy saying, *sotto voce*, to mummie, 'Well, he might at least have taken her back to London.' By now she was slightly tight, and for good reason. Here she was at Marlow, Sunday evening, stranded, 'stood up'.

I could not have been more than nine years old, though I may have been less, and for me, this scene was appalling in its poignancy. Also, it brought to the surface many of one's hidden childish horrors. Here was a woman left to get home without an overcoat, without a ticket, without money, and, what was worse, she was obviously wicked: as a child, one heard one's elders making jokes about drink and sin being synonymous, and here she was, drinking brandy and soda all by herself. I recognized the poor old thing as a 'bad lot', and my mind worked feverishly imagining what could be the sin she committed. By degrees, she became the embodiment of such appalling evil that, today as an adult, I am shocked that a child, in its ignorance, can, in its mind, evoke Kraft Ebbing scenes and practices that only exist in the most elaborate and depraved Berlin brothels.

So, since twenty-five years ago, this wretch has been waiting for the beau who welched. Why had her day been such a failure? Had the two of them bickered when the rain came down? Had she plied her girlish wiles too relentlessly? Had the shock of seeing a phantom of the night in broad daylight been too upsetting?

Perhaps she realized the humour of the situation, if indeed there was any, for she looked over at our domesticated family group and smiled. Like an old dog that has snapped at a fly and caught it, she winked at me. My parents were rather discomforted. We were bundled together and hurried out of the presence of sin.

NEW YORK AND BACK

White-faced and swollen-eyed, Margaret Case, a great anglophile and one of my first, and certainly one of my most loyal of all New York cronies, was at the docks to greet me. She had a sheaf of newspapers under her arm, and asked if I had read the news? Three hundred and thirty thousand troops had landed safely from the exodus from Dunkirk. It was a miracle, she said, that the whole British Army had not been wiped out. I was too numb and uninformed on the latest developments to understand that a retreat on such a huge scale could be considered anything but disaster. But, by painful degrees, I learnt the full horror of all that had been happening during the past week while we were at sea.

Yes, my visit to the United States was profitable: I took a series of advertisement photographs — which seemed to me in odd contrast to the times — in which society ladies must appear as if they possessed complexions of finest alabaster. If my spirit was not entirely with the undertaking I was able to call upon the technique I had developed during the years. The advertisers and the ladies were both delighted, and the addition to my bank balance helped the financial stalemate which continued until the end of the war.

However, these weeks, spent living in unaccustomed luxury in the Fifth Avenue palace of a beautiful and kind friend, were made into a nightmare of anguish and horror by the progressively deteriorating events in Europe.

Each morning I woke, heavy from a semi-sleepless night, to find the newspapers folded beside my breakfast tray on the pink *crepe de Chine* sheets of my large bed. The banner headlines blared forth the news of the fall of France, and of the refugees from the appalling onrush of Panzer divisions: every hour the radio bulletins told of further tragedy. Nowhere could one find solace from the prevalent gloom. One's worst fears were confirmed each hour by friend and news bulletin.

When I was free to return home, my good, but misguided, friends begged me to remain with them for, at any rate, a few days. They said: 'England will probably be invaded any day now — and there can't be much resistance. Why not stay here a few more weeks, and then it may all be over. In any case, what are you going back to?'

But terrible as the prospect might be, I was impatient to return to where I knew I belonged.

My American friends have never shown more sincere devotion, or more loyalty to the Allied cause, but New York has a very large German population. As the liner was sailing down to the ocean for our return across the Atlantic a pleasure steamer that tours sightseers around New York, manned by a German crew, came across our bows, and as it passed close by, its crew grinned with macabre grimaces as it jabbed its thumbs down at us.

Back again — after an eventless journey on a half-empty ship — in my servantless, small house in Wiltshire, my spirits soared. The war situation had in no way improved: any day now an invasion by the Germans could be expected: the future might well be gruesome, but, somehow, to be in the midst of this maelstrom was far less painful than to hear of it from afar. I was positively amazed and comforted when my Aunt Jessie, pottering in bedroom slippers in the greenhouse, with a broad smile on her shiny cold-creamed face, said, 'Do you know, those dashed Germans dropped a bomb only a few miles from here? What were they up to? Scared a lot of rabbits, but what good could it do? Just blasted cheek!'

Part III: Air Raids, 1940

IRENE VANBRUGH AND A SHORT PLAY PROJECT

Summer 1940, 8 Pelham Place, London

It was a new adventure for me to call upon a renowned actress to discuss, as author, the play in which she is to appear. The fact that I, with John Sutro, was only part author, and that the play was but a short twenty-minute affair, did not detract from the magnitude of my visit.

I was shown, with the script under my arm, into a room filled with theatrical photographs and paintings, and any old vases of flowers, real and artificial. Irene Vanbrugh was waiting over the teacups. The years have made her increasingly like her sister, Violet: square-faced and gaunt. But, in spite of the physical disabilities which are the scourge of old age — the twisted rheumaticy wrist and bent fingers, huge ox-tongue feet, deepset sunk eyelids and false teeth — I had soon yielded to her attack of personality and became a victim of her charm.

The tea and brown bread and butter were disregarded as Miss Vanbrugh told me she liked my quarter-playlet. She wanted to take on the part at once. A few minor changes should be made but, as she explained, this was customary: if the author is unknown he is likely to be more willing to make alterations from the suggestions of others; it is only the old hack who knows his job too well to learn and to permit even a word to be altered. We went through the play line by line. She was completely forthright and took it for granted that others would be as business-like as she. Each typewritten speech came to a vivid life with Irene Vanbrugh presiding over it. She became a sort of microscope through which one could see all the faults and qualities of the written words. I felt nearer to the play than I had before while creating it with John. I was encouraged that so much was there that could be effective.

The professional's skill was also shown in deleting little bits of business which, she assured me, would be unsuccessful across the footlights: the leading lady must not leave the stage for even a second during this short play; the audience would always be conscious of that revolver she was holding; while it was in her hand she must not reminisce about Austria or talk of scones. Besides, it was, at this juncture of the playlet, too late even to mention Austria and scones. 'You have already registered the atmosphere and you must not plug it too long. Coquelin used to tell me that when playing Cyrano's death scene he no longer wore a large nose. It would merely have got in the way of his performance, and the audience did not miss it for they had long ago established the fact that he had a big nose.'

'Theatre' is created by these effects which can be learnt by experience. How fascinating a medium! I do hope one day to master its intricacies.

When, at length, I left Miss Vanbrugh I was even more her admirer than before. Only now did I realize how much the effect she creates on the stage (and even off) is the direct result of a quick brain at work experimenting and using intelligently her long experience.

The blitzkrieg started. Theatres closed in the provinces as well as in London, and John's and my playlet has yet to be taken out of a forgotten drawer.

Only a few minutes after the 5 o'clock to Salisbury had left Waterloo the air raid sirens sounded. Then the guard, a little man of over fifty years, came along the corridor crying 'All blinds down.' Above the noise of the train we heard thumps and bangs. We went on with our reading or minding our own business with lowered eyelids. The English behave with impassivity even in the face of disaster. Imagine this carriage filled with Latins! The screams! The hysterics! Our train came to a halt while, still silent, we sat in a shuttered carriage and just waited. Then, somewhat grudgingly, the train continued. Contrary to the rules, we peered through the blinds and saw that a bomb had started a fire: from a small house a huge black plume of smoke curled into the sky. The general gravelike quietness was extraordinary. Still no one spoke. We heard more thumps. Our train once more came to a halt, as did another shunting slowly towards us. It was empty — its passengers having disgorged themselves fifty yards down the line. All its windows were broken. Eventually, we moved into the station of Malden, and I remembered that at St Cyprian's, my preparatory school, there was a boy called Reggie Malden who was small, pudgy, with pale suet complexion and protruding teeth; he was a lord. Today, Malden Station was a nasty untidy mess, its glass roof blown to smithereens, the general waiting-room a shambles. The local ARP in tin helmets were busy with lorries, bicycles, motor-cycles. We had not realized that we were in the centre of a raid, that we had missed a bomb by fifty yards and by half a minute or less.

The 'All Clear' sounded. The women and children burrowing in their shelters surfaced again, laughingly jerked up their thumbs, and waved. We all trooped on to the line to inspect the damage: the usual story of walls blown away, of cement dust, crumbled bricks, and bomb craters among the runner beans and rambler roses of the cottage gardens.

When later we were on our way to Salisbury again, the damage all along the line was already being cleared up, and the craters in the open fields were quickly being filled before cows could fall in and break their legs. The guard of our train became emotional when the crisis was over. Waving victoriously out of the windows at the women and children clustered together, rejoicing in their safety, he *ad libbed*, 'Those women have had a lot to put up with... It's a hell of a strain for them with the responsibility of all their children to look after...'

On the somewhat halting journey (because of delayed action bombs, our train was diverted to Southampton, where another raid was in progress) miscellaneous snippets of information were picked up. Nine people had been killed at Basingstoke. Overton had got it badly.

Four hours late we arrived at Salisbury at 11 o'clock at night. While a friend gave me a lift to Wilton, friendly voices stopped us, 'Lower your lights, there's an air raid warning.' The blitz seemed to be everywhere. The local yokel who had charge of my car had gone to bed and refused to let me get it from his garage. The night was spent at neighbouring Juliet's,[9] who, like everyone else, enjoys her own personal bomb story, and remains incorrigibly gay. 'Fire bombs in the park!' She raised her eyebrows. 'What a whimsey!'

BOMB DAMAGE AT CROYDON

Pelham Place

Went to Croydon to see real air raid damage. It is *pathetic!* The sirens didn't go off and 300 women and girls were killed in

---

[9] Lady Juliet Duff.

factories there. The relics are poignant: a picture of the King and royal family among the cardboard containers that lie by the thousand among the white cocaine-like debris! A residential quarter also suffered, and one dwelling — luckily deserted — was completely demolished, its *art nouveau* decorations scattered far and wide. 'If you go there you'll find an unexploded bomb — maybe a dud — maybe a delayed action. Better keep this side of the fence.' Along one road, where a stick of bombs dropped, they've made a guy of Hitler, railed off a section and collected scrap iron — twelve and a half tons of it! In Germany everything is done by order. Here much is left to personal spontaneous effort.

The funeral processions pass down the highway; everyone is calm and quiet. But one street beyond, life goes on as if nothing had happened, as if nothing could happen from one particular day to another — unless of course our number is called and, if it is, we are not likely to know it, luckily.

I dined with Sybil Colefax — her usual 'ordinary': when everyone present pays his share. Diana was there, and Knickerbocker, the American journalist, an interesting, Lawrencelike Major Wingate with a Chinese-doll wife, the Minister of Agriculture, etc. As the raid was above us and we could not move, the evening was a success for the hostess. Wingate fascinating, a dynamo, but over life-size and, as the night wore on, the rest of us smothered yawns. When at last we did leave, the sky presented such a spectacle that again we were prevented from going to bed. The heavens, sparkling with every star in the constellation, were patterned with nearly half a hundred searchlights. Occasionally coloured flares were dropped, but these seemed to die after a short descent.

BOMBS ON LONDON

August 30th, 1940

The air so clean, the sun so pristine in its sparkle; only the dried trees and biscuit-coloured grass betrayed that summer was passing. It was more like a spring day in Italy than late August in London. I went down to the city to photograph the damage done by Sunday night's raid. When I found myself at St Giles's church the sirens again went. Everyone ran for shelter. It was as if a squall had suddenly sprung up and everyone sought cover from the raindrops.

The sun slanted through the broken stained-glass windows making it a pleasant place in which to seek protection. I marvelled at the freaks of air raid damage and the unfathomable laws of blast. Scattered cherubs' wings and stone roses were strewn about — whole memorial plaques of carved marble had been blown across the width of the church and lay undamaged. The entire frontage of the deserted business premises opposite was wrecked, and Milton's statue had been flung from its plinth. Yet the lamp-post was standing erect with no pane of its lantern broken. A cluster of workmen, shielded by a few wooden planks, were making jokes as they gazed into the turquoise sky.

In the one week of air raids London life has entirely altered. Most families are closeted together in their basements. Few people go out at night, and if you wish for company you must invite your friends to stay the night: everyone dosses down in the basement. No theatre is open.

I had had enough of being alone in the house and was fortunate enough to find Harold Acton free for an evening. We drank and ate to the roar of bombs and felt extremely safe in each other's company. I must say Harold is a most entertaining person under any conditions, but tonight I feasted on his talk! In his deep, unctuous voice, he takes a roistering pleasure in overstepping the conventional mark into often acceptable, and always entertaining, obscenity. The nearer the bombs dropped the louder we laughed, and the delicious French wine gave us courage to explore the night.

The sky was rose-coloured, and each vast explosion was preceded by a flash of blinding light. Every time a whistling bomb was heard we threw ourselves flat on the pavement close to some railings, and the relief that the bomb fell the other side of a block of flats was such that we were quite elated.

Having been out in all this turmoil, I was able to sleep more peacefully than I have for some weeks, for nothing plays havoc with one's nerves so much as imagination.

Life started slowly next day. Reports of further damage trickled through: a bomb had fallen in the grounds of Buckingham Palace making the suffering of the East Enders seem a little less in that they are not alone in their misery.

Again I went about with my camera. At the Natural History museum nearby, the curator showed me the wreckage. *The Times*, he complained, had minimized the damage. Why, the herborium had been burnt out by an incendiary bomb! And that was the centre of interest of all the botanists of the world! Vitrines by the acre were smashed to smithereens, the carcasses of pre-historic animals had gone to dust — and the force of an explosion had caused a sheet of writing paper to cut a crack right through a mahogany cupboard door.

Ashcombe

What balm to escape to this haven of peace, after the nights we've had in London! For one continuous week London has been terribly bombed. Everywhere people were shivering in shelters and cellars while above, too high to be picked up by the searchlights, were the Hun planes, droning like a slow swarm of bees: jerky bees — buzz-er-buzz-er-buzz. Every moment a distant 'crunch' would be heard, and then a whistle: an inverted rocket sound, and the terrible explosion of the bomb followed. Since listening to this noise so many of the household sounds, the crackle of a fire in the hearth, the crashing of the tray with all the glasses on it, the thud of a banging door, or a housemaid thumping upstairs — all these become the noises of destruction.

For ten hours each night my poor mother remained cowering in the basement at Pelham Place, and flinching at each crunch. Then my secretary, Maud Nelson, managed to get her off to the country, but not before they had had a further air raid while waiting at Clapham Junction. Here they saw a *Boche* brought down amidst cheers. I was unnerved at seeing my mother's ordeal, and was relieved when I was alone at home, sleeping down in the basement in the room vacated by the maid, Dorothy. Sleeping? Well, not sleeping — just lying awake listening to the symphony above. The basement room is a sort of sound box and there is no note that I miss. Worst, perhaps, of all, is when the whistling bomb ends in silence, and you know a time bomb has been dropped, perhaps even in your own backyard. Eventually one became so sleepy that the monotonous recurring arrival of German planes, and subsequent bombing, acted as a soporific; and one's slumber would only be disturbed by the 'rat-at-tat' of a silly little gun, or a particularly shrill swish of a close-by bomb.

The beginning of the week had been the worst. The waves of planes droned above while they took their time to deposit their loads. Searchlights were impotent to locate them, and there were no anti-aircraft guns. But, now that our guns have come into action, we are comforted. Even if they prove themselves to be of no practical use they have created among the civilian population a wonderful feeling of confidence. The din is deafening. The night after the AA guns had answered the bomb explosions, people appeared with sparkling eyes, and clasped each other with the greeting, 'Oh, the lullaby of the guns!'

WAX MASKS IN ALBEMARLE STREET

Pelham Place

I went to Albemarle Street to see if the wax head I had seen among the debris of a former hairdressing establishment was still there. As I arrived a demolition squad was pulling down a large top-heavy façade. Whrump! The cloud of black dust eventually settled. I clambered over the rubble to find a new wax head lying, bald but smiling, among the cracked mirrors, glass fragments and wreckage of the ladies' beauty shop. The men working on the job were helpful, and when I asked one if he had seen lately the head with golden hair flying wild, he said he thought it could be unearthed. It was. The ghoulish head was produced from a mound of rubbish, and I proceeded to photograph it against the dreadful surroundings.

Suddenly the usual officious passer-by appeared. A little man with ferret eyes and a pointed red nose. I must show my papers. Yes, there was nothing wrong with the papers, but it didn't say you could photograph those wax heads — it wasn't right — the Ministry of Information would not want to show anything like that. I explained that, in any case, my photographs had to be submitted to the censor. But the discontent had started and now gathered momentum. The newspaper seller, who before had been so blithe and friendly, became truculent and grumbled that he wouldn't let me leave the spot until a policeman appeared and proved that everything was in order. A plain-clothes man edged his way through the gathering crowd, and whispered that everything was straightforward but that the feelings of the people must be pacified.

It was some time before the constable appeared and I was escorted to the nearest police station. After a few telephone calls everything was put right, but the constable explained that I had done wrong in provoking the antagonism of the crowd and a record should be made of the case. This seemed a somewhat empty formality since all the records had been destroyed by last night's bomb.

When one looks around at the damage, one realizes that the people have every reason to be highly-strung and super-sensitive. I felt thoroughly sad and somewhat unnerved as I walked down the havoc of Savile Row and Conduit Street, where scarcely a window-pane remains intact. And the East End is far worse.

ZOG QUEEN

Another day I photographed the Zog Queen. The cortege came up the awful old staircase of the squalid *Vogue* studio in the middle of Bloomsbury with such a clatter that I thought a demolition army was arriving. Three blackish, dirty, greasy bandits appeared, smoking furiously, and spitting, hands in pockets. Then appeared a German nurse carrying an albino child in a yellowy-white bearskin coat. Followed the tall young Queen in a red velvet tambourine hat, and an old American crone, a Baroness something, who is supposed to be lady-in-waiting, but who is said to be the Queen's grandmother. All the *Vogue* assistants and secretaries came out of their lairs and dark-rooms to join the circus.

The Queen, with her ever-ready, eager smile and bright popping eyes, is so pretty that she would make an ideal appendage to any chocolate shop.

An air raid had long been in progress and we no longer paid any attention to the gunfire, but the Queen, as she sat on the arm of a property sofa in front of the camera, was scared stiff at each bang.

'Is that a cannon?' she kept asking.

We pretended it was nothing, but each time the guns roared the entourage grabbed at the child in a half-hearted movement to save it. The child is two years old, yet looks four, with unhealthy pale skin, long pointed nose, and receding chin like a rodent.

The studio, now windowless with tarpaulin nailed where there was once glass, was frigidaire cold, and there was a question of whether or not the child, for its photographic 'turn', should be relieved of its heavy coat. The grandmother piped up in broadest Chicago accent, 'We can't take a chance with its health!' The Queen spoke German, French, English and Albanian, the last being a language that sounded comic with all its pffts, pees, wees, pings and fitts. When practised by the bandits in an effort to attract the attention of the gyrating little child, the scene was hilarious.

While the Queen and her male escorts did a war dance for the edification of the child, with no success, I listened, trigger poised, to Mrs Redding, the studio manageress, making conventional headway with the Baroness.

'It must have been awful when you had to leave Albania so hurriedly?'

'Oh, my dear, we had to leave everything, everything, everything! And we had to get in motors, and she there — she — the — er — Queen, was about to have a haemorrhage any minute, but we had to go round and round and round the mountains, and all the while we were just crazy with fear that we'd fall over the precipices, and then, dear, what do you think they did to try to get the — er — the Queen *and* the child? They started to throw stink bombs!'

The Queen, now tired of dancing, resorted to screwing up her nose and making funny faces to attract in vain the child's attention from one of its fly buttons. The Baroness continued her gossip.

'Of course, we'll go back there one day. Meanwhile, we have to make a new life for ourselves at the Ritz!'

But the Foreign Office has no intention of ever setting Zog back on the throne and, one by one, the circus will be broken up, and one wonders if the scruffiest bandit will remain loyal once the last gold nugget has been taken from underneath the hotel bed.

RAID ON LONDON DOCKS

September

The War Office arranged for me to take photographs on Salisbury Plain. It was pleasant to be able to work with my base at Ashcombe. However, as always happens, if I am away from London for even a few days, the accumulation of work there becomes alarming, and when I returned it was to find Talleyrand's desk heaped with packages, papers, letters, telephone messages and cables. I hurried through them to see if any spelt disaster, then, relieved that they didn't, bolted off for dinner with Ivan Moffat, in his flat on the top of a huge house in Fitzroy Square.

There were eight of us, the majority socialistic young women with lank hair. No sooner had we sat down to the table than the alert went. Eve Kirk, the painter, whose potato features are compensated by an innate elegance of manner and speech, had to leave immediately as she is warden in the square.

When the guns were heard some of us went on to the roof to see if there was anything to be seen — and, my heavens, there was!

The Germans were dropping chandelier flares all the way from the docks along the river to Chelsea. The spurts of shells looked like exploding stars. An enormous red glow lit up the sky against which domes and steeples, and the bobbles of near-by plane-trees, were silhouetted.

It was cold on the roof, and so much shrapnel was falling all around us that it was foolhardy to remain. But a raid is more exciting and stimulating, and somehow less unnerving, when one is out of doors.

However, we came below. Ivan was excited and kept repeating in his rich port-wine voice, 'It's terrific! It's a full-scale raid against the London river!' But the bombs were not confined to the docks. A terrible swishing noise, like the tearing of a giant linen sheet, ended in a vast explosion preciously near the house. The windows were broken, the doors of cupboards blown open, and the entire solid building rocked. Then followed the sickening noise of air raid wardens running to the scene of the crime.

Some of Ivan's guests now became really jittery and, moping and wailing, descended to the shelter. Others quarrelled with one another. At various stages down the circular stairs people whimpered, 'I'm going home.' — 'No, don't! Wait!' — 'I'm going now.'

During the lull in the storm Ivan and I made intermittent visits to the roof to look at the flaming panorama. Old fires were extinguished, but new ones were forming. One conflagration was so near that I felt it might be a target, and that we might easily be hit by a stray bomb that was intended to add fuel to the main objective. The licking noise of the flames was horrible. Vast sparks flew across the skies looking like aeroplanes themselves. One's eyes were smarting in the smoke-filled air.

Eventually I went home by taxi. The driver was rather frightened, but the girl I took home was strangely unmoved. We discovered that bombs had fallen on almost every part of the city and, in fact, were continuing to do so. Whole streets were paved with broken glass, and it was macabre to hear the rows of burglar alarm bells heedlessly ringing away in the shops whose doors and windows had been broken by the blast. The awful buzz of hundreds of aeroplanes above was made less sinister by the lion roar of our guns.

Back at home I felt I was still in the centre of the raid for, again and again, one's heart almost stopped as another terrible bomb shriek shot towards one, and ended in a crash that shook the house to its foundations. What to do but tackle the mountainous pile of papers on Talleyrand's desk? I started to reply to various business notes. I wrote a lot of letters to friends abroad, and, at last, became so exhausted that, in spite of the din being no calmer, I decided to go to bed.

In my half-sleep the noises were unbelievable: there was such a continuous banging and thumping that all the remaining glass in my windows was broken, and the appalling bee-buzzings of further planes seemed to drone ever nearer and nearer so that I felt they were about to come right through the bedroom curtains. Several times I put my head under the clothes while a bomb exploded not, mercifully, on my roof, but on someone else's nearby. Next morning I heard a plane had come down as near as Kensington High Street.

FRANCIS ROSE

Ashcombe

Francis Rose[10] has spent many months at Ashcombe. He has nowhere to go, and precious little to scrape from the bottom of his once overflowing cornucopia, yet he seldom complains about the tide of events. He seems unworried, and is oblivious to everything including the elements. For six hours on end he can paint, hunched in a thin overcoat in icy gales on the Downs, not minding that his face and hands are literally frozen blue.

Francis has not been an easy guest. He has left hot taps running, burnt a hole in a sofa and, oblivious to rationing, has helped himself liberally to stimulants. One night he left the light on in his bedroom while he slept. Heedless to blackout rules, he had not even pulled down the blind, so that a policeman from miles away had to trudge over the Downs in a raging tempest to knock up the house at early dawn. Worse, he has been quite unadaptable in asking my mother, who has been doing the housework, at all unsuitable times of the day if she doesn't think the room with the painted animals in the Palais des Papes at Avignon is the most beautiful thing in the world, and whether she has ever eaten orchid salad — a favourite salad in China. Now, to my mother's relief, he has got some job as an aircraftsman in the RAF.

---

[10] The painter who had lived in France, where I met him as the protégé of Gertrude Stein.

WALTER SICKERT

September 21st (Saturday)

Having scrounged two cans of petrol, and as the autumnal sun warmed our spirits, we decided to take the opportunity that might never again present itself, of motoring from Ashcombe to Walter Sickert at Bath.

Quite a family party it was that set out, for, in addition to my mother and Aunt Jessie, Oggie Lynn and Maud climbed into the car. We were blessed: everything went smoothly. It was a real 'joy-ride'. In spite of there being no signposts we found the way without difficulty. Bath lay in a vivid blue mist in a bowl of trees and grey stone. I recognized the Sickert house, with its large spreading chestnut and lions on its gatepost, from the latest pictures that the old boy — he must now be over eighty — had sent to the Leicester Galleries. The box-like house is of stone with tall well-proportioned windows. Inside it is somewhat sparsely furnished in the civilized taste of England in the late eighteenth century: a solid chair, a fine Regency sideboard, a Chinese bowl filled with fruit, and drawings and pictures in simple bevelled gold frames. Walter Sickert's room was white and bare but for a vast bookcase, some of his own pictures, a step ladder, easels and on the chimneypiece a row of wonderful plaster caricatures by Jean-Pierre Danton (who is considered to have caught so wonderfully the fire of Paganini's playing in his Paganini statuettes).

Mrs Sickert appeared — a tired, drab little woman, in faded, dark colours with untidy hair. Suddenly one realized that she was, in an oriental way, an exquisite *objet de vitrine*: her flat shoes on her spindly feet became those of a ballet dancer, and she showed herself to be a sensitive artist. She is also the gentle nurse and perfect wife for a painter, and like a little Chinese *amah* she slid around in the near distance attending her husband with infinite tact and devotion.

The great old man, smoking a cheroot, was lying deep back in a large leather chair with outstretched arms, displaying sensitive bird-like hands. His magnificent wild and farouche head was adorned by brilliant white shocks of hair and square beard. Behind him a huge window framed a salad-coloured view of Bath.

From where he lay his eyes fell upon an early portrait of his mother — a rather dark, Ingres-like painting of a woman with hair parted in the middle: a gold brooch at her throat. 'It is by Fuseli, that's a good name, isn't it? And it's well done, the brown of the hair and the gold of the brooch.' Occasionally Sickert's brain would give off a flash of brilliance, but suddenly he could not remember what he wished to say. Then his imagination would take control, and he would blurt out all sorts of inconsequent things like a wise lunatic or a highly cultured child. It is astounding to think that this old man should be able to take control of his senses when it comes to painting, for it soon dawned upon me that poor old Sickert's brain was in a state of advanced decay. Yet in front of a canvas he seemed to regain all his power; his pictures are as solid, well constructed and bold as only those by a man in his prime could be.

Enthusiastically I photographed him in the studio and, in answer to my 'Please keep still', Sickert would gesticulate, 'Enchanted — Of course I'll keep still. I won't even talk if you don't want me to'; but, nevertheless, he demonstrated his latest work — a dry, scaly, solid piece of architectural painting done in greys and brown, of the Kingsway Arch (now taken down). 'I will make that like a lily of the valley!' he said. But I think the lily of the valley thought came into his head at this last minute.

An omnibus was being sketched in. He explained, 'You see, I always wanted to be a bus conductor. That coat over there' (he pointed to a buff coat with a darker velvet collar) 'I like, because I feel like a bus conductor in it.'

'May I turn on this light?' I asked, thinking it might help my photography.

'Oh, but are we allowed to turn it on?' The old man knew vaguely that we were at war and must conform to the blackout rules, but he couldn't quite understand that it was only at night that the light must not be switched on if the windows were unguarded.

'Now we can go down on to the terrace in the garden,' he suggested. But the procedure of getting the old man out of his deep chair was a laborious one. Sickert would lean forward to hoist himself to his feet, then start talking about his father and the doctor who operated upon him when he was a small boy, about Islington and the Trinity, and then, oh dear, he'd sink against the deep leather back again. However, eventually he was upright and on his feet. Sickert's study was next door: again a huge bookcase and leather chair. The tables and floor were papered with leaves of the various books he'd been studying. Ingres was everywhere, and there were certain illustrations with the edges turned back for special reference. Sickert was himself reading a French book on Millet, and the margins were enlivened by his pencil notes. Written in a very fair and sure hand were his reactions: '*Comme il a raison!*'; and the various prices mentioned as having been paid for certain pictures were annotated. Meissonier was always selling pictures, it appears. So Sickert wrote: '*Le cher Meissonier toujours réussi.*' And he would translate the French francs into pounds, so that for one picture Meissonier received 10,000 francs — or, as Sickert wrote, 'Forty bloody pounds.'

A long digression was staged in the hallway while engravings of Venice — Sickert's great joy — and Sylvia Gough's paintings were shown. The garden was below and to reach it we must all descend a winding stone staircase that presented many hazards. 'This is something that has got to be done,' Sickert laughed. 'We have to go down it — that's the only way of getting to the garden — and then we have to come up again — a lamentable state of affairs!' Sickert was not at all sure on his feet, moved in little jerks with a heavy use of his stick, and as he hobbled about he took great trouble to avoid stepping on one particular flagstone which, he then explained, was something to do with the 'waterworks'. There was an awful stench of urine, and I gradually realized that poor old Sickert no longer has any control over his bladder; his heavy blue tweed trousers were stained with dark wet patches that must make him feel terribly uncomfortable.

Once out in the garden, the terrace, effulgent with a jumble of nicotianas, petunias, asters and stocks, gave hundreds of opportunities for photographs, and for Sickert's mind to run free in its fancies. His wife listened attentively to everything he said. He was trying to be gallant and uxorious: he threw his thumbs in the air with a jerk and said, 'This is the job for the husband — no one is going to interfere here!' Then he laughed with salacious enjoyment at a story he told of a girl in the neighbourhood who had gone out and got her skirts somewhat torn. 'And after that, she continued in that life.' Suddenly he sang *Deutchsland über alles*, and asked if I liked music — oh, how he liked music. And did I like Canonbury Crescent in Islington? To him it was so beautiful — as all things rounded were beautiful, like those two hills over there. He pointed with his stick to the distant landscape. 'Do you see those two thick trees! They have seats under them, and every afternoon tea is served.'

The terrace on which the Sickerts were now walking had featured in some of the master's most recent pictures: they conveyed the spirit and essence of quiet English country atmosphere and light. Suddenly Sickert took a dislike to a certain path, 'It is too wet; it can never be dried up' — and he stumbled when the flagstones were uneven: once he nearly fell headlong into the nicotianas. Like a toddler, he was afraid of going too near the parapet of the terrace. Then, stopping in his tracks, like an old actor, he started to recite, and sing snatches of early songs. Then he would enjoy some happy formal laughter: laughter that did not arise from amusement but was created for its own sake.

Sickert's mind was now darting unexpectedly in every direction. 'Do you patronize Despenser?' (or some such name). 'No, who is he?' 'He was Whistler's tailor, and I like your suit and your trousers. It appears they were very much impressed by a wet cucumber.' The Trinity were often on his lips, and suddenly he threatened he would write to Queen Victoria to overthrow the State.

In spite of his infirmities his brain is powerful and grandiose. He used beautiful English, and spoke in a flowery way that is no longer fashionable, but no less delightful. 'Do you observe where that little bust of Queen Anne has been on the bookcase? It seems that her head has been purposely struck off with a walking stick.' And: 'You wish to remove that rose branch? And for what other purpose, pray, is a penknife?'

We all had tea in a blue lattice tea house. The artist's hand was steady as the cup was raised to his lips. Sickert enjoyed being host. 'Can you stay to dinner? Well, come to lunch. Come and have a meal — after all, a meal is a meal. Show them everything!' 'Everything?' 'Yes, all turned up!' Mrs Sickert laughed. We all laughed.

After a short sojourn in a red and gold wallpapered room, hung with miscellaneous Sickerts, we drove away. Although we had welcoming invitations to return to meals it may be that the war will prevent our seeing the old man again.

In his happiness with his wife there is a smooth and mellow friendship, made more poignant with a certain play-acting as master and mistress occasionally stage little scenes of obedience and revolt.

Sickert is living almost entirely in the past of his youth, with only a few flashes of the war of today. He is completely happy for his pictures are always with him and he sees everything in terms of painting and more pictures to be made.

DIANA AT THE DORCHESTER

Pelham Place

I go to see Diana at the Dorchester. She lives in a bilious-coloured suite on the top of the hotel. Her old maid, Wade, comes up from the bowels of the building to make some tea in their own pot: war-time room service is not all that it should be. Sibyl Colefax then appears. Diana washes out her own cup, finds there is not enough hot water. A half-empty cup of very strong tea is refused by Sibyl who explains she had never really wanted it. Then Venetia Montagu comes in. 'What, no tea?'

'Have a drink — or no?'

'Yes.'

'Oh!' says Diana, rather flummoxed.

Search is made for a corkscrew. A bottle of sherry is about to be opened when the sirens sound. A gale is blowing, the windows rattle and the wind howls down the fireplace where an electric stove is embedded. The park guns below fire to crack your head. We go downstairs.

In the lobby the scene is like that on a transatlantic crossing, in a luxury liner, with all the horrors of enforced jocularity and expensive squalor. The people are the same as those we always see on board: Mrs Simon Brand and Harriet Cohen. But now they are prepared for an all-night vigil with rugs, torches, cushions. Diana is nervous: she darts, every so often, with inquiries to the hall porter. As she staggers down the lobby like a doll with its legs put on sideways, the fellow passengers point, 'That's Lady Diana — doesn't she look Bohemian!' (Diana is a 'day-dream' dresser. She wears velvet slacks, pearls, neckerchief, yachting cap and a fur cape.) Duff is late. Why hasn't he come home? Has he had a heart attack, been ran over, bombed? Then the Minister of Information arrives. He reminds me of a little pug dog. He stands staring boss-eyed with surprise at the whole scene. Diana totters towards him. Instead of saying, 'Evening, darling,' she stands at bay ten paces from him and snorts and snarls while he snarls back. They throw a few statements at one another, then dash lovingly into the elevator.

NO 10 DOWNING STREET: MRS CHURCHILL

September 1940 (Pelham Place)

I often forget the address to which I have to go, so that a taxi driver looks on superciliously while various door bells are rung in vain. Today no such difficulty: No 10 Downing Street is a number even I could not forget. I was going for the Minister of Information to photograph Mrs Churchill — possibly the great man as well: but that was indefinite. A breathless skivvy showed me up to the secretary's room and left me. For the first half-hour I beguiled myself prowling around, looking at the stacked files of newspaper articles and accounts of speeches, and the boxes with their ordered headings. It was enjoyable to note the presents sent to the Prime Minister from fans, with letters thanking him for what he was doing for the nation. But I was anxious to get to grips with my electrician, already established in the drawing-room, so in a fever I used the house telephone to ask to be freed from my imprisonment.

The suite of rooms where the pictures were to be taken had tall ceilings, with long windows looking on to herbaceous borders. Here, in the heart of London, bees were wafting in through the open curtains, and the quiet was a country quiet. It was the hottest day of the loveliest summer (climatically) we remember, and the rooms were a delight with sun streaming in from beneath the blinds on to bowls of sweet peas from Chartwell. There were some fine English portraits, Adam fireplaces and Georgian silver. Mrs Churchill has typically arranged the rooms with her usual pale colours of pistachio green and palest salmon pink. Pamela,[11] enormous with child, announced the imminent arrival of Mrs Churchill who appeared with her hair set for the occasion like Pallas Athene. Mrs C. announced that Winston was not able to be photographed. He was inspecting New Zealanders somewhere. This was a disappointment but, at the same time, a relief. If I had felt that, at any moment, he might come through the door I would have been most uneasy, for he has a paralysing effect on me.

Mrs Churchill, a bright, unspoilt and girlish woman, is full of amusing and shrewd observations about people and the afternoon's photography passed breezily and easily. She insisted on showing me the whole house, and I was an avid

---

[11] Mrs Randolph Churchill.

sightseer. The three reception-rooms give on to a small passage room which Philip Sassoon turned into a dining-room where Mr and Mrs C. have their evening meal, the big parties taking place in the panelled hall next door. Mrs C.'s own bedroom with chintz flowers is as pretty as any country bedroom, and all the corridors and bedrooms look like part of a manor house. On the pale-coloured walls were Sickert sketches and Nicholson still-lives, family photographs and Victorian sketches. The Prime Minister's bedroom was simplicity itself. A small single bed: some drawings of his family and his mother by Sargent: a bedside table mounted with telephones galore: boxes of cigars: a wash basin with shaving soap and brushes in evidence: a few books: some files of Parliamentary speeches, and that was all — except for the view from the windows on to the Horseguards Parade and the Admiralty. Mrs C. pointed out a truck full of pigeons. These are being trained in case all else fails. Pigeons to send last-minute SOS's — in extremes we revert to the primitive.

While we had a break from photography for tea Mrs C. talked of the terrible days when France was cracking and Winston had to keep bolstering up the French. But Winston had been so convinced of France's weakness that he had to refuse them the help of all our own fighter squadrons lest we ourselves be wiped out. They are, Mr and Mrs C., both pro-de Gaulle, whom they consider a great engineer-officer responsible for many new methods of mechanized warfare. He is full of courage, the maker of many magnificent speeches, but a difficult man to get along with.

Mrs Churchill recalled having sat next to the General at luncheon. During one of the many silences Mrs Churchill pondered on how difficult must be the life of Madame de Gaulle. Her daydreams were interrupted by the General addressing her: '*Vous savez*, Madame, it must be very difficult, Madame, being the wife of Mr Churchill.'

LONDON UNDER FIRE

October 12th

One still feels a sinking of the heart at the sight of ever more bomb damage: windows blown in and tumbled wreckage of rubble in the road. A small dwelling — its front cut away — gives a doll's house effect, with the parlour, where the evening meal was being eaten on the cloth-covered table, a teapot and bowl of tomatoes exposed to passers-by. Pictures have been knocked crooked by the blast. Skyed high in the air remain the useless bath and lavatory with the pathetic little roll of toilet paper still affixed to the door, and the staircase leads to an upper floor that no longer exists.

James[12] is writing a book called *London Under Fire* for which I am doing the photographs. Besides the vandalistic damage, we must show the tenacity and courage of the people, and we do not have to look far. Signs are posted: 'We have no glass, but business continues.' As soon as the worst rubbish is cleared away, the notice appears 'Open as usual'.

Londoners have had one month of this so far, and they must look forward to a whole winter of it. The planes arrive each night at dusk. One hears the drone, then the bangs, crunch, zumphs of the bombs. The AA gunfire, which is gay and heartening, is like a firework fiesta: and then an interval. During the lull one tries to read a book, but one's thoughts wander, and soon the hum of more approaching planes is heard. The zumphs come perilously near, and one leaves the

---

[12] James Pope Hennessy.

chair for a vantage point under the lintel of a door. The restless night continues.

By degrees many people have grown accustomed to being frightened. For myself, most evenings I have beetled off to the Dorchester. There the noise outside is drowned with wine, music and company — and what a mixed brew we are! Cabinet ministers and their self-consciously respectable wives; hatchet-jawed, iron grey brigadiers; calf-like airmen off duty; tarts on duty, actresses (also), *déclassé* society people, cheap musicians and motor-car agents. It could not be more ugly and vile, and yet I have not the strength of character to remain, like Harold Acton, with a book.

In the infernos of the Underground the poor wretches take up their positions for the night's sleep at 4 o'clock in the afternoon. The winter must surely bring epidemics of flu, even typhoid. The prospect is not cheering, and Churchill makes no bones about the ardours of the future. The electric trains are bombed, so typists fight their way on to extra buses. Telephone exchanges are out of order, and hardly a clock has its face intact. Yet the life of the city manages, more or less, to continue as if in normal times. Nothing can really dash the spirits of the English people, who love to grumble, and who, in spite of their complaints, are deeply confident of victory.

In the absence of printed posters, the newspaper sellers chalk up their version of the news. 'Tragic Death of James Joyce.' One old man at South Kensington had written: 'Bomb in cellar — horrible mess.' Another outside Waterloo Station had scrawled, 'We are winning!'

PAMELA CHURCHILL

Week-end with Pamela Churchill. She has just moved into a Queen Anne rectory house at Hitchin which she shares with her sister-in-law Diana (Sandys). The object of my visit was to take the first photographs of Winston Junior who is now five weeks old. When the great man saw his grandchild for the first time, he bent down and kissed him, and said, 'What sort of a world are you being born into?'

Pamela, with Raeburnesque red curls and freckles, was looking radiant and triumphant. But she had been through a turmoil — for the child had been long overdue. The air raids had not hastened it, yet they had unnerved her. One day the doctor was hurriedly called — in vain: no luck! In desperation Pamela caught her white Pekinese dog, dressed it up in the expected child's clothes, and sent it out of the room to Mrs Churchill. What a joke! Mrs Churchill rushed to Winston with the dog dressed up. 'Look — look what a surprise I've got for you.' Winston at once asked, 'Is it a boy?' Pamela realized more than ever how important it was to Winston for her to give birth to a son. But the one person who did not take the story well was Randolph. When it was related at Max Beaverbrook's, Randolph was profoundly shocked.

The child was born in deep secret at Chequers, with bombs falling all round. The London house is now evacuated: the back staircase is unsafe, and the ceilings have come in in a few rooms.

Diana Sandys, like the rest of her family, has this reverent worship for Papa. 'Papa is so kind and gentle, is better, is more good than anyone!' A. J. Balfour had said it: 'You, Winston, can forgive — I can only forget!'

Diana told me of the terrible rumpus there had been at No 10 when Winston was broadcasting his recent bolstering speech to France. (*'Et les poissons aussi*, meaning that the fish were fat, according to rumour, on the German soldiers that had been drowned in the 'false invasion' of Britain.) The Churchill family were assembled around the radio waiting and gossiping, the knobs were all prepared — and then, Time! An aunt pressed a knob to turn the radio on, but it was the wrong one. Someone else switched to Radio Normandy and then to Rome. The feathers flew: Mrs Churchill grabbed the radio and broke it and, after an hysterically chaotic scene, everyone rushed upstairs to listen in to the remainder of the speech on a servant's set.

Diana described the results of her sister Sarah's nasal operation. Sarah was still black and blood-red, swollen and unrecognizable, four days after her ordeal. Diana went to call on her sister and, at first, Sarah hid behind a fan. When, at last, she dropped the fan Diana's jaw dropped, but she managed to spurt out the sentence she had prepared on the way up the stairs: 'Oh Sarah, you *have* been going it!'

Finally the nose was ready to be seen, and Winston made a call to scrutinize it at Westminster Gardens. The great man shuffled backwards into the room, blowing his nose. He turned to the fireplace, his back to Sarah, and addressed the chimneypiece: 'Now, Sarah, whatever happens, Sarah, remember, I shall always love you more than anything on earth. Now you've had your nose altered, and I want to see what it's like.' He turned: 'Oh? Oh — Oh, charming! Charming! Not my old Sarah, of course, but still — very nice. Now then, what were we discussing? Victory, of course...'

When Diana got a job as an interior decorator she told her father of her doubts. 'Do you think it's wise to work in such a dowdy shop? They make money — do awfully well — but so dowdy!'

'Dowdy? Why, all England's dowdy!'

PHOTOGRAPHING WINSTON CHURCHILL

The prospect of photographing the Prime Minister next morning prevented me from sleeping most of the night. I knew it would be a difficult job, but it was most important that I should succeed. As with anyone whom I enormously revere, I am always paralysed with shyness in the presence of Churchill, and I knew I wouldn't be able to wear down his gruff façade in the short time that had been allotted for the sitting.

It was a cold grey morning and Dorothy, the maid, was slow in bringing the wretched little pot of hot shaving water (we have been two months without a bath at home — still no gas!), and I was late in starting off. When I got to No 10 they were all rather feverish, Mrs Hill, Churchill's secretary, saying she had tried to call me to come earlier but my line was always busy, and now the Prime Minister was already in the Cabinet room and would not allow the lights to be rigged up there while he was working. Would we like to fix up something somewhere else? I was whisked down to see Mrs Churchill. On my way I noted that the symbol of Western survival had evidently hurried out of his tub that morning, and there was a trail of wet feet along the corridor, together with damp bath towels and a dripping sponge on a window-sill. Far from being surrounded by footmen or valets who ministered to his needs, Churchill has to manage his own bath, and however late he might be for a Cabinet meeting or an audience with the King, there are no short cuts even for his daily ablutions. Very feverish and excited Mrs C. seemed to be and said, 'You must come and see Winston right away.' Before I demurred that my preparations were not complete, all a-flutter, all flurries and staccato darts and jabs, Mrs Churchill put her head around a succession of mahogany doors. 'Is the Prime Minister in there?' Further doors leading to Adam rooms were opened, and from the final secretary's room I was able to catch my first glimpse of our goal. Through a double door, heavily lined, and framed by a couple of white columns, at the centre of an immensely long table, under an eighteenth-century portrait hanging above the noble chimneypiece of white marble, sat the Prime Minister. The huge Cabinet table stretched to left and right. The tall windows were, here and there, pasted with improvisations of brown paper. Mr Churchill appeared immaculately black, white and pink; fat, white, tapering hands deftly turned through the contents of a red leather box at his side. A vast cigar was freshly affixed in his chin. He was deeply engrossed.

But Mrs Churchill's entrance broke the solemnity of the atmosphere. All smiles and femininity, Mrs Churchill beamed, 'You know Mr Beaton, don't you? He's come to take a photograph of you.'

'Ah, yes!' He pierced me with his cold blue eyes, and barked, 'I hear you're very clever!'

The interruption was obviously displeasing and who, indeed, would wish to be deflected from the business of running a war by a photographer? The Prime Minister grumbled gruffly, inarticulately, huh-hummed. In desperation I threw down my trump card. The first photograph, just rushed through, of his grandson, Winston Junior. The atmosphere lightened for an instant, but then what else to do but leave the presence immediately, for what use is a photographer without a camera or light? Mrs Churchill had disappeared, smiling, into thin air, perhaps as embarrassed as I, perhaps oblivious. I made a hasty retreat and threw myself on the mercies of understanding and competent secretaries. Where could we most easily and quickly fix up the fights? No 10 is now a nutshell, most of the furniture and pictures are gone, only a few secretaries' rooms have the necessities.

Mrs Hill, always kind and helpful, hurried from her silent typewriter opposite the Prime Minister to whisper that perhaps the reception room would be most suitable, but we must hurry as there was an 11 o'clock appointment. In a frenzy we tried to arrange the necessary paraphernalia, but the devil was in my Indian assistant, Haupt, today, and the lights would not go on. The big antediluvian camera was still buried in its case, and even the procedure of unpacking it was a lengthy one. Already panicking at the thought of the rush there would be at the last moment, I compromised on making a half-hearted arrangement of portable lights and smaller camera trained on to a yellow marble pillar in an upstairs room. Haupt and I then hurried down to the ground floor to await our fate outside the Cabinet room armed, just in case, with a Rolleiflex and some flash bulbs.

At ten minutes to 11 o'clock we were still waiting outside the mahogany door. Senior secretaries, who were playing their important roles in fighting the war, passed by. I noted with relief that they all seemed cheerful and at ease. Perhaps the war was not going so badly after all. At 11 o'clock the butler took a glass of port into the Cabinet room, and came back confiding that the Prime Minister had just started dictating to Mrs Hill.

The Whip, David Margesson, appeared and talked about the latest air raid damage: minor secretaries crossed and re-crossed the hall. It was 11.10. At 11.20 some more Government servants appeared. Without doubt the Prime Minister must leave at 11.25. He had a Cabinet meeting at 11.30!

Mrs Hill, white and worried, put her head around the mahogany door. 'No time to go upstairs. Would you just come in here and take a few pictures now?'

I went into this noble room again. Churchill, still with cigar in mouth, looked so lonely and alone in this large room. This would make an aptly symbolic picture. From my distant vantage point, I clicked my Rolleiflex, and Haupt let off a flash. This surprised the Prime Minister. Although his sentences were not perfectly formed, I would hazard that the following would be an interpretation of the barks, wheezes and grunts that turned my blood cold: 'Hey, damn you, young fellow, what the hell are you up to with your monkey tricks? Stop all this nonsense! I hate candid camera photographs! Wait till I'm prepared: the glass of port taken away, my spectacles so — this box shut, the papers put away thus — now then — I'm ready, but don't try any cleverness on me!'

The PM settled himself and stared into my camera like a bulldog guarding its kennel. Click! 'One more, please.' By slow degrees I stealthily stalked my prey, coming at last within close range of him on his left side. He glowered into the camera, and by slow degrees dissolved into half a smile. Good humour prevailed. 'Sorry I can't go upstairs to the lights, but come again — come another day!'

By now three minutes must have ticked away on the clock. Dare I venture? 'Would you turn this way?' To my intense relief he turned his head and in reply again I clicked the camera. 'But come again another day. I'd like to see something that isn't just another photograph.' He rose from his chair. I asked, 'May I take a flash of you as you walk along the corridor outside towards the front door?'

'Certainly, so long as you don't photograph me putting on my coat and hat — no fooling about!'

We are in position; the PM, ready for the day's business, was about to make his stately progress along the hall. The flash went off twice. I moaned an aside to Haupt, 'But that was a double flash!' The PM stopped. 'Does that mean it's ruined? Does that mean it won't come out?' 'Yes, sir.' And once more he turned on his heel and walked back the length of the hall to repeat the exodus for me.

Yes, indeed, the devil was in Haupt today. He took for ever to put the new bulb in. Lighting his cigar Churchill waited patiently, while Haupt, all fingers and thumbs, tried to reload the flash lamp. Finally Churchill said, 'I must go now. I can't wait.' Haupt at last was ready and let off his flash — but far too soon. Oblivious of the disaster, Mr Churchill now in excellent mood, smiled benignly at me. I had not the heart to let him know that his magnanimous gesture had been unrewarded. Nevertheless, I was later able to beam with satisfaction myself, for although less than five minutes had elapsed since we had been admitted into the Cabinet room, one of the results on our negatives made a little history.

FIRE OF LONDON

December 30th

The city was still in flames after last night's raid when eight Wren churches and the Guildhall were destroyed. It was an emotionally disturbing experience to clamber among the still smouldering ashes of this frightful wasteland. It was doubly agonizing to realize that, had precautions for fire-spotters been taken, much of the damage could have been avoided. But it was too late, and some of the best churches have gone with little to indicate what was there before.

St Bride's in Fleet Street is now just a gutted orangery; St Andrew-by-the-Wardrobe, a hideous black mass with a molten copper roof like a blanket pall over the charred remains. No signs can be found of Gog and Magog at the Guildhall, and only a few baroque memorial tablets with sorrowing cupids and skulls remain at St Vedast's.

In the biting cold with icy winds beating around corners, James P. H. and I ran about the glowing smouldering mounds of rubble where once were the printers' shops and chop houses of Paternoster Row. We have trundled under perilous walls, over uncertain ground which, at any moment, might give way to the red-hot vaults below. We have known Ypres in the heart of London. We could not deny a certain ghoulish excitement stimulated us, and our anger and sorrow were mixed with a strange thrill at seeing such a lively destruction — for this desolation is full of vitality. The heavy walls crumble and fall in the most romantic Piranesi forms. It is only when the rubble is cleared up, and the mess is put in order, that the effect becomes dead.

We went to St Paul's to offer our prayers for its miraculous preservation. Near the cathedral is a shop that has been burnt unrecognizably; in fact, all that remains is an arch that looks like a vista in the ruins of Rome. Through the arch could be seen, rising mysteriously from the splintered masonry and smoke, the twin towers of the cathedral. It was necessary to squat to get the archway framing the picture. I squatted. A Press photographer watched me and, when I gave him a surly look, slunk away. When I returned from photographing another church, he was back, squatting and clicking in the same spot as I had been. Returning from lunch with my publisher, my morning's pictures still undeveloped in my overcoat pocket, I found the Press photographer's picture was already on the front page of the *Evening News*.

Part IV: Friends and Relations, 1940-1941

STEPHEN TENNANT

Wilsford

Because Stephen is so delicate his friends have felt that every day was made more precious in his company by the fact that any moment he might disappear for ever. But Stephen has learnt how to conserve his strength. I have now come to look upon him as someone who will beat us all and be the last to go — the tortoise among his contemporaries, the hares.

During this latest visit I have never appreciated the comforts of his house so much as now when in my own there is no hot water, the mirrors are blown out, and the blackout regulations are inadequate. Here, in a house that is heated to a uniform temperature with lights blazing, one relaxes into deep beds with fur coverlets or into steaming scented baths. The war — even the winter — is being defied.

Stephen himself is so untouched by the war that it is a comfort to be with him. He came to London for shopping. His reaction to the bomb that burst near him in Stratton Street was that it shot him and the page-boy through the swing doors of the Ritz 'like Peter Pan and Wendy'. He said, when the manager came down saying, 'Is everything all right?' he was only looking to see if the chandeliers were intact.

While staying at Wilsford, there has been much reading aloud. Stephen intoned his favourite authors: Conrad's stories (for he loves the sea), Suarez's work on Marseilles, descriptions by Firbank, books on sexual aberrations, the next world and spiritualism, and poems by Madame de Noailles. Stephen is the greatest paradox of heart and heartlessness, sensibility and cruelty, taste and vulgarity. He has untold strength. He laughs ruefully at the idea of becoming old, and manages to consort with younger people with facility.

Stephen, in his bathroom amid a great juxtaposition of face creams, scents, soaps, antiseptics, coal tar mouth wash, celluloid goldfish, and every sort of sponge and loofah, described a visit to a perfume counter in a Bournemouth store. At last the shop assistant had met someone who knew as much about scent as she. Stephen and she huddled together. This little woman essayed to describe the subtleties of every perfume that even a writer would blanch from setting forth. She said, 'When I use this, I become all dizzy. When I use this, it's like a shot of chloroform and I lose consciousness. And when I use *this*, I am followed!'

Rex Whistler asked Stephen, 'What are all these creams?' 'They are preserving creams.' 'But I don't see the point. What are they preserving you for?'

Yet incarcerated as he is in his ice cake fortress, how alive and susceptible to impressions he is! Tancred Boraneous said that the house should be made airtight and preserved intact just as it is at the moment, so that future generations may see these incredibly delicate and vivid colours, the vases of artificial roses and lilac, the fishnets hanging over the banisters, the tinselled postcards in the revolving stand, the whole paraphernalia of Stephen's taste, which astonishes even his few intimate friends and would be quite incomprehensible to future generations.

WITH NANCY AT FROYLE

Dorchester Hotel

There could be no more striking example of the changes that marriage can bring to a woman than that of my sister Nancy. She used to be gay, effervescent, with a streak of circus fanfare about her. She was full of fantasy and fancy. From the day she married Hugh the metamorphosis took place. She is now completely content (as far as anyone can be during this war). She has aged hardly at all yet her face wears a pensive look. In her teens she was plump to an extent that she used to diet and take foam baths. Her figure is now lean, her hands and face positively bony. In fact, she has become the typical English lady of tradition.

There is little today to stamp her of her own epoch. She says she would like to have lived in the time of Jane Austen. Her house, her clothes, have nothing modern about them, and her mind is full of the leisure and the domestic quiet that is not part of my own life. She has infinite time for her house, for her child and the country neighbours. It is only in gossip that she likes to have contact with the great world. She receives, and writes, large quantities of letters, copies poems in a flowery handwriting, does embroidery, is amused by the things the villagers say — and gives imitations of their voices, their toothless accents.

Staying with her for one peaceful week-end was an agreeable contrast to my week in London. We did nothing — yet were always occupied.

I came back, laden with lettuces and magnolia leaves, to find that the windows of my room had all been blown by the blast of an enormous bomb that fell only a few hundred yards away from the house.

I went upstairs to find my mother's room disfigured with soot, a wall bracket smashed, and looking-glasses littering the floor. This, of course, is nothing to what is happening to many others. But a succession of minor irritants were added to make this week an unproductive one. Maud was stricken with flu, the telephone was dead, telegrams impossible, and still no gas. I left to live at the Dorchester and this, in spite of its advantages, really only added to my displeasure for it has become a vulgar escape hole filled with foul-tempered, bombed-out people like myself. It is costing me the eyes of the head to stay on here paying for drinks and dinners every night.

DIANA AT LOELIA WESTMINSTER'S

I went to bed for dinner in the hotel but later, when the usual racket outside became unbearable, went downstairs to the gaieties of the restaurant. I was glad I did as my rather bitter mood was sweetened by a description of Diana's week-end at Loelia Westminster's.

On Sunday night Diana finds herself useless and unwanted. There is a bridge four and she and Ian Fleming remain over. After dinner Diana suggests to Ian they should play backgammon. No, he has some accounts to run through. He is poring over figures. Diana takes herself upstairs to write reams to her son, John Julius, in America. Envelope addressed, downstairs Diana comes. Ian Fleming still full of absorption in his figures. Diana thinks she'll make a joke. 'Awful to be the wife of the Minister of Information when the Minister doesn't give his wife any information, and so no one wants to ask her anything.' Silence! The bridgers continue their calls. Ian Fleming still absorbed. Diana in a huff goes up to bed. She creams her face, puts on a nightcap net, and then hears the

Boche aeroplanes overhead. What use to try and read a book with that din? She becomes really frightened. Duff and bridgers still at it downstairs. The intermittent buzz of engines above sickens her. Damn these unheeding swine below! She gets out of bed, explores the corridors and finds a room exactly above the bridge table. Here she jumps high into the air and lands as heavily as possible with a bang on the floor above the bridge table. With beating heart she rushes back to her room and, as was to be hoped, Duff appears.

'Did you hear that? It must be a bomb nearby. The whole house shook.'

A few intimate words between Duff and Diana. Music to Diana's ears. Duff agrees they are all shits downstairs, paying no attention to her — shits, absolute shits they are. Loelia's cheery face appears around the door. They are waiting to get on with the rubber. Duff goes downstairs, and once more Diana is left alone to listen to the enemy above. What could she do? Go downstairs and delight them with her greasy face and nightcap?

No, she'd done that last night. She couldn't keep on appearing in that garb.

For an eternity the bridge continues. Diana is scared, cold and desperate. Once more she explores the corridor, this time wearing high cork soles and heels to her shoes. Carefully she mounts a table and jumps. The whole house rocks. The bridge players rush upstairs, followed by Ian Fleming shouting to know if an incendiary bomb has fallen on the roof? Diana has raced to be in bed and appears drowsy by the time the door is opened.

'Did you hear that?' they ask. 'Must have been jolly near!' But the required result is obtained and Duff stays with her. When he asks, 'Was that you, Diana, who made that noise?' Diana lies, 'Certainly it wasn't!'

She told this story to Hutchie[13] and myself, sniggering and biting the air like a little child, on condition we swore we would tell no one. But I did not swear to exclude it from my diary.

THE SPHINX

How fortunate to have known, even a little, the Sphinx, Ada Leverson, who has already gone into history as the friend who with superb courage helped Oscar Wilde in his darkest hours. Perhaps none of us today realize quite what courage it took on her part, also that of her husband, to support Wilde at a time when feeling ran so high against him. His name was such anathema that even pet dogs could no longer be called Oscar.

When I met her in the company of Osbert Sitwell, for whom she cherished a passion, she was an aged figure in large black picture hat and long black trailing dress. Her hair was pale yellow and her face and neck so heavily powdered that some of the flecks had fallen on to her bodice.

I was extremely timid at this early age, and I found her wry smiles and lascivious winks somewhat alarming. No need. It was merely that the Sphinx was intrigued by all good-looking young men, and she used to write postcards to say I had eyelashes like ostrich feathers.

The Sphinx had great zest, and in her declining years never declined. Ever ready to accept any invitation or proposal, her youthful enjoyment of a jest was not dulled by the years. She had at least one good new joke a week. She knew this joke was good and preserved and polished it for the delight of her friends. I remember a little poem about Osbert Sitwell and

---

[13] St John Hutchinson.

Adrian Stokes, also a conundrum 'what is the difference between Oliver Messel and Oliver Twist', but I fear neither the poem nor the answer to the riddle are printable.

Of course the Sphinx also adored Sacheverell Sitwell, and when he became engaged to Georgia the Sphinx was obsessed with jealousy and curiosity. She was determined to be the first to see 'the new wife' on the return from her honeymoon. The Sphinx winked and asked, 'Well, Georgia, how did it go?' To which Georgia, furtively looking to left and right, answered in a hoarse whisper, 'Perfectly, thank you, but I want to ask you four questions — quickly now, Sphinx. What is the difference between romanticism and classicism? What is behaviourism? Who is Harry Melvill[14]? And is Julie Thompson[15] received?'

STEPHEN SPENDER

Stephen Spender was at dinner with Cyril Connolly. Stephen is a genuine character and one must admire his pristine integrity, but it is strange that a poet should be so insensitive to his audience. At the table he leant forward and in super-sibilant tones held forth: 'I do think, Cyril, some encouragement should be given to these Czech poets. Their poems are, in my humble opinion, very remarkable. They are Marxist in theory — but their Marxism is a safety valve, a check — and these Czechs need a check on their emotions. Some of them are slightly Kafka-ish — but Ida Crispi says she thinks they are remarkably interesting, and Albert Sessions,[16] whom I saw yesterday, thinks the same. So we must do something to encourage Czech poets.'

---

[14] An elderly wit about town.
[15] A fashionable American-born lady, famous in Paris.
[16] Or some such names.

He continued, 'The men at the fire station where I work for 148 hours each week were very much interested when I lectured to them about these poets. But then they are highly sensitive and listen to anything that I tell them. They like me — but they think of me as just number three on the pump drill. They don't know that I go off and make money by writing. They would hate me if they knew I made money. But I do — in my spare time, and during the time I'm supposed to be on duty too. I ought to be on duty now, as a matter of fact. But, anyway, to return to the subject of my making money, I wrote an account of an altercation between Joan and John Rayner to illustrate the present day mentality as bearing on tensions in modern war-time in spite of the teaching in secondary schools and the absence of essential facts — and I got three guineas for it. If I admitted it at the fire station the boys would be furious, for there's nothing that causes such a deep intellectual and spiritual rift as money.'

DIANA AT BOGNOR

Bognor

Duff has been ill for some days with a cocci infection. Three doctors have been brought in to look after him. At last his temperature is normal, though he has become deaf in one ear, and he is sufficiently recovered for Diana to send me a wire to come after all to Bognor. I've missed her deeply. It is a month since she left London and had to give up her work at the canteen. Each morning at 7 o'clock she walked through the park to do the breakfasts at a canteen. If, as a result of the previous night's raid, the gas was off and no hot water available, she had to improvise some sort of cooking.

She has been such a boon to have at the Dorchester and made the hotel life seem less squalid, and the evenings dining with her — while the blitz burst outside — have been delightfully escapist. Always a live wire, surrounded by interesting people and bits of news, Diana, nevertheless, became more and more unnerved by the horror of the bombing, for she is at heart a pessimist, and although she refused to show it, was terrified. Bravery does not consist of not being frightened, but to hide your terror is courageous. Diana pretended to take everything in her stride, and played up with bravado until she became positively ill. She, more than the doctors, knew she must quit.

The small Regency house in Bognor has been part of her life since her childhood holidays. Later her mother bought the beloved property, and now it is Diana's haven. Although even here the sirens sound thirty times a day and night, it is a comparatively peaceful existence for her running the place as if it were a farm.

Diana has bought a cow called Princess — a feminine equivalent of Ferdinand, for there never was so clinging and affectionate an animal as Princess. Twice a day Diana milks her, at 7.30 am and 6 pm. Princess delivers enough milk to keep the household and to make one large cheese every other day. The goat, less docile, produces milk that makes equally good cheese. Diana's hens produce ten eggs a day, and the pigs, named after the St John Hutchinsons, their children and children-in-law, are extremely clean for pigs.

But there is no nonsense about Diana posing in Le Hameau. 'To begin with, it gave me a mental hernia to put my hand inside a rabbit and pull out its insides. Now I give a good tug and don't mind, and it's the same skinning a hare.' It is hard work. Every day, by breakfast time, Diana has been looking after the farm for two hours. After breakfast she motors into Bognor with a trailer attached to the car to see about a hen house, or she collects swill from the neighbours, or the fish for the pie from the bus stop.

The latter part of the morning is spent in the dairy with large bowls of blue and white china, butter muslin nets and spotless efficiency. Here she sets about the technical jobs of cutting whey, taking temperatures and heating to certain degrees large bathtubs of milk, which with the addition of rennet drops from a calf's innards will be eventually turned into the required number of cheeses and arranged in rows on the storeroom shelf.

Like everything she takes up Diana works with enormous, business-like enthusiasm. Many amateurs set about their latest hobby with most elaborate equipment, little patience and no knowledge. Not Diana: her house is now littered with dogeared, second-hand textbooks on bee-keeping, on chickens, cows, goats. Her equipment consists of improvised utensils. A tinselled red embroidered Mexican saddle bag is filled with heavy stones. This, she considers, placed together with a log of wood on a wooden tray, makes a suitable enough press for the cheeses.

The guests — who may come down to keep her company while the Minister is busy at his desk — help bring the swill pails, add bone meal to the animals' fodder, or measure the dairy nuts for Princess. Diana makes all these chores such fun, and gives the impression that the animals' food is every bit as good as her own. Diana galvanized me into collecting in sacks some hay she had earlier cut from a neighbour's field. The job was a pleasant form of relaxation and an accompaniment to conversation, but, that task finished, there were many more to do while she fed the Khaki Campbells — her latest addition to the farm: a dozen ducks.

At the end of a long day she cooks the dinner. We sit at a table covered with pale lime green Macintosh. The fish pie is highly flavoured with a lot of onions. The news is turned off directly the raids start.

Moments of pleasure and relaxation are savoured to the utmost in this cluttered personable house — so live a picture of its owner — with the pale limedrop cushions, the grey-lilac walls, the Empire mirrors and candlesticks, the taffeta-bowed muslin curtains and the cases brimming over with books. It is a house feminine in its colour but broad in its effects. There is no time for arranging nick-nacks for, as soon as *The Times* crossword puzzle has been completed, there is some mending to be done. Diana sews some yellow fringe from discarded dining-room curtains. She picks at the yellow braid and twists it around thumb and little finger in the professional way that drapers' assistants had perfected when she watched them, awestruck, as a child. Enough twilight remains for Duff to read aloud some stanzas of Andrew Marvell, and to compare Cowper's description of Cromwell to Hitler. Then early bed and a lot of books on the counterpane.

Diana has always been attuned to the time and circle she adorns. Today she is beautiful in the only way she could be admired at this moment. Wearing dungarees of blue canvas, flecked and splashed in many colours, her head tied up in a kerchief over which she wears a straw hat, she manages artlessly to look as beautiful as she did in *The Miracle*. Hardworking and vital, close to essentials and yet, in her simplicity, so highly civilized.

It is a lovely picture: Diana, in her garden grown wild with gangling flowers blossoming under the trees, or scything the paddock: Diana, painstakingly putting entries into the farm ledger or, after carefully reading the instructions supplied by the local decorator, successfully hanging paper on the walls of an improvised guest room.

Dorchester Hotel

The bombing of London has slackened. Each week becomes more like war-time and less like war. Prices soar, commodities are more difficult to come by, and for the ordinary person the difficulties of housekeeping must be deeply depressing. All essentials are taxed or rationed: tea, butter, eggs, bread, bacon and onions. For those that can afford to, it is cheaper comparatively, to eat in hotels. But the luxury hotels are in cruel contrast to the existences being eked out under the arches in the Commercial Road and on the Tube platforms.

Moura Budberg dined and we found that with the help of a good bottle of claret the evening went easily. Wars, we agreed, knocked one from one level of age down to another. The Russian revolution had kicked Moura from youth to middle age (and had completely cut off her romance with Bruce Lockhart who joined us from a neighbouring table for coffee). This war was knocking her to old age. It has already aged us all so much, and to look around the Lansdowne House tonight was a ghastly revelation. Girls who used to be frivolous, fatuous and fast, and whom I had known dancing all night at the Embassy Club, were now dried-up old hags blinking at another generation at play. One or two lanky-limbed airmen were out for a quiet evening with some unsmiling granite-jawed ghouls who were no doubt tonight's substitutes for romance. These apparently casual young colts seemed quite content — for they are cynical about everything, including fighting dangerously for a future that possibly holds nothing for them, or getting into the hay with a dried-up old trout.

Maybe civilization advances in ratio to the horrors it invents. (The drowning or burying of old ladies in their shelters under their bombed homes makes Goya's *Désastres de la Guerre* look like picnics.)

This war seems to have been faced by England in a calmer, more cold-blooded mood than in 1914. Today there is no fanfare of drums, few pulses throb to the bugle-call that summons heroes to lay down their young lives for a freer and better world. The new VC's are calm, unassuming young men who deprecate their bravery in a way that is new. The cold, patient, brave bomber pilot has come to be regarded as the paragon — rather than the reckless fanatic.

And, thank God, that ghastly recruiting racket with hitches singing 'We don't want to lose you but we think you ought to go', and handing out white feathers is a thing we are spared.

For the present lack of hysteria we must be forever thankful.

AUNT JESSIE

Ashcombe

This last spell of London has been frustrating because it was so difficult to get any work done. Not that the bombing was bad: it has let up a bit. But life at the Dorchester is unnerving, Pelham Place is no longer habitable: the street is roped off with an unexploded bomb in the vicinity. So I am particularly blessed to have Ashcombe as a retreat. There has been no petrol for gallivanting in the neighbourhood, so I have stayed looking at books, reading, eating and sleeping. Perhaps I do not fully realize the vast benefit of this quiet. For four days I have been nursed and coddled here, tended with care and sweetness by my mother and my Aunt Jessie.

At last, Aunt Jessie, so hard-working and so full of life, is showing physical signs of age. It is hard for her to discover that her body is not as young as she feels herself to be. No child has greater enjoyment of this world. The smallest little details afford her acute excitement. Having been pampered and rich, accustomed to the highest echelons of the diplomatic world, she is now an impecunious widow. Yet she is a lesson in courage and simplicity. We walked as far as the sweet snowdrop wood, my only outing of the cold, sunny week-end. 'What do you think this is?' I asked in a somewhat blasé manner, handing her a piece of metal. Aunt Jessie was filled with awe. 'Oh, it's a thunderbolt!' she shouted, 'Oh! Oh! Oh! But we're standing on the snowdrops! Let's go in quickly. It's such a shame, now they've come out this far, to spoil them.'

Later Aunt Jessie said, 'I've failed terribly this winter! I can feel it. I know. I've coughed so much it's tired my old heart. I realize I've not got many days left now. I've been to the bank and got out £300. I've given some to my church, and put some aside for my funeral expenses. It always costs so much to die, and one has to have some ready money. Oh no, I'm failing very fast.'

NAPIER ALINGTON

September 22nd 1940

A milestone has gone. Napier has died. It is still too soon to realize it. His frail carcass had been wracked with appalling tubercular coughs for many years. Yet his system was of such ironlike strength that, whereas most other people would have succumbed long before, he had hung on. Sometimes he looked desperately ill, like a pathetic wastrel, but he was always courageously ready for fun. Now that the inevitable has happened, one wonders why the impossible should not have continued: It is perhaps more shocking when someone near extinction for so long suddenly disappears.

Napier had always a great preoccupation with death, and felt that each summer was perhaps his last. When Juliet and I bade him good-bye at the Ritz before he left on a mission to Cairo, he had said maybe this was the last time we'd meet. How beastly of me to consider that he was being a little theatrical!

None of his generation was more readily loved than Napier. Throughout the world, no matter what city he happened to alight upon, he exuded such warmth and charm that everyone threw their friendship at him. He treated such exuberance with kindness. In turn he was devoted and, genuinely devoted, to hundreds of people. But his friendship never became facile; it was never turned on just in order to chalk up another victim. Although he had such a large, warm heart his smile and charm were not circulated indiscriminately. He was easygoing only until he came across something of which he did not approve. Suddenly he could show anger and his granite sense of right and wrong. But for someone so sparkling and brilliant he was exceptionally benevolent; nearly every lame dog found a Samaritan in him.

I was not one of Napier's intimates, in fact I felt always a little removed from him, perhaps on account of my considering myself so much less genuine and sincere than he was. But Napier could not bear to be alone, and whenever I was at Ashcombe he would call me from Crichel to join him and his myrmidons. Sometimes the company he would invite encouraged him to sit up and drink all through the night, but the weakness in his nature was also encouraged by his illness, and lately he had seemed to wish, by any means possible, to escape the harsher unpleasantnesses of the way the world had gone.

Napier had always a spontaneous exhilaration and enthusiasm, a boyish glee in whatever surprising circumstances he found himself. In spite of the responsibilities and conventional ties of Crichel he was able to be as free as a bird, and felt just as at home in Persia as in France. He appreciated the nuances of luxury but could put up with any squalor. No matter where he found himself, he always behaved just as he wished. In New York exalted circles were scandalized, but in London he never became *déclassé*; however much pitch he wallowed in, it never stuck.

Today, when we motored through the sad rain to Crichel for the memorial service, I felt desperately miserable that we were not going over just once more to bask in his charm and enjoy the comic situations he created with the help of such a diversity of people surrounding him.

Crichel, with its noble porticoes, ornamental lakes, gazebos and Adams decorations, was still beautiful. All the things Napier has done with such exuberance to improve the place were paying their dividends today. But without Napier's glowing spirit to welcome us, Crichel could never be the same. (Maybe the house will remain empty for ten years or more — until Mary-Anna, his small daughter, God willing, comes back to live there.)

The service in the home chapel was a travesty. The arrangements were in the hands of a housekeeper-secretary whom Napier disliked, and the date had been peremptorily fixed without asking advice from relations or friends with the result that, war conditions being as they are, few intimates were able to be present. The vicar who gave the address assumed that Napier had been a conventional young peer, and obviously knew nothing of his audacity and courage, his sophisticated taste, bubbling fun, naughtiness and kindness. Napier would have chuckled at the description of himself but would have been pleased at the way his favourite extract from St Paul to the Corinthians[17] — on charity — was read by old Lord Shaftesbury.

At the macabre tea-party which took place afterwards, I managed to escape to Napier's small sitting-room. It is a room replete with so much personal charm and relics of his epoch, showing its owner as a dilettante in the arts. He was on no subject a connoisseur but had an avid interest in, and tremendous appreciation for, Chippendale furniture, Chinese jades and porcelain, jewels, English and French literature, the stage, the Russian ballet — almost every form of aesthetic manifestation. The room had been over-tidied, and the Casati portrait by John had disappeared, but the McEvoy portrait still hung over the chimneypiece. This sensitive impression completely conveys Napier's spirit. It is a portrait to inspire a novel — a portrait of someone who spells a distant mystery, who emanates a rare romantic and untamed quality.

Napier died at forty-three, a boy. A tired boy in appearance, but essentially young, with the willowy figure of a bantam-weight champion, a neat head covered with a cap of silken hair, pale far-seeing eyes and full lips.

He made life seem almost bearable to a large number of people, many of whom will be hard put to continue without him.

---

[17] I Corinthians xiii.

UNCLE WILFRED

December 1940 (Sunday), Pelham Place

I'd meant for some days now to go and see my funny, eccentric, Ally Sloper-Adrian Boult-looking Uncle Wilfred. For the last two weeks he has been in a hospital recovering from an operation. Impossible to go empty-handed, but since fruit and flower shops would be shut today, I hunted through the bookshelves for something that might be suitable for him. He has a definite taste in literature, but wouldn't be able to tackle anything heavy just now. I took some time to find anything to the point; then Edith Olivier's *Life of Cruden* (of *Concordance* fame) also a book on Mary Tudor, seemed the thing.

The telephone bell had not rung once during the entire day but, just as I was about to slam the front door, a pale tinkle came from the dining-room. It was one of the strangest coincidences that this should be a call from Mrs McGregor, Uncle Wilfred's Scottish housekeeper. She said my uncle had had a relapse and was most disquietingly ill — in fact, she was worried lest, during the night, she should be summoned to his death-bed.

Two days elapsed before Uncle Wilfred died. We were all upset and distressed. He has always been kind and good-humoured, and with his walrus moustache, bulbous red nose, and fishy eyes had given an air of fun and festivity to all our family gatherings. As a conversationalist he was excellent company, and his letters were elaborately witty. He was like a character out of Dickens — in fact, a character.

Now we felt remorse that in his later years we had done so little for him. He had had such a lonely life. My sister Nancy, it is true, had been quite solicitous and enjoyed inviting him down for an outing at Froyle. In fact this had somewhat irritated my mother, who considered Uncle Wilfred should not be encouraged to go on in his mean ways. He was a hermit engrained with stinginess, she said. Certainly the stories of his undressing by the light of the street lamp outside his windows to avoid electricity bills are pretty preposterous. Some people said he lived so simply because he had no money; others that he was a miser by nature. Nancy now telephoned and said rather excitedly, 'The great mystery is about to be solved!'

I hurried off to the funeral. This was my first visit to the flat at Palace Court, and never before had I seen Mrs McGregor, the legendary figure who had looked after my uncle for thirty-five years. A small, wizened, cobwebby little Scots woman opened the door. Now nearly eighty, her legs were twisted and bent, her grey tousled hair was topped by a large black hat. She wore a long fur coat of sorts. Almost unable to see or speak, so terribly upset was she, Mrs McGregor's face was both lined and swollen. She blurted out a few remarks that she was grateful for my sympathy and led me to the drawing-room where our remaining Beaton uncle awaited me.

So this grotto was where the hermit had hidden himself from the world! It was quite an expensive, old-fashioned series of tall rooms, polished, immaculate and trim, filled with mahogany furniture — the whole richly sombre effect as impersonal as a Victorian flat could be.

Uncle Cecil blinked at me with his baby blue, starry eyes. He had once bought a brewery, and when we were young we used to laugh at the way he used, when telling us about his beer, to bark out with such relish the word 'bah!-ley' for 'barley'. In fact he used to be known as Uncle Bah-ley. But with the years beefy Uncle Bah-ley, with the red cotton thread on his big cheeks, had shrunk. Today he looked a ghost of his former burly self. He, like Mrs McGregor, was also very upset. Rather distractedly he pleaded with me to do the honours at the funeral if there should be anyone to look after at the service.

We went off to Golder's Green in a hired Rolls, Uncle Cecil, Mrs M. and myself, and arrived at the crematorium to be met by a fat, self-satisfied, old aunt of a priest who welcomed us with a glinting smile as if he had swallowed another canary. There was only one other mourner, Clement Janes, who had married the Beaton sister, florid Florrie, and was considered a bit of a scallywag — no doubt because of his gambling instincts. No flowers by request, so that the purple coffin had only one bunch of mixed chrysanths upon it. The service had dignity, for the fat, Alice-in-Wonderland, cat-grinning priest managed to speak the English of the Bible with a certain sonorous gravity.

But that only four people should see the old hermit to his ashes was poignant! — yet understandable! for in war-time it is difficult for people to receive personal news or to travel.

The coffin was cranked past the thick doors towards the furnace, and another pair of doors facing the East was opened. That was that. We walked out into the cold wintry morning to a loggia strewn with half-dead wreaths. The Cheshire cat priest now became a gossiping aunt with my remaining uncle: 'Oh yes, it is *tragic* — tragic ...' He pursed his lips and frowned. I watched his performance wondering that he could run through it at least six or seven times each day.

Clement Janes now showed himself to be a high-spirited, opinionated gas-bag of the old school. Through whistling false teeth he confided, 'God! I had to read the notice three times in the paper. Gosh! It gave me a jolly good old shock, I can tell yer!' Then Uncle Cecil, limp and sagging, with typical hanging silk scarf and wide, tragic, Beaton-dog eyes, said, 'Now we'll go back and have a glass of wine!' In the motor-car Mrs

McGregor was alternately weeping and gossiping with equal spirit. Clement Janes was only gossiping. 'These days I feel die cold — I've even got chilblains — and I put it down to not having enough liquid refreshment! It's so damned expensive you know, old boy — it just can't be managed!' I wanted to hear the cause of Uncle Wilfred's death, but C.J. was tossing his conversational snowballs in the air. In spite of his shabby shoes, his long hair and frayed collar, his tall hat, gloves and speech bespoke the dandy.

Back at the flat, Uncle Cecil announced, 'Well, the trustee tells me that although I must give away no definite information yet, Wilfred has, in fact, left a generous will. Every member of the family has been remembered. He has been most thoughtful and kind. Now, Mrs McGregor, bring that sherry — and the port we opened last night.' Decanters were produced, and a vast box of Scotch biscuits just sent as a Christmas present to Uncle Wilfred. The two other men were soon in high spirits. Uncle Cecil was galvanized into talking like an uninhibited child about anything on its mind. He was swinging backwards and forwards on his toe points in front of the fire. Clement Janes relished his glass of sherry. It was a rare treat, and I was impressed by his refusal of a second glass. 'Oh no-no — dear old chap — not any more than one glass of sherry! I don't take breakfast these days.' Not having tasted port since I had too much at a Beefsteak club at Cambridge, this glass of rich tawny ruby was a revelation. 'So you're working for the Government!' Clement Janes turned to me. 'My dear man, I wish you'd get me a job in the Ministry of Information!' I was amused that he should refer to my piffling work with such ceremony. 'You laugh — you think I'm not up to it! Ha! Ha! Well, you're damned right. I can only say what I think. I can't write anything — wish I could!' One could not but admire this somewhat faded ne'er-do-well, down on his luck — cold, threadbare — for his braggadocio. In a grandiose way he talked about getting back to Golders Green 'where the Jews had let down the tone of the place', but since the *blitzkrieg* they had abandoned the neighbourhood and he, personally, hoped they would never go back again.

Clement Janes wended his way. Uncle Cecil shut the door on him. Now fully in his conversational stride he did not wish me to leave for a while. 'So, you see, your Uncle Wilfred — well, I hate all these uncles and aunts, and cousins and nieces — it's all right for babies, but let's drop it — well, Wilfred's death — has been such a shock to me. I never thought I'd be the last to go. However, Bentley, the family solicitor, came here and we had dinner here last night, and he was so tired, poor fellow, I thought he was going to faint, and I said, "Bentley, you'll have a bottle of champagne won't you?" And we did, and it was jolly good, for my brother had a splendid lot of wines and spirits and cigars — and that's all he has left me — unless there's anything over from the residue when everyone has received something. Well, it appears to me like this — reading the will — that each person has his own hobbies. I collect stamps, for example, and your uncle — well, Wilfred — he collected money. He was so careful in his lifetime: it upset him if anyone were to spend any money on him. He used to like red clove carnations, and I wanted to take him some to the hospital, but I asked the price — eightpence each. Mind you now, he would have been simply furious if I'd spent eightpence each for a carnation for him: "What are you wasting your money for?" he'd ask. I brought him some rotten little chrysanthemums, and when I asked him what he'd like, he said, "Nothing, you've already brought me some flowers." But I bought him some bananas: first I bought him three, and another day I bought him two, and he liked that. He sat up in bed and ate one in front of me. But extravagance enraged him. Mrs McGregor used to buy a grouse as a treat if it were four and sixpence but not if it were five shillings. Of course he liked his glass of sherry with his dinner, and his glass of port, but he was very Victorian and often said, "What was good enough for me as a boy is good enough for me now." Sometimes when we went away together on trips I'd come across all sorts of little traits that were part of his character. We'd dine, and the waiter would say, "Coffee?" "How much?" he'd ask. Abashed, the waiter would say, "Sixpence." "Nonsense, no coffee is worth more than fourpence," and he'd go without. I'll tell you another story that is typical of him. You know he used to walk home every day from the city. Well, he knew the fare of a bus ride from Marble Arch to Whiteley's Corner was a penny, so, as it was raining one day, he got on to the bus and gave the conductor a penny. The conductor said that for the distance he wished to go the fare was twopence. "No, it isn't, my man." "Well, I ought to know my own job. I tell you the fare isn't a penny, it's twopence." "Well, I pay under protest."'

On arrival at home Uncle Wilfred wrote to the bus company complaining of what had happened. Later he told Uncle Cecil the story and of how, the following day, he was to go to the courts about the case. 'Now, really, you mean you'll go to all that trouble just over a penny?' 'I don't care how much it's over — it's the principle of the thing. I'm not going to be rooked!' The next time the brothers met, Uncle Cecil asked, 'Well, did you waste your time at the courts?' 'Waste my time? Nonsense! I won my case, and got back my penny!'

Now, after years of really denying himself all the luxuries, and even many comforts of everyday existence, Wilfred has died, and the scattered strangers with the fluke of a Beaton surname are to benefit. It is an extraordinary stroke of fortune for us, and, judging from the way in which Cecil talked about the legacies, I should not be surprised if Wilfred has not died an extremely wealthy man. It is a great comfort to know that Mummie has not been forgotten, and I only pray that it may be substantial enough a sum to give her a certain feeling of freedom. Nancy, Baba and I will benefit, as indeed does Olive Mary Beaton who, it appears, is a daughter of Theodore Beaton in Liverpool, and a few obscure relations will also receive a pleasant shock.

Suddenly, with Russian cigarettes, Scotch biscuits and French champagne, the atmosphere became highly keyed. It seemed so unlikely that any member of our family should be connected with money. Of course we may yet be disappointed, but I have never expected a penny.

Another surprise was to find how human and entertaining is Uncle Cecil. He has the quality I love of being able to describe people in imitations. Completely unselfconsciously, he could do exaggerated impersonations of our relations, of Mrs McGregor (now weeping outside so loud that I thought a dog was howling), and other intimates in the circle. He was really inimitable describing his night sleeping or waking here in the flat, with Mrs McGregor's snores (she had said she couldn't sleep a wink) and the chimes of the clocks. He gave imitations of Uncle Wilfred blinking in bed as he sank into his final illness, of the blustering doctor and pernickety nurses, and of the dreary, cautious, indoctrinated family solicitor. He also told me in character many amusing family stories about flushed old Aunt Florrie, who always spoke as if she were trying to prevent a burp, and her son — who is considered a crank for he does no work, but knows every date in the world's history. He is good enough, Uncle Cecil said, to be featured as Datus was at

the Tivoli in the old days. Datus was fired at with questions at
the rate of one a second but he was never once 'pipped'; even
when the trap of Leap Year was sprung, he would reprimand
the questioner by saying, 'Don't you remember that that
happened to be a Leap Year?'

Poor old Wilfred whom I last saw, more walrussy than ever,
flying about wild-eyed and hatless, in the middle of a traffic
roundabout in Paddington during an air raid — he'd popped
off very quickly, and we had now lost the opportunity of being
nicer to him, of giving him a better time. We'd missed that bus,
and we didn't really deserve to benefit. Yet instead of returning
home depressed, Uncle Cecil and I came back somewhat
galvanized by the morning to my house for a lunch of cold
pheasant. When, during the meal, I gave a telephone message
to Dorothy, the maid, for Peggy Ashcroft, the actress, Uncle
Barley barked out, 'Tell her you're lunching with her
godfather'; and it was true. The morning had been a succession
of surprises.

I was sorry to have to put an end to this adventure in a new
world of family life. But a blonde tartlet of a movie actress and
the usual ratty concourse of film scavengers — publicity men,
yes-men and no-men — were awaiting my degrading services
at the costumiers.

End of April, Ashcombe

The spring, though it came late, has been such a welcome joy
after the long and frightening winter. Here at Ashcombe,
paradoxically enough, the garden has never been in such trim.
Dove, the new gardener, is a gentle creature, who has not only
put up a desperate fight against asthma, but has battled
ruthlessly against nature. Nettles, six foot high, and weeds have
surrendered to his onslaught, and favourite flowers have grown

larger than ever before.

It was here last Sunday that the radio informed us that London had been badly bombed — the heaviest raid yet. We've been so remote and peaceful in this fold of the Downs that it was only the nightly drone of German aeroplanes above that gave us any sense of war. Even the drone ceased on Saturday. We did not realize that the planes, instead of being on their way to Plymouth or the Midlands, had taken a course to London.

Immediately on arrival in London one realized the chaos and damage. Great yawning gaps gape around Waterloo Station: there was little traffic on the roads, and rubble was all that remained of thousands of bombed-out houses. The Temple church and many city buildings that survived the Great Fire and the *blitzkrieg* of September have gone in this last onslaught. By some fluke the house in Pelham Place remains intact, but its survival becomes ever more remarkable. One realizes that the odds against remaining immune are drawing in.

It is characteristic of the British always to be convinced that all goes well. But I begin to wonder secretly whether all good things don't come to an end, and if, this time, we have been caught bending once too often. Events are very dark. At the collapse of France we said, 'Things couldn't be worse.' Now the Balkans have gone, Greece is in the throes of a final agony, and we have lost there our last foothold in Europe. I know we cannot afford to give up, but if the Suez Canal goes we are likely to be terribly maimed. In a year's time, maybe, we shall be living on capsules.

Each month one learns of more victims: Robert Byron, torpedoed on his way to the East, is a great loss. He was such an original scholar. His *Birth of Western Painting* led the way for others to re-discover Byzantine art. I recall him dressed in exaggerated tweeds, as though just in from the moors — a man of great wit and with the grandeur of a Roman emperor. And he was still so young. Each month the net of tragedy is pulled tighter. Each month one looks back on the last with a nostalgic regret as for the 'good old days'. Growing hardened to more and more rationing we cannot believe that once we went shopping casually for a box of matches, a roll of photograph film or a bottle of soda water. As Vic Oliver quips, 'Do you remember razor blades?'

NEWS OF BABA

Nancy came back from Baba's. The atmosphere had been gloomy. Baba apathetic: she feels there is nothing further to live for now that Alec[18] has been killed. Nancy reported that the youngest child had an angelic disposition, but that Xandra was going through a difficult phase. Perhaps out of deep unhappiness she seemed determined to show no feelings of friendship or affection for anybody. She even remained outwardly unmoved when told of her father's death, and remarked that for her mother to buy a lot of black clothes was 'a waste of coupons'.

Xandra looks like a gipsy child, burnt as brown as leather, very stringy, with long lank hair: she wears a cotton smock with nothing underneath it, leather shoes and no stockings. Each morning, as soon as she is awake, she is round at a neighbouring farm milking the cows. She is lost all day, seldom returning at meal times. She only likes driving the cattle. She will wade them across a river, and spend the rest of the day in her muddy shoes. She swears like a trooper: when a rabbit she is feeding scratches her, she holloas, 'You bloody so and so!'

---

[18] Alec Hambro, married to my sister Baba.

She spends her days with the village boys and enjoys a good fight with them. The other day there was a hideous scene at the back door: Baba was appalled to find an irate mother shouting, 'I'll have the police on her! She's thrown a brick at my Tommy and got him right on the nose. She's a menace to our kids, always fighting with 'em. I'll put the police on her!'

Part V: With the RAF, 1941

Torquay

Cooped together in a two-seater motor-car one is apt to get to know one's travelling companion pretty well by the end of a ten-hour journey. Jolly lucky to have, as my cicerone on a photographic tour of RAF bases for the Ministry of Information, someone whose company is so easy to enjoy and who, in turn, is so appreciative, as Derek Adkins. Our many expeditions across and around England and Wales have the aroma of adventure. Derek, blue-eyed and beefy with fair crinkly hair, is very much the average man in the Service, and it surprises and pleases me to discover that his sort has so much sensitivity and understanding of others. In the washroom of the officers' mess, meeting fellows in corridors, his contacts are easy, gay and mysterious in their simplicity. Perhaps his breeziness is part of a tremendous assurance; without being braggartly or conceited he keeps his own independence and individuality through every circumstance. Derek is in contact with life at first hand, all day long and every day. He does not need any of the escape-screens behind which I like to hide. Figuratively, I am lost without a secretary. Derek prefers to overhaul his fountain pen, fill in his own income-tax returns, pay the bills, interview the judge, and cope with everything as ordinary citizens of the world should do. He even mends the carburettor himself, or jumps out of his car to argue with the man who is advising him on the road. Enough...

Diana Cooper suggested that Alfred Mason[19] should have us to stay at his rented house in Torquay for our tour of hospitals and rehabilitation centres around there. Alfred would be away, but he would be only too pleased to have his copious staff tend to our wishes. Until a few months ago when she died, the house belonged to a Victorian woman with a religious mania. It remains exactly as it was when she decorated it sixty years ago. Such a mass of rich Victorianism is now rare — windows hung with heavy cut velvets and starched Nottingham lace, piccalilli-coloured carpets, buhl, over-upholstered sofas, love-seats and ottomans, and gilt-framed religious pictures, crucifixes and porcelain reproductions of Florentine Madonnas. Severely uniformed Edwardian parlourmaids serve port, sherry, turbot, and gooseberry tart. Miss Andrade (Alfred's literary secretary) comes in, every now and then, to stifle our bewilderment: 'Mr Mason always has this tantalus of whisky.' 'Mr Mason doesn't realize the food shortage.' 'We can get fish, but it's terribly dear.' 'We've opened these windows ever since he's been away, but we still can't get rid of his cigar smoke.'

I am innately shy, but I have to overcome this. It is often hard when it is up to me to take the initiative before a group of servicemen and try not to display my abysmal ignorance about things in general: the strain of trying to learn and memorize facts, statistics, names and ranks begins to tell by the evening. It is like convalescence to be able to return in the evenings to the Villa Borghese, and to relax in front of a huge fire.

Yellow cartons of exposed film accumulate by the gong in the hall into such a bulky pile that I long to take a morning off to potter out to the rock-garden with its Scotch heather, cacti, and stones looking like petrified spittle. Or I would like to browse with a book until the sun sets against spiky palm-trees,

---

[19] A. E. W. Mason, the historical novelist.

over the Bay of Torquay. For then the effect of light on the harbour is completely Mediterranean. But no — Derek is conscientious, and has the strength, the vitality, of a lion. If I show signs of weakening he bullies me into further activity, and the pile of yellow cartons by the Indian gong in the Victorian hallway grows ever higher each evening.

Biggin Hill Fighter Station

It was from here that much of the Battle of Britain last September was fought. The CO of a squadron, whose name is Robinson, was particularly amicable, and suggested my going up in the air to photograph him in his Spitfire flying in formation. I was taken up in an old plane, 'Miles Maggie', to fly at a height of 4,000 feet and circle around above the clouds.

Out of the cumulus Robinson suddenly appeared, like a shining fish, alongside our wing. He smiled, and continued to grin as he kept level with us, and we travelled thus while I photographed him. The wind blew my eyelashes into my eyes, and it was difficult to focus. Suddenly, I saw myself reflected in the viewfinder of my camera. The crow's feet around my eyes were those of an old man. Oh God! Was there no escape from oneself even under these unusual conditions?

When my pictures were taken Robinson, still grinning, put up his thumb, pulled back the stick, and the Spitfire climbed, its nose soaring backwards into the heavens like an inverted dive. Climbing higher and higher he was triumphant over space and time; defying gravity he had attained a means of expression that had given him an elasticity denied to all the earth-bound. With this new element at his disposal he had attained exquisite sensations of power and purity.

We, in the 'Maggie', continued to fly across the empty blue, weaving arcs and patterns up and down. It was a sultry day below, but this mountain freshness was refreshing and cleansing to the soul. The clouds beneath dispersed and I watched the insectlike shadow of our aircraft gliding smoothly over patchwork squares of fawn and green fields and squares spotted with rows of corn-stooks. Our shadow coursed over the orderliness of walled-in gardens, their secrets of washing pathetically revealed on the drying lines: it hurdled over haystacks and the miniature church with its steeple smaller than a pepper-pot. It flew over avenues of trees, and counterpanes of woodland and the stationary arabesques of small rivers.

Cruising along so smoothly like this, watching the slow-moving scenes below, there was the added balm of escape from terrestial troubles. It seemed impossible that such turmoil should be fermenting down there. These troubles suddenly seemed as childish as the world itself looked childish. For this neat and efficient toy world belonged to a child's nursery. By now I had forgotten myself, my human frame, and worldly cares. This escape into the skies had been also an escape from war. Just to leave the earth even for these few minutes had given a perspective to the problems that daily assail us, and suddenly life, and even death, seemed relatively unimportant.

As we came back to earth the warm air engulfed us like a towel. Like a gull coming to rest we glided down, then taxied around jerkily, bumping to our resting-place. The airscrew blades turned visibly as they rotated more and more slowly and finally jerked to a stop.

Robinson, whose smile across the sky had been so euphoric and intimate, was already back at the dispersal unit. His mood had changed: he was no longer smiling; he had become somewhat matter-of-fact and pedestrian. When I told him how much I had enjoyed our encounter in the skies, he replied, 'Yes, it's always wretched to have to come down.'

De Havilland Aerodrome and Training School

The training school here gave me a glimpse of the concentrated effort needed to make each pilot accomplished enough to take to air combat. Although the pilots are now being rushed through the elementary school in less than five weeks, by the end of that time their receptive heads are crammed with knowledge that would take me years to imbibe. It is deeply impressive to see the seriousness with which all these young men tackle their job. They have the perseverance of a kindergarten child, but none of its recklessness. They set out on their afternoon flights with the same attitude as a surgeon tackling an operation, and it all seems far removed from the dare-devil conception of an airman that my brother Reggie gave me the impression of aiming at.

The training wing presents a microcosm of the entire RAF. Every aspect of activity is emulated with care and imagination. The trainees rehearse the ritual they will ultimately perform, but with dummies and 'props' instead of the real thing. One pupil sits lidded down in a wooden box and must go through the entire procedure of a long solo flight under all conditions of weather. (He is sometimes four hours in this contraption, complete with thermos and sandwiches.) Classes are occupied doing Morse signalling, navigation, winding airscrew wheels, or you will see trainees squatting under the belly of a skeleton bomber loading the racks with bombs filled with sawdust. To an intent group of would-be gunners a sergeant instructor demonstrates the working of an electrically operated gun turret, and aims his sights at the *art nouveau* or Paul Klee-like diagram of swirls and convolutions marked on the wall. No moving-picture studio can make more careful models than the miniature enemy towns used in bombing practice.

One is astonished at the youthfulness of these seventeen-year-olds with their subtle English looks, clear complexions, and thatch of hair shorn closely over the ears. One bright young man asked when my pictures would appear, and in answer to my 'in six weeks' time' said, 'Oh, most of us will be dead by then!' But it was pleasant to discover that most of the RAF volunteers are utterly fulfilled in their job — they live and breathe flying. During their spare time they make models of aircraft from odd bits of wood, or read aeronautical magazines. They are neither pining for home, lusting after girls, nor fretting about danger. It is all much happier and simpler than I'd imagined, and the discipline is freer than in the army.

Air Commodore Critchley agreed with the article in which Ingersoll, an American journalist, stated that, if the Germans had been prepared to go on losing 150 planes for another week the Battle of Britain would have been lost: but not for the reasons Ingersoll claimed. Critchley explained that we were on the knife-edge of disaster, not from the point of view of bomb damage or of services breaking down — but because our pilots could not be got into the air. They had been on the alert to surprise and danger continuously, and had become so overtired and unnerved that they could not sleep without such strong sleeping draughts that, when eventually pills had taken effect, the men could not be woken again.

London

Looking at a batch of photographs I had taken — the result of cursory visits to various RAF stations — Hugh Francis at the Ministry of Information said, 'It's rather surprising that you enjoy doing this — they're so different from the stuff you used to publish.' But although my subject matter had changed so violently, often my approach with the camera was the same in that, wherever I went, I was trying to find groups and settings that would compose into a design. Often the bare walls or the struts of a hangar lent themselves as usefully to a pictorial scheme as any more calculated effects of decoration.

The fact that here were people of character living under dramatic conditions inspired me to adopt a more realistic approach, and the freedom of doing a straightforward piece of *reportage* was something that I found stimulating. My equipment consisted of one Rolleiflex and a flash bulb, so my powers of ingenuity were given full rein.

Hugh Francis told me he would authorize my making a complete study of the RAF. Apart from the uses he would make of the photographs, I should write a fictional composition, written for propaganda.[20] At last, I felt, I was able to do something to assuage my pangs of guilt at being unable to make a more worthwhile contribution.

LIFE ON THE STATION

Somehow, it always seems to be that light is fading when, after a long and hazardous train journey, I arrive, cold and stiff and full of trepidation, to be met by some cheerful PRO. In fact, it is sometimes an early afternoon arrival, yet at this time of the year, and at this stage of the war, daylight seems something always on the wane. Yet I have not been in the company of my new friend for more than a few moments before he has succeeded in assuaging my pangs of anxiety. 'You will enjoy seeing this set-up; it's bags of fun.'

---

[20] This resulted in Hutchinson's publishing *Winged Squadrons*, drawn from my diaries.

We drive to the outskirts of the town where, on a bleak strip of land, the aerodrome is situated. All air stations, with their widely-spaced bungalow buildings, seem to be laid out on an identical plan and, with their protective covering of olive greens and khaki, the long, narrow buildings themselves are so impersonal and anonymous that, each time one arrives, one is baffled by the strangely familiar feeling of 'I have been here before'.

Work never stops in the 'Ops' room. The electric bulbs burn continuously upon the maps and charts that show the progress of the latest sorties. Day and night the Met. people foretell the weather conditions of the future. In the vast dark hangars the electricians are making major repairs to every sort of aircraft. In the bomb dump armourers are loading on to trucks the explosives destined for the pressure points of the enemy's arteries. Sunday differs in no way from other days, and only when completing their forms and log books do the constantly changing occupants of these warren-like buildings know the date of the month.

Here the necessities of life are provided, the food is good, for pilots are too valuable not to be kept in top condition, but little emphasis is placed on comfort.

The community itself creates, by its own fervour, the warmth and cosiness in which it lives. Former existence, ties and interests are intentionally forgotten: family or fiancée are secluded beyond the barriers. The farther removed from a large town with its girls, colour and distractions, the better is the spirit and morale of a station.

The aerodrome itself is the orbit of these men. It is simpler not to rely, or even embark, upon friendships when life is so precarious. The RAF encourages a loyal *camaraderie* rather than deep individual friendships. Under an armour of carefree gaiety there is an inner core of quiet and reserve. On an off-duty evening men divide into groups of four or five of those who are in the same flight (or have the same amount of spare money) to drink a tankard of beer at the local pub. Yet, living within their realm of local jokes and rounds of beer, pilots undoubtedly have a fuller life than we groundlings outside. The aerodrome is confined within its barbed-wire palisades, but from that constricted space, by day and by night, the inhabitants audaciously invade the domains of the deities.

Perhaps I have not yet seen enough to generalize about the character of each Service, but it does seem to me that RAF men acquire a certain similarity of outlook: each man shows an enthusiasm towards his duty — everyone is always trying to learn more about his own job. Even while waiting at the ready by their aircraft the pilots 'talk shop', exchange experiences and suggest new tactics.

The RAF has had less time to create traditions than the older Services, and one notices that there is less of a uniform style of manner than in the Army. In appearance, too, there is more variation in dress: personal preferences are shown in boots, shoes and coats. Some wear the top button of their jacket undone with a civilian scarf worn at the neck. Those who are old enough to grow moustaches do so, emphasizing their personality in variations of style, shape and proportion. None the less, tradition, together with training, does play a large part in the maintenance of morale. Morale is highest in the presence of a leader, or when dangers can be faced in company with others. Flying is a solitary form of duty, and pilots have not always the presence of their companions to support them, as the soldier has his regiment. It is when the individual is called upon to face danger alone that the greatest strain is placed upon him. Yet if he has a crew with him, the comfort their company gives may be outweighed by the added burden of this responsibility.

The spirit of a squadron is also enormously influenced by the personality, vitality, or even wit, of certain of its members. A squadron is keyed up to produce its best results only when it feels itself to be in good form. The whole fabric can become slackened by the removal of a few of its compelling personalities. It is just the same as during the run of a play: the acting can deteriorate if a star member leaves the cast. Each individual counts in the structure of the whole.

When a pilot of a fighting squadron does not come back, the others, after waiting about an hour or two, disperse rather quietly. If the reports show the missing man to be safe, these fellows show their relief. But if no word comes through they are likely, that night, to drink a tankard or two extra, to have a determinedly cheerful evening, so that they may forget the gnawing at the back of their minds.

Shirley Woolmer, who is an intelligence officer attached to Victor Beamish's heroic squadron, told me about a party that had been arranged at North Weald. A few hours before, a sweep was called in which three of the pilots were killed. No one suggested, however, that the party should be put off. Everyone got rather drunk. That was the way of demonstrating that in all circumstances 'the show must go on'.

At first, so lighthearted appeared the general atmosphere, I had the impression that on these RAF stations no one felt very deeply about anything anymore. There was little interest in activities outside, no talk of Whitehall, and all unpleasantness, danger, and even the war itself was banished from conversation. In a unit where, from one hour to another, a friend may 'fail to return' (how heartless a phrase with its ignoble note of censure!), gloomy subjects are forbidden by tacit consent: mention of the possibilities of disfigurement or being seriously burnt is unthinkable. An intuitive wisdom dictates these rules. If emotions were allowed free play the shocks would be even harder to bear. Death may be mentioned flippantly, if at all. Someone had 'gone for a Burton' or been 'bumped off'; the men seldom again referred to anyone once 'presumed lost'.

But I now realize that feelings are controlled and smothered by a self-preservation instinct. Realization of their nearness to danger is never far removed from the minds of these youths, in spite of such easy grace of heart.

These men bring the art of living into the aerodrome, knowing that the best has been provided. They value their aircraft, and appreciate that it does only what the pilot makes it, that without him it cannot fly, and that its weakest part is the pilot. Their respect even for their rather arid-looking mess is shown by the scrupulous care with which, having returned from the air, the pilot takes off his coat, washes his hands, combs his hair, and brushes his shoulders before entering. Airmen are surprisingly formal. Even the bad language and the slang they use becomes part of a code of behaviour. Even the CO feels that he must use the 'good shows', 'wizard prangs', and 'gens' that are part of an anonymous language pattern by which the RAF expresses itself. He even thinks in the special phraseology of the RAF, thereby associating himself utterly and entirely with the communal spirit.

April 1941, Tangmere

Fighter pilots have a daredevil *bravura* quality, and seem to be rakishly gay and heroic in an offhand way. They are the more reckless ones, slightly temperamental, perhaps even a bit selfish — but only in comparison with the rest of the RAF, for selfishness, as known in the outside world, cannot exist here.

Though the fighter pilot generally flies alone he is always a part of the squadron, he is often flying in formation, and receives his instructions from the squadron leader or wing commander. However, we have the impression that the fighters are the tough ones, irresponsible young sparks who might risk all for a lark. But the daredevil who, without reckoning the odds, would go 'flat out', would 'shoot up' his aerodrome, diving down between the refuelling bowsers, has long since gone. Erratic feats of devil-may-care recklessness are less admired today than the calculated courage of the new type of hero with his 'cold guts'. His bravery needs no aids. His attitude, without heroics, even a little cynical, is sobered by his sense that so much depends upon him.

Under fine weather conditions any fool can fly a straight course. To manoeuvre a Spitfire in rough weather for an hour is as fatiguing as any normal day's work. To compete with the unexpected danger, and to control the hundred-and-one 'hot and cold taps' on the dashboard, needs a concentrated clarity of mind: to be able to fight in the air demands enormous ability and intelligence.

The fighter pilot must learn to have such instinctive mastery over the complicated controls that within a split-second he can take action. Simultaneously assuming the duties of navigator, wireless operator and air-gunner, he must be as alert as a highly-trained racehorse, never off guard for an instant, craning his neck lest an unsuspected enemy forestall him or creep up from behind. Taking into consideration position of the sun, wind speed, his height and petrol reserves, he must be quick enough to make any immediate practical decision. For his life he alone is responsible.

Although so much can happen within the few split-seconds of combat, the fighter is rarely for more than an hour and a half in the air. Most of his time is spent waiting near his Spitfire 'at readiness' from dawn to sunset.

These young pilots stand about in loose attitudes, flexing the muscles of a leg, kicking a corner of the door with a heavy foot, or tossing a pencil in the palm of a hand that has a piece of sticking-plaster on it. Intent on nothing particular, they are absorbed by the waiting. Yet this lassitude is neither as casual nor as utterly carefree as it seems. At any moment the alert may sound — and then all hell breaks loose.

They are a blue and yellow group in their yellow life-preservers, their blue trousers tucked into sheep-wool lined boots. In the RAF colours take on new significance. They are not chosen for aesthetic reasons or personal taste. They become intelligence symbols that change according to the code of the night. Red chalk on the boards of the operations room shows what has been achieved, yellow chalk that which has been the aim. The coloured lights flash their signals to the traffic in the air above where, for obvious reasons, the Defiant night-fighter and the Manchester bomber are painted black. Yellow, however, according to the scientists, is the colour most easily seen in the distance. Yellow becomes the symbol of faith. The skull-caps, like buttercups, that the pilots wear when they bale out into the sea, and the dinghy which contains them, are yellow, and it is often by the streaks of yellow fluorescine chemical with which they stain the sea that they are seen from above and saved from drowning.

Hallo! What's this? One of the squadron back already?

'What happened to you, McCarthy?' McCarthy, of the large, pale moustache, is 'browned off'. The door of his machine had come unhinged and might have flown off, hitting his tail. So he'd had to turn around, hanging on to it with all his strength. He settles down in resignation to read a detective novel until the others return.

A dramatic silence pervades the operations room with the flashing lights of its batteries of telephones through which come information, orders and inquiries to the controller. The men working here are older, now considered unfit for operational duties although, having been previously through similar combats, they are able to give confidence to the younger men fighting in the sky.

The pilots, when many miles away over enemy-occupied territory, are comforted if they know the controller on duty and recognize his voice. Henderson, with the long, lean face of a sad greyhound, said, 'Yes, I want to know whether the bloke is fat, stupid, or if he knows what he's doing.' The controller can become a sort of godfather to the fighter pilots — a sympathetic link with the ground; they like to hear the deep, pleasant voice which warns them: 'Bandits behind you, but don't worry', and in answer to their, 'I think I'd better come home', replies: 'Yes, come home right away.'

Though conversing with one another in the air is not encouraged, for it may add confusion and their bad language prove embarrassing to the WAAFs in the 'Ops' room, the fighters can often be heard calling to one another on their radio sets: 'Look out for your tail!' 'You take that one on the right, I'll take this.' Leslie, with his tombstone teeth and mop of yellow straw hair, is recognized, when soaring above the clouds, by his imitation of Donald, the squadron's mascot duck. It never fails to send a shiver down the spine when you hear the cry 'tally-ho' as the fighters dive to engage the enemy.

One by one the returning aircraft circle before landing. An intelligence officer is there to interrogate the fighters as, with surprising agility, they jump from the cockpit. As all men when they arrive from the skies, they appear a little remote from this planet. They have acquired the ecstasy that only pilots know. They have become a particle of the great kingdom of the skies — attained the sense of freedom of a bird. This has been achieved by complete mastery of the aircraft and the element in which they fly. Now, ambling along towards the hangars, harness thrown over their shoulders, they smile the smile that conveys more sentiment than a whole host of words.

The questions surprise them. 'How many does that make? How many missing?'

'Yes, I got one, but Brownie's not back, nor Leslie.'

'Anyone see what happened to Brownie?'

'Someone saw him shot down in flames.'

'See him bale out?'

'No. Don't think he got his hood open.'

'How bloody!'

Another aircraft circles above. It must be Leslie! Yes, it is. Leslie appears, straw thatch on end, in such a state of wild exultation that his very teeth are flashing as he punches the air.

'Oh, boy! Oh, boy! Never had such a time! I got two, two down. Never had such a wonderful ten minutes in my life. Oh, boy! Oh, boy!'

Often the pilots return in such a highly-keyed condition that it may take several hours for them to calm down enough to remember clearly what happened. Sometimes, in order to get his story, the PRO will give them a drink. 'Had an interesting time? What was it like?' But, in all probability, he will only be told that it was a 'hell of a party' for, so innately modest and selfdeprecating are the pilots, so self-conscious about 'shooting a line', that they are seldom willing to give a graphic description of their fight.

COASTAL COMMAND

June, Lossiemouth

The work of Coastal Command and Fleet Air Arm, concerned as it is with our seas and shores (and those occupied by the enemy), is the least spectacular, if perhaps the most strenuous, and even dangerous. Coastal Command is relied upon to be the eyes of the RAF and is an air force within the air force, with its own land planes, bombers, fighters and flying-boats to ward off attack from the air. Its fleet services the flying-boats and high-speed launches, and co-operates with the Royal Navy. The men, wearing navy blue, using nautical terms and measuring in knots, whether in landcraft or not, escort or sweep ahead of convoys in search of U-boats.

The pilots seem to have a quietness that results from their long days of patient endurance on reconnaissance trips, from which they bring back valuable photographic and other information of activity along eastern and western coasts. They must be able to report fully to Intelligence on every detailed item of interest they have seen on their long journeys, keep constant watch on shipping, give positions of the mines, upturned boats, or the small loads of escaping foreigners they may have seen. (To these latter, compass courses, food and brandy are dropped from the air or, should they be in distress, rescue launches are sent out.)

During the first year Coastal Command was said to have 'had the war to itself', and became known as the 'Green Line Bus'. As one officer said, 'A lot of petrol ran through the engines at that time — the boys saw a lot of water, and did they work! Yet somehow they still had time to take out the WAAFs in the evening!' One, Corporal Ball, did over 180 flying hours in a month.

Coastal Command, besides patrolling the shores of Great Britain and Northern Ireland and stretching its arm from the north of Norway to the Spanish frontier, carries on a twenty-four hour watch over almost the entire eastern world, while a 'strike crew' always stands by waiting for orders to attack enemy shipping. The pilots have to read visual Morse signals and know as much about navigation as a ship's master. They must be able to manoeuvre a flying-boat and, though its wings are caught by wind, to bring it 'alongside' in roughest weather. They must recognize the types of stern of all ships, so that they may learn what class of ship has been seen and from whence it comes. Enemy ships must not be confused with friendly ones, nor islands be mistaken for ships. (Sometimes small islands have been torpedoed!) From early morning until moonlight the marathon of routine patrols continues. Sighting reports are sent every two hours, and a 'nil' report is always welcome.

A jovial, red-cheeked officer with a ginger, lavatory-brush moustache, completes his conscientious report of yet another monotonous daily sortie. He scratches his sandy head and asks, 'How many G's in Skagerrak?' The pink and perky flight orderly who comes in with a wicker cage of carrier pigeons does not know. The use of homing-pigeons to carry messages is as old as Solomon: the early Persians trained these birds for the ancient Greeks to dispatch the results of Olympic races.

Today, when more modern methods have failed, they are considered the most reliable means of communication, and many men have been saved by these birds flying as quickly as forty miles an hour back to their home loft. The last act the navigator performs when his wireless fades out is to release the two pigeons carrying messages giving the position of the aircraft.

The fighter pilot is never away for more than two hours, but Coastal Command pilots, on their long flights hundreds of miles out over the Atlantic, must exercise enormous patience and, in an effort to make time pass more quickly they prepare large meals of soup, steak, vegetables, fruit and coffee. A tea towel is kept on the stove. One gunner does the washing-up, the other the drying. The navigator, having given the pilot his course for the next half hour, crawls about the aircraft doing odd jobs or composing light verse. In his turret the rear-gunner is singing Rabelaisian songs into his radio transmitter. The crew has to fly until the clock shows it is time to go home. It is ungrateful work and seldom spectacular, yet these men are doing a great national duty.

Nearly all the while flying at a low level over the waves (to fly at 2,000 feet is considered mountaineering), often in slow, cumbersome landcraft, they go out as far as their petrol can carry them, 500 or 600 miles at sea, and can be blown thirty miles off course by the gales. If forced down, they have poor chances of survival. An aeroplane sinks rapidly in rough seas, and it is only a miracle if a small yellow dinghy and its buttercup-capped occupants are sighted from the air.

Night after night, day after day on end, these men endeavour to track down, sink, or even capture submarines. 'If you spot a "sub" it's a hell of a scramble to get to it, and, in any case, it's probably seen you first and already started to crash dive.'

Coastal Command pilots have been known to circle over a certain patch of sea, their eyes glued to the spot where they have sighted a submarine, until the help they have signalled for has finally arrived, hours later. Jim Osman, a seasoned pilot of twenty-three, told me that once he had strained the muscles of his neck so that, for several days afterwards, he couldn't turn his head back to its normal position.

Maybe word is sent by cypher from a patrolling Hudson of a convoy creeping past the coastline. These men have dislocated enemy communications, have laid their mines, have attacked with torpedoes a ship carrying bombs from a height not higher than 500 feet at a level with the gunfire — unless, in fact, it skims beneath the fire angle of the guns.

Some of the feats of endurance do not bear contemplation. Gunners are clamped in the medieval vice of the narrow fuselages where they have bled to death. Sometimes they fly in temperatures so low that a thermos of tea becomes frozen the moment the cap is unscrewed, and icicles form on the chin.

Patrick, a tall, cub-like youth who pilots a reconnaissance plane, baffled me with his incomprehensible allusions to 'the enemy'. At last I realized Patrick was not referring to the Germans, the Japanese or the Italians, but to the weather. When he spoke of the front, it was not of the battle-front, but of the weather-front. Weather is his greatest problem. Weather can bring him down to his doom more readily than any gunfire. The weather is mysterious. This enemy springs so many surprises. Suddenly, in a warm atmosphere, the pressure valves may begin to ice up, and our friend must go up and over, not below, as one might have thought, to avoid disaster. The strangest phenomena occur in this element: fickle and contrary winds can beat and batter the aircraft and cause it to go 'off trim', or bear down upon one wing or the other and blow the pilot irrevocably off course; electric storms can turn his aircraft into an electrical conductor; the strata above and between clouds can contain 'up and down' currents of 100 miles an hour: cirrus clouds, flat and small and wispy, are so cold that they are non-ice-forming in that the ice snaps and bounces off the wings. Patrick may dive down into a warmer cumulus cloud where, within a few seconds, ice forms on the outward edge of the wings, destroying the vacuum of their upper surface, and therefore depriving them of their lift. The air speed indicator and the other instruments are thrown out of control. Patrick opens up the engines faster as the icing proceeds faster. He puts up the nose of his aircraft when gradually he finds himself stalling and then falling uncertainly, like an autumn leaf, towards the earth until control is regained.

The stars have also been known to lure pilots up and up to their doom, for they have sometimes been mistaken for night-fighters and gunners have blazed their ammunition at them. The stars can be familiar signposts telling a pilot within five miles his position in the sky. By astro-navigation he has been able to fly thousands of miles with the aid of the constellations, and before setting out on their night flights you can hear the pilots joking to the CO: 'Can't you give Sirius a bit of a polish up for us tonight, sir?' Cloud is good cover, at the right height, in which a pilot is unlikely to be discovered: cloud can provide him with the stepping-stones on which to hop towards and over his target — but the clouds may fail him, may close down and prevent his landing; sea fogs and mists are calamitous.

Yet certain Coastal Command operations are so dangerous that those undertaking them pray for bad weather conditions during the execution of them. Patrick himself prefers to navigate weather which, over England, would be considered too bad for flying. Sometimes it is necessary to go down 400 feet in order to photograph a well-defended port where it is said the 'flak' is so thick you could land on it! To launch a torpedo the pilot must descend as low as twenty feet above his target. It is easy to understand why he prefers not to perform such feats out of a clear sky.

For minelaying the aircraft approaches the coast as near as possible, gliding in quietly 'like a cat in a crypt'. Pilots have been known to fly along the hostile cliffs so close that they were supposed to see what appeared to be fireflies, but were, in fact, the pocket torches of the Germans running to man their guns! So vivid is the feeling of stealth during these occasions that the pilots, forgetting the noise of their engines, instinctively talk in whispers to one another on the intercom.

The typical Coastal Command pilot has a sailor's sense of distance, and like a sailor he learns to depend a great deal upon himself. He is an aviator, a true wanderer through the sky, and is never for long at one home station. He may find himself unexpectedly working anywhere from the Far East to the Shetlands. Compared to pilots of other commands he is perhaps more adult and more at ease when conversing about the universe.

BOMBERS

Mildenhall

These dark grey weeks spent at a bomber station have given me an appalling sense of guilt. Not only am I a stranger and one who is incapable of sharing the dangers of this terrifying life, but I am an interloper prying into the private existences of these airmen.

Of course I am 'chaperoned' wherever I go, and there are certain activities too secret for me to witness (I am seldom allowed to be at the briefing when the crews are given their targets for the night), and, of course, my pictures are submitted to the most rigorous examination by the censor who indicates which maps, diagrams, log book or paper must be 'airbrushed out' from my prints before they are sent to propaganda bureaux throughout the Empire. Yet, in spite of my being the tweed-clad civilian in their midst, I am treated with the solicitude of an honoured guest. At Cambridge the idea of taking my seat at the dining-table in Hall, and 'making my number' with my fellow colleagues, was an anathema that I avoided whenever possible. Now, I enjoy the friendliness (and the food is better than to be found in most war-time restaurants), and this in spite of the innate reluctance of the whole Service to participate in anything so indiscreet, and even vulgar, as propaganda.

Napoleon called it 'the 2 o'clock in the morning unprepared courage', the cold-blooded kind, that is needed to pilot a heavy bomber on long flights over well-fortified enemy country. For what bomber can enjoy finding himself, in an Arctic temperature, flying through the enemy's searchlight belt while every piece of metal melted down from all the statues, railings, pots and pans in the neighbourhood, is hurled up at him? Yet, for the bomber with his poor manoeuvrability, 'flak' holds less dangers than interception by patrolling night-fighters. Unless he has sufficient height to dive low, thereby gaining speed — but temporarily becoming more vulnerable to the ground defences — he knows his chances are desperate. Some pilots have said that their sternest moment is when the target for which they are making is 'thirty minutes ahead', already illuminated by the gunfire loosed at the 'early take-offs' who have already arrived. Once in the centre of this bombardment they are less conscious of their peril. The tracers flying past, the orange lights of the 'flak', the bursts of cannon that from the air look similar to bomb-bursts, the green explosions from the blazing factories below, and the coloured 'flaming onions', create an effect that would be 'very pretty', they say, 'if you had time to admire it'.

Hugh Francis suggested that a picture 'feature' — hackneyed enough in idea, but, none the less, one to be approached with sincerity and freshness — would be to show 'a day in the life of a bomber pilot'. Initially to find the right type was hard enough, but then to assuage his natural aversion to being picked out for prominence from his fellows created a tougher problem. However, when the CO suggested we should use Robert Tring as our star — he was handsome, nineteen year old and had brought back his crew and aircraft, B for Bobby, from twenty-nine bombing trips over Berlin — Bobby could not demur with impunity.

B for Bobby was, in fact, an excellent choice with his photogenic, cat-like features, rather wild, dark eyes, and black silken curls. But to see him, as I did for the first time, sitting bolt upright in his cell-like room, legs folded, with *Tarka the Otter* held in his slender, feminine hands, you would never suspect that he had enough strength of muscle to take up, and bring down, a heavy Stirling bomber. Yet Bobby is one of the most steady and reliable pilots of the squadron. The son of a clergyman from the Cotswolds, his is the dark quiet voice of the scholar. He is the perfect antithesis of the brutish type our enemy produces.

At first Bobby suggested several other 'buddies' whom he thought better for the job of being popped at by camera flashes as a change from enemy guns but, being an amenable type, acquiesced to being a guinea pig.

Slowly he went to the basin, washed his hands, and brushed smoother his hair. He looked abashed that this action should seem worth recording. Again, before lunch in the mess, when he drank from a pewter tankard, he seemed surprised that this conviviality should warrant more pictures.

After lunch Bobby and all the crews on tonight's raid were given their preliminary briefing. Every available inch of wall is covered with large scale maps and photograph mosaics: the balloon barrages, the known ground defences and hostile fighter bases are indicated by blobs of purple ink; threads are stretched over the route the bombers are to take. Seventy-five per cent of the bomber's work must be done before he leaves the ground, so he must be of a patient, persevering disposition, ready to take infinite pains over his preparations.

So great is Bobby's absorption that he has now become quite oblivious to the camera's presence. No lecturer ever had a more attentive audience than the senior intelligence officer. Heads crowd close together around him, intent, earnest, solemn; they are surely those of mere schoolboys. Their faces and hands are smooth and pale without any suggestion of down upon them. Rows of cats' eyes peer up at a blind which is suddenly pulled down on which the details of tonight's target — the Ruhr — are flashed by the vast epidiascope. The navigators are given their special conundrums and immediately start to make their calculations, and to copy the various codes and cyphers to be used. They must recognize the fake German towns — and not release their valuable load on dummy targets.

These youths are quite objective about their task: they do not feel hatred for the individual German. How can he hate someone he does not know? Bobby asks. Yet he will have no mercy for the enemy, knowing he will show none for them. Incentive for revenge is given when a submarine sinks a ship without warning, or a friend is shot down on his parachute; but in most cases the assault is an impersonal one.

The crew ask few questions. They show little interest in why this certain target has been selected: they just get on with whatever they have to do and make every effort to ensure good results. Thus the explosion from an effective hit causes them satisfaction, for a technical feat has been accomplished. But they do not like to think too much about the punishment they inflict.

The weather is rough again — perhaps too rough for tonight's sortie: nothing to do but wait for further reports to come in. This tension of anticipation has a frustrating effect to which no pilot becomes totally inured, however hard he tries to accustom himself. Sometimes a pilot will remain keyed-up for weeks before it is possible for him to play his part.

By now Bobby is showing distinct signs of becoming tired of me. In fact, by the way he chain-smokes and casts a slightly haunted look out of his stag's eyes, I wonder if he is not showing signs of over-fatigue and nervous stress. But, one more trip, and Bobby will be leaving this station. He wishes to be sent 'out' East, but it's more likely that he will be posted to a training school to become a flying instructor.

The wind has blown away some fog. The Met people now seem to think conditions are becoming more favourable.

'We'll be on tonight,' says Baker, who puts his head around the door, then is gone. Baker is Bobby Tring's second pilot, the heavy Etruscan type, with a shock of black silk fringe falling to his jet-black eyes. Sitting by Bobby's side in his heavy leather suit, he has been a monolith of strength throughout the perils of the past twenty-nine trips.

The Met people were right and the 'big trip' is on: those valued and terrible jewels of destruction, the enormous torpedo-shaped bombs, have been taken from the prison-like vaults where, in the silence of the tomb, they lie in row upon row, rack upon rack, and are now placed in readiness in the under-belly of the aircraft.

All sorts and sizes, all characters are here in their crumpled, weather-cracked harness. There is Miles, a born leader of men, who worked in the gas industry before the war. He is wearing a long, thick, grey sweater that reaches almost to the knees. There is a blond Yorkshireman — the wire-haired variety, with small seed-pearl teeth and a voice like a razor. There is the dark Cornish boy, heavy, with high cheekbones and a slow regard. An overgrown gangling youth, with an enormous Adam's apple and a voice from the depths of a well, he has just missed being an Adonis, and this failure makes him slightly ridiculous. And there is Hardy, the typical English school hero, coarsened a bit, with bull neck. His colouring is still vivid, with rosy cheeks and the azure eyes which associate him with country-house tennis, followed by a quick dip and vast quantities of lemonade and strawberries for tea.

The crew-room is crowded and full of smoke for the final briefing. The weather expert gives his latest information and last words of advice. The navigators put maps, dividers, and protractors into their satchels. The crews stand about, fastening the clasps or pulling at the straps of their parachute harness, buckling on the life preservers, or adjusting the electric tubes of their 'hot suits'. They are laughing and in high spirits.

The provisions for the trip are handed out, carefully selected Christmas packages: energy pastilles, chewing-gum, raisins, chocolate slabs. The scene is as light-hearted as that of the locker-room before a preparatory school football game.

'What's happened to my gloves?' asks Bobby's gunner, a tough-looking little runt from Lancashire with a face that screws up like rubber when he smiles. The missing gloves are found. Then a pair of white silk ones (one had forgotten that sort since the days of juvenile dancing classes) is put on; over these he wears the leather gloves, and on top the fur. A ten-foot scarf is coiled around neck and shoulders. Bobby, serious and somewhat aloof, still wears his service cap, for he does not wish to be photographed in a helmet and will only put it on when once in the cockpit.

Outside they lie about on the ground, looking suddenly like strange Bank Holiday-makers, waiting for the lorry to come back to take another load to the dispersal points. Bobby is taking a light from Baker, their last cigarette for an unconscionable time.

'Wonder how much we'll see tonight?'

'From the look of it we'll be lucky if we see the Rhine.'

I now realise that in any further photograph I take it would be tactful to make Bobby's presence only incidental.

The lorry's here. In their cumbersome harness the young men clamber up and are jostled together, laughing, jerking up their thumbs and generally behaving as if they were getting a lift as far as the local Odeon, instead of for a journey of 1,100 hazardous miles.

Arrival at the aircraft seems as vague and casual as if no definite time were set for the take-off. But there is no hitch or delay. The ground crew have put their final touch to the vast machine that towers, like some prehistoric beast, against the grey-blue sky streaked with apricot-coloured islands. Daylight is waning, but the decline is gradual, and you are barely aware of it before semidarkness envelops you.

Two of the crew are standing rather stiffly against the hedge, with their backs to us; then they come towards us and burrow into the bowels of the aircraft.

Aloft in the cockpit, at a height where the top windows of a tall house would be, Bobby at last straps on his helmet. The navigator is laying out his chart, adjusting his astrograph, arranging his sextant and numerous papers and bundles into position. The wireless operator is tuning up his set; the second pilot testing his RT, while the engineer checks his instruments. In his protruding glass 'blister', the rear-gunner, with barrels depressed to their fullest extent, takes a careful look to see that no one is 'in line', and fires a burst of fiery sparks to make sure his guns are working correctly.

'He's taking no chances,' an officer standing by explains.

'Don't blame him either,' smiles another.

As the airscrews jerk and, one after the other, the four engines roar, the wall of noise becomes deafening. The wind of their power flattens the grass and drives away stray leaves, twigs, dust, and some old canvas covers in the slipstream. The ground crew, their flapping trousers flattened to one side of their legs as the engines rev up ever more furiously, are standing on the side lines and, like comic people in an early cinema farce, are quivering paralytically, their hair on end. The vast chocks are pulled aside. The prehistoric beast is navigated into position for the take-off. From the control tower the instructions are given to stand by. The first monster crawls forward, gathers speed, rushes to the boundary of the airfield, and rises with a roar. Another has taken up its position and starts its run, along, now off. One by one the 'giants with stings in their tails' have circled the pale night and float like a slow moving frieze against the sky.

Those of us who are left behind can only guess what the experience must be for those who undertake this awful journey. We see the men who come back and receive their travellers' tales: we hear them discussing amongst themselves the excitements and terrors of that nine or twelve hours' ordeal. Time itself becomes a black eternity as the aircraft, without even giving its passengers the comforting sensation that they are in motion, bores its way through the night. ('Will there really be a morning — is there such a thing as day?') We know that the heating apparatus often 'packs up', and in an attempt to relieve with some counterpain the agonies of frostbite and lack of oxygen these boys have butted their young heads on the metallic floors of the aircraft.

Meanwhile, in the control room, situated at the top of a sort of land lighthouse, the signals and reports come in. To avoid being located by their radio, the bombers seldom break wireless silence on the outward journey, but they must send a message when their mission is completed. To this polished, rather empty operation theatre of a room, the dramas of the raid are relayed. Tonight as ever, the lights burn stale and yellow and a loud crackle is heard, a crash of static from the dark world outside, and a hollow voice comes over the air a few minutes after the aircraft have left. One of them is in difficulties. There is a commotion as various officers and men run to their telephones to give special instructions. 'C for Charlie is returning,' through the mouthpiece the voice recites in a cold, almost Chinese, sing-song. 'Hallo, Talisman here. Hallo, Rabbit. C for Charlie. Talisman answering you. Are you receiving me?'

At his desk in front of an elaborate series of coloured lights, one of the engineers, a rather wizened little man in plimsolls, looking like a boxer's second, barks into the mouthpiece: 'Is the ambulance warmed up?' 'Beacon!' an officer's voice orders, and an aircraftsman presses a button.

Someone else is instructing, 'Yes, you may land. Circle prior to landing. Circle prior to landing.'

Another strident, disembodied voice calls that the flarepath shall be lit. From the terrace of the control room the men stand watching the skies and listening. The night is quiet. A young owl squawks into the night, or a rabbit screams, caught in a snare. The radio gives out a heavy slumbrous sound. Distant gunfire may be heard; a newspaper crackles; a shrill bell rings. Presently a distant buzzing drone is heard. 'That's him, C for Charlie.' The buzz becomes an intermittent hum, and at length a slowly moving star is seen. The star makes a semicircle above the perimeter of the aerodrome. More requests and acceptances by radio transmission — permission is given for C for Charlie to land.

The beacon light shows a red welcome. On the flarepath the coloured glow-worms somehow remind one of the far-distant days when fairy-lights betokened a gala. But how can we digress at the very moment that C for Charlie is turning into wind, about to land laden with her full load of bombs? Everyone watches. Lower, lower, the light descends. She turns on her own headlamps. The purring sound is heard when her engines are throttled back; a soft bump. There is a moment's pause, and someone turns, 'Perfect landing that.'

Meanwhile, the other businesses of the night must continue. The commanding officer is being shown the photographs, straight from the drier, of the damage done in today's daylight sweep. The interpreters have marked with arrows on the negatives the latest results. The CO, a trained spotter of damage, gauges the crater holes which show where the bombers have dislocated traffic at railway junctions and marshalling yards, or have fallen wide with the result that the civilian population suffer the terrible degradation we well know at home.

In Shakespeare's wars night was quiet for men and animals, and the birds slept. This war knows no such night; the crepitations of darkness are shattered by the bestial shriek of enemy bombs, or, as we now hear, the magnificent roar of returning friends — the giant Stirlings circling above.

How long must we wait until they are all back? This is the zero hour of suspense; soon the vigil will be over; we will hear of their achievements and of the price that has been paid.

Up on a vast board the arrivals are chalked; there are still half a dozen to return, but already the lorries will have brought back from the dispersal points the first crews who, peeling off layers of gloves, jackets and scarves, explode into the guard room. Accustomed to being buffeted by various vibrations in their cramped confines, they tell you how wonderful is the moment when the engines are switched off, the noise is over, and they can drop out and pull deeply at a cigarette. With hair awry, these boys are still part of the nightmare that has engulfed them. After the hours of inspissated darkness, interrupted only by blinding flashes of deadly light, they screw up their eyes on coming into the unshielded lights, and appear as if waking from a deep sleep. Here they are — yes, the same men whom (secretly) you prayed for at their outset at sundown. But the interim has told its tale and every one of them has aged by several years.

However, soon their tongues are loosened, and they tell one another, with an exuberant relish, of their adventures. For the time they quite forget that 'brave men hide or make excuses for their deeds'.

'We gave the Hun a pasting all right — took him by surprise — must have had too good a dinner, for it was some time before he started any "flak".'

'Thank God!' says one of the men as he flings his helmet on a bench. 'But they're bastards. Don't know how they do it. We fly so high that it takes their "flak" a minute and a half to reach us, yet by the time we've travelled a mile and a half on anything but a straight course, there's the stuff waiting to meet you! And doesn't it just bump you about when it hits you!'

The CO moves among them. He learns that the squadrons hopped over clouds on their way out, and, instead of having to come down low on to their target, the clouds had parted to show the way for the bomb-aimers.

The CO hides his relief, and casually asks, 'Any news of B for Bobby, or D for Donald?'

'No, sir.'

The crews are now wolfing sandwiches and meekly saying 'thank you' for the thickly sugared milk and coffee from the urn.

A gaunt, ghostlike youth tumbles in, his face of a grey pallor.

'Feugh! I've never sweated so much in one night! For sheer sweat this trip takes the cake! I thought those photographs that you took of us, Beaton, were going to be our memorial. Jerry got us in a cone of lights, and did he jib us about, eh? I certainly thought it was our last "ops" — the worst I've had yet!'

The flight sergeant returns, 'B for Bobby just down, sir,' and before long Bobby Tring strolls in, still very erect, but with the look in his eyes even wilder. He wears his peaked cap on the back of his curly head and smokes nervously.

Soon the formal interrogation has started. The epic legends of the night are pieced together. At one table they discuss the fighter opposition met on the raid, and how L for London had pinpointed a factory with a load of incendiaries. A senior intelligence officer points with a pencil to the map in front of him. 'And here, how was the "flak"?'

Bobby, leaning on the palm of his hand, with wrinkled forehead, mumbles, 'Pretty bad, sir, really pretty bad.'

The older man wrinkles his forehead in sympathy and nods. 'Still here,' he said, again pointing. 'Over Holland at this point it would be fairly quiet, wouldn't it?'

'Oh, no, sir!' affirms Baker, the second pilot, and the others join in. 'Not a bit of it, regular Fifth of November firework display.'

'Hm! And there — did you make that target?'

'Yes, sir; we had to make a second run though. But I think we can be certain of it,' says Bobby, drawing deep on his cigarette.

'Oh, yes! We got that all right,' corroborates the rear-gunner in his Lancashire accent. 'Yes, sir, we got that one — and what a flame that dump made!'

Again the CO turns to a corporal. 'Any news of D for Donald? — must be getting short of petrol now.'

'Nothing's come in yet, sir.'

At another table a group is arguing about the colour of the 'flak' at Gelsenkirchen. 'It was red, definitely.'

'No, I'd say pink.'

'Absolute rot! It was orange with a white centre.'

'Aw! You mean pink with green spots.'

At yet another table a Canadian youth, with long curling eyelashes, is refuting some point with determination, 'Now, let me show you what happened.' The others fit in around him respectfully as he prods the map. He is doing a tough man's job with a stout heart, though he looks as if he should still be at prep school. Certainly he should be abed long before this; for, unnoticed, the dawn has crept up outside the blackout blinds. Time, at long last, for breakfast and that well-deserved egg which, they say, tastes like none other.

So these young, but quickly ageing, men sit at the breakfast table, politely conversing with the CO and with one another. Bobby Tring cuts the rind off the bacon that accompanies the egg, carefully prepares his next mouthful, and pauses with it poised at the end of a fork, while the blue-eyed tennis player with frayed collar puts up a silencing finger, 'There's our friend the cuckoo!' Turning to me, he says, 'We often hear the cuckoo when we're going out on "ops", and then again when we get into bed.'

'Well, you'd better be getting along now,' the CO suggests.

'Right-ho, sir, I was just thinking the same — good night, sir,' says the tennis type, drawing back his chair.

'Good night, Bobby — and now I must set about my day's work; there's a lot to be done.'

'But,' I ask, 'you haven't had any sleep, have you?'

'Oh, I'll be all right after a hot bath.'

'But a hot bath! I know it's very pleasant,' I suggest — 'but without any sleep whatsoever?'

'Oh! I mean a *really* hot bath,' the CO smiles, 'one that wakes you up good and proper. Well, I must be sending in my reports. Too bad about D for Donald, but the raid has been successful.' Now everyone is too tired to think, to worry, or to hurry — even to hurry to bed.

Lying on a hard metal bed, under a coarse, wiry blanket, I watch the flashes of different coloured lights against the frosted window, listen to the footsteps along the corridor, hear the sounds of laughter, and I wonder what is the secret which sustains these men in a life of perpetual sacrifice, of successive risks, the probable end of which is calmly discerned by their clear and disillusioned eyes. Do they go out in the faith that the world will be a better place because of their sacrifice? Do they see their own eternity beyond the death of the body? I doubt if either of these conceptions consciously actuates most of them. Like the Roman soldier of long ago their 'dark sense' of discipline and duty takes the place of religion. Who can say that it is not religion?

Part VI: Acquaintance, 1941-2

OLGA LYNN AND LILY ELSIE

Summer 1941

Olga Lynn,[21] evacuated from the bombing of Belgravia to the overcrowded purlieus of Windsor, has often suggested arranging a lunch in order to talk over *les temps perdus* with the old musical comedy favourites Lily Elsie, Gertie Millar and Zena Dare. Now that people are dispersed far and wide such a meeting would be improbable. But, quite by chance, Oggie met Lily Elsie on the platform of Windsor Station and discovered that she was also living close by. So a Sunday was set aside for the three of us to meet.

As I took the train to Windsor, I was beaming with anticipation, for I found that I still received the same elation at the prospect of seeing Lily Elsie that I would have had all those years ago when this goddess wrapped the whole of my adolescence in a haze of roses.

As a child of not more than three I was lying in my mother's bed — an early morning treat — while she breakfasted and opened her letters. There, one morning, on the eiderdown, lay a picture postcard of the most beautiful lady that I had ever seen in the whole of my life. Wearing her hair in a mass of Greek curls adorned with a diamond fillet she thrust forward a flawless profile. Her lips and cheeks were tinted, her diamond necklace and *décolletage* were spangled. Thus was I first conscious of Miss Lily Elsie.

---

[21] A former concert singer, now a music teacher and social figure in London.

My flamboyant Aunt Jessie spoilt me outrageously and I loved her for it. It was she who a few months later took me to a children's party at the Carlton Hotel. The floor of the large circular hall was covered with a stretched canvas which was liberally sprinkled with imitation hoar-frost. I was frantically scooping up iridescent crystals with an opal and silver trowel (which I had just won in a raffle) when a smiling lady in furs was presented to me. Immediately I made my Uncle Percy, Aunt Jessie's Bolivian husband, buy the lady a huge bunch of Parma violets — for she was none other than my goddess of the picture postcard.

I was four years of age when my father considered that I was old enough to go to my first matinée. Having bought dress circle seats for *The Merry Widow* he returned from his office for an early lunch prior to setting off for Daly's theatre. But he brought bad news. 'Owing to indisposition' Miss Elsie would not be appearing. Would I prefer to wait for a later performance or would I be content to see the understudy? Over-excitement had caused me already to bite my finger-nails to the quick. How could I brook further delay?

As it happened, all I remembered afterwards of the euphoric afternoon was the astounding surprise of seeing a lady at Maxim's dance on a table top. However, Lily Elsie became a household name, and after Aunt Jessie and Uncle Percy chaperoned her on a trip to Biarritz they invited her to lunch. The smell of melon and cigars struck my nostrils as, with my brother Reggie, I was allowed in the dining-room, at the end of the meal to perform our version of *The Merry Widow* waltz in front of its originator.

Today I went off as a man who has seen most of the living beauties of the world, and I had complete confidence that I should not be disappointed with my first favourite.

It was high summer; the day was one that one dreams of — blinding sun and roses spilling in profusion. It was arranged that we should have luncheon by the riverside at that Wren house which has recently been turned into an hotel.

Oggie, Jack Gordon, the fourth of our party, and I waited on the terrace watching the boats glide up and down the river as they did when the Thames was fashionable at the time of our heroine's hey-day. The rambler roses tumbled over the wire umbrellas as they do in a musical comedy. Only our leading lady was late. Oggie became nervous that our guest might have forgotten the rendezvous. We passed the time working up an electric atmosphere for the star's arrival.

'Now, let me see — she was the "Merry Widow" in about 1907 — she married Ian Bullough before the war, at twenty-five — she must be over fifty now.' Brought up in Salford she was said to be the illegitimate child of Lord ... and his cook. Her mother boasted a strong Manchester accent, but Elsie with her natural elegance, the antithesis of the archness of the actresses previously in favour, was said to have brought a new, contemporary grace to the role of leading lady. To see her merely walk across the stage was a poem. Not a man, woman or child was to be found who did not fall for her charm. One elderly gentleman — a distant admirer — sent her a duplicate of her stage jewellery — only in real diamonds. She had always retained a certain mystery and even those fortunate to know her off-stage found her slightly elusive with this unattainable quality that was utterly romantic.

Windsor clocks chimed the half after 1 o'clock and still no Lily Elsie. Oggie was frantic. Jack was sent as outrider to convey the missing guest to our meeting-place. Moments later, the doorway to the terrace held two figures. From a distance of thirty feet one still felt electrified by the aura surrounding this lady who 'filled' with her presence the door through which she came. Without being 'stagey', she 'made an entrance'. Tall, slim, spruce, she hovered, turned to ask a question, fumbled a little, and then walked towards us with the familiar straight-backed, loose-legged, slightly coltish walk. Yes, here walked beauty. Or was I confusing a period-prettiness with the real thing? Was my critical judgement being led astray by sentimental associations and prejudice? A shady hat and dark spectacles hid the eyes so that now, at last without competition, her nose and mouth could be seen in their unchallenged beauty. I realized, for the first time, how important an attribute to her charm is the way that she moves the lips in speech. They are thrust forward into a sort of open pout which reveals the slightly receding teeth yet still retain their smooth, shiny cherry-surface. Certainly these features are not those that one finds in the greatest paintings, though there is an affinity in the roundness of early Botticelli. They are more the features that one sees in Boucher, Greuze, or, alas, Burne Jones, who would have exaggerated the fullness of the lips and the ivory bosses of the nostrils. To be hyper-analytical, the shape of the face is a little too round, and there are planes of the cheek and jaw in three-quarter view that are slightly coarse; but on the stage, and in photography, this is a positive advantage. The complexion is of a flawless veal-white quality even today, and the hair, curled in the shapes of the current fashion, though it has become streaked with white, gives the effect of being fair. Although Lily Elsie does not do so with a definite effort, she retains her youthful quality.

I was able, thanks to my own dark glasses, to stare concentratedly at the lady opposite without her being conscious of such intense scrutiny. In the half-light, caused by the shade of her hat, I peered at the same features that I had pored over in a dark snapshot taken at an Edwardian garden party, or on a seaside hotel terrace, ('enjoying a well-earned rest' read the caption) nearly a half-century ago. I think my blood tingled as I recognized the curve of the arm inside the elbow — a curve I had drawn many hundreds of times from those shiny Beagles postcards. I corroborated that the elbows protrude at a strangely gauche angle, and her thumbs have never been expressive.

The past came surging back over me like a torrent. It was an uncanny experience to realize, of a sudden, how well I knew this face. How little I had forgotten from childhood! I remembered, with a shock of familiarity, that little lump hidden in the crevice by the left nostril, and the small dewlap that falls from the centre of the sensuous upper lip. For me it had once seemed the heart of a rose and the centre of the universe! Still after the intervening years, after coming to admire Piero, Greco and Blake, the Diaghileff Ballet, Paris, New York and Hollywood, here was something that compared favourably with all that I had subsequently learnt to think of as beauty.

And what would Lily Elsie prove to be as a person? A trifle genteel? A bit too ladylike? Even a bore? I had not really feared this, for artists of a certain calibre can be counted upon always to strike the right note. From the moment she joined us she made the atmosphere easy and cosy, proved herself instinctively bright and amusing with her way of picking certain words out of sentences and making fun of them. She laughed with a deepchested relish.

As we sat having our skimpy war-time lunch (hors-d'oeuvres with diced beetroot but with no sardines) on a Windsor terrace in 1941, I was being transported to the realm of my first stage inspiration that was still, perhaps, more real today than the nightmares that engulf us all.

Oggie, bright and bursting with vitality, helped by giving confidence to our guest and encouraging her to reminisce. Lily Elsie talked about the experience that led to her taking the part of the Merry Widow. Elsie Cotton had gone on the stage as a child impersonator known as Little Elsie, later she toured the provinces before coming to Daly's as a chorus girl. George Edwardes, the manager, or 'the Guv'nor' as he was called, dropped in unexpectedly at a matinée, saw Elsie throw a balloon at the audience, so gave her notice for insubordination. Some time later, meeting her in the street and hearing that she was still out of a job, he took her back to play small parts. When she appeared in a Chinese musical, having been impressed by an oriental Tree production, she wore a strange wig and slanting eyes. Her appearance created a stir, for in musical comedy nobody bothered about realism. When Edwardes found his Daly theatre unexpectedly empty, and wanted to find a leading lady quickly for his stop gap, *The Merry Widow*, he took Little Elsie to Berlin to see the German version. They arrived just in time to have high tea before going to the theatre. The leading actress was huge, fat, and sang the part with tremendous operatic gusto. Edwardes asked Lily Elsie if she would play Sonia in London.

'Oh no, I couldn't possibly.' Lily Elsie was always shy and unsure of herself. She considered herself too thin, too ineffectual, and her small voice was never properly trained. Edwardes and Elsie returned, somewhat crestfallen, to London. But the Guv'nor, search as he did, could find no one else for the role, and the production had to go into immediate rehearsal. He eventually cajoled Elsie into becoming his Sonia, and by accepting, she made history in the English theatre.

Yes, she enjoyed arriving at the stagedoor and putting on the grease-paint, but she could not understand that overnight she had become a living legend. She had never understood, nor was fully conscious of, the effect she created, or the success she enjoyed. She remained exceptionally shy and only occasionally did she go out in public: an exception was made on the Sunday after her 'Widow' opening when she was prevailed upon to make an appearance among the fashionable crowd on the river. She bought a dress for twelve pounds and a vast mob cap of blue and white broderie anglaise from Swears and Wells and went off by train to Henley. After a long day in the miasmas of the Thames, the hat flopped, the brim fell low over her face, and when, at last, she returned home, the turkey carpet covering of the train-seat had left a large, indelible red patch on the dress.

'Once the Guv'nor realized that the "Widow" was a success, he ordered a new set of clothes for me from Lucille. Everything she made was a work of art. After that I couldn't go to anyone else. But I never understood why that black hat I wore in the last act was such a sensation. It arrived from Paris a few days before we opened. It had a few black wisps of paradise on it; it wasn't particularly large, but it created the craze for huge hats. It became the Merry Widow hat.'

'And what about the blue osprey hat you wore in *The Count of Luxembourg*? Weren't you very pleased with that?'

'I always thought it a common hat. It was badly made by Gracie Ansell. I never liked it, but I thought it would look well on the stage.'

Elsie told how she and Gabrielle Ray had contracts to be photographed exclusively for picture postcard sales by Foulsham and Banfield once every month, how artificial light was never used but they were taken in a 'sort of conservatory'. Gab Ray was the bright one: she always insisted on marking the proofs herself for the alterations, and she arranged to be paid £400 a year for posing whereas Elsie had signed too soon and only received £100 a year. Our guest talked of Gabrielle Ray being a great perfectionist in her work and in her appearance, rehearsing her dances forever, and experimenting with strange new make-ups, putting them together like a Pointilliste artist, with dabs of all sorts of different colours — mauves, greens and reds — which created in the distance a strange luminosity. She told also, of Gab being spoilt, moody and always so jealous of Elsie that it was painful when the two of them were staying together in the country and were riding or playing tennis.

Lily Elsie told us how the four remaining years of her stage career following the 'Widow' had gone by as if she were in an incubator of unreality. It was only on the stage that she became less painfully shy. Invitations came to her from the greatest in the land but she never accepted them. She had never been brought up to answer letters, and she was hopelessly casual, although she had never realized she was so. Many distinguished people had sent her interesting letters, but nothing of her past had been kept except a few picture postcards.

It was in hearing of such senseless, forgotten minutiae that the summer afternoon passed in halcyon retrospect.

We went over to Oggie's new dwelling nearby, and listened to Maggie Teyte on gramophone records singing Fauré and other French songs. At fifty, today, Maggie Teyte's voice, being so beautifully trained, is more perfect than ever it was. Lily Elsie sorrowed, 'I had no stage training, no singing lessons. My voice has entirely gone — everything's gone!' Oggie commented that Elsie's singing had always had intuitive style, and that at the first performance of the 'Widow', Maggie Teyte had sat with her in a box, and said that so fresh and exquisite was Elsie's voice that it gave her to despair.

Somewhat tentatively I took a few snapshots of Lily Elsie in Oggie's garden. In the hard, out-of-door light her face suddenly became pulpy, coarse and plump, and the liquid melting stag eyes lost their brilliance.

'Don't publish them without cutting off a little lump from the hips, and don't choose one in which, like a hen, I'm sitting badly!'

Lily Elsie is now a middle-aged woman (to write that sentence is, for me, a tragedy, for how could that exquisite heroine ever become old?), yet there seems little cause for sadness. She still exudes the quality that only those who have been greatly admired can possess: and once they have it, it remains with them for always.

At the end of a long day Lily Elsie dropped me at the station on her way home. I had known her all these years by her stage name and it came as quite an embarrassment to call her Elsie, for I had not known that Lily was a name never used by her friends. Dear Lily Elsie, her memory will always have a fragrance that none other possessed for Cecil Beaton.

NOËL COWARD

1942

Wet feet — cold feet all day long — in the snow and in railway carriages going to and from a Ministry of Information job. Particularly discouraged to arrive at night at Denham to find no John Sutro to meet me, as arranged, at the station. Waving a lantern in an endeavour to find a telephone box, like Lear on the heath, I staggered down a snowy road. At last a pair of headlamps, a call from the darkness, and I was saved. John motored me to his temporary home where we found his wife, Gillian, waiting for us in front of a glowing hearth. With her was Noël Coward who is preparing his film *In Which We Serve* at the neighbouring studios.

Although each time we have met we have become friends Noël and I have never got along well. In between meetings we have said bad things about one another and obviously they have been repeated. It's true that I have been bloody about him, and I have never quite known why I should have felt so intolerant and bitter. There was no reason to be that jealous of him. It isn't that we cross one another's paths. I don't resent successful people as a rule. However, here we were irrevocably face to face and, as usual, and, of course, we were pleased to see each other.

Noël was extremely generous and, at once, said some kind things about my recent work. I was pleased. Life suddenly had a glow as I sat in my socks, my shoes baking by the huge fire. The very cockles of my being were thawed even more by the praise than the embers or the cocktails. However, after two enormous Martinis I felt I should keep a check on myself in case I should say something that could be taken in evidence against me by my newfound friend. This was ungenerous of me because the white flag had been accepted by us both, and Noël was being completely frank and opening himself up to me on a platter. Who was I to hold back? A lot more gin loosened any remaining constraints I had.

Soon an extraordinary evening, which the Sutros watched in comparative silence, was under way. Noël is nothing if not articulate, and his analysis of us both was excellent. His command of words is quite fresh, and only occasionally did he resort to the use of words like 'glamour', and 'hiccupping off', 'flouncing off' which have been appropriated and ruined by people without his ability. Suddenly I confessed, 'I've never really minded your being bloody about me, but it has baffled me that a person of your perspicacity should have shown no interest in me.' To which he answered, 'Don't you believe it, sister, I've been madly interested in you! But I've been a fool, I've misjudged you. The war has shown how wrong I've been. You've done a great job — you've whipped off in a bomber to Iceland,[22] you've earned great respect in the RAF; and it just shows what a mistake I made. You've been yourself always, and how right you've been! I've been hiccuping off at the outbreak of the war, thinking it was a wonderful thing to give up those two plays that were already in production to do a job that anyone else could have done. You've done much better than I by just sticking to your guns: people respect you more for that. You used to stand for everything I dislike. I've been beastly about you being Elsa Maxwell's darling and Elsie Mendl's puss. But I've been wrong. Let's be buddies! Life's going to be tough for us all for the next years of the war, and much tougher after the war, and it's better that people like us should be friends rather than enemies because we really have so much in common — powers of observation, wit, industriousness and professionalism. Ring me up, or I'll telephone to know what you're doing at the last minute, and come to stay here, while we're making this film, in my guest room any night you're free.' The Sutros were silently amazed. During dinner they doled out great libations of burgundy and apricot brandy. Noël never stopped the pace for four hours. He got a bit squiffy — his eyes closed up and his face became drawn and haggard, but he spoke with lucidity and brilliance. Luckily I never saw myself in a glass, but I slurred over certain words. We lurched over to Noël's rented villa near by to drink a huge container of cocktail. Noël has never acquired a taste for comfort, and these temporary quarters showed no signs of

---

[22]I hadn't.

his tenancy apart from a 'Little King' cartoon on the wall and, in silver frames, signed photographs of the Kents, Mountbattens, Toscanini and Rachmaninoff.

I asked Noël about his method of writing plays, but he elaborates little on the birth pangs of creation for the reason that there are none, or if so, they are not interesting to him. 'If I type easily then I know the stuff is good!' The way he goes over the appalling obstacles of play construction is done with the ease of a surf-rider skimming the Honolulu waves. He spoke with emotion of his childhood when his mother took him to the pit to see Gertie Millar, Gracie Leigh and the other stars of his formative period. He is first-rate when discussing the theatre in any of its branches. He dismisses Broadway as of little interest. I asked, 'And Geo. Kaufman — what do you think of him?' 'Nothing — why do *you*?' Broadway is too easy meat for Noël. He admitted to having had such success during the last fifteen years that he wouldn't think it terrible if a bomb killed him today. '*Blithe Spirit* is a bloody good play, and *Private Lives* will always be revived and will go into the history of comedy like a play by Congreve or Wilde.'

It was 1 o'clock: the unexpected evening was at last at an end. We embraced. We reaffirmed that we are friends now and it is, as he says, better and nicer that we stop being so jealous of one another. Gillian had long gone to sleep. John did impersonations of nonogenarians while I lay chuckling in bed.

Next morning John woke us with an imitation of a ship's steward doing his rounds and calling for all luggage to be ready in an hour as we were landing before midday in order to catch the tide. It was one of his best improvisations. Gillian and I took an ice-cold early morning train to London, and it was little wonder that I had a hangover and felt a bit weak from the shock of last evening.

January 14th, 1942

Thirty-eight! January 14th, 1904, I was born thirty-eight years ago! I've never liked birthdays — not even at fourteen did I want to be older. But birthdays used to be a festivity — now another nail in my coffin. Was busy this morning — didn't have much time to think about it.

Lunch with Cecil Day Lewis who talked about the way he writes poetry: gets a clue line, writes it in a notebook. Later, when he has a stomach-ache that denotes it is time for him to deliver, the poem is evolved around this line. Half of poem is due to the way he works it out — half inspiration — half technique (or idiom).

Like C.D.L. *so* much. He looks as if he's disintegrating, his complexion almost malarial and his thick, but lustreless, hair donkey-coloured. But he has reserves of energy, an inner vitality, and his eyes express everything and pierce you with their penetrating, but compassionate, curiosity. Knows how to write. He went through my RAF book carefully, making brilliant suggestions; never missed up on a piece of bad style.

Whole day spent at Ministry. Took my MS to censor. Slept a bit before dining with Colefax — nice party — Marjorie Anglesey, Cranbornes, Duchess of Devonshire, Ivor Churchill, Victor Cazalet fresh from Russia with General Sikorski.

As I had slept before dinner it took longer than usual to get off at night, so thought about my life and wondered about the past in comparison to the future. Had it been a good past for preparing for older age? Doubt it. Long to write for stage — virtually without any talent for it. Have cold feet. Thought about Daddy — how little I'd had to talk to him about — yet how like him I'm becoming in so many recurring ways. Find myself behaving like him often — laughing like him — polite interest shown when obviously bored — childish whimsical look when walking alone — or in the dark. Wondered a lot about my childhood ('picking daisies' were my first words), my earliest drawings, aged four, were signed by my nickname Toto. Remembered how I fell in love when I was still at Harrow, and the thrill of working in a proper theatre at Cambridge. Wished Peter had rung but not surprised he didn't — he never even thanked me for Christmas books — likes teasing me — let him have his little game.

Nothing as ageing as a war. The Americans now visiting us say we have aged ten to twenty years in two years of worry. It's the anxiety that makes us so old.

High spot of week: Long evening with C. Day Lewis over my book, discussing styles and forms of writing and writers. It snows. He described the sounds of everything muffled in snow: postman's tread — even the birds' twitter. Snow reduces London to a village. A black cat comes into its own: everything else white: cat a-hopping.

Randolph[23] to suggest to B. Bracken I am sent out to Cairo to photograph the war in the desert. Thrilled at idea of escaping and doing some more useful jobs. Besides, London palls.

DINNER WITH MARGOT OXFORD

January 24th

A deux — Margot at her most delightful, at her best. Edythe Baker, with a slimy Cabinet minister, shrugged her shoulders and made an expiring grimace at me from across the restaurant. For someone thinking only in terms of sex, probably my dinner companion *did* look a little unappetizing.

---

[23] Randolph Churchill.

Margot presents a rather macabre sight these days with the strangest make-up and clothes. Tonight she had applied two very rough black eyebrows and burnt-corked eyelids. She wore a lot of thick underclothes beneath a transparent green Russian blouse, and on her head, at a perilous angle, a Russian cossack toque of long-haired fur that kept tickling one eye.

During the last war Margot was at Downing Street; she was one of the great figures in England, a pivot of interest and excitement. Today she has no position and has been too frank for her friends. It is remarkable how graciously she takes her back seat. She remains completely un-bitter.

Never was she as mellow or warm-hearted as tonight. For three and a half hours a most galvanizing and witty performance on her part overcame any superficial deficiencies. I feel she will not be 'with us' for long, and she has so much to teach. She is never afraid of showing her *naïveté* and childishness. Her knowledge of geography is as poor as mine; neither of us could place the counties of England. She professes only a superficial gift for politics, cannot speak German although she lived a year in Dresden, Berlin and Munich, and she has little French. But her sense of humour gives her a bond of sympathy with everyone who can understand anything funny. Her understanding of human nature is deeply sympathetic. She also possesses the freemasonry of the artist.

She discussed her frankness: 'When I'm tired, or bored, I always start undressing in the drawing-room.' When her dinner guest rises and apologizes, 'I'm terribly sorry, I must leave,' she replies, 'No one can leave too early for me.'

She spoke of her husband with deep admiration for his character and humour. In Leicestershire her hunting friends said, 'But you can't marry a man with long hair!' (They were later surprised to find that Mr Asquith knew the names of all Derby runners and their jockeys for the past twenty years; and quite dashed when he said, 'You see, I have a wonderful memory for all trivialities.') Four prime ministers signed the registry book at their marriage.

Certainly the one man she loathes with venom is Lloyd George. She obviously dislikes him for having dislodged her husband from power, but she has made herself believe it is because of his dishonesty and crookedness. In one passage-at-arms he turned on her and said, 'My dear lady, you are morbid about the truth.'

She told me of how, when Lloyd George was living at No 11 and Herbert, as the Prime Minister, was away visiting the King of Italy, Lloyd George determined to overcome her hostility. He even thought he might make a pass at her, and appeared in her bedroom one night. Margot sat up very erect and behaved as if there was nothing strange in his sudden appearance and said, 'Now do tell me the news — all the news.'

When Asquith was out of a job and Margot and he found themselves without a penny, Thornton Butterworth offered her £30,000 for her autobiography. When the money arrived, Margot asked, 'I suppose we'd better save and invest this?' 'No,' said Herbert Asquith, 'Let's spend it and enjoy it,' and they did. Today Margot is poor and really rather lonely. It is true she can be a nuisance and a bit obstreperous, but it is an indictment of her contemporaries that they do not put up with her any more, treat her as a bore, and are without the imagination to appreciate her shafts of wit.

Of course Margot can be extremely difficult. At Vaynol recently she slapped Lady ... across the face for allegedly cheating at cards, then rushed into the next room to beard the husband. 'Sir B., you're a nice man. Your wife's terrible. You should never have married her. Let this be a lesson to you!' At the same house-party she appeared at midday dressed in tweeds, with bootees and leggings, and a tall pheasant's feather in her hat for the shooting lunch. Sitting in the improvised tent, she fervently inquired what the local shots thought about the latest political events and the morning's leading article in *The Times*. When the locals excused themselves by saying that they had left the house before the papers had arrived, Margot turned in disgust, and in a stage whisper opined, 'Ignorant fools.'

On another occasion she stood in the hall at a wedding reception and, as the guests endeavoured to go up to the drawing-room to shake hands with the young couple, confided in a loud aside, 'Don't go upstairs, the bride's hideous!'

Especially since the bombardment, with London empty of all except those who have to work here, Margot has time to permit fate to play a large part in her existence. When I told her that, unfortunately, I seldom allowed destiny a chance to act its part in my life, she said, 'But you're so busy! You see, I've got nothing to do at all! Yesterday I saw two young RAF men lunching at that table over there. I asked if they wanted a lift afterwards anywhere as I was fortunate enough to have a car and driver. The young men explained that one was the groom and the other his best man. So I took them in my motor to the wedding in Hanover Square.'

Another day Margot saw a woman waiting in the rain for a bus and took her to her destination in Esher.

'Now I am without a maid and I have to ask the liftmen at the Savoy to get me out of my dress.' Her butler, Whitmore — a great character who has been with her seventeen years — comes to see her each day. He knocks on the door. 'Can I come in?' (Never a m'lady or anything like that.) 'Just a minute,

Whitmore, while I put a Shetland shawl round my head and get myself ready.' Whitmore comes in and asks, 'Do you know of a good life of Voltaire?' Then he proceeds of his own free will to ring up Mr Cyril Radclyffe or Mr Cecil Beaton to see if they can have her to dinner. 'But Mr Beaton has only a small house, Whitmore; I'm sure he can't have me tonight.' They go out in the car. Whitmore, sitting in front, says to the chauffeur, 'How can we amuse her?' To save the embarrassment of hearing the reply Margot pulls-to the intervening window.

When talking of prison reform she remarked, 'Wormwood Scrubs! What a name for a prison! Dickens couldn't have done better!' At one moment, on the subject of suffragettes, I interrupted and said, 'Surely they were *before* the war!' Very sweetly Margot continued, 'It doesn't matter if it was on Thursday or Friday.' She relishes a good story, especially if it is long and full of complicated labyrinths! She chortled with deep enjoyment when I told her about Bridget Paget whose maid told her she was going to the races, 'in a charabanc with fifty friends'. 'Fifty friends?' exclaimed Bridget, pulling at her wisps of hair. 'How lucky you are, I've only got five!'

Margot also reminisced about her lecture trip to America: how she was invaded in her cabin on the boat by the reporters before she was dressed. 'Go to my hotel and wait for me there — I'm not dressed yet!' she shouted through the door. 'But we have to make the evening papers!' By degrees the reporters wormed their way into her cabin while she kept asking questions of them. 'Why do you sit on rocking chairs?' 'Why must you continuously use spittoons?' They laughed.

'Now, now, Lady Oxford, we want an interview.'

'When does it begin?'

'It's begun.'

'Oh, well, perhaps I oughtn't to have mentioned the spittoons.'

The lecture tour may have been even funnier in fact than Margot imagined it. She must have looked quite fantastic in a silver tissue dress given to her by Callot. At one time she was asked to become a member of the Culture Searchers' Club, and when invited to a 'hen luncheon', she inquired, 'What's a "hen" luncheon?'

'Oh, isn't she lovely!' they laughed.

Margot has her dislikes: she once told Shaw his plays were too long. 'It's the only way I have of emptying the theatre,' was his reply.

She said she was not fond of Sibyl Colefax of the dark curly hair. 'I don't care who people know, and it is so tiresome that Sibyl is always on the spot. One can't talk about the birth of Christ without that Astrakhan ass saying she was there in the manger.'

It was here at the Savoy that Ivor Novello had recently gone up to Margot's table and introduced himself. Margot looked nonplussed, then uttered: 'Novello? Novello? Ah yes! You smile too much and Eddie Marsh loved you!'

Each time one sees her she is apt to say something one will long remember. Tonight she was full of good things. The waiter asked, 'Will you have spring chicken, m'lady?' 'Which spring?' she asked. She told bright little stories: Maud Tree and she were passing Lutyens' newly-erected cenotaph. Lady Tree breathlessly exclaimed, 'But that's not a war memorial! I want angels — angels — angels — I want angels mounting higher and higher!' Margot replied, 'But you don't want a Jacob's ladder.' Lady Tree replied, 'I don't want a Jacob's lift!'

When Margot is at her best she can envelop you with her charm as she did this evening. She even kissed me and put her face close to mine in a most surprising way. I find her love of humanity, her bemused outlook and abundant affection are her greatest merits. The years have given her a kindness and mellowness that, I am told, she lacked before.

Tonight Margot has had a treat, and so have I!

DEBATE IN THE HOUSE OF COMMONS

January 29th

This was the third day of the debate on the progress of the war.

There is a lot of unrest and anxiety throughout the country. The news has been unrelievedly bad, so far as Britain and the United States are concerned, and Mr Churchill demanded a vote of confidence. He knew he could get this, but the House wished to make it quite clear that they were dissatisfied with the output and the work done by members of the Cabinet.

On the first day Mr Churchill had made a brilliantly adroit speech in which he devised many ingenuities and surprises which succeeded in causing a number of members to tear up their speeches of protest already written. On the second day there had been criticism — stinging and useful. On the third day it so happened there were no fireworks left: everyone knew the Prime Minister would succeed, and must succeed, for the good of the country. Mr Shinwell, Randolph and Jock McEwen (who said that the work of Lord Beaverbrook had the same effect as a strong cocktail — exhilarating for a time but leaving a bad hangover) had done their best. Today Belisha had been unconvincing and bored, and Lord Winterton made references to Mr Churchill being like W. G. Grace the cricketer, who would play with village elevens so that he could bat all the time and bowl when the others on his side were out.

Everyone laughed. This really 'got' them. I felt it strange that, in the middle of this war, the House of Commons could be so amused by references to the traditional sport. Somehow I felt the whole procedure was quite unrelated to the war. It seemed like a performance that had little bearing on the world outside. The newspapers would bring this scene to every doorstep, but it seemed so muffled in tradition that all sense of actuality and urgency was lacking. It was up to Mr Churchill, in the final contribution of the debate, to bring the proceedings to a high level. He became twice his usual size, as he always does when making a speech. He was like a bird that ruffles up all its feathers. When after the debate he wandered about the floor, talking to all and sundry, he again became quite *svelte*.

Mr Churchill spoke well and enjoyed a few well-phrased jokes. Nevertheless, it was obvious that the speech was not costing him much, that by taking an even path he knew that no great effects were necessary. But he appeared so exaggeratedly like himself that one had the impression of watching a rather uninspired historical film about the great Winston Churchill. From where I sat, an effective cinema shot could have been made looking down on him as he stood by the Mace, a bald, waxen figure, with chin and nose of a pig-pallor, and of a rather powdery consistency, with the large empty expanse of the green carpet as his background. The camera would then pan up to Mrs Churchill, an impressive figure with hair worn in a high diadem of blue-grey curls capped by a fan-like arrangement of the transparent material of which her turban was composed. She behaved with impassive calm whenever criticism was particularly waspish.

Churchill became his most grave when explaining the loss of the *Prince of Wales* and *Repulse*. But the real drama of the day came with a moment of pathos and tragedy when, after the victorious result of over 450 votes to 1 in favour of Churchill, Sir Roger Keyes sprang to his feet, and, full of emotion, delivered an incomprehensible little speech. His son has been killed on one of the Commando raids and Keyes looks as if his own life were about at an end. He is wizened, with staring eyes, and did not remember what he had started out to say.

Beverley Nichols motored me to North Weald to photograph Michael Duff looking after his squadron of American Eagles. It is Michael's triumph that, by remaining just as fantastic and full of eccentricities as ever, these tough, amusing and witty pilots love him.

Michael does not attune his manner to them in the slightest degree, and appears more 'British' and ramrod of mien than ever. He is completely lacking in self-consciousness. What an enviable quality this is! For me it is quite an ordeal to go alone into a mess. However, today's expedition, under Michael's aegis, overcame even the more sombre aspects of war, and private terror was lost in laughter.

Beverley has obviously been struck hard by the war, and did not seem capable of mustering much gaiety. But I liked him so much for relating a story about his visit, earlier in the war, to a bomber station. It might so well apply to me (or, I suppose, to almost any frightened stranger). 'Would you like to go up?' they asked Beverley. 'Sure.' 'Sign these papers just in case you meet with a fatal accident. Now put on your parachute.' They assembled under the belly of an enormous bomber. 'This is where you get in.' Beverley looked up at a cylinder of shining metal above him. How on earth could he get to the top of that? His parachute was very heavy on his behind. With a tremendous effort, and, of course, with the incentive that under no circumstances must he fail, also out of nervousness and desperation, he performed a most tremendous physical feat. He jumped up into the air, with galvanized strength jumped higher than he has ever jumped before. He then stretched higher than he has ever stretched before. Somehow or other, by a miracle, he was able to reach the summit of the cylinder: not only did he hang on, but with one further effort he pulled himself and parachute up into the cockpit. When, with bleeding fingers and thumping heart, he looked down the funnel at the others below, their faces were upturned in amazement. 'How in hell did you manage to get up there?' they shouted. 'They've not yet lowered the step ladders!'

Luisa Casati had been telephoning frantically. Every block in the house was filled with messages to say I must call her urgently. Something catastrophic had happened. Could I see her? Sure. Lunch tomorrow. Oh lunch, how kind — do you really mean it? Isn't it too *much*? To save her the taxi fare I called at her flat — a dirty room on the top floor of Catherine d'Erlanger's former house, where Byron lived, in Piccadilly. Luisa, wild black eyes and yellowed tresses, in the inevitable black velveteen and leopard skin, said that *everything* had gone wrong. It was a day when the devil was in everything. She sat at a table in the middle of the room, adding kohl to her eyes while the taxi ticked up. Now to tidy the room, to hide — in a locked wardrobe — the electric stove a friend had lent her so that the landlady would not charge her for extra electricity. She opened the cupboard to display a sight of degradation: old artificial flowers, methylated spirit, broken bottles, and jet evening cloaks.

Luisa is a product of the D'Annunzio period, a Gustave Moreau painting or Aubrey Beardsley drawing to the life. Her appearance is so exotic, and even frightening to many, and seldom do her acquaintances have any idea what goes on behind the white and black mask of her face. In fact, Luisa is a very human and wittily comic character who worships beauty in its more fantastic forms and enjoys the incredulity her personality creates in unsuspecting strangers. Luisa also possesses a cruel streak and has been known to annihilate many an enemy with a phrase; she can be unsparing in her sarcasm and bitterness. Not only does she look like a witch but, believing in witchcraft, she can become one.

In the past her glittering riches justified her eccentricities in the eyes of conventional Roman aristocracy. Even so her highest flights would only be tolerated with difficulty. The *beau monde* would be bidden to a soirée to find their white-faced, scarlethaired hostess, entwined with cobras, had decorated the ballroom with caged monkeys gibbering among branches of lilac. Dressed by Bakst in Persian trousers, she was once accompanied by a negro slave, named Larbi, who led a chained panther in his wake: it was said that Larbi died from poisoning as a result of having to appear at another ball naked, but gilded from head to foot.

Luisa's vagaries took her to Capri, where she created a remarkable house like a Greek temple that Axel Munthe later made famous. At the end of one Venetian season, she found herself unable to pay the gondolier's bill, so, in settlement, took off a row of heavy pearls and tossed them at him. Dunned by bailiffs, the *Marchesa* migrated to Paris where she lived in Boni de Castellane's Palais Rose. Francis Rose told me of the first time he, as an extremely impressionable young painter, saw her. Luisa was in her bedroom wearing, as a hat, a gold upturned flowerpot from which sprouted an enormous salmon-coloured feather to match her salmon gloves. She was clipping the artificial daisies from a grass carpet she had had made in imitation of a picture by an Italian primitive. Her maid stood by, holding the basket into which the daisies were put. No doubt she not only enjoyed this highly aesthetic activity, but was secretly amused at the effect she must be creating on this somewhat incredulous Englishman.

It is really ghastly to see to what straits of poverty this wildly extravagant woman, who has spent two of the greatest fortunes in Italy, has fallen. She hasn't even a tosser left! A few English friends club together to give her a stipend each month, but she blows the lot on fodder for her cat. Occasionally she hires a cab and, in desperation, beseeches one of her benefactors to buy the relics of the Countess Castiglione's fancy dress as the Queen of Hearts, a tarnished, theatrical necklace, or bits of worthless finery from the bottom of a trunk. Sometimes they accede to her entreaties, but most of them eschew the bargain, giving her instead a present, only to become irritated when they learn that their contribution was used to buy imitation orchids or sets of false eyelashes.

Even Augustus John has turned. Luisa's frequent requests for fivers have at last got him down. He says she should be, like some beloved household pet, shot and stuffed. She would look so well in a glass case.

Luisa and I came back home for lunch. It was a bitter February morning but my guest wore no overcoat over her only day dress: doubtless she still possesses some old gold-cloth ball gowns, but they would give her even less protection from the icy blast. My rooms were warm and, suddenly, the sun came through the library windows and everything looked comfortable and congenial. Luisa became as happy as a child. She said she worshipped the atmosphere of my house — the scent of the rosemary that we burnt at the grate — and she felt that she 'lived again' now she was in this dark-red room, sipping this glass of amber.

We started lunch. Oh, she liked so much the plates — the food! Everything she imbibed with a passionate enjoyment. Her enthusiasms are so much stronger than mine! I really adore her, in spite of her wickedness and suspiciousness and vitriolic wit. For what tenderness, warmheartedness and *camaraderie* she possesses! She has the spirit of an artist, and, as with all artists, one can learn a lot in her presence. I was fascinated to watch her reactions.

'Now, tell me, Luisa — what is wrong?'

'You have a little time to spare for me after lunch? Then let us mention unpleasant things later. Now let us enjoy this pigeon, this good glass of wine that is so rare.'

She talked brilliantly. Luisa sees ordinary Chelsea flappers as archangels: Augustus John a patriarch; Tilly Losch looks 'like a rifled drawer'. Apropos of two friends of ours, she said they are like love birds which sit touching one another and chirping at one another all day, not 'I love you' but 'I hate you'. Their proximity — from which they cannot escape — prevents them from loving one another. Luisa has a good memory for funny stories: Violet Trefusis brought a lanky lover to her mother. 'Mummie, this is the man I wish to marry!' '*Mariage, Violette, non! Collage, oui!*' She considers Henry Moore's 'Shelter' pictures were for 'alltime': she was deeply moved by my Fuseli painting.

Then came the story of her catastrophe. A. John gives her two pounds a week, but he has been away for five weeks. For Christmas Augustus had sent her a letter enclosing a present, but no present was enclosed! He has forgotten to write the cheque. His wife, mistresses and daughters swarm around him and forbid her to talk to him on the telephone in the country; they are jealous. Meanwhile Luisa has no money. She telephones Mrs Brougham, who asks, 'What has become of that pound you had last week?' Luisa, outraged, answers, "*J'ai mangé, j'ai bu — et j'ai encore de l'argent dans ma pochette.*' Alice Astor has sent her some shoes and artificial flowers which have caused her to walk on air, but she has no hard cash, no prospects, and is incapable of helping herself. As Augustus says, 'She can't even knit!' Yet she is never depressed and complaining — only frenzied in the direst half-hour of need. I felt enriched by her company, stimulated by her unusual presence, and my eyes rejoiced as I watched this stringy black scarecrow undulate down the garden path to the extravagant taxi which, of course, she must take now that I have given her a small present.

Three days later, and again catastrophe. Luisa telephoned that she could not reach Augustus on the telephone. I called his number and there he was. Luisa, cruelly, had been given a wrong number. Yes, Augustus was wanting to see Luisa. *Must* see her, in fact, for he would be going away again to the country tomorrow. Luisa, for a few more days, was saved again.

A couple of weeks later poor Luisa arrived, unannounced and unexpectedly, without even the money to pay the taxi at the door. I had brought her luck before, and being so superstitious she had had to come and see me again.

But her plight was again extreme. Well, how could we ward off another evil day?

I had an idea: Luisa makes, for her own amusement, strange and surrealist *collage* screens or blotters composed of fragments cut from engravings and any odd pictures that strike her fancy. 'Could you not do some of these for sale? You could *make* money!' Luisa flapped her false eyebrows and bared her huge teeth.

We went forthwith to the Charing Cross Road and I spent a fortune on eighteenth-century and Victorian prints. Although Luisa chose with care, and seemed enthusiastic and grateful, nothing came of the expedition. She will not commercialize her talent.

Is it not curious that this exotic creature should not warm her old bones in the warmth of an Italian sun rather than choose to end her days in — of all cold, dreary places — South Kensington? Yet perhaps there is method in her madness: she knows that her 'old friends' in Rome, who tolerated her when she was a millionairess, would cut her ruthlessly and give no help now that she is stony-broke. Whereas in England there *are* always a half-dozen cronies who can be relied upon before the very last gasp of her cat.

'I love England,' Luisa claims. 'It is so mysterious and unexpected. It is much more highly civilized, subtle and difflcult to know than any other country.' It cannot have been easy for her living here with an Italian passport without occupation or permanent address. But her proudest moment came when the police wrote to her: she showed me the letter. 'In future you will be considered a friendly alien.'

SCHOOL FRIENDS' MEETING

He sat opposite me in the train. 'We haven't met for twenty-five years,' he said. He told me his name. He is bald, but perky, full of assurance and enthusiasm. He remembers vividly every detail of Harrow life, which, to me, is now in a haze of oblivion. We were not particular friends but he knows a lot about me, as he does of everyone else there. He tells me things about myself that I had not remembered. He's a type of school-bore, but rather fascinating.

He informed me I went to Harrow in the summer term of 1918, just before the end of the First World War; that I got my shoes from Chathams, my clothes from Wards; I had a damn good time there and never did any work. Used to draw different *coiffures* for women on the back of my notebooks. He said he thought I was by no means silly but never concentrated or worked, was screwed in examinations, and never got out of the same class. He reminded me of our doing 'stinks' together — and I vaguely remember putting sulphuric acid on pennies — but other divs and classes that he mentioned were, to me, something that I might never have experienced.

Yet he was able to conjure up again the taste of Gillettes' ham sandwiches (they cost sixpence each). Gillettes was the snobbish shop where any outcast schoolboy, entering without the necessary credentials, was made to feel so out of it that he'd not dare to defile the precincts a second time. He reminded me also of Gillettes' cold sausages and tomato ketchup, the Patum Peperium, and the *marrons glacés* in silver paper. Gillettes' cold, white, little emporium was an exciting meeting-place, and it was here that many strange friendships and emotional upheavals began.

Yes, he repeated, I always had a good time, and was particularly amused when, in evening class, Tregoning used to crawl along the floor and turn out the gas, so that for twenty minutes the whole room was in darkness. By the time order was regained, the hour had come for the end of the lesson. He talked of the Beaks. He remembered how Ponto (du Pontet, four feet in height) bumped into Morgan (a tall man with a squint) who said, 'I do wish you'd, look where you're going,' to which Ponto replied, 'I do wish you'd go where you're looking.'

What a strange life this man leads harking back to those early days, stopping people in the street — 'A. C. Kinahan, late of Bradby's, isn't it? No, you wouldn't remember me, but you did this and that in such and such a year. Do come and have lunch with me one day and meet some other Harrovians ...'

DESPONDENCY

February 15th

I don't believe the morale of the country has been so low since the beginning of the war. Not even the desperate period after Dunkirk compared in gloom to this. There was something rather exciting about the appalling sequence of events that ended in the collapse of France. But nearly two years have intervened. It is the fact that, even now, we still seem to be muddling and unprepared, that has, after a dark winter with long periods of snow, ice and dirty skies, given so many people at home a feeling of cynical desperation or what's worse — sheer apathy. I believe that for the first time the English now do seem to realize the possibility of defeat.

Of course that possibility had always existed, but it was our great strength that we would never face the fact. Now we are beginning to lose that strength. Churchill is undoubtedly a great man, but the pendulum of popularity has swung away from him and people talk of his faults and ask, 'Who else is there?' From having had to admit there was nobody they now answer 'Stafford Cripps'. Overnight, Cripps has sprung towards the top of the class. The country has built him up to be a force since his return from Moscow. His radio talk has had wide success: letters have poured into the newspapers suggesting he should lead a new Government.

Meanwhile the news for which Churchill is responsible, and yet for which he is not to blame, gets ever worse. The Japs advance. They have occupied Malaya, they have landed in some numbers in Burma. The Russian advance on Germany seems to be held up. The Americans are talking. The German battleships *Gneisenau* and *Scharnhorst* and *Prinz Eugen*, on whose attempted destruction we have wasted many lives and, reputedly, forty-two bombing machines, have been able to leave their positions at Brest and sail undamaged along the Straits of Dover past the English Channel to the comparative safety of Heligoland Bight. This all happened on Friday the 13th — but worse on Sunday the 15th! We hear that Singapore, to which we have been sending reinforcements, and which was defended by 80,000 men, has surrendered. This is one of the most shattering blows. The country is bowed in shame, furious with indignation and impatient of further setbacks.

Churchill has hurried to the microphone and made a speech that is strong and rallying. He has said that when Russia was being harassed, and the fall of Moscow seemed imminent, the people did not lose faith in their leaders and demand a change of Government: internal disorders were just what the Germans hoped to achieve. It is a bad period for Churchill. It is a bad period for us. Personally, I do not wish a change in Government — and one never knows what sort of a prime minister Stafford Cripps or anyone might make. Yet it is comforting to the country to realize that, at last, an alternative looms on the horizon.

The gloom is all-pervading. Increasing restrictions — without any visible signs of results in production — the cold, the untidiness, the ugliness of people in London, a lack of smartness in our army, and, above all, the off-handedness and apathetic laziness of the people, has become a slight obsession with me.

Now that my RAF book has been sent to the printers I am looking around for my next job. My ambition is to be sent to the Near East. Randolph Churchill, on leave, was enthusiastic and helpful. I go to see Brendan Bracken on Wednesday, and there is a chance that the Ministry of Information may send me to Cairo to take photographs and do articles for another book. It is a thrilling prospect, and there is now a star shining brightly in front of me.

Part VII: Middle East, 1942

CAIRO

March 1942, Cairo

'He's away in Malta,' said Walter Monckton's secretary, wearing what at home we used to call a Henley Regatta dress, when I called to present myself at the office of the Minister of State. 'Perhaps you had better see Mr Tweedy.' She rattled the telephone exasperatedly. 'You've no idea what the phone service is like here' — and while she waited with the receiver to her ear she explained, 'It's a strange place, and you'll soon find no one keeps a date on time.'

Mr Tweedy said, 'We want "might" in our propaganda here. Don't photograph one aeroplane, photograph sixty at a time — never four tanks, but a hundred! Get them to "lay on" some important demonstration! Ask for the impossible! You've come at a good time. We're prepared for the balloon going up at any moment: we're not worrying though; Rommel's no bogy; we made a mistake in building him up as a great figure. The Germans themselves don't star him.'

Wing-Commander Burn, at the RAF Public Relations Headquarters, went to a map and suggested itineraries for me to start upon in the desert. 'Begin in the canal zone and work up here, this way, then down here, along there and then back here, on to Palestine, Iran, Iraq, Transjordania and Syria. But first you must wait for a Service identity card.' Philip Astley at the Army PR suggested other places to visit.

In London the Ministry of Information were baffled as to whether I, being 'a special case' should wear a uniform or not:

if so, to which Service was I to be attached? Would I be a private or a non-commissioned officer? 'Best to leave it till your arrival in Cairo. They'll know what to make of you.' But HQ were equally baffled. 'He can't go into the desert without a uniform. Someone, sooner or later, would be bound to shoot him for a spy.' 'We can't possibly make him an officer,' said a grey-haired group-captain, scratching his head. I was rather sad to hear this, as ever since my childhood I have suspected I would never get beyond being a private. In the end it was arranged that I should wear RAF uniform with 'Official Photographer' on the shoulders instead of a badge of rank.

This morning I went to order my uniform. As I looked in the glass, trying on a cap and jacket, I felt it was a pity I was not fifteen years younger for, although no apparel is more becoming than uniform, a bare bullock face suits it best. There is altogether too much going on in my face — it reveals all sorts of nasty bits of character that I do not like at all.

On my first few, rather tentative, outings in this uniform I was self-conscious about matters of saluting on which I had not been briefed. I caused great surprise by the smart manner in which I touched my cap to some men on leave casually buying souvenirs. I was alarmed to notice that important old men covered with tabs should look, in a somewhat bewildered manner, at my shoulders rather than at my face. Small wonder they were bewildered because I have now learnt that I was supplied with a heterogeneous collection of garments that would ordinarily have belonged either to a high-ranking officer, or to someone in the ranks, but not to both at the same time.

Many of those in high authority have been out here for more than three years. To an outside observer like myself that seems far too long. In this war, fresh ideas come so fast that even a man capable of adapting himself to new ways of thinking is soon apt to get 'behind the times'. Moreover, the clammy heat squanders a man's patience and plays upon his moral fibre as relentlessly as on his physique: unless he resigns himself to running in low gear his nerves are soon frayed and the Kipling epitaph applies: 'Here lies the fool who tried to hustle the East.' Thus, the Cairene climate, producing a *laissez aller* policy, procrastination and delay, is a great ally to Hitler.

I was bidden to 8 o'clock breakfast at 'Air House'. This official residence of the Air Officer Commanding-in-Chief Middle East is where he lives and entertains any distinguished RAF commanders in transit or on a visit to Headquarters. It looks like a house you would find at Godalming, and its drawing-room and dining-room suites are furnished with a strange 'unlived-in' formality. Park and de Crespigny, the AOCs of Egypt and Iraq respectively, had already finished breakfast when I arrived, and Tedder came down saying, 'Shall we nibble?' What sort of a man is this who has one of the most responsible jobs out here? He looks like a bilious schoolboy. His complexion is sallow and rather dry with very small wrinkles. Thick hair, twinkling eyes, bat's ears and wiry body, with legs that stretch back at the calf like a bow. It is impossible to believe that this coltishness belongs to someone of fifty-two. He does not wish to impress — rather to put everyone at ease, so that talk will be at its most natural and interesting. He puffs at his pipe, smiles with his eyes, and invites you to a conspiracy of friendship. He is, you feel, always storing up impressions, and that the opinions of anyone with whom he comes in contact are grist to his mill.

Tedder has been accused of being too full of charm, of not being forceful enough. He is a man of undoubted charm, but I would not like to cross him. He can suddenly become granite, as he did when describing some of the remarkable things against heavy odds that the RAF boys had achieved out here in the desert, and in Malta, from where he had just returned.

I was somewhat anxious lest he should give me technical instructions that would be above my head, or that he might discuss warfare in the Near East as if I were as knowledgeable as some recent American woman journalist had been. But, knowing that someone else was in charge of my programme, he showed me crayon sketches he had done of the bombing of Malta. Although quite naive in technique these little pictures gave a better impression of these war scenes than the Press photographs. Tedder always carries this small notebook in his breast-pocket, and produces it when he sees something he'd like to record as a 'souvenir'. 'You're going to Syria? Well, hurry up and get there before the spring flowers are over.' This remark surprised me pleasantly. 'Yes, the wild flowers are a bit late already, but they're amazing — in one square yard of rock garden I counted twenty-seven different varieties.'

After the comparative 'austerity' of England, Cairo presents a luxurious façade with ultra-fashionable Egyptian, Greek and Syrian women giving lavish entertainments, servants without number, and none of the usual restrictions. The torrent of optimistic war news in the Anglo-Egyptian newspapers gives many of the English people here the complacent feeling that the war will be over in two months. Even Churchill's speeches are not given in full if the import is not sufficiently encouraging. This policy of pap feeding is aimed, it is said, at 'heartening' the Egyptians. But surely we have a grim enough example from France of what happens when the newspapers refuse to face the gravity of events?

What a joy to find good old Flick[24] out here! One would have thought him too self-effacing and elusive to find for himself any pigeon-hole in the framework of a war, yet, in his quiet way, he has become an expert on camouflage and has been disguising the Takoradi oil route. And Felix has sufficient strength of character not to allow a battle to divert him from his interests in all forms of art and architecture. Felix has become my guide, combining erudition with an appropriate frivolity on our sightseeing expeditions to medieval Arab houses in the Old City, the early Mosque of Ibn Touloun, the late-Napoleonic Palace of Mahomed Ali, and the painted Palace of Shubra.

Yesterday, in one of the local carriages — gharries — we toured the Arab town, the largest Moslem city in the world. The gharry provides the most delightful and leisurely way of surveying the narrow, overhung lanes, with the pretty, wiry balconies of the harems almost meeting above the jostling crowds. The tarboosh and coloured turbans of the various sects, dynasties and families formed a bobbing sea below us. We sat aloft, jogging along lanes lined with brilliantly coloured sweets, or butchers' shops, or alley ways with gold necklaces arrayed in glittering splendour.

A whole thoroughfare given over to engraven brasswork rolled past us, followed by another of pearl inlay. The spice quarter exuded the fragrance of the *Arabian Nights*. In bulging, buff-coloured sacks, mint, cedar, sandalwood and innumerable varieties of curry powder comprise still life arrangements ready for the brush of Braque.

---

[24] Felix Harbord.

The signs of poverty are very distressing: so many lives are devoted to the most inhuman tasks. Young men swing a large heavy shell-shaped weapon pounding the nutmeg as they sing in unison a loud and monotonous dirge, the rhythm of which helps them forget their physical agony as they heave to and fro, like Blake engravings of tormented souls writhing in purgatory. Once they give up this work their muscles contract and they are unfit for further effort. Some extremely aged men have spent their whole existence doing the same work every day of the year until now they have become human machines.

How depressingly ugly is the Egyptian of today! The veiled women are an unfortunate, unlovable lot. On badly-balanced, high-heeled shoes, they lope along sloppily, without looking where they are going, continuously colliding with one another or stepping under the wheels of the oncoming traffic. Above their noses, which are squashed by a cotton spool keeping their veils in place and looking like a misplaced Hitler's moustache, their eyes wear a perpetually wronged, hang-dog expression. Scanty, sagging breasts swing low, and their stomachs bulge as if about to deliver yet another unwanted brat whose eyes will be food for flies. The men are avaricious, and look it.

Screams could be heard coming from the centre of a group of Arabs who were eagerly huddled together. A small child whose head was covered with bleeding sores was having its scalp shaved. The child wriggled and screamed as it was held down by a dozen dark hands. The razor was unstayed. The blue, shaven scalp, the flash of the blade and the bleeding sores produced a ghastly effect.

Wives of officers in Cairo were given the alternative: either to be vacuated to South Africa or to work fifty-two hours a week. There was a rush of women to General Headquarters for jobs as telephonists, typists and secretaries. Many experienced professional men were ousted from their jobs and chaos reigned. It became even more difficult to make a telephone call than before — an exasperated voice was heard bellowing, 'I've tried all day to get hold of the Colonel. Is that the Colonel's secretary? Well, I shall report you for incompetence for not giving him the message. What's your name?' The voice came back apologetically, 'I'm very sorry, but this is the General's wife speaking.'

Today the British colony turned up in its shantung and duck at the Embassy in celebration of the visit of the Duke of Gloucester. Flags were flying from the balcony and cut flowers were wilting in the sun. A brass band played. 'God Save the King' was struck up, the Duke stood at the top of the steps. A pause — a silence while everyone stared. Everyone waited for His Royal Highness to move, but nothing stirred, except a fly which Her Excellency, Lady Lampson, whisked away. This whole scene could not have been more typically English, in spite of Egypt, the palm trees and the sun. The Embassy, with its shuttered windows and balustrades, might have been a country mansion near Henley, and the Nile was reduced to the Thames. Yet coming from England it all seems a little astonishing, for although the buffet could not be criticized for extravagance (orangeade and cakes were provided), the whole set-up appears so definitely removed from this epoch and certainly from this war.

My British forces identification card, No 55561, has arrived, stamped with a photograph of myself in uniform, and I am off to the desert via Alexandria.

ALEXANDRIA: LILIA RALLI

Alexandria

On Sunday, a great friend of mine, Lilia Ralli, a young Greek lady, wearing a child's dress of bright red, with red bows in her hair and carrying a hat in her hand, took me for a walk to the canal banks. Here life cannot have altered since the days of the Pharaohs. The barges were being propelled very slowly by men in clothes dating from the sixth dynasty. Women walked past carrying a mountain of clover on their heads, and the little mule accompanying them would be hidden, except for its delicate, bird-like hoofs, under the load it had to bear.

Lilia has inherited from the Greeks an enviable basic simplicity, a contentment which stems from the philosophic acceptance of the immediate present. She is full of the joys of intense intimacy. To her, her family and friends are the most priceless of jewels — an apt metaphor for someone to whom jewels mean more than they do for most people — and she will remark of an expedition she made, 'Yes, I went there with my brother Stephan,' giving his name an ardour that others would reserve for a beloved king or poet.

The peasant things of life are enjoyed by Lilia to whom a melon cooled in a rusty can of cold water and eaten under a tree can be the best of the year. A lunch of bread and cheese, sardines and grapes, is enjoyed as much as the *truffle fondu* at Giovanni's in Milan.

I had not met Lilia since she had escaped from Athens when Greece was overwhelmed. It had been a nightmare experience for her to see her country, after enduring so much suffering in the Italian campaign, like a savagely maimed person assaulted by a fresh foe, fighting against Germany without the necessary strength and with little outside help.

Yet the spirit of belief in final victory had been almost mystical, and had sustained her people through the worst tragedies. Liha does not feel that same spirit here in Egypt. It makes her deeply unhappy, and she longs to be able to go back to Athens to collect food or cook communal meals. Her maid, Heleni, who had lost four stone in weight, had written describing the tumbril of their dead that passed through the streets of Athens each day, yet whenever she heard Lilia's canaries sing she felt that her mistress would be soon returning.

THE DESERT

Derek Adkins is to be my conducting officer while I am with the RAF in the desert. This is a godsend, for Derek has toted me around so many air stations in England and he knows my interests and how to intervene as soon as I am getting out of my depth. Today Derek and I went shopping for necessities and commodities for the desert trip. There is so much to buy that it seems like marriage, getting a trousseau, and setting up house. Pots and pans and special clothes are needed. Goggles, towels, desert boots, a mirror, soap, toilet paper, hook to hang clothes on, wash-basin — all these you must provide apart from the bed equipment of Lilo mattress, blankets and rubber groundsheet.

This evening the sun lowered itself on the windscreen of our lorry, and when the ball of light sank behind the horizon we were treated to a show of great beauty. The landscape in the sky was more varied than any terrestrial *paysage*, more fluid than any architecture. Islands of gold and silver, peninsulas of black and rose, floated against a background of many shades of turquoise and azure. The activity of the sky changing so quickly, yet apparently motionless, made the earth below look even more barren and forlorn. Only the straight ribbon of road in front of us became reflected pink. The wisps of gold islands in the sky dispersed; the moon came up in exchange. At twilight, or by moonlight, the desert becomes beautiful: tonight the undulating landscape and white hillocks sprinkled with clusters of thick black bushes, solid and squat, and clumps of feathery palm trees, reminded me of the Patinir landscape in the National Gallery.

Once you have shown your passes and are admitted into the fraternity inside the barriers of the desert — yes, there is a barbed wire entrance to the desert — the newcomer, no matter to what Service or Allied nation he belongs, will be received, without question, not only as an honoured guest, but as a long-lost friend. No matter to what strain the cookhouse has already been put by the difficulties of communications, invitations to share what rations remain will always be pressed, even if an acceptance means your host 'tightening his belt' or 'going dry'.

Mess secretaries, like housewives out on shopping expeditions, are always on the look-out for the means of 'coming by' fresh additions to their stores. They will swap sugar and tea for small eggs from the Senussi tribes. Some of them keep a dozen hens, and they travel with them in the back of their trucks when they move their camping sites. Although under battle conditions the hens may not produce sufficient eggs for breakfast, they supply enough for an occasional omelette.

Some of the dining tables in the mess tent are adorned with wild flowers picked from the desert scrub. A certain rivalry stimulates the various messes. I heard one squadron leader, after seeing the glass display at the mess at which he had just lunched, telephone back 200 miles to his orderly, telling him that last night's Chianti bottle must be saved and used in future on the table as a water jug.

In the motor transport, piled like a pack mule, with every cubic inch of space taken up with our camp-bedding, wash basins, beer bottles, tinned fruit juices, bully beef and other provisions, Derek and I started our trek forward into the desert. Rattling over a rough road running parallel to the sea, we passed a featureless, forlorn desolation, a world seemingly without end, its emptiness broken occasionally by some scraggy fig-trees that never grow tall or bear fruit. This scrubland is without interest, a drab mottled procession of dim colour stretching in all directions like an emptied sea. This desert of slag is a very different desert from the Sahara where beautiful dunes, elaborately combed and dappled by the zephyrs, are composed of a soft canary-coloured powder. This is desolation. It is as impure and drab as a dump heap. The plains are of small useless stones, grit and rock splinters, and the vegetation is dry and unsympathetic. One wonders that even a camel can digest the patches of prickly veitch.

To find oneself at the Army and RAF Public Relations camp at Bagush was like arriving at the Ritz. The tent in which I slept was large and spacious, equipped with an electric light bulb, garden furniture and telephones. In the mess before dinner, an officer was instructing two orderlies to swot an uninvited moth. What would they say at home, with their diet of Woolton vegetable pie, spam and nettle soup, if I wrote to tell them of our dinner tonight? Eggs, tinned salmon, steak and a chocolate pudding, all served with a formality that might have irritated me if it had not seemed so humorously incongruous. The mess quartermaster, in an intimate, confiding manner to the orderlies, kept up, like a nervous hostess, a running whispering campaign during the dinner. Out of the corner of his mouth he would make an aside to a corporal, 'Clear away the salad plates.' 'Crockery away again' — 'butter away' — and, a little later, 'Tell that orderly to pull up his sock.'

The bedouins, in the wadis near the shore, watching the battle wage backwards and forwards along the tableland, consider the protagonists mad. They see first one army and then another retiring in haste, leaving behind a wonderful amount of loot. The bedouins steal forward and sell their spoils to the conquering army. A few months later the victors are vanquished; again the Arabs find great booty. They are the only people, so far, to win on this hazardous chessboard, where invariably the winner loses with his long lines of communication. Only the Arabs understand how to live here in the desert. They have learnt little else. After the battle, in which tanks are set on fire and their occupants fried alive, the fluid field of battle moves on, and the Arabs arrive to pick up, among the useless relics and impediments of destruction, the gold rings, wristwatches, cameras and souvenirs from the stiffened bodies lying in the sun. They will sell the silver strap of a wristwatch that is worth fifteen guineas for a few pounds of sugar. Occasionally they are punished with the loss of an eye, hand or arm; for the Germans sometimes leave behind them fountain pens and thermoses which, when opened, ignite the secret fuse — then bang!

I came to the desert thinking I was nearer to war; yet even here war seems distant.

Where then is war? In Whitehall, where the planning is done, thousands of miles from the sound of the guns, it necessarily seems remote. Here I see how much spade work goes on continuously behind the lines, the running of maintenance units, of repairs to telephones and cars, the arranging of the never-ending difficulties of transport. I see how many hours of dreary waiting and inconvenience must be endured each day, or how much time can be spent repairing an accumulator or a lorry, bringing in trays of tea, or doing chores that make life here similar to what it might be back home. I see that human existence in the desert has not the proportion of the surroundings. Yet I realize that all these aspects are as real a part of war as another.

'I've never had so much fun as now,' said a friend of mine while firing at the Germans, but he was carried away by his enjoyment and was soon taken prisoner. Can he be considered a more intrinsic part of war than the orderly lighting the Primus stove? The chores are as actual a part of war as the excitement.

Lunched with an all-Greek squadron in a tent decorated stylishly with large squares of blue paper, the colour of the Greek flag. This in contrast to English tents, whose tatty decorations are more artlessly improvised. The Greek lunch of macaroni and meat stew was well cooked and savoury, the ingredients being the identical rations so unappetizingly served in many of the English messes. The Greeks, like the Free French, are flying Hurricanes, and while we were with them two of their aircraft took off in answer to a report that a possible enemy bandit had been sighted. We watched in the operations room while the course of the stranger was plotted. The Greek controller gave his advice to the pilots. An Adonis with classical profile and dark ringlets, he issued his instructions in clipped English on the RT, and the hoarse replies from the pursuing aircraft were also heard in English, but, when they became most excited and eager to make themselves more clearly understood, they would gabble a translation, as an aside, in Greek. The others watched the plot and listened to the latest instructions with growing enthusiasm as the 'would-be' bandit flew down to the coast from the north-west towards their zone. But what a disappointment! The message came through: 'Aircraft presumed friendly.'

Mersa Matruh

On the way to Mersa Matruh, a patch of fig trees in a dip of the road gives the impression, after the miles of unending desolation, of an oasis; but the surprise of coming over a hill top, to find Mersa lying as a panorama below is so delightful that one imagines a town with clumps of dark trees, of domed buildings with minarets, startlingly white against the blue and emerald sea. But, on arrival, one discovers that this is an abandoned, shell-torn seaside town. The white façades still bear the Egyptian signs of the old shops, the baker, the laundry and the hairdresser, but they are empty shells. The few people hanging about seem lost and pointless. At the Toc H Headquarters a few soldiers appear quite bland, despite the sinister dreamlike atmosphere of emptiness and decay.

An eighteen-year-old negro soldier, born near Freetown, staggered into the barracks to put himself at the mercy of the English. He was frantic to join the English army, having fled from his French commander twenty-five miles away. 'What is your story?' The boy gulped in an effort to keep back the tears. He did not like his commandant; he had never done anything wrong to him; but he would never go back to him. If he were made to do so, he would kill himself. 'But just what is the matter?' The dark young boy cried he had refused to sign a chit, saying he did not expect pay of two shillings a day and would be satisfied with eightpence. For his insubordination he had been thrust for three days into a hole in the ground (this, it appears, is how he refers to the Congo form of solitary confinement). He escaped while the guard was asleep in the middle of the night. He walked and slept and had nothing to eat, but, much worse, he had no papers: the commandant had taken possession of them. The English officer was sympathetic. He said to the boy, 'Go and get something to eat over there, by the cook-house.' But to me he said, 'As the commander has his papers, there is nothing for it but to report him to the police, who will turn him back again where he belongs.' The small boy, who had slept in the desert and had not eaten for days, walked with distinction and elegance, and though his face was black he looked cleaner, smarter than most of the English soldiers who had come out of their quarters to listen to his tale. I watched the boy squatting by the brazier, eating carefully and fastidiously. He looked around him with a trusting expression that all would help him. But a feeling of helplessness, the undercurrent of tragedy that is so often near the surface in this war, had a disturbing effect upon me.

Halfaya Pass

Now to the forward areas. The packing up was like moving house. Bags, folding beds, Primus stoves, provisions, water cans. Derek and I took crates of drink. We bumped and banged, ricocheted from rocks into pot holes. The hideous roads seemed endless, with many miles of scrub and muck extending as far as the eye could see.

Quite unexpectedly, and within a few minutes, I was given my baptism of sand. Hot winds blew particles into every crevice of the sealed car, into one's throat, eyes, nose. The wheels of the car added their individual dust storms and the sand poured over the mudguards like clouds of sulphurous smoke. Sometimes it was impossible to see even a few yards ahead, but occasionally patches of road were clear. When the storm was at its worst, the smell was, according to Derek, like new linen.

The sandstorm had abated when we got to Sollum, a badly bashed fishing village. The waves were washing through the skeleton of a wrecked ship by the shore. The houses were pockmarked with shell wounds, and not a roof remained. We drove by hairpin turns up Sollum Pass, past long-haired, immaculate, turbaned Indians, running glibly over Halfaya Pass in pistachio-green tanks. The relics of the battle of Halfaya are now half-buried in sand. A clothing stores must have been blown up; hundreds of shirts, neatly folded, were strewn on the sand; some tanks were blown up, so that a rhythm of circular discs stood in diminishing recession. The ground was littered with ammunition, gas masks, water-bottles, old boots and letters. The surrealist painters have anticipated this battleground with its eternal incongruities: the carcasses of burnt-out aeroplanes lying in the middle of a vast panorama; overturned trucks; cars that have been buckled by machine-gun fire, with their under parts pouring out in grotesque, tortured shapes: some unaccountable clothing blown into the telephone wires, or drapery in a tree seen against sunsets of bright, unforgettable colours.

A north country soldier was wandering casually among the graves of the German soldiers, their topis, rotting in the sun, thrown over the crosses that bear the beastly swastika. A beer bottle, with a piece of paper inside, up-turned with its neck dug into the sand, was all there was to identify the young man who had died in obedience to the Fuehrer — 'Adolf Gross, born 14.11.19, died June 1941'. The north country soldier put back the bottle. 'It makes you think,' was what he said.

One of the worst aspects of desert life is the men's lack of reading matter. However conscientious they are about their duties, much of their time necessarily must be spent 'hanging about being bored'. In the whole of the Middle East there is a shortage of books (such a thing as a Baedeker is nowhere available). The paper shortage is worse than it is in England, and transport cannot be spared for the printed word. Randolph Churchill has worked wonders by not only inaugurating, within a week, and editing a *Desert Press Review*, but by devious means, seeing that it has reached even the most remote outposts.

Coningham[25] welcomed us in his immaculate trailer. Of its interior he is justifiably proud: no grain of sand had penetrated past the meat-safe mesh of the entrance. In leather frames were photographs of his good-looking wife, like Norma Shearer, and family. The atmosphere was peaceful, as if he had everything in control, a most encouraging feeling. Huge, good-looking, strong, sunburnt like an apricot, with a wide column of neck and massive chest. When he talks he shows his lower teeth — there is a gap between the two front teeth. When he laughs, the upper row appears small and in bad condition. In every other way Coningham gives the impression of perfect health. His bright clear eyes turn up slightly at the outer corners. He sits, a colossus at his desk, and waves his arms in broad masculine gestures.

He considers Cairo a bad place for a headquarters. English people cannot fight against the climate and sooner or later become static. Yet, on account of communications it seems

---

[25] Air Chief Marshal Coningham.

impossible to transfer to Heliopolis or Alexandria. He described the desert, without trees or water, as an ideal battle ground. He quoted the German General Von Ravenstein who, when taken prisoner, called it 'the tactician's paradise and the quartermaster's nightmare'. Not more than one man out of every 500 is ill, that is 0.2 per cent. Of the difficulties he encountered in the desert one of the most frequent was the wish of the men to 'build themselves in'. Whenever he found someone had made himself a cement floor to his tent, Coningham would move the camp a mile farther on. The men should be mobile at a few hours' notice and feel that they are nowhere permanently. For the Germans, with their Teutonic orderliness, it was even more difficult. Each time they move camp they start lining little pathways with stones, so soon (we hope) to be abandoned. To keep them in good mental health, Coningham insists that his men work every hour of daylight so that they are pleased to go to bed: with nothing to do but try to look for ticks and scorpions they would become so apathetic that they would not even walk the necessary mile to their mess for a hot meal, but would prefer to open, on the spot, a tin of bully beef for their lunch. Fortunately we had troops here before the war who have the instinct of the desert by now.

But the desert absorbs so much it alone is the victor. To fight here is like trying to fill a bath without a plug, where everything gets washed down the pipe. Two hundred thousand gallons of petrol are devoured each week, 80,000 vehicles are maintained in the knowledge that each can survive only about six months' duration. The waste was terrible; especially on aeroplane machines, which had continuously to be overhauled. A man returned from a raid on Benghazi with, it was discovered, eighty pounds of dust in the wings of his aircraft. He said he thought it felt rather 'soggy'.

The lack of privacy of the desert latrines is something that gives the novice a bit of a shock. The more private of these toilets are encased by a transparent flapping sacking which reaches as high as a man's waist, through which the occupants can be only too clearly seen silhouetted, sitting like Buddhas, oblivious of the world around them. At first I did not know if one saluted or looked the other way when, among a row of men squatting on a wooden 'throne', one recognized an awe-inspiring acquaintance. Out of shyness I was loth to visit such excessively public conveniences. I hoped for an opportunity when I could find somewhere to retire more discreetly. As a result, I suffered from headaches due to constipation, and felt a kindred sympathy for the Edwardian Baroness Burdett-Coutts who, I believe, died as a result of not being able to face the lavatory on a continental train.

Tobruk

In Tobruk Derek was fortunate in getting three fresh loaves at the bakery where all the bread is made for the front lines, and the areas reaching back almost as far as the base. These bakers work at astonishing, almost paralytic, speed and the 300,500 loaves that they produce each day use up 250 tons of flour a week. Pommelling and kneading, they develop tremendous stomach muscles. A machine is too delicate an instrument to stand up to desert conditions, and out of necessity we have been brought back to this simplicity of hand-kneaded bread. Nothing tastes better. The master baker with his badge on his sleeve and his rank of staff sergeant-major fully realised his monarchical powers ruling over this unique white kingdom.

HOSPITAL CASES AT TOBRUK

The General Hospital at Tobruk has suffered remarkably little from the bombing. At this time one of the senior surgeons, named Simpson Smith, with the rank of colonel, a fair goodlooking sportsman, was bemoaning the fact that most of his cases were accidental. 'It worries me so much that there's this terrible continual waste. The other day we had seventy-four cases all in at once: burns — very bad. But out of 220, only three have died. That's because we have this new method of dealing with them. We re-burn them with this silver nitrate. It used to be said that if one-third of a patient's body was burnt he couldn't survive the shock, but now with the present-day processes a man can recover even if five-eighths of his body is burnt. The nitrate forms a skin, a coating that protects the nerves and, at the same time, prevents the life juices from flowing out. Now let me show you this.' The doctor bends over a shrouded figure. 'Now let's have a look at you today.' He uncovers a body. The doctor has tremendous enthusiasm, vitality and charm. If some of his remarks shock me, it is because I am squeamish. 'Yes, you've got it badly, old son. Of course that man represents a good deal of work. He's been a grand patient, taken it very well too. Four pints of plasma were pumped into him. The trouble is he need never have been burned; if only he hadn't thrown down his lighted cigarette next to that petrol can.' The doctor passes down the ward, pauses at another bed and explains: 'This man stepped on a mine, both arms and eyes were blown away, also a large lump out of each thigh — yet he manages to live.' However, another patient was not progressing at all well. 'I got very cross with him,' says the doctor. 'We don't want to have another death and send up our averages.' His earnest, unflinching, matter-of-fact quality was inherent in this remarkable personality. In the way that friendships spring up in the desert, Simpson Smith and I became friends.

The calm fortitude with which the young nurses attend these cases is beyond admiration. They smile and are gay, and refuse to be worn down by the atmosphere of disaster around them. Suddenly, I see something that, from a distance, seems strange and beautiful: shrouded behind a veil of mosquito-netting lies a young Greek god, with long, fair, curly hair bleached by the violent sun. But, on closer inspection, I see that the head is the greeny-black of certain bronzes. The face, with closed eyes and open lips, is racked in torment. 'What is this?' The sister says, 'He's very bad, I am afraid he's going to die.' Apollo Belvedere begins groaning, whimpering and later shouting.

The doctor's enthusiasm for me to photograph his various exhibits is sometimes hard to face. He rubs his hands. 'Splendid, Beaton. There's a great deal to show you — burns all the colours of the rainbow. But best of all, we've got in a field case. You *are* lucky! We've just received a South African, who was driving in a truck when a mine went off. We're operating on him tonight. Just you take your time; there'll be plenty for you to photograph there. We're having him X-rayed now. We'll start at 9 o'clock.' He slaps his hands.

'You'll have dinner with us, of course — in fact, you and your party will be our guests in the hospital tonight — and then we'll go on together afterwards. Meanwhile come and have a shock-injection.' While I drink a most welcome whisky and water, the surgeon talks about his work. 'When I have leave, I go farther up to the front line. If I were to go back to Cairo or somewhere like that, I'd find my place taken when I returned here, so many people are after it. I'd like to be up in the front line all the time, but they can't spare me: I'm too valuable for such rough work. The doctors on the spot do the jobs that have to be attended to immediately, or else the patient would be dead by the time he reached here.'

At dinner the doctors were a cheerful lot — with relish relaying local jokes that were greeted with gusts of laughter — but they became transformed when afterwards we all retired to the solemnity of the operating theatre. Here was complete silence except for the whimpering of a negro writhing on a high bed on wheels. He was starting to come round from the anaesthetic, administered while his badly burnt legs were treated. Time for another injection. A glint of terror came into his eyes as the needle of morphia was pricked into his arm. 'We always have to have someone standing by: sometimes they try to fight their way off the table,' Simpson Smith explained. 'Let's go into the adjoining theatre.' About eight men in white overalls, their khaki shorts showing at the back, were pulling on rubber gloves; over their faces small squares of white linen were tied with white tape bows. My new friend was obviously disappointed that he himself was not to be performing the operation. 'You see, we take it in turns here,' he remarked. 'Major Bingham is on tonight.' The results of the X-ray photographs were handed around. The colonel showed me the negatives, which were interpreted as revealing little bits of dispersed metal, but their whereabouts could not be gauged precisely. 'My God, you're lucky, Beaton! This'll be a great opportunity for you. You can take your time: it's a big operation. It all depends where we find the metal is lodged, but it may last an hour and a half. There's a fly!' With a fly whisk he swotted it. 'If that fly were to alight on an open wound, it might at least give the man dysentery. See this stuff?' My friend blew some powder out of a rubber squirt. 'It's sulphanilamide and it's the most wonderful medical discovery since Pasteur discovered antiseptics and bacteria in 1865. You just put some of this in the wound and there's no chance of gangrene or any poisoning.' Another fly. He got it. 'No, this stuff is extraordinary. You'll see; Major Bingham, the surgeon, will undoubtedly use it continuously during the operation.' Major Bingham, with his bright eyes, looked little more than a schoolboy.

A South African of strong physique with olive skin, flashing eyes and curly black hair was wheeled in on a stretcher. The doctors read his history. 'You were driving a truck and a mine went off: your pal is all right, but you got it in the leg a bit and in the arm here? Where does it hurt?' The surgeon gently placed his gloved hand on the brown skin of the abdomen. 'Does that hurt?' 'Yes, doctor,' said the man with an expression of disgust caused by the pain. 'Well, we will see what we can do for you.' Quickly the anaesthetist fixed a rubber mouthpiece over the man's face and soon he was breathing stertorously, his chest and belly heaving as he inhaled the ether and oxygen. The breathing became desperate as air-hunger increased and was all that could be heard in this small white-tiled room. The patient's forehead began to sweat. Now he was unconscious. A nasty little safety razor began to shave the torso. A bowl containing the wisps of hair was taken away. The body was now painted orange with iodine and the operation could start.

The lights were centred on the abdomen. The remaining parts were hidden beneath cloths and towels. The patient sucked air through the rubber mouthpiece which, connected by a tube, caused a glass cylinder of liquid to fill with bubbles each time he breathed out. The muffled instructions of surgeon and assistants were difficult to hear. A nurse, masked like the others, was busy with her tray of instruments, producing, one by one, the necessary knives or scissors. An assistant mopped the surgeon's sweating brow as he slowly cut a large slit down the patient's outer gut that was held back to reveal the intestines. My friend came up to me and whispered, 'Don't hurry, Beaton. Take your time. He'll be an hour yet. It'll get much better later. If the metal has got into the intestines or liver it's a tremendous business with masses of blood everywhere.' The white figures hovered. The patient breathed a little less desperately, and the anaesthetist changed over his apparatus to gas and oxygen.

I concentrated hard on my drawing, yet I felt a little weak when looking up to see the surgeon's gloved hand penetrating down through the newly-formed cavity deep between coils of entrail. 'Beaton, you're a lucky bloke and you've brought this man luck, too. He's one of the few lucky ones. The metal has got lodged in the kidney where perhaps it'll form an abscess which can be dealt with later, but we're not going to do anything more now than sew him up. It may never bother him. If it does, it won't be anything of a job. The sewing-up will take nearly as long as the rest of the operation.' The brilliant lights shone down on to the dozens of silver pincers that stretched wide the gaping chasm of the wound. One by one the nurse was handed back a pair which was forthwith placed into the sterilizer. The incision was now sewn up.

Since the most serious part of the operation was over, the spirit and atmosphere changed in the operating theatre. The surgeon talked more freely and his assistants offered comments and suggestions. Now the patient's arm was to be the focus of attention. The white figures altered their former composition as a group: some leant forward holding the arm in position while others retired from the ring of light. The blood flowed down the side of the stretcher on to the surgeon's shoes and on to the floor. A bigger and yet bigger cavity was made in the search for the elusive metal. 'It's a bit tricky to probe when we're so near the joint: we don't want him to lose the use of his arm: as it is the poor bugger will have a stiff elbow for a bit!' The cavity was squirted with the new discovery and wrapped in fresh bandages. The old blood-stained things, and the support on which the wounded arm had travelled, were thrown into a bucket.

'Now, what else is wrong with him? Serious grazes on hip and leg.' Again the South African's dossier was read. 'This is one of the bad things about this war, there are so many multiple wounds. A shell explodes and a man is lucky if he doesn't get hit in six different places. But we've a lot to be thankful for in this desert. No horses, so we don't get cases of glanders. This arm has had to be explored very carefully for grit and bits of the road, but there are few camels about and so little chances of tetanus.' The patient's body was turned over to enable another operation that was lengthy but was not serious. The strongest lights were turned off for the heat had become almost overwhelming. The surgeon and his assistants chatted among themselves as they worked now on this minor job. 'What sort of a time did you have on the hospital ship coming out?' 'Oh, I travelled like a lord, but it was slow, of course. Arrived at Suez. Got there just a year after a friend of mine came out but he had a bad time of it, got pneumonia, and died. It took me a long time to find his grave.'

At last the South African truck driver was wrapped in layers of blankets, and the mouthpiece taken from him. His face was sweating and white, his closed eyes weeping tears. The anaesthetist wiped his nose. Soon the patient was making spluttering noises like a baby in its cot. 'Now he's for the hot box,' said my friend. 'He'll be all right. He'll be heading for home in a hospital ship in thirty-six hours.' Men with leather yokes, like those from which old-fashioned farmers hang milk pails, came in to bear away the stretcher to a cave-like embrasure covered with an awning of electric lights. The victim was said to be 'quite comfortable', but a man stands by 'just in case'.

Now that the operation had been successfully performed even the spectators realized how drained of energy everyone had become. In the colonel's room we drank a night-cap. The young surgeon came in, his shoes still witness of his recent exploits; but the doctors all laughed and talked of cheerful things.

Corps Headquarters

To visit a regiment in the desert, it is necessary first to report at Corps Headquarters, then at a Divisional Headquarters, before proceeding down the line to Brigade and on to the Battalion Headquarters. With the aid of a compass four of us — Derek, a conducting officer, a minute Scottish driver named, of course, Jock, and myself set sail to pay our formal calls. For most of the day, surrounded by miles of scrub, we could see nothing on the horizon. My guide did not appear too sure of his bearings. Several times we stopped. He took our position again. He stood on the roof of our transport and scanned the distances through field glasses. Nothing in sight. We proceeded. Again we stopped and peered. Yes, there's some sort of signpost there. We drove towards a mound of stones, but found it to be without any markings to indicate our whereabouts. Further mathematical calculations were made, and once more we went on.

We arrived eventually at a group of camouflaged, dispersed lorries, somewhere in what might be the centre of nothing. Yes, this was the 13th Corps Headquarters. A small unit of sophisticated young men with exaggeratedly cultured voices, whom one would expect to find in the quadrangles of Christ Church or at the bar at White's, invited us to a drink or a piece of chocolate. They made telephone calls to say that we were on our way to Division, and with another car to guide us we set off again, heading for an invisible point on an empty horizon. After a while we stopped for, according to instructions, we should long ago have reached our goal; a new reading of the compass was taken. It appeared that somehow the metal vibrations of our transport affected the true bearings. We started again. Suddenly our car crashed down at the back with a thump, followed by a grinding noise that continued until we stopped dead. Violently we sounded the horn to indicate our plight to Derek in the accompanying car ahead. Dispassionately we watched it becoming smaller and smaller in the distance, unmindful of our signals.

Jock was under the back wheels, his straddled legs all that could be seen of him. 'Ai think it's a gurruge jarb this taime.' But where was the local Lex? Meanwhile our other khaki-coloured transport had missed us and turned back; both the drivers now got together under the car, and pronounced the breakdown irrevocable. Someone must return to 13th Corps to telephone for assistance.

One of the great paradoxes in the desert is the *richesse* of its telephones compared with the poverty of its domestic arrangements. The RAF communications (the air formation signals) alone have fifty static telephone exchanges with 600 subscribers — and as many as 3,500 calls are put through from Rear Headquarters each day, while during last April the number of calls at Advanced Headquarters increased from 900 to 1,900 a day. On one landing ground alone there are 1,200 miles of field cable. The maintenance difficulties can be imagined.

Jock and I remained by the broken-down car. We felt remote and alone in the desert. My companion said, 'Ai niwer thaght a year agoh ai'd her sittin hayer in the muddle of the dessert. It's a straingh laif and noo mistaik. Donn't ye thaink whee'd bettair huv oohr deener?' We made some tea. We opened tins. By now the sun was hot. In Libya at this time of the year the evenings are autumnal, the nights positively wintry, though clear and with stars full out. The early mornings are nippy, like springtime, but high summer is achieved by noonday.

The hours passed, the sun was strong, and the furnace of the car provided the only shade. Later we were relieved. Derek and the others came towards us. 'What news?' 'The rest of the journey must be made in the lorry, while this car and the luggage are left here until the repair unit call.'

Once more we rely upon our unreliable compass to take us across stony, scrubby bareness. Jock, stranded, waiting alone in the desert, looked very pathetic.

We drive in a thirty-degree direction for half an hour. 'That looks like a camp over there. Get on the roof once more and look through the glasses. We should see something by now,' said Derek. We drove on but again no luck. Derek suggested another direction: 'Perhaps they gave us the wrong instructions. What are those little dots on the horizon? Are they boulders, hummocks or tents?'

We had come across a dispersed camp. Just to make sure that we were at our destination, the conducting officer drove up to a caravan to ask our position. To his surprise, humiliation and shocked embarrassment, he found he had bearded the Corps Commander, General Willoughby-Norrie. Many generals might have blown off a fuse at such an informal encounter, and stormed furiously about such things as the dangers of bad navigation; but Norrie is said to be imperturbable. Certainly his immaculate perfection of appearance gave one the impression that he had just fitted his uniform in Sackville Street. Amused by our haphazard arrival, he tried to put us at our ease, and passed us on to the care of his staff officers. But I did not think it was at all funny when I realised how easy it is to get lost or to walk into the enemy's hands.

Stirling and the Long Range Desert Group, the highwaymen of the desert, have made a legend for themselves with their extremely scientific, yet romantic, pirate-story adventures. Sometimes for months on end they patrol the desert ocean in armoured vehicles equipped with radios. Often they penetrate miles behind the enemy's lines, take him by surprise at night, burn army lorries, destroy tanks, and blow up vital equipment. This war is one of machines and technical efficiency: it allows little scope for individual escapades by groups of men. But the very specialized warfare that the Long Range Desert Group have perfected is an exception. It is one which the Germans, thus far, have ignored or have not dared to undertake.

Stirling, Ramsay and the other officers seemed to be a serious, sophisticated lot — like members of an olympian club. The easy laughter and childlike ragging that whiles away time in many messes was absent. A most impressive group, too dedicated for small talk, they plot and carry out a primitive and savage form of warfare with a buccaneer's courage and a philosopher's mental refinement. The men, coming from all walks of life — chauffeurs, bricklayers, policemen, professional soldiers — were drilling in the heat of the day with as much precision and smartness as if they were outside Wellington barracks square.

Clump, clump, clump. A patrol commander came in, heavily-bearded, covered with sand, matted hair on end, sunburned so that the white shining teeth were his most brilliant feature. He had just returned from an expedition of many months' duration yet his fellow officers welcomed him as if he had returned from short leave. 'Had a good time?' 'Everything go well?' No doubt on account of the stranger in their midst, few questions were asked. Everything was taken quietly as a matter of course. Yet, undoubtedly, this man had come across tremendous excitements. Lunch over, the newcomer took us round to see his men. A more grotesquely assorted, more frightening-looking bunch of bandits it would be hard to imagine. Bearded, covered with dust, with blood-shot eyes, they were less of the world of today than like primeval warriors, or timeless inhabitants of a remote hemisphere. One apparition with ginger matting for hair, and red eyes staring from a blue-grey dusty face, looked no more human than an ape. They were now avidly reading the mail that had arrived during their long absence. One man, who had been a professional swimmer, chuckled as he read aloud: 'I cannot wait until after the war, when we can get married and live together for always.'

Siwa

To arrive by the caravan route taken by Alexander the Great 330 years before Christ and, after an infinity of desert, to come upon the oasis of Siwa is to witness a miracle.

Suddenly your eyes are refreshed by the sight of bubbling emerald pools, streams, date-palms, limes, grapes, olives and other trees of feathery richness; the small hills, minarets and towers are like illustrations from a fairy story. Siwa casts a spell on all who behold it. Most of the tall pinnacles of white mud in the old city built thousands of years before Christ still remain intact, though others are but lately fallen. The new city, moulded of the same white mud, is an extraordinary honeycomb of terraces built into the hillside. The Ammonium or Temple of Jupiter Ammon, where Alexander consulted the oracle, is a noble pile of masonry as incomprehensible in its way as Stonehenge and its white stones are almost on the same scale. A painted cornice frieze of the Ptolemaic period is still in good condition and the effect is startling against the intense blue of the afternoon sky.

The inhabitants are so secretive and furtive that I had the impression that the town was completely deserted. A child running out of a doorway, immediately to retreat in alarm, was the only sign of life to be seen. Occasionally a bulkily laden white mule, attended by its owner wearing white egg-shell cap and draperies, trod delicately along the bleached rocks, past the streams and trees that throw a dark pattern of fanlike shadows on the white ground.

The late afternoon sun was casting elaborate patterns through fronds of palm-trees when a group of soldiers arrived from a long trek in the desert. Imagine their surprise and delight! Here were natural bubbling springs for bathing! Immediately they stripped off all their clothes. In a small pool they soaped and scrubbed themselves, scrubbed and soaped one another, lathered their dust-covered heads, and shouting and smacking each other with joy they ran headlong over the sides of a huge circular pool. Surfacing a moment later, they were entirely transformed, hair and bodies a different colour: they laughed and spluttered and performed aquabatics in the warm water: again and again they dived in every attitude, and swam for sheer exultation until, tired, they unconsciously created a living classical frieze as, letting the sun dry their apricot-coloured bodies, they sat against the silver palm-trees along the side of the pool in which Cleopatra is said to have bathed.

Cairo demands too little of a man, and the desert too much. Existence in the desert is, in its way, as unnatural as that of Cairo for a false reality prevails. The desert is an unnatural habitat for the average human being. It may be possible to dominate your surroundings for a certain length of time. But after a long spell you may, though physically healthy, grow mentally lax.

Yet although there can be no more wasteful, heartless and purposeless theatre of war than the desert, still it possesses advantages. It is a healthy battleground, unlike the disease-spreading mud and miasmas of the 1914 trenches: most men are physically fitter than ever before in civilian life. Life here is primeval, and from this very simplicity seems to spring a new contentment. Often the men become so contented that they are said to be 'sand happy'.

Geoffrey Nares, the son of Owen Nares, the matinée idol, whom I knew in theatrical circles, suddenly appeared as if from nowhere. He is much changed from the elf-like boy I used to know. He is now captain of an armoured car. He told me that in the desert he was continuously frightened. During a patrol, through all the hours of daylight, he must watch the enemy through field glasses. Sometimes during an entire day he would be lucky if he could snatch a cup of tea. Perhaps if the order came through on their wireless set to advance farther, the strain became almost unbearable. Yet an indication of fright is the one thing that must never be seen. A man showing alarm can contaminate a whole group. If, to his officer, one of the men says quickly, 'What's that over there?' the officer must never open an eye just that little much wider that indicates shock. He must maintain a complete calm. If one of his men says, 'I can't go on,' Geoffrey must answer incredulously, 'What do you mean?' He must pretend that it takes him some little time before he even understands the man's plight. Geoffrey said that a certain type of man, often brawny and tough in appearance, when frightened, becomes absolutely hysterical. When a man whimpers, 'My nerve's gone, sir,' nothing remains but to send him away.

Geoffrey told me how for months his men had perched on a little hill facing the enemy. They had come to think of it as 'their' hill, but one day the Germans brought up a big gun and forced them to retreat. In the excitement one of Geoffrey's men left behind an enamel plate. When later the fortunes of war changed and they were able to throw the Germans back from the hillock, they found a little pile of German magazines, on which was the plate bearing the message: 'You left this behind you — Fritz.'

RETURN TO CAIRO

Cairo

For my part it is pleasant to be alone again: to rediscover my own individuality. Certainly to become part of a unit frees one of responsibility, gives an escape from many personal troubles, but I have always been my own master. It is a habit of mine. So it is good to get back sole charge of my days. There is a great deal of work to wade through — thousands of captions, some articles to write, censors and many people to see.

Looking at the enormous batches of photographs I took in the desert I sometimes feel disappointment. Before these pictures were developed they represented a limitless set of vivid memories which could be conjured up at any moment in the mind; but, as soon as the results are produced in black and white they banish the fleeting, but more real, memories.

Geoffrey is here on leave, and I have seen a lot of him. He does not seem to know what to do with his days — the days to which he has looked forward all those months in the desert. Maybe Geoffrey has always been a sad, striving, rudderless young man. I knew him at first when, dabbling on the stage, he appeared with my friend Caroline Paget. They struck up a romantic friendship. However, the moment war was declared, though hating the idea, he joined the army. He did well. He is now a grand officer in a grand regiment. Yet he still seems to be lost.

While we sat at a café or restaurant table Geoffrey, with his attractive, sallow, tired baby's face and dark, melting eyes, talked obsessionally of his life in the desert. Most men there pass the time wondering what it is they most look forward to on their leave: luxury, comfort, food, sex life, or drink. Yet whenever Geoffrey heard the troops discussing their future, their one desire, no matter how poor their conditions had been, was that life after the war should be exactly the same as it used to be. They don't want a 'better world'; they dream only of the old days.

Geoffrey considers the ordinary German soldier is no less frightened and no more efficient than ours. 'But, until last month, we felt the Germans were bogies and couldn't be beaten. In the great retreat we couldn't get out fast enough, and there was a certain amount of pandemonium. One officer had got so lost that he had to ask a quarter master where he was.' Geoffrey smiled. 'Now things are different. We all believe this time it'll be non-stop to Benghazi, and the most encouraging sign of all is the number of young men occupying important positions in the army.'

The night before his leave was up Geoffrey and I dined together: he looked particularly poignant, his large brown eyes deep pools of sadness. As we got into the hotel lift to go to our rooms he appalled me by saying, 'Good night! I shall never see you again — give my love to Caroline and all those people.'[26]

Perhaps not until this moment did I realize how different is it for me being here merely as a visitor. Geoffrey is a real part of the war: he knows that a major campaign may be launched at any moment, and that casualties are likely to be heavy.

Thursday, May 21st

Two months by the calendar since I left home yet none of the literally thousands of photographs I've taken have yet been sent back! Can't imagine why there are such delays. The organization at HQ is frustrating beyond endurance. Bray excuses himself saying he wants to wait until all my stuff can be sent off in one vast wad, but I know it would be used much more advantageously if it didn't arrive like an avalanche.

I get to my office to start work soon after 8 o'clock each morning but even now there is another solid week's work of cutting, sorting, and giving the last of my pictures the most uninspired captions. Then there are articles still to be buffed to their final polish. Bray is obviously not interested in my work, makes me realize my tremendous unimportance, and even seems unable to bring himself to choose pictures for a propaganda book that is to be produced locally.

---

[26] Geoffrey's premonition was correct. He died in hospital a few months later.

Monday, May 25th

It is a nice thing to start the day at 6 o'clock before the sun has dried out the cool of the night from the streets and trees. Everything was so fresh and clean when Lady Russell, wearing an Edwardian picture hat, took me to see the gardens of the zoo, where there are particularly good varieties of flowering trees. The gardeners had just appeared with their brooms to do a little pretence at tidying before the opening of the gardens to the public. Zebras and pelicans were given their breakfasts, and when a keeper thrust his arm and a bunch of dried clover way down the glutinous gullet of the hippopotamus, with its foot-long teeth protruding from the blubber, I recognized that the animal looks just as ugly as I feel at my worst moments.

By 8 o'clock Lady Russell had shown me flamingos, pelicans, the absurd-looking secretary birds, and all the animals of Piero di Cosimo. We had admired the huge grotto built overnight in honour of the Empress Eugenie's visit to the Suez Canal, then returned to the Russell home where a marvellous English breakfast with eighteenth-century coffee pot and sausages and bacon in sizzling silver dishes was served under the white flowering oleanders.

While Lady Russell dispensed this charming hospitality, her husband, Russell Pasha, stroked his particular favourite parrot on his shoulder, and regretted having to hurry off to some camel trials. I wondered, but fortunately did not ask, if they race camels here. (Do they jump hurdles?) The Pasha, as head of the police, has almost succeeded in stamping out the drug traffic, but explained that there is still one way of smuggling opium and hashish across the frontier from Syria. This is done by filling a metal container with drugs and thrusting it deep down the camel's throat. Recently a sort of radio-location contraption has been invented by which it is possible to detect the presence of these containers. The Pasha, of whom it has been said, somewhat cryptically, 'He has spent his life making camels sick', was off to watch the reaction of this machine to three suspected camels.

Friday, May 29th

At last a wad of my stuff, as large as the pyramids, was put into the bag for England! The Ministry of Information will be deluged at the other end. There are so many, so many, too many pictures: yet I am sick of them all by now.

Dudley Barker asked excitedly, 'Do you want to take some action pictures?'

'Then it has started in the desert?'

'Yes, this morning.'

This was how I heard that Rommel had attacked. One of the Anglo-Egyptian secretaries squeaked up, 'Oh, I can't get a thrill out of the desert any longer. It's always a case of someone going backwards or forwards.'

Dudley Barker again: 'Will you help us out by taking a picture at Heliopolis of the arrival of an important prisoner.'

Top speed to the aerodrome to arrive simultaneously with the unnamed prisoner. Fun if it would be Rommel. But no. It was his second-in-command, his General Officer Commanding, General Cruewell, a good name for a German general. He had been shot down by ack-ack as he was circling over the battlefield in an aircraft with some Italian staff officers.

Wearing a florid uniform covered with red tabs and buttons like an old-fashioned Tyrolean beater, a good-looking old man with white hair sat smoking a cigarette in a car, and looking like something stuffed in a cage. But maybe this was because we knew that here was Exhibit (A).

The whole air station was in high spirits. Barker, full of enthusiasm, said it was like the old days of Fleet Street journalism when a news story broke. The Army Film Unit sent a sergeant to take a movie of the prisoner, but this young sergeant, so as not to appear too encroaching, hid himself shyly in an oleander tree. It is extraordinary how the English behave to their prey. This man, our deadly enemy, had by chance, been delivered into our hands. What do we do? We treat him like royalty. In the forward areas of the desert where rations are extremely scarce, as soon as our men take a prisoner they offer him their rations of cigarettes and beer.

An officer who had escorted General Cruewell here by air had received a signal that the pilot must be well protected, but the officer said he found it embarrassing to show his revolver and had, therefore, sat on it the whole way. When they had taken off in the air, the General had buried his face in his hands and remained bowed in despair, then shook his head from side to side and clubbed the air with his fist.

The General said his wife had died a week ago, and that it was hard that his marital life and military career should be at an end within the same week. But are we becoming sorry for the old brute? It is alleged it was he who had ordered the execution of 2,000 citizens of the town of Jogordina in Yugoslavia when the civilians mined a bridge to hamper his advance to Belgrade.

Sunday, May 30th

The news of the moment is that the two armies are locked in combat: a mêlée of tanks in this heat must be like an Armageddon. Barker thinks the campaign will fizzle out: others consider it will be decisive one way or the other. A crazy photographer here, known as 'Glorious Devon', said it would not surprise him if Rommel soon appeared marching down Solman Pacha Street.

Stacy, the pilot who has been flying the Duke of Gloucester around, told me he had to go and identify the crew of an aircraft that burnt out at Heliopolis this morning. He said a well-cooked body is not too bad to look at — it's quite unrecognizable; it's when it's partially cooked, as these were, that you feel weak.

Saturday, June 6th

The news from the desert still is that we are locked in a death struggle with the enemy. The losses in men and machinery must be colossal, but this seems quite remote from the war that the Egyptians see. They only take the war seriously if it means they are able to do just a bit more profiteering.

Monday, June 1st

Rabbits. We are told at the office that the battle in the desert is not going well. That instead of retreating down the gaps in the minefield the enemy has dug its toes in, has become solidly reinforced, and is now impossible to attack. There, at the moment, the situation remains.

I was restless throughout the night with the prospect of an early rise. I was to be called at 4 o'clock, but my anxiety was caused by a fear lest the night porter should ignore my instructions; that I should miss my aeroplane to Iran, via Iraq.

The hotel staff is unreliable. I visualized having to complain to the concierge while he laughed at my plight. I have seen him unable to contain his mirth at so many irate young officers who, on account of him, have missed their trains. However, all was well. It was still dark while we waited to be taken to Heliopolis — two Russians and myself.

The Russians were travelling with diplomatic passports, and looked like characters out of the film *Ninotchka*. One, swarthy, uncouth, rugged, with a heavy cold. The other, entirely globular with rose-red cheeks, pince-nez and a sweet smile. Both were neatly, if badly, dressed.

They had recently visited England and were impressed by the spirit. Splendid, if surprising.

I asked them where they stayed in London.

'Oh! The Ritz.'

'How was the food?'

'Hmm! Yes, it was good — but not much of it.'

Teheran

The city of Teheran rises against a purple screen of the snowcapped mountain range. The water from Mount Demavend gushes down through the streets: in this torrent the inhabitants wash, throw their slops, and collect their drinking water. Many of them, as a result, are victims of an appalling boil that takes a year to subside and leaves a scar for life.

After the gloomy ugliness of modern Cairenes in their drab draperies, the Irani people in their brightly coloured clothes are a delight to the eye. The men of Aryan stock, with olive complexion and regular features, are lean and ferocious-looking. The women, heavily painted, with eyebrows elongated to join on the bridge of the nose and carrying a turkey, the elephant bird, under each arm, strike us as being rather too plump; but the Persian poet, in a panegyric note on feminine beauty, wrote: 'Her face is like the full moon, and she waddles like a goose...'

I went off expectantly with the RAF chaps, to take pictures of the latest arrival of American bombers. The aerodrome at Teheran presents a heartening sight. Phalanxes of newly-arrived American bombers were standing ready to be wheeled into line for the final 'take off' to Russia. The Russian ground crew, with shaven heads, Slav cheekbones and khaki blouses, had meticulously gone over every screw and cog before signing the acceptance sheet for these latest deliveries and covering the American white star with red paint. At this time, over forty aircraft of different types were arriving here each week; even as we watched, yet another couple of bombers circled and landed. Repetition of almost anything on a large-scale is generally impressive to the eye. These rows of identical aircraft were most imposing. I was pleased with the designs created in the camera viewfinder. But I had not taken more than half a dozen pictures before a Russian guard came up and asked me to accompany him to the police. The American captain and some of the RAF men argued on my behalf for twenty minutes. Out of the blue appeared a serious young woman with a bun and dry lips, wearing sandals, a cotton dress and a topi. She was the Russian interpreter.

The American explained I was an official RAF photographer, also working for the Ministry of Information. These pictures I had taken would be censored, of course. I had come a long way especially to take pictures of the Middle East Command.

'But no,' said the dry-lipped blonde. 'No. The film must be liquidated.'

'Nonsense!'

I got good and mad. But before we found ourselves in further difficulties we would at once seek out the air attaché. Meanwhile, I was forced to hand over my films. But I gave them to the Americans. While waiting for my conducting

officer to get some papers from his office, I stood on a parapet
by the barracks, where the Russian soldiers are billeted in the
same building as the RAF. The RAF entrance happened to be
in the sun. The Russian soldiers, boys of about seventeen, all
looking like brothers, were sitting in the shade. I walked ten
yards towards the shade, and stood for a moment trying to pry
a splinter from one of my fingers. A Russian sentry with a
bayonet and a flick of his hand sent me packing.

It was not for several seconds that I realized what had
happened, and began to smart at such treatment. How after all
was the sentry to know that I was not a bona fide RAF officer?
I told my conducting officer what had happened.

'It is very difficult,' he said, 'but we have to keep calm.'

SHAH AND FAMILY

The snow-striped Mount Demavend, 20,000 feet high, is
seventy miles distant, but so clear and bright, so dry and fine, is
the air in Tehran, that the extinct volcano seems to overhang
the summer palace. The palace is as new as any Hollywood
movie house, and its 'modernistic' decorations, the colossal
silver sphinx bastions to flights of marble steps, the geometric
furniture, the furnishings of triangular patterned materials of
squashed strawberry and chutney colouring, strike an
anachronistic note in this country, which knew civilization
before Greece and Rome. But it is a fitting setting for someone
so young in ideas and years. Shahpur Mohamed Reza believes
in democratic government, has abolished many forms of
despotism and dictatorship in favour of reforms towards
liberty and progress.

A young man of courage and independence, he has thrown
in his lot whole-heartedly with the Allies, and today his country

provides the great supply lines to Russia; upon its roads thousands of workmen can be seen.

The Shah, with his family and entourage, stood rather shyly around the swimming-pool. He looked surprisingly untidy with long curling hair, unshaven chin and black and white co-respondent shoes that were in need of a going-over. His wife, Queen Fawzieh, a sister of the King of Egypt, appeared little more than a child although wearing the maximum of *maquillage* and a knee-length dress, probably from Shaftesbury Avenue or Buenos Aires. On slender arm and leg were bandages.

Princess Ashraf, the Shah's sister, with flashing eyes and long black curls, wore beach shorts. A chamberlain was busy picking up dogs and children, while minor court officials stood by on the terrace and in the neighbouring rooms. On guard behind the colonnades of trees, half hidden, were numberless unshaven Charlie Chaplins.

The Shah, agreeable, well-mannered and serious, submitted to being photographed while his wife and sister tittered and occasionally burst into explosions of laughter which they ill-concealed behind their hands. The Queen as a model proved to be more photogenic than many a film star as she posed on the edge of the bathing-pool with skirts and scarves trailing in the water. But my intention was to use the Queen as a figure in a photographic version of one of the miniatures of the golden age of Shah Abbas — the contemporary of Queen Elizabeth, under whom a renaissance of Persian art flourished. Although here was the perfect sitter we were missing suitable garments. Surely there must be some embroidered coat or a piece of material to turn into a turban? An old woman servant brought an armful of Riviera foulards and garments trimmed with swansdown or ostrich feathers. 'We have a large garden party hat upstairs.' No, never mind. It was my mistake. How unwise to try to link the past with the present.

My visit to Teheran was flavoured by the wit and originality of outlook of my old friend Christopher Sykes. He has been out here for over a year acting as the Hon. Second Secretary to HM's Legation. In his company one can only relax, and any feeling of strain at finding oneself meeting strangers in a strange place melts into guffaws of laughter. I stayed with him in the Legation compound at Gulhak, about six miles out of Teheran. Here, in his offhand way, he explained the political situation, and introduced me to the Luards (he is AICO) and other close friends who have apparently acquired, if not Christopher's charm and stutter, his somewhat debunking attitude to everything from the romance of a Persian garden ('Look at those moth-eaten roses and that piddling little f-f-fountain!') to the war itself. Yet Christopher is one of the most talented of his contemporaries and his seriousness of purpose has been recognized.

He was to report to GHQ at Cairo, and I was fortunate to travel with him in the same aircraft as far as Habbaniyah. The Bible is his Baedeker, and we had no sooner left Teheran than he indicated the places over which we were flying. 'That is the tomb of the Three Magi.' Over Hamadan he showed me the tomb of Esther, and pointing to Azerbaijan he roared, 'That's where the Ark came from.' He laughed, too, at the place where Jonah spent three days in the belly of a whale. 'There's some half-witted yarn about this town being named with a word that could easily be mistaken for the sound 'belly of a whale'. Nearer to Baghdad he pointed to Babylon, and as we looked down upon the mountain range of Pai-Tak he remarked that the strange formations looked like fortifications, though I thought they looked like nothing so much as serried ranks of pagodas.

IRAQ

Habbaniyah

It is fortunate that I am invited to stay with the Air Officer Commanding, Air Marshal de Crespigny, for he lives with his staff in a building appropriately called 'Air House'. Its pagoda roof, with slits to let air into the high-ceilinged rooms, allows it to remain cooler than most buildings. For this I am particularly thankful, as although I have never suffered from an excess of heat this is like a scourge. Each day starts with a bathe soon after dawn in the surprisingly rough and choppy Lake of Habbaniyah. By 11 o'clock the sun has become so piercing that one can hardly bear to remain out of doors.

The air station of Habbaniyah, with its power works, workshops, water supply, electric plant, native cantonment and messes for Service men and civilians, built at the cost of many million pounds in the desolation of the Iraqi desert, is a self-supporting town of 6,000 inhabitants. All building was done by British contractors: all fittings and furnishings for this desert mushroom brought from England. Its thoroughfares are called 'Kingsway' and 'Cheapside', its circus is named 'Piccadilly'.

In spite of the terrible heat, the enthusiasm of the 'levies' on the parade ground never falters throughout the day as they salute, stamp and beat their rifles. These are the Assyrians who arrive from the hills in their turbans, draperies and wide elaborate belts. Soon their hair is shorn, and the moment they are put into uniform they become so fanatical about their training that they drill in secret, behind cover, on their

209

'afternoons off.' They are trained to guard the airport and, at the time of the recent rebellion,[27] showed a complete contempt for danger under fire.

The latest batch of recruits has just arrived. Some of the men are noble-looking creatures with long plaited hair and white flying skirts, like figures from a nativity play. One of these men, for our benefit, performed a war dance called the Khigga, to the accompaniment of weird screams and whistles from the pipes and the gourd-like instrument of a three-piece orchestra. I went up to another in a speckled mongoose turban, who with a look of fury on his face withdrew a dagger from his cummerbund and adopted a menacing pose. The young English captain with flowing, blond moustache, who escorted me, remarked disgustedly to this fearsome warrior, 'Oh, stop that bullshitting!' Farther along were groups in their national dress of Kurds, Yazidees, and Assyrians.

In another part of the drill ground, a group of recruits, after three weeks' training, has attained clockwork precision. Near by the cantonment live the wives and families. Each man has an average of six children. The interiors of their small mud homes are immaculate, the officers' rooms furnished with embroidered antimacassars, coloured pictures of our King and Queen, and silver trumpet-shaped vases filled with stiffly arranged asters and zinnias.

Today, at luncheon at Air House, a group of four American officers, of the Army Air Corps stormed in. Their deep voices rolled out in the reverberating high-ceilinged room with such volume that it was hard to hear what they said, but it seems they had just brought down a Messerschmitt. They are *en route* for their home station on their first operational trip, the initial American air operation in the Middle East. They had been to

---

[27] Raschid Ali's abortive anti-British hostilities in 1941.

bomb oil stores near Lake Constanza, had flown at a tremendous height, using oxygen for many hours, so were now suffering from innate fatigue. Even so, they have an enviably easy flow of talk that shames the English officers who sit dumb, without making any attempt to break a silence.

The colonel telephoned for news of the other crews: 'There are five here, one at Mosul, another somewhere nearby; another has given wireless signals recently; as for the others, let's hope that Messerschmitt hasn't been repaid.' But, for the time being, they bothered little about the others, as they described their own adventures. One growled in a voice like the breaking of coke, 'The ack-ack was jurst like a fluhr gordon, vurry purty!' My neighbour growled, 'I'm taking quite a small part in this war, but I'll be playing a really big one in the next "blow out" in twenty years' time!'

KING FAISAL AND THE REGENT

Baghdad

This morning early an Oxford was waiting with a crew of three young English boys to take me to Baghdad.

When our aircraft circled over the aerodrome of our destination Stewart Perowne, whom I knew at Cambridge, hurried down the steps to welcome me and, with a frog of excitement in his voice, to take me off to photograph the King and the Regent.

The Palais des Fleurs is of white marble, white stucco and white wood. In the throne-room the chairs and tables are doubtless intended for a chain of hotels, while in other rooms the furniture is chromium plated.

The Regent brought us, by the hand, his nephew, the King, wearing white knickers. The Regent, quietly assured, modest and gentle, is one of the great figures of the Middle East. Politically he is courageously pro-British. The seven-year-old King is a phenomenon, a child with adult poise and sense of responsibility. Yet he is not precocious. Much credit for his being so well brought up must go to Miss Boland, the grey-haired young Scotch woman, who hung around in the middle distance knitting a khaki scarf. The child enjoyed changing the films in my camera and watching my impromptu methods, such as putting one table on top of another to act as an improvised tripod. Generally I am loth to end most sittings; but after two hours, when the heat of the day had begun, I felt we had really got more than we needed, and the Prime Minister was awaiting his appointment to be photographed, so we said good-bye to the child with such a remarkable destiny.[28]

Stewart escorted me from one national figure to another: I was in complete ignorance of the significance of many of my subjects; I only knew that they were excellent photographic sitters, and the language barrier provoked laughter and childish mime. The unusual heat, and an unaccustomed amount of spiced food, inspired ideas for a long siesta. However, the sleep of the whole household was continually broken by the strident alarm of the telephone bell. Always it was the indefatigable Miss Freya Stark. 'Would we come at 4 o'clock?' Later: 'Could we come at 5.30 instead?' Later still: 'Could we come at 4.30? Or could we come at 6 o'clock?' When at last we drove around to her home, it was just in time to see Miss Stark, dressed like a child in scarlet and white with a bow in her hair, tottering out on to the lawn to a committee meeting. An assortment of English neighbours, spotty youths, old men in Panama hats,

---

[28] When the King was assassinated in 1958 a mangled photograph from the day's sitting was found in the ruins of the palace.

and chicken-like women in voiles, were sitting on deck chairs in a large circle.

Later this evening we visited Adrian Bishop,[29] and sat on the terrace of his Turkish house, overlooking the Tigris, built around a series of courtyards with pretty grill balconies and elaborate capitals painted white. The bathing-boys below 'showed off', splashing, holloaing and diving from pale-blue boats. Twilight faded; the lights, one by one, were turned on in the distance and the scene was peaceful and soothing. We reminisced about Cambridge. Since those days, when we were all 'up' together, Adrian has taken his vows, entered a monastery and is only 'out' for the duration of the war, doing propaganda here for the Ministry of Information. We talked about Cambridge personalities and were glad that Maynard Keynes had, today, been made a peer in the King's Birthday Honours. In the old days the newspapers would have written stories of Lydia[30] headed: 'From Ballerina to Baroness'.

PALESTINE: TWO PATRIARCHS

Jerusalem

The Patriarch of the Greek Church, today the most powerful in Jerusalem, in black robes with a magnificent array of jewels at his breast, appeared with outstretched hand for his ring to be kissed. Princess Peter of Greece, making a curtsy to him, gabbled, 'If you are to be photographed, your Beatitude, why don't you put on your ceremonial garments? The Easter garments are particularly magnificent.' But the Patriarch benignly refused: why must he be glamorized? No, there could

---

[29] Some time later Adrian Bishop fell from a balcony here and was killed instantly.

[30] Lydia Lopokova, the Russian dancer, who had married Lord Keynes.

be no question of wearing the Easter garments. From the liturgical point of view, it would be impossible, for the robes have to be donned in ceremony in front of the altar. With no one to witness the ceremony, how could he wear the robes? The Princess suggested that she should come and watch. No, she got short shrift. The Patriarch, with enormous white, tin-loaf beard, wearing a square, pork-pie black hat, provided a magnificent target for my camera as I lured him around the various rooms of the Patriarchate and down the stairs into the garden. He sat on the throne, stood by a black and silver door, by a richly carved holy water well, by a mother-of-pearl model of some church, and by the hollyhocks. I had lately photographed a large variety of people, hospital matrons, master bakers, desert cooks, and stokers. I have given instructions to Majesties and Air Marshals; but not before this had I the opportunity to say, 'Please moisten the lips, your Beatitude.'

The Orthodox Patriarch and the Latin Patriarch are not as friendly as twins. Monsignor Barlassina, the Latin Patriarch, is an Italian and considered, in general, unfriendly to Englishmen. But to me he could not have been more hospitable. He was wearing black, with a wide magenta sash and a magenta skull cap; he said the colour was the purple of a Roman iris, but to me it was more the colour of those wild cyclamen they used to sell in the Piazza in Venice. His head bald, his pale face with wild humorous eyes, a beak and false teeth, gave a parrot-like impression. A jolly old boy with lots of fire and laughter, he reminded me of a wicked character out of an Elizabethan tragedy. Sitting on his throne he looked like the Cardinal in *The Duchess of Malfi*. When I told him I thought he should have been painted by Tintoretto, his heart melted; he was delighted.

'Turn your head more to the right, your Beatitude.' 'No, that is too much,' he said. 'Not at all, your Beatitude, no, have more faith in me, your Beatitude.' He laughed. He roared. 'After all these pictures the police will have no difficulty in tracking me down! I believe you have been sent here to take my photograph in every position by the CID,' he roared, his false teeth sagged.

I enjoyed his irony. He once said to Ronald Fleming, the Aide-de-Camp to the High Commissioner, 'Oh, your English towns are so wonderful! I remember so well your beautiful old city of Glasgow!'

TRANSJORDAN: EMIR ABDULLAH

Amman

'Just a little bit of drift weed' was the name of a song I once sang in the ADC at Cambridge, and that was how I felt this morning when I left for Amman. What the immediate future would bring I had no idea. I had been told to report to the Resident, and he would be responsible for my wherewithal. The cab was late in arriving, and we had not started more than ten minutes before the old Arab in the front seat turned round and said, 'Give me three pound!' 'Nonsense!' I knew that if I acquiesced now, the blackmail would continue all day. Half an hour was wasted while we argued, and the resources of my indignation amazed me.

It is now late in the summer here, and the enormous mountain slopes and pastures are burnt to a biscuit colour; but in the wadi there is still an extraordinary richness of green and the oleanders are in flower, pink by the mile. As we drove on, the valleys became more tropical with palms unlike any others I have ever seen — the green very juicy and dark — and much of the landscape was dotted with small bushes and dark green tufts like the backgrounds in Piero della Francesca's paintings. When we reached desert land, it seemed a more sympathetic wasteland, with more personality to beguile the eye, than the appalling, ugly flatness of the Libyan Desert, where I remember that for hours one day the shining reflection of the sun on the telegraph wires was our sole distraction.

Now we passed through Jericho, its famous walls encircling nothing but a small village. On and on through many other villages whose names I could never discover, and eventually we arrived at Amman — the ancient capital of the Ammonites. Now, after many earthquakes, it is a modern town recently carved from the craggy precipices, with few remains of antiquity except the Roman theatre for 6,000 people — an impressive ruin built into the towering hills.

The Resident was rattled at my late arrival; the Emir had wanted me to go to lunch, but he did not know whether it was not too late now. It was not. The interpreter, in a sharply pressed suit and tarboosh, arrived to take me away forthwith. Suddenly I found myself having to make conversation to a nice old man with painted eyes who smelt of musk and was immaculately starched in white shift and turban. The Emir Abdullah is the brother of the late King Faisal, and grandfather of the present King of Iraq. He speaks no English or French, so the interpreter had to work hard, seizing the gist of one's halting utterances and turning them into brilliant witticisms; or, at any rate, so it seemed from the reaction of the others at table. The meal was a succession of a dozen dishes of the same consistency — mousses of cheese, of eggs, of marrows and cucumbers. Rice was the nearest we came to any 'roughage'.

The Emir is interested in politics: he is seldom away from the radio and its news bulletins. He said: 'If you win, we are saved.

If you are not saved, we are lost.' His Royal Highness asked, 'What do you consider the greatest feats you have accomplished in this war?' I gulped: 'The achievements of the pilots in the Battle of Britain, and General Wavell's campaign with improvised forces and inferior numbers against the Italian Army in the desert.' There I stuck; but the Emir had a copious list at his fingertips of the great events of the war, both those that 'were good for us, and those that had been bad'. This was politics told in fairy-story epigrams. 'When the Germans took Athens, they did not beat the Greeks; they succeeded only in capturing Rome.' The Emir, nodding, said the English courage in waiting and fighting alone was the most remarkable feat of bravery, and that the English spirit was exemplified in Mr Churchill. He was disappointed that, instead of using the Free French Forces, we could not make an Arab army from Transjordan, Syria and Iraq to fight in the Western Desert.

In search of interesting backgrounds for my snapshots the Emir unlocked with a Yale key various doors of his palace. Some of the rooms of gigantic size were almost empty and smelled of disuse, but whenever we ventured out of doors, even so far as a loggia, we were almost felled by the heat. The Emir, sweating through his *maquillage*, lasted out pretty well the course of a strenuous photographic sitting.

ARAB LEGION

Wednesday, June 17th

The evening sun was sinking slowly and casting long blue shadows when, after two and a half hours' drive through the desert, we arrived at the Arab Legion at Azraq. On our way we had passed Glubb, in a khaki *tajrifa* (headdress) with two highly coloured henchmen in the back of his car, returning to

Amman. He looked baffled and miserable to see me, which I later realized was his normal expression. But, thanks to his introductions and instructions, we had an adventurous evening. In an oasis of emerald grass and rushes, of palm-trees, of birds and mules drinking water, is the Casa el Azraq, where Lawrence had his headquarters. It is a ruined battlemented castle, made of lava rock of an ugly leaden colour. Here, stranded miles from his big home and family, lives one of the great English eccentrics, Colonel Sir Philip Brocklehurst, who lost two toes from frostbite when on an expedition with Shackleton. Now he is the Commanding Officer of the Second Company of the Legionaries. He lives in a circular mud hut, does his own washing and cooking, eats practically nothing, but is obviously content with such adventurous simplicity. He sent us to visit his Legionaries who, in scarlet, pink and khaki uniforms, with resplendent headdresses, were being taught to use a Vickers gun, others running about in armoured cars or, at a range, doing shooting practice.

They thoroughly enjoy this life which transforms them from desert pirates into lawful soldiers. They did well in the Syrian campaign and are disappointed that they have had no opportunity to fight the Germans in this part of the world.

GLUBB PASHA

Whereas Lawrence now is a name only to a handful of Arabs, Glubb is known throughout the Arab world. He is quiet and self-effacing. Nothing riles him more than to be called 'the second Lawrence'. He is childlike in many ways, without much grace or facility of manner; in fact, facility is something he does not possess, with the result that greater effect is given to his every action and word. In the last war part of his jaw was shot away; his teeth have grown together and look like a beak. The Arabs now call him 'The Father of the Little Chin'.

All day long dozens of Arabs hang around Glubb's headquarters to be able to talk to him on some personal matter. The sheiks come in, just to remain in his room without talking. They do not mind the silence, but rather are honoured if allowed to be for twenty minutes in the presence of the Pasha. Glubb is like a squire with his tenants, listening to their troubles, answering with just the right amount of sympathy, not too warm so that he could never again be left in peace, nor frigid so as to appear proud. He is obviously devoted to the Arabs and himself lives almost like a Moslem. He speaks Arabic fluently, has given up smoking and plays with beads behind his desk.

Glubb said, 'You want to go to the 9th Army. No good taking it from its perimeter. Go to its source. Don't go to Damascus, go to Beirut.' And forthwith wrote letters of introduction.

Outside in the corridors and hallways, which are always crowded, a greater excitement prevails when Glubb is due to leave. When he appeared at lunchtime, his two henchmen enjoyed a tug-of-war, pulled each other's arms and skirts, and tussled their way down to the waiting car, roaring with laughter, in which Glubb joined.

SYRIA AND LEBANON: BAD NEWS FROM THE DESERT

Beirut

Joan Aly Khan is a subtle and kind creature. To find myself sheltering under her roof is one of the greatest strokes of good fortune I have ever enjoyed. We talked of the Syrian campaign, of the Free French difficulties, of Spears's mission which, starting as a liaison organization, is now almost a local government, while Spears is invested as minister. He has a brigadier as his military attaché and a staff of really first-rate, hand-picked men. In certain circles Spears is unpopular, and the plea has been heard that Syria should be 'French without Spears'.

Ali, who works as secretary for General Catroux, came in depressed at the news: 'The Libyan battle has been lost by us — we have announced as much on the radio.' There had been no indication that things were not going well; the campaign started so successfully, but now it is likely that we shall lose Tobruk in less than a month, for the Navy can't afford to supply it. What then is there to prevent Rommel from making a nice straight run to Cairo?

June 22nd, Fouglass

It was cold in the night. By degrees the brilliant sun warmed my cold feet. I started with reluctance upon a day I did not look forward to: we were to watch an army demonstration — a giant tank battle to be fought from 9.30 until 3.30 in the afternoon, before driving all the way back to the patch of desert, another five hours away, that was considered 'home'.

Altogether, today I was more miserable than I have been for years. A long line of cars drove out in sandstorms of our own making, to a certain mound far away in an airless stretch of desert where, assembled to watch the demonstration, were about 3,000 soldiers, airmen and sailors. The heat was pitiless. Of course there was no shade.

Jumbo Wilson arrived, and then another general spoke into a microphone, fixed up from a van, telling us what we were about to witness. To me the technicalities were incomprehensible; a rat-a-tat was heard in the distance and some small specks of dust flew up from where the guns had aimed. That was that.

The next demonstration, also first explained at full length, took place in a large plain many leagues away to which we again drove in a cloud of dust. This incident was indeed impressive. A 'make believe' attack by a Panzer division was staged. The Panzer division was represented in half strength; but, even so, one was given a graphic impression of the size on which these operations are fought. The tanks, moving like lice, were specks in the distance, hardly visible but for the clouds of dust they and the motor-bicycles churned up. The sun beat down with such force that it reduced the world to the palest colours; yet, in the middle of this haze of misty blue, the flashes from the tanks blazed like fireworks; explosions rent the air with a thunder of rolling reverberations.

The sight was impressive, though I could not interpret the various units represented by each group of vehicles. I did grasp that a motor-bicycle was an armoured car, a lorry a tank; but the tactics and strategy were far beyond my comprehension. Most of those present seemed to be only mildly interested, and only a small percentage were listening to the loudspeaker's endless monologue.

General Wilson, however, was enjoying the whole proceeding with relish, as well he might; for this demonstration was Jumbo's particular toy, a toy costing thousands of pounds with 2,000 men taking part.

Suddenly I heard one of the officers saying, 'Hell take it, I'll tear a strip off him for that! He shouldn't say such things in front of the driver!' 'What did he say?' I asked. 'Well, as a matter of fact,' lowering his voice to a murmur, 'he said that Tobruk has fallen, 25,000 prisoners have been captured, and that the Germans will be in Cairo in a week.' As Jumbo's toy battle continued the crushing disappointment of the news was whispered from man to man. The campaign had turned into a major disaster. The prospect was now alarming; for if Suez goes, linking the Germans with the Japs, where then can we stop them?

Last night I had a nightmare that the Germans had arrived in Cairo, and had discovered my excessively indiscreet diaries left behind at Shepheard's Hotel, which were now receiving a very mixed reception among my friends, relayed over the air to England by Lord Haw-haw.

Whenever I am asked when I am going home, and I reply: 'Soon, perhaps,' the eyes that once regarded me in a friendly way are suddenly filled with loathing. The men are resigned to remain out here in one solid block; but to see a man who is returning to England is disquieting. One Major said, 'I shall be lucky if I get back in five years' time!' Another, 'I would give my right hand if I could get to England now!'

I was shaving and washing under desert conditions when the AOC's personal assistant informed me casually that the Germans have captured Fort Capuzzo, and if they get Barrani then there is only Mersa Matruh before Suez!

I felt quite panicky and most irrepressibly upset. In a beastly, selfish way, unmindful of the hundreds of thousands of other men who are in much worse a plight than mine, I thought only of my own troubles. With tremendous enthusiasm I had come here to do a job for a certain length of time, but I had not faced the prospect of remaining here for the rest of the war. Now I saw this the possibility. Any ideas of home might have to be abandoned: my mind wove all sorts of unprofitable theories, and I felt disgusted at my own alarm. I realized how enviable is a dispassionate courage, a blindness to misfortune.

I walked over to the 'ops' tent. The Group Captain was busy, everyone was busy with their morning's work; but I had nothing to do but wait for the mail plane to take me to Beirut that afternoon. I wandered towards the mess tent aimlessly; perhaps there was a mug of water to spare. Someone had forgotten to place the mugs in the water cans so that they should remain cool, with the result that standing on a table they had taken on the temperature of the tent and might really have been heated in an oven. A man with a handkerchief tied around his neck hung up the receiver and said to me, 'I am afraid you're unlucky today — there's a three hour delay on the mail plane, it has broken down.' 'Isn't there any car I could horn in on?' After many delays I succeeded in getting into an RAF van, and we motored in the heat of the day for six hours. Inside, the metal of the car was almost too hot to touch. My razor, wrapped in a leather case in a dressing-gown in a leather bag, was heated as if by electricity. I wondered how the human frame could survive such contrasts of temperature as it does.

On our way, we came suddenly upon the ruins of Baalbek, the earliest city built in the world. Like Nimrod, the great grandson of Noah, who is the legendary founder of the first city to be built on this site, the early history of Baalbek is lost in mystery. In the centuries which have passed over these rough monoliths and noble pillars Baalbek has withstood two major earthquakes, attacks of Crusaders, a siege by Saladin, and the victory of Tamerlane in the fifteenth century. Long forgotten are the great licentious festivals in honour of the Goddess of Pleasure when negroes were sacrificed and the golden statue of Jupiter was carried in procession to be worshipped by prostrate crowds. A priest was hidden in the hollow body of the god, having entered it by a subterranean passage which can be seen today, and from the image itself issued the mysterious responses to the questions of those who came to consult the oracle.

With the lasting record of all these fleeting centuries before my eyes, it was an outrage to complain of the heat of the passing day; and yet, as I stood in the presence of so much grandeur and beauty, it seemed to need more energy than I possessed even to click my camera. I loathed myself for my petty thoughts in so vast a setting as I mopped my brow and felt sorry for myself.

The sun dropped lower but became no less burning. For the first time I hated the pitiless, merciless sun. The mountains provided a respite, and as we neared Beirut the avenues of shady trees were a special balm. Then, at last, we arrived! Oh, the coolness of Joan's house! The treat of a bath! Someone produced freshly pressed clothes — what luxury!

The news is terrible, London and Washington in an uproar; in fact, so bad that most of the day, even in the lovely airy spaciousness of Joan's house, I've felt stifled. But Joan has a protecting soothing quality. She seems calm, and thinks that we might be able to make some sort of final stand. We discussed the hunger that English people, in particular, have for home. They crave, when out here or in the desert, to hear thrushes and blackbirds and to feel grass under their feet. They yearn for a softer fight, a sun reflected from grass and not from white stony scrub.

Joan is interested in everything from music to medicine. She is an artist in the way a great surgeon is. She told me of a German doctor who had instruments designed by himself, so beautiful that they should be preserved as *objets d'art*. She herself was a great friend of Martell, the French brain doctor who shot himself when the Germans arrived in Versailles. Joan's life has been varied and thrilling. She has lived in the four corners of the world, yet remains Cornish at heart.

Toby Milbanke, a friend staying in the same house, is extremely grim about the position in the desert and envisages my personal troubles as being quite serious; for now, he calculates, I may have difficulty in getting on to an aeroplane — surely a great number of people in Cairo at the moment must be wishing to do the same thing. Cairo is the terminus for England and, in order to return, I have to go to Cairo. He hopes that my arrival there does not synchronize with that of the Germans.

I went to the RAF headquarters and took some pictures half-heartedly, for my enthusiasm had left me and these photographs were redundant. A chap said he thought I could be got on to a mail plane to Lydda tomorrow; but could not promise what would happen from there onwards.

Thursday, June 25th

While I was in my bath, the angelic Joan shouted, 'You can go on Misery tomorrow, if you want.' Action, splendid! Determined Joan had managed to get me on the Egyptian transport MISR passenger aeroplane to Cairo.

CAIRO FLAP

Shepheard's Hotel, Cairo

Cairo is full of rumours. Stories of reinforcements are encouraging: a convoy is said to have arrived at Suez just at the right time; de Gaulle is reported to be flying in, and Wavell, too, is on his way. Shepheard's Hotel is already lousy with generals; General Messervy in the telephone booth, General le Gentilhomme standing by the revolving doors with General Catroux, General Ritchie coming out of the wash-room. There is a great deal of talk as to who must be punished for the fiasco in the desert. The Egyptians have behaved surprisingly well and have not panicked in the face of unpleasant news. In fact Cairo, outwardly, seems quite calm.

Lilia Ralli has appeared from Alexandria where tearfully she bade good-bye to her parents: 'They are too old to be chased about by Rommel,' she cried. She described Alexandria as a dead city: all Wrens and sailors evacuated; roads without traffic; windows open on to empty rooms; telephone bells ringing unanswered.

Derek Atkins turned up with stories of the retreat. Yes, it was sad leaving the 'Ritz' at Bagush, the camp which we had considered our desert home, and awful to have to blow up the recently built cookhouse of which they were so proud.

Randolph Churchill, who was smashed up in a motor accident in the desert, is out of the hospital for the first time today. I had dinner off a tray by his bed. He was at his most enthusiastic for four hours on end, shouting with relish, 'The situation's splendid!' He'd like to see the Germans come to within fifty miles of Cairo, then, with their long transport lines, be cut off. He said he was glad I was going home soon so that I could tell 'them' what had happened at Tobruk; but when I asked him what did happen at Tobruk he was unable to answer. Randolph's stout heart makes me feel ashamed of my anxieties. Just to hear such exuberance is encouraging.

June 28th

The German radio announced that their armies would be in Alexandria on the 6th and in Cairo by the 9th. Someone at the office said that, if that was so, the end of the 'shooting match' was in sight. Dudley Barker gallantly remonstrated, 'Oh no, we should have to stop them somewhere else.' The front lines are so near that the journalists go up to the battle for the day.

June 29th

The Germans have announced the fall of Mersa Matruh. All army and air force personnel must remain indoors after 8 o'clock. Cairo, at last, seems in a state of alarm with queues outside the banks and crowds milling in front of the shops that sell luggage. Rumour is rife: forty tommy guns were found in a priest's house. In offices everyone is busily burning documents: black charred pieces of paper drift down from the chimneys — a storm of black cinders, a hail of funeral confetti; the air thick with a pungent, peppery smell of burning. Out of doors there are more braziers heaped with piles of smouldering paper.

Tuesday, June 30th

Cable came from Air Ministry requesting I do a job in Lisbon on way home: this makes my departure seem more probable. When I lunched at Gezira with Bruce Bennett he was so determined not to discuss the news as to be alarming. 'I know naught,' he said. But I nagged, 'Would you say the news was hopeful or grim?' 'Grimmish,' he said. But I was not fooled by his apparent calm when he asked, quite casually, if I would take back to England his gold cigarette case. He explained he didn't want to pay for its being stored here in a bank.

Later. Houghton came in again. 'Look here, you're in luck, Beaton! You can get a plane to Lagos on Thursday.' The photographs of my Palestine-Persia trip arrived and there was a lot of ordering and captioning to be done.

Wednesday, July 1st

Houghton came in again. 'As things stand, on account of the mighty flap, it's difficult to say for sure if you'll be leaving tomorrow or not.' Probably this office will be evacuated before tomorrow morning, in which event, should I remain and risk getting on to the plane, or retreat with the office staff?

Houghton and I looked at a map. A pencil line showed how perilously near to Alexandria we have now taken up our positions with back and flanks against the last wall. A heavy weight seemed to press against my diaphragm. It made me feel somewhat sick: how could I fill in the day? What was there to be done now? No work for me to do. After I had sorted some negatives and thrown away some old papers and letters it was only 10.15 in the morning. Still so much of the empty sickening day lay hopelessly before me.

The stage was set more in terms of defeat than in victory — why? Was it because we had lost confidence? Everyone carried his revolver; luggage was to be brought to headquarters in case hotels were picketed. In order to do something, in order to do anything, I walked round to the propaganda department of the embassy to submit my latest batch of pictures. The propaganda articles and magazines became a mockery. On the walls the posters proclaimed that we were 'Mightier Yet'. One of the old women who has been working here was experiencing her second exodus, having escaped from Athens; but this was my initiation into the waste and despair of an evacuation. I left the bureau, my pile of photographs still under my arm; no one would look at them now.

The day passed with a few welcome opportunities of activity for me, luggage chores and visits about permits and tickets. The Passport Office was in an uproar: my passport had been sent, by mistake, for a Belgian visa instead of a Portuguese one. With difficulty, I managed to retrieve the passport and take it personally to the Portuguese.

At lunchtime I ate, by myself, an omelet at a French restaurant. Suddenly, the *maître d'hôtel* rushed out, waving his napkin, gesticulated wildly to an Egyptian soldier, who in turn picked up his revolver and left forthwith. 'What's the hurry?' I asked. The *maître d'hôtel* said, 'They've telephoned from Alexandria to say that the town is surrounded.' 'Nonsense!' I argued with him furiously. It was disturbing, nevertheless, to realize how inflammable feelings were.

The 'flap' grew in intensity. 'Flap' was the word of the moment. Everyone put a stopper on his emotions by calling the crisis a 'flap'.

At HQ still no news from the desert. Neither was there any personal news about my proposed flight. I long to leave Cairo, but feel guilty at being so selfish as to be worrying about my own departure in the face of such gigantic disasters. If 'things go badly', as the current phrase has it, other people's lot will be so much more awful than mine. Those wretched men, for example, the 'burnt-out' cases, still, after many months in hospital in the throes of having new features grafted on their faces, what would happen to them?

HQ: Burn is convinced the Germans will conquer Egypt; thinks there is chaos in the desert; says a caterpillar of strength is arriving continuously from Germany through Crete, and that our best tank crews have gone. Watson, the Australian, and Denis Johnston of the BBC, and incidentally the author of that beautiful play, *The Moon in the Yellow River*, appeared from the desert. Johnston was riled and rattled: he had been badly looked after; couldn't get transport for his electrical equipment. He thought the battle did not look too good, that Auchinleck had lined up in the wrong place, that our armies were too stolidly backed and had no flexibility. He says the Eighth Army is tired and discouraged, realizing their equipment is not as good as the Jerrys': our shells just bounce off their tanks at 500 yards' range, and once again we are out-distanced by their guns. Watson, on the contrary, was optimistic: he admitted our armament wasn't as good as the Germans', but thought the fresh troops would 'make all the difference'. The RAF are doing as many sorties as they ever were, although we have not many landing grounds, and the German aircraft are never seen by day. Another comfort: we now have aircraft fitted with a cannon that dive on to tanks firing a gun as big as a Bofors. To score a direct hit is difficult: a tank does not look a very large target from the air. But if a success is scored the tank is not just put out of action, it is completely obliterated.

In case I do leave tomorrow I ordered some valedictory drinks in the office. Everyone was busy, but it was nice to know how friendly these chaps would be if I have to spend the next six months with them in Khartoum.

Thursday, July 2nd

I woke to find a light sky, and a dog on the roof outside my window gnawing a bone. The electric light was on in the service pantry so I rang to know the time: there was no answer. I walked down the corridors. No one about. Had they forgotten to call me for my aeroplane? I went down the main stairs and hung over the banisters looking into the oriental hall. There were a few servants moving quietly, and some luggage men sitting on trunks. They looked stupefied when they heard my voice echoing through the columns: 'What time is it?' They did not know: 'Well, get someone to find out.' At last, the reassuring answer came back. '3.10.'

The first rays of sun filtered through on to Heliopolis Airport. So this was escape! I suppose I am the first of the rats, but I prefer to think of myself as fortunate in having finished my contract perhaps just in the nick of time.

The aircraft was not yet fuelled, and even now I feared some general might start a row about reservations and have me thrown off the plane in his favour. What news of the battle? We heard nothing. At last the plane mounted the skies over Cairo. With what tremendous relief was I leaving this restless, corrupt, unfortunate, suburban town, with the Germans only ninety miles away, for England, where the Germans are only twenty miles distant.

Part VIII: Homeward Bound, 1942

Lagos

At Khartoum the hall of the Grand Hotel was stacked with the luggage of many English families, part of the evacuation scheme. Some sailors whose ships have been sunk, boarded our plane here to return home to join other ships. They cheered the atmosphere so that a general who had earlier been irate — after a late night — became merely petulant. 'You don't need much brains mucking about in the desert,' he told us apropos our generals in Libya! 'It's an awful thing to send a general home. It means his military career is finished. Take Gort — a stupid man, but the men love him! What's he doing now? Malta! Well, that's not really a military job in any case. He deserves better — after all, he did get the BEF Army away from Dunkirk.'

We flew over desert — what the sailors called 'Bugger All' — for over 1,000 miles, and at sundown we arrived at El Faschir. From the radio in the rest house we heard Churchill paint the news in the darkest of colours. Fifty thousand men have been lost in Libya: over half are prisoners. In one day of battle we started with 350 tanks and ended with seventy. Any moment he might announce news 'from the fertile valley of the Nile of grave importance'. After being away so long it was odd to hear the war interpreted from Whitehall. In Cairo news from the desert comes first-hand, but Whitehall's version of what one has seen on the battlefield, relayed through the mouthpiece of a genteel BBC announcer, seemed far from reality.

It is only partially true to say we have flown across Africa. This, in fact, we have done, but we have had no sensation of travel. The places at which we have stopped for refuelling are merely pinpoints chosen on the navigator's map. The aerodrome is invariably impersonal, the meal anonymous. It is a way of travel that encourages ignorance, cynicism and boredom. One does not know or care how the aircraft is flown or how the route is found: one resignedly accepts the improbable and negatively achieves a result.

While we were flying through afternoon sunshine and I was reading *War and Peace* the wireless operator picked up the BBC message: 'Forces are fighting seventy miles from Alexandria. German Army was repelled continuously throughout yesterday. British Army launched a surprise counter-attack from the south — results not known yet.'

After another 100 pages of Tolstoy, the scenery below changed. Hitherto unadorned desert now sprouted little trees; there were pools of water and hills. We cut through the bright blue sky into a floor of marshmallow pillow-clouds. These were the first cumuli we have seen for months. We had said good-bye to the dry, flaky dust and grey palm-trees of Egypt and had come back to the lushness of West Africa with the impenetrable jungle below like tightly-packed bunches of broccoli.

At Lagos, the rich earth smelt suddenly damp and good. On the way out to the RAF camp, seven miles away, blades of banana trees touched the roof of our van. The chocolate-brown natives in European shorts and shirts walked with incredible dignity and grace while balancing huge crates of melons or cutlery on their heads; the women lilting along in enormous fish-finned turbans and cotton draperies of barbaric colours and fantastic Braquelike designs. (It seems these materials come from Manchester and are not available in the UK. These fortunate women can choose a motif of fans, parachutes or even Singer's sewing machines while their equivalents in England have Hobson's choice.)

In the mess, RAF men of various ages and rank were sitting about in silence. All of them were waiting patiently to leave. Lagos is a bottleneck, and, without a 'priority', it often takes weeks, or even months, to board an aeroplane for home. Here was a wan-looking crow of a brigadier who had been waiting forlornly for ten days to go back to England; he pulled at a lock of his dark black hair, wondered if it would not be quicker to go by boat to Freetown. A squadron leader had been hanging about on call for three weeks. They looked at me, the latest arrival, with scorn or pity, or as a possible enemy. Suppose my 'priority' was better than theirs, then perhaps my presence here would delay their chances again. Not a pleasant place this — Lagos — famous for its humidity and mosquitoes — but nearer to home than Cairo.

There is not much to do, but last night I got a lift to see the outdoor movies. It was interesting to watch the reactions of the native populace to the entertainment. Two curiously unsuitable comedies with a snow background about winter sports. Snow is an element that most of these West Africans will never know; but the dark audience roared with laughter when someone fell from his skis on the white slopes. They applauded most when the comic strip showed thousands of little sheep tied with blue ribbon that someone was counting in order to attain slumber. During the big film, a clumsy effort at American whimsey — *The Wizard of Oz* — I slept; but not enough.

Sunday, July 5th

Everything is damp — the bed, clothing, papers. Soon one's luggage becomes mildewed. The earth is red, so that the swamps are like lakes of tomato soup. It is an uncomfortable billet, too: the beds are granite, and the other men in the dormitory make such varied and horrible noises that one longs for earplugs. Even deep in the night there are continual disturbances with latecomers turning on lights and bawling at the top of raucous voices. Early calls start before dawn: again doors are banged, young men whistle bits of my least favourite ditties ('A Wandering Minstrel I' or 'She was poor but she was honest'), and the songs are accompanied by the most explosive gurkings and lavatory noises.

The meals are in strange contrast to the tropical surroundings: everything comes out of a tin. Quite resigned to the unsympathetic surroundings is an old air commodore with a far-away look in his topaz-coloured eyes. He had been two and a half years in East Africa and is now going home on leave. He finds himself stranded here without any priority. This morning the 'Movements' people telephoned to say that the next bomber load is full, but would he tell them if his return was urgent or important. This sounds like an improbable story yet, miserably bored as this old man is here, he said, 'No, I'm going home on leave, and I can't honestly say I deserve any priority — or that there is any urgency in getting back.'

Radio latest: The desert battle has raged for five days: we are still holding the enemy. Dimbleby said, 'There is no cause yet for optimism, but we need not be pessimistic,' which seems a fair statement of the case.

Denton, the Information Officer, told me that the women journalists visiting the Middle East have made themselves pretty unpopular. One who is known as the WOV (World's Oldest Virgin) boasted that she acquired most of her information in bed. Eve Curie was by far the most popular, and she was a beautiful, smiling woman until she transformed herself into a journalist; then her mouth became contorted and turned down at the corners, her eyes popped, and she barked, 'How many aeroplanes are passing through here a week? I must have hard facts and figures for the great American public.' Least loved of all was Clare Boothe. She had been so insulted that the red carpet of Lagos had not been unrolled for her that she made it her duty to tell everyone how to do their own particular jobs. She was full of machine-made epigrams, and did not ingratiate herself further by calling the fighter pilots 'flying fairies'.

As Lagos is becoming a more important port each month, Denton thought some pictures of the wharfs might be of use to the Ministry of Information, so he put the Information van at my disposal and telephoned the military police for a permit. We must visit them straight away. No, the CID were not empowered to give me the permission to operate in a prohibited area. My papers reiterated 'Every reasonable facility must be given'. Yet, in spite of the undertaking that they could have my negatives, a lobster-faced man named Titmus displayed himself as a first-rate histrionic obstructionist. As a result, the afternoon was spent photographing the more peacetime aspects of Lagos: the Rousseau-like scenes were not at all suitable for wartime propaganda, but a delight from the aesthetic point of view. Some of the women carrying bunches of frangipani, or clusters of squawking hens, fled from the camera. One woman threw some water at me while others hid behind stacks of plates; but a crowd of excited children longed to be taken and they cheered each time I clicked the camera. It was a strange Pied Piper's progress surrounded by about fifty naked piccaninnies who clapped and shouted in unison.

There have been many opportunities recently in which to contemplate and take stock of one's life. There is much about which to feel dissatisfied. Perhaps it was my greatest mistake to have spent so much time taking photographs. Not enough energy has been left for other activities. It was disturbing to me when Geoffrey Hoare, *The Times* correspondent, seeing my book of war photographs, said to me, 'How you must hate doing this!' In fact, he is wrong. I derive satisfaction from taking almost any sort of photograph, and photography has been the means of my seeing many exciting aspects of this war. Nevertheless, I do realize that only certain compartments of my mind are at work while dabbling with the camera, and this will find me out in the long run. Chunks of my brain-matter will have become petrified. Even when taking photographs one must use one's intelligence over one's instinct. A lot of my work could have been taken by the automatic pilot.

On my return to England I must shut myself up at Ashcombe and buckle under to some very hard work and quiet reading. Then, when I've got all the present assignments delivered, I shall try to get a whole-time war job: it is not good enough being free to carry on in the ways of peace.

Tuesday, July 7th

Perhaps as a result of the above, I decided to spend the day in a manner unlike any other since my travels started: so remained at the mess doing nothing but reading. It is quite uncanny how Tolstoy, in *War and Peace*, has chronicled this war. The personal emotions are exactly the same. One can look up almost any aspect of today's events in its pages as if it were a dictionary.

How many must feel like the soldier who goes off thinking that war will be so gloriously exciting — that he will become a hero — and how events misfire leaving him terrified, helpless and unscathed.

I dressed only in time for the 'News' before lunch. The battle has reached a lull: the Germans have made no progress, but a lull is not very healthy if it allows the enemy to bring up reinforcements. However, the situation is so much better than it was a week ago: the onrushing tide has been stopped. Yet the Germans seem to have got a foothold in Russia: really, is it not astonishing what they have achieved? It is a terrifying thought that we should probably have been annihilated if Germany had taken us on before Russia.

'There's a place for you on the clipper to Lisbon. 2.30 start in the morning: you must be called at 1.30.' Action again. The air commodore stirred his after-dinner coffee and wistfully mentioned the lucky people who were able to get on to an aircraft, but he himself would not wangle any pull, although it would be easy for him to do so — a most remarkable man.

At the last minute two Wellington crews were put off: they have been waiting for six weeks and are accustomed to last-minute disappointments.

The magazines in the mess are dog-eared to the point of falling to bits. A chap who had been looking through the torn pages of *Country Life* came up to me to chat about English houses. In memory we travelled from Wiltshire to Cumberland. One of the acutest pleasures for people stationed far from their home is to spend long hours reminiscing nostalgically. In fact, later, as I lay on my pallet unable to sleep with excitement at the prospect of the journey before me, and the anxiety lest I should not be called in time, I pulled out various drawers of memories and re-lived many happy events of the past: my earliest remembered holiday, as a child of two or three, trussed up in a starched suit, driving in a carriage under the trees at Shanklin in the Isle of Wight, to pay a teatime call — a rather plebeian dog came out to the gate to welcome us; my first visit to Scotland — where everything smelt so pure and fresh and the food was better than any; my initiation into Californian life and meeting my idol, Greta; then the long summer holidays spent motoring in Austria and Germany with Peter when we became *habitués* of the music festivals, and on the way to Munich were stopped at the frontier by a most brutish-looking Hun in uniform, with shaven head and leggings. 'Why are you going to Munich?' he demanded. 'To see *The Roseti- kavalier*,' Peter replied. In the most raucous tones he replied, '*Aach, sie werden die schöne kostüme geniessen!*' Suddenly, my halfconscious reveries were broken by the nice native boy calling me and bringing me back to Lagos.

Thirty people assembled with their lugagge at the shack pathetically named 'Airways House'. The long and incessant delays were easily borne for we all knew at the back of our minds how darn lucky we were ever to be getting away. I was told to change out of my uniform into a civilian suit prior to landing at Lisbon. Portugal, being neutral, does not welcome Service men, so they must hide their uniforms in their overnight kitbags while they meet Germans on 'friendly terms'. It was still dark when we got into a launch and sailed on a long journey before we boarded the Bristol clipper (the flying-boat that took Churchill to America), an enormous machine, like a vast air-train with silk-lined walls, desks, Pullmans or hotel-lounge chairs, and various compartments for sleeping, eating, smoking. A great adventure this, for none of us before had been in a flying-boat. We took off so smoothly in the blackness that we could not tell when the aircraft had become airborne. We slept, and awoke above a carpet of white clouds with breakfast awaiting us.

We have juggled with time so much that it has little meaning left for us. Once we did a spurt of twelve hours and came down to refuel in Bathurst: we eat up two gallons of petrol per minute on our 8,000 mile journey home.

When, eventually, we circled a mountainous coast line and swooped down into the blue Bay of Lisbon, the door of our flying hotel was opened on to a gay, sunny scene. Small flags fluttered and turquoise wavelets splashed a white jetty that might have been painted by Tissot.

At once we found ourselves in the pre-war atmosphere of holidays in Spain or the South of France.

LISBON

Did they know anything about my visit? No, the Press attaché had heard nothing. But two young men at the embassy, Stewart and Herbert, looked after me with interest and enthusiasm and telephoned several departments to inquire if there was a job awaiting me here. Yes! The Air Ministry *had* called about my arrival, but further inquiries only brought a blank. I felt I was here under false pretences. Stewart was of the opinion that I should not stay, since there was nothing for me to do here in Portugal. Herbert said he thought they should wire the Air Ministry as it would be too bad if I were to go back home only to be sent out here again. Stewart smiled to himself as he booked me a room at an hotel, and conducted me there himself.

No wonder he smiled, for the Aviz Hotel proved to be a phenomenon. More like a Victorian millionaire's mansion, it was decorated with gigantic pieces of heavily-carved mahogany, medieval statuary, Portuguese tiles, eighteenth-century wrought iron, vast Spanish carpet and unliftable tureens of encrusted silver filled with ugly flowers. The whole atmosphere was so rich and unlike anything we have known since the war, that it was as if that over-size baroque clock in the hall had been put back twenty, even forty, years. Stewart left me, having inquired who my next-door neighbour was (in case she was a German or Italian), to bath, to shave, to dress in different, cleaner clothes, and to have a meal.

Lunch was an event. In a shrouded rose-reflected Louis XVI dining-room a few tables were filled by a varied assortment of pre-war personages of various nationalities. In a corner, his back to the wall, sat Mr Calouste Gulbenkian, the oil and caviare king and art patron. A portentous silence prevailed as the most sumptuous and extravagant meals were served. My eyes were out on sticks as the wagon of hors-d'oeuvres was wheeled over the thick carpet towards me. These proved to be a banquet in themselves. How I managed after this to swallow three more courses I do not know, particularly as I had eaten almost nothing during the last weeks; but there was no room for the gargantuan strawberries.

My bedroom, with its apricot-coloured furnishings, silk flounced lampshade over the bed-head, and palm tree rustling outside the balcony, was an oasis. The bare dank cell of the RAF mess at Lagos was forgotten until I brought out my dressing-gown from the bag, and once more my nostrils were filled with that smell of mould and I remembered that other bed and pillow of damp moss and fungus.

Yes, I am glad I'd been ordered to stop off here (for what reason I am still ignorant!) I wandered down into the town and with what relish did I regain my appetite for sightseeing! The lovely eighteenth-century buildings and ornate rococo decorations are something of which I have been starved since the war.

The façades are often painted deep coral red and white, and have ornate stucco decorations sprouting from the caps of pilasters, whilst above the balustrade on the roof, obelisks grow out of stone urns. By chance I came into heroic white marble squares ornamented with ornamental arches and statues. I admired gardens with classical busts that appeared out of pillars entirely grown over with foliage. It was a great pleasure to sit and enjoy the green shades by the Neptune who watched a fountain spring from the pot he held in his arm.

It is astonishing to see the shops so crowded with rare foodstuffs, sweets and liqueurs, and all those things that are unprocurable at home — silk stockings, watches and lipsticks. I am likewise amazed to note how many kiosks carried so many English newspapers and magazines (many more than there are to be had at home). I looked at an *Illustrated London News* to discover if any of my war pictures had yet appeared, but only saw how the English months have passed, that everyone is wearing entirely different clothes, and how Princess Elizabeth has grown from childhood to be a young lady.

At the secretariat I looked through a pile of German propaganda magazines. Their photographs of the war, both in colour and black and white, are so much more original than ours. Not only do they know the value of restraint in colour, but their attitude is so bold. They show dramatic blurs — pictures taken in semi-darkness, in smoke, in rain or fog that create a tremendous dramatic effect. Yet it is baffling that these magazines, which are so much in the contemporary spirit, should still harp on the abolishment of 'decadent art' when, in so many other ways, their minds and tastes are more flexible than ours.

Friday, July 10th

The Rip van Winkle aspect of Lisbon has its disadvantages. Portugal is undoubtedly the refuge of the 'rats', and the Hotel Aviz caters for the richest of the collaborators who come here to do their deals. Perhaps her blindness to the world situation has cost the country her former greatness and has resulted in Portugal living now in the twilight of her days. But maybe my vile ruminations have merely been caused by my not being able to get a taxi. In this land of luxury there is one shortage — petrol. The streets are almost bereft of traffic, and since coal is in short supply electricity must be saved so that even in the Aviz Hotel lights are turned off after 10 o'clock.

The Ministry of Information have at last telegraphed that they wish me to photograph the entire Cabinet and all local celebrities. They have sent a list of proposed sitters ranging from the President to Salazar, from admirals to cardinals. I cannot think this can be of much help to anyone, and it is certainly of no 'importance'; but it will provide me with a contrast to the recent pictures I've been taking.

The business of setting about this task was dire. At the Secretariat a man named Almeida was to give me a permit to use a camera (it appears that in Lisbon you are arrested for taking pictures, and once in prison it may take weeks to get out), but to find him at his desk was our first difficulty. Owing to stringent economies resulting from Salazar's reforms, and the balancing of the budget after many years of financial chaos, sacrifices have been made by many people including Government officials. This may be the reason why many civil servants live by another job, and therefore arrive at their government office only at 5 o'clock in the evening. When at last Mr Almeida appeared behind his desk he treated us to an extraordinary histrionic act. Surrounded by telephones like a Hollywood agent, he carried on long conversations each time the bell rang. He would dial numbers without ceasing, curse the operator, hang up and dial again immediately. He would throw wild gestures at the telephone and grimace like a tortured madman. Having kept Herbert and me as spectators for half an hour, Almeida then, for our protection, got on to three policemen. But oh, how sad he looked that he, Almeida, was at his desk so late in the day when most other people had long since gone to drink beer or eat ices at the cafe! At length, after his hysterical performance on the telephone had reached a crescendo he confided, 'Things are moving fast!!' I could not help laughing, but Herbert explained that this was comparatively true: patience is the first thing one has to learn in Portugal for time, as we know it, does not exist. (No war correspondent had ever been able to send a word home before ten days of incessant, dogged hanging around.)

When I am free, Marcus Cheke comes round to take me sightseeing. Free? What have I to do but wait? My delight is all the more keen since this fellow, who wrote a fantasy about the *Directoire* called *Papilée*, was one of the most surprising of my early literary discoveries. No Englishman knows more about Portugal; he has recently written a life of Pombal, the great eighteenth-century dictator. In fact, Cheke himself is an eighteenth-century character: vague, eccentric, temperamental, what is known as artistic, and full of quiet charm.

I am finding him an excellent guide, rich in fascinating information. He is fond of the Portuguese but considers the people of Lisbon are polluted by the artifices of the world. Yet they are unsophisticated, feckless and childlike: one of their great pleasures consists in letting off fireworks, and one bullfighter-nobleman, bearing a name that has stood for courage through several centuries, visits the zoo twice a week where he throws firework squibs into a den of monkeys.

Our taxi today, bent on pleasure, dashed with a fury only known to Portuguese taxi drivers, up the cobbled steeps of the Moorish quarter — the Alfama. It climbed huddled streets hung with balconies, bird-cages, morning glories and washing. This is part of the town that has survived the catastrophic earthquake of 1755 when two-thirds of Lisbon fell down in fifteen minutes. When surveyed from the summit of the town the jumble of roofs appears like a patchwork quilt with its texture of coarse weaves. Here is the fish market, and the women, bearing huge platters of fish on their heads, become excited and fight continuously, smacking one another across the face with a turbot or a lobster.

The taxi then darted down the hills. On two wheels, it navigated the hairpin bends that are protected from a drop of great precipitousness by a delicate ironwork grille, depositing us before the beautiful eighteenth-century riding school. Here is the great collection of gilded coaches. In addition to these carved marvels of locomotion, one can also be amazed at the taste displayed in the uniforms that were worn in the processions by the coachmen, heralds, musicians and footpads. The embroidered suits of the aristocracy are incomparably rich in colour with gold and silver embroidery and buttons of mosaic, porcelain, enamel and jewels. Even the shoe buckles are like precious jewelled picture-frames. This, my first visit to a museum since the war, brought me back vividly to those distant days when, the Sitwells having 'discovered' baroque, Bavarian holidays were spent sightseeing in their wake.

Is it possible to convey one's pleasure of a first visit to the Palace of Queluz? Even Beckford in his letters was unable to do justice to the pink and pistachio green, Cinderella-like palace. It is prettier than anything in Bavaria: with a greater licence and fantasy than anything in France. It is the apotheosis of all 'fondant' architecture. One building, with Dutch gable and double mansard roof, boasts a façade ornamented with sphinxes, angels blowing trumpets and lacework balconies. It is a startling display of architectural fireworks.

Tuesday, July 14th

The battle of Alamein has been brought to a lull for five days now. We have even made a few nibbles into the enemy's lines and have taken 2,000 prisoners; yet the danger is as serious as ever. Human nature is such that we can accustom ourselves to almost any set of conditions. The enemy's proximity to Alexandria, which first caused panic, is now accepted with calm.

Wednesday, July 15th

No more slothful mornings. At last arrangements have been completed for my camera to be used as part of a goodwill gesture. An early start from the Press Office presaged many full days of flattery to the leading citizens of Lisbon. Statesmen, marquesas in black with fluttering fans, an eighty-year-old admiral, a cardinal patriarch and other Church dignitaries, the head of the army, the home guard and the Red Cross, a woman poetess — all these figures were set apart, in a scene of their own, far from the intensely living and dying world of Africa.

In a castle entirely renovated in the nineteenth century, President Carmona, who has been called the Botha to Salazar's Smuts, received me with old-world graciousness, in spite of the fact that he had just been given a painful *piqure* in the leg. Born in the 60's President Carmona led the *coup d'état* of 1926 which eventually resulted in the foundation of the present Portuguese New State. Now, after fifteen years as President of the Republic, he enjoys as much prestige as a regency sovereign, has the army as a solid block behind him and is respected and loved by all classes. The revolutionary has become a grand old *seigneur* with grandiose manners which he now exhibited in spite of obvious disappointment that none of us proved to be the colonel the secretariat had told him to expect. Looking like an illustration by Caron d'Ache with his straight, lithe figure — a legacy of his army days — in a black coat and striped trousers, with his white moustache turned up at the ends and his hair parted with a flourish, he posed like a dandy of another day. The Victorian decorations of the castle lent themselves to delightful pictures with the mustard brocade walls, portraits like oleographs, and the huge gilt clock under the glass dome. In some of the many silver frames were photographs of a lady who was reputed to be his cook, whom the President had recently married. Maybe she was a good cook; certainly she was no beauty.

Each day brought forth more sitters: old men in resplendent uniforms and aristocrats in blue and white tiled gardens. But each day also brought forth more prevarications from Salazar. At last I prevailed upon my superiors to call a halt to this tiresome hide and seekery, and to allow me to return home without the Garboesque leader in my portfolio.

After my final sitting (the chief of the naval staff, an admiral with a long nose pointing to the left and grey hair cut in a fringe), I dropped my camera on his stone staircase. This Freudian accident made me realize with what foolish confidence, yet incredibly good luck, I had embarked on my Middle Eastern trip with only one camera. The Rolleiflex, which had seen me through sandstorms and the roughest jolting in jeeps, with typical German efficiency, was now put out of action when, psychologically, I must have wanted my mission to be completed.

A CHILD FROM OCCUPIED PARIS

I am now awaiting permission from the Ministry of Information to return home. The frivolous eighteenth-century delights of this pretty pistachio-coloured town, and the unaccustomed luxuries of a peacetime existence are beginning to pall and I'm starting to fret for home. Moreover, knowing not one native and being unable to speak a word of the language, I feel I have imposed too much on the hospitality of Marcus Cheke and others at the embassy, and am conscious of becoming a lounge lizard.

Today I lunched — instead of alone — in the hotel restaurant, with the little Castellane girl whose parents were out to lunch. I enjoy so much the company of girls of this age; they have an appealing quality that I always come back to. This one is particularly enchanting with a sort of poignant hopelessness. 'Oh,' she said, 'it is a terrible thing to be fourteen!' She didn't mind being eleven, and she looked forward to being nineteen — but twelve, thirteen, fourteen, fifteen, sixteen and on — oh, it was horrible because she wanted to behave in a grown-up way but couldn't help being childish. She is writing her memoirs. They start with the 'exode' from the Germans when France was falling.

It is a curious sensation to find oneself on neutral ground and to listen to first-hand stories from enemy-occupied territories. This little girl talked about Paris under the Germans, and how everybody loathed the *Boche* but dared not show animosity for fear of being chucked into jail. When her father took her to Luna Park two Germans decided to get into one of the revolving cages that rise like a windmill high into the sky. The owner of this attraction saw his opportunity for a bit of fun and made the cage revolve in mid-air at double speed. A crowd of Frenchmen below looked up, roaring with laughter, as the frantic Germans above bellowed ever louder. In the crowd a young German soldier went up to a girl who was yelling with amusement. 'Very funny they are, aren't they?' he said conversationally. The girl was silent, looked haunted, then fled.

Jews must wear yellow stars on their lapels saying, 'I am a Jew.' This child saw one of her school friends wearing this badge in the park, and was so embarrassed for her that she dared not talk to her. 'Aren't they terrified, the Jews?' 'No, they seem to be doing very well — the "black market" is run by them entirely.' My small friend also told me a lot of gossip about mutual friends, of their political sympathies, and the effects of the Occupation on trade. ('Business is thriving — the Germans pay well!') 'What do the French say about the RAF raids over France?' 'Oh, they're very amused!' 'Aren't they terrified?' 'No, they are confident that the RAF will only hit the factories. They hear the bombs drop, and then later the warning siren goes.' We laughed at anti-German stories, and became ribald about a party of eight brutish Huns that were devouring an eight-course lunch at the next table.

HOME BY FLYING BOAT

Friday

At last word has come that I can return to England. I am fortunate in having a friend at the embassy who not only facilitated my departure, but lent me money to do last-minute shopping for presents of all the things that are unprocurable, or rationed, in England: sugar, marmalade, preserved figs. I've bought a dozen Comice pears. They are marvellous specimens and will be like gold when brought home for the family.

Saturday

As I sat in the bar, acquiring dutch courage before my departure, the manager of the hotel passed the time of day with me. He was like someone from another planet for, until a month ago, he had been working at the Hotel Adlon in Berlin. The German people never discussed the war; there was nothing on which to spend their money; the shops were empty; very little food, no commodities, certainly no antique furniture or jewels; but the theatres were thriving.

At last it was time to go to the port. My fellow passengers had all provided themselves with baskets of fruit to take home for wife and family: some had pineapples in string bags, and General Willoughby Norrie, whom I had last seen when I was lost in the desert, clutched a large bunch of bananas. The weighing of the luggage seemed to be a lengthy business. 'How long will it be before we take off?' 'It is very doubtful if you will be leaving.' The wind had got up yesterday and blown with a fury ever since. The flags were beating themselves in an attempt to free themselves from their masts. One had been vaguely conscious of the wind, but now it had become the prime interest in life. The sea was rough indeed with white foaming horses. The flying-boat, enormous as it is, was swinging up and down on the waves. The launches that went out could not get near it. When it was announced definitely that there would be no take-off tonight I was somewhat relieved.

No good even trying to go back to the Hotel Aviz — they would have disposed of my coveted room long ago. In any case, the *cafard de grand luxe* has set in. The dark panelling, the heavy furniture, the pile carpets and endless meals had become indigestible. A bus took a party of us to a gimcrack hotel in near-by Estoril. The wind hammers the panes of my bedroom window as if we were on a ship in a gale.

Sunday

A bright sun but still blustery: the wind may not abate for several days. A strange gathering of people is assembled together just on account of the wind: a good subject for a short story. I spent my day reading *War and Peace* and, in the late afternoon, went to the Casino. It being Sunday, the place was crowded, and I watched a fencing contest. The participants were wired electrically with a long string coming out of their backsides which connected with an electric box. Each time one of them was *piccuéd* a bell rang — a more ridiculous installation one could not imagine. There were cinemas, tango teas, bar and *chemins de fer* rooms. I enjoyed watching the types of old people, ravaged, and ravenously playing for gain, but desperately losing chips.

Wednesday

On Monday evening preparations were made for another departure. A gale was still blowing, but 'they' said we *might* start. We got into the bus again and, on the road, passed another busload returning from an abortive 'take-off', filled with the disappointed faces of those who had been all the way out to the sea only to be told they must return. Would the same be our fate?

When we arrived the usual formalities were gone through, including the lengthy weighing of luggage. I was rather worried that my pears would be over-ripe when the Customs men were again 'very doubtful if we start'. A launch had gone out to reconnoitre. The captain, it was said, was as impatient as anyone else to turn his back upon Lisbon.

When the word was given that we were to try our luck, my feelings were mixed: I was glad to go, yes — but none too happy at the prospect of taking off from such a mountainous sea. We walked, with much buffeting, to the end of the jetty. It was quite an achievement to jump into the small boats tossing about below. After a choppy journey, with our luggage falling about us, we were thrown aboard the flying-boat. Once we were locked inside everything seemed calmer — for one heard and saw less. We taxied through the waves for what seemed in itself a complete sea journey. Then we turned in our tracks. The engines revved-up, snorting and backfiring furiously: it was as if some monstrous, enraged dragon were at bay. Now we were cutting through the waves at great speed. The sea, in its fury, came down upon us like walls of steel. For minutes on end we continued with a desperate determination to lunge, lurch and rivet forward. Suddenly the man next to me threw his thumbs in the air — and we were off!

At dawn, we dove through a hole in grey clouds to find ourselves among a lot of slate islands floating in a brackish sea. We were at Foines.

The neutral Irish came out in launches and were meticulous in their inspections: the brogue sounded supercilious at this early hour. A doctor examined us before we were allowed ashore for breakfast. A wet, drab morning with Ireland's trees bushy, thick and lush.

Another take-off. The windows of the aeroplane were curtained so that we should not see our island's defences, but one young man peeped and saw that a Spitfire was escorting us. After two and a half hours' flying — England! At last! England — green — such dark spinach green — so damp and rich. Poole looked rustic: very village-like and 'sea-sidey'. A group of young folk, leaning on their bicycles, watched our arrival with benevolent curiosity. The English atmosphere seemed remarkably peaceful until we went through a gruelling at the Customs; even our personal papers were read. Yet the Customs inspections are always somewhat harrowing for, surely, everyone cheats just a bit: there are very few who would declare that pot of jam without hiding a slab of chocolate. However, I paid in duty really more than I should have — though a few things did get overlooked! The pears I bought in the market, many days ago, were safe. General Norris still had his bunch of bananas, and the others their pineapples.

Now for the train to take us to Victoria. We passed rows of cottage gardens, so strange and yet so familiar, that appeared, after the parched climate of the East, so opulent, lush and dark green. When I left England, winter had still been upon us: now I tried to gauge the time of the year: There were scarlet runners in the gardens, and hollyhocks and marguerites, and avalanches of rambler roses. Yes, the summer must be drawing on. Heavens! it will soon be August Bank Holiday — but the holiday season doesn't count for so much in wartime. How lucky I have been to get back to enjoy much that is left of summer! This was what I looked forward to while I was away. This is the goal — their homecoming — that all the men in the desert dream of during the years they are existing in such unnatural surroundings.

In spite of the shortages of war, and even after the opulent food of Cairo and Alexandria, I would not now exchange all the rich meals of the Hotel Aviz for this English train meal — this plate of cold tongue with the new potatoes, and such green, sweet-tasting peas. I must take stock of my good fortune. Yes, without this luck I might still be awaiting my return from Cairo or Lagos, or even have been 'put in the bag' or sunk on the sea.

The train rattled on, but it is a longish hop from Bournemouth to London when one feels desperately impatient. My mind was already filling up with the events that would be part of life at home. I longed to see the garden at Ashcombe, and Peter, Diana, Juliet, Clarissa and James P. H., and have news of Rex, and new surprises in the theatre.

It was quiet at home. Mummie was upstairs, but rushed downstairs looking thin but well. Aunt Jessie screamed with extrovert surprise and sing-sang in her long-acquired foreign accent. The dog bounced up and down. The house was filled with faded flowers from friends: they had been awaiting my arrival for several days. There was such a lot to hear — news of death, divorces, and of the immediate family; so much to talk about or discuss; letters and clippings to read. Francis of the Ministry of Information rang and said they were pleased with my work. He is a kind man. I had a lot to tell him.

During my quieter moments away I decided that, on my return, I would not dash at once to the telephone and become involved forthwith in the lives of my friends, but would settle more quietly in the bosom of the family.

I enjoyed the tranquil dinner at home with so much glowing of hearts, and warmth of sentiment. The presents I had brought were received with delight especially the ripe pears.

At last, after so long, my well-travelled suitcases have been finally emptied and taken away. At last, the bed of my own, that I have so often remembered. At last!

Part IX: London Interlude, 1942-3

THE ROYAL FAMILY AND MRS ROOSEVELT

August 8th, 1942

Edith Olivier's hair has become white. We shall soon forget that she was all these years the dark-haired gipsy for ever on the move, laughing and scratching her scalp. The white hair, while being more becoming, is not so striking. She appears more of a conventional little old lady and less the violent character that her conversation still proves her to be.

While staying with Edith in the park at Wilton, I walked one afternoon, while she was out at a meeting, to the Close at Salisbury. Here I wished to feast my eyes again upon the rosy brick façade of the Wren school that, together with Mompesson House, and twenty other exquisite small houses, is part of the most beautiful domestic architecture in England.

It was a leisurely afternoon, and so peaceful that it gave me the feeling that often accompanies such an unexpected pause — that of presaging great activity — which is exactly what it did. Returning to the Dayehouse, I found Edith at her door, bidding *au revoir* to someone from the Women's Institute. Edith saw me and called, 'The King and Queen want you to photograph an unexpected visitor with them tomorrow — you must go up to London by the earliest train.'

I had been working on my Middle East book and had not taken photographs for some weeks. In my mind I felt so far away from photography that this summons came as rather an upheaval. My night's sleep was punctuated with half dreams in which all the usual fears had eventuated, with fuses blowing, lamps falling and confusion reigning in the subsequent darkness.

Sir Eric Miéville rang me at Pelham Place to say the visitor, though expected, might not arrive: the aeroplane had left Iceland but there had been fog, though now it had lifted. On getting to the palace there was still secrecy, but eventually I was told that the expected arrival was that of Mrs Roosevelt. Messages kept coming through. As I waited I was treated to a furlong by furlong account of Mrs Roosevelt's progress as if she were a Derby favourite. 'She's coming round now — she's at Tattenham Corner — she's leading by a head — she's getting closer — now a straight run for it and she's here!'

The royal family came in quietly and shyly, the King showing restrained embarrassment by a muscle moving in his cheek, the children meek with furtive side-long glances. The Queen smiled blandly and said, 'Mrs Roosevelt is just taking her hat off. After she's had a cup of tea, we'll come in again right away.'

The lamps stood in readiness in the Bow room — its walls decorated with rather pretty gilt medallions containing copies of Winterhalter portraits. The glass cupboards, because of bombing, were bare of china and the fireplace was empty. The palace has conformed to wartime strictures and sets an example in austerity. The temperature in corridors and many of the rooms was little above freezing. There were no flowers in vases. It very likely *is* true that the King allows himself only a few inches of bath water, but this somewhat dour atmosphere did not make my job of picture-making any the easier.

After a slight interval the royal party, with their tall powdery-haired, powder-faced guest, swept in. Hurriedly I stage-managed a group around the chimney piece. A few suggestions from the King were graciously acknowledged. At last we were ready. 'Now still! Quiet, please!' Whereupon Madame President turned this way and that — her head high in the air while she shouted, 'I haven't put a comb through my hair since New York. I haven't had any powder on my face since leaving Washington. Now that's very nice of you to arrange to have him for dinner — I didn't know where I'd contact him!' Meanwhile, the family smiled nervously and the youngest child tittered. I asked for quiet, and waited by the huge camera with trigger poised. I felt like an old-fashioned Victorian photographer trying to take an exposure of a scalded cat. Mrs Roosevelt leant forward this way and that, threw her head back, and kept up a monologue while I waited with the trigger poised in helplessness. I shouted hopefully, 'Still! One second's exposure!' Yet Mrs Roosevelt talked!

It was much later, after reading of it in the Press, that any of us realized that Mrs Roosevelt has become somewhat deaf, and this, of course, had been accentuated by the recent throb of aeroplane engines. I now realize that this deafness gives her the expressionless voice and the baffled look that these unfortunates possess.

Personal vanity is something of which Mrs Roosevelt is not conscious. Obviously it made no difference to her how she looked in these pictures. It seemed ridiculous that I should ask her to cross her feet, lower her chin and moisten her lips. Mrs Roosevelt was much more interested in going upstairs in order straightaway to write her column 'My Day' — which, in fact, is what soon she did. In any case the wife of the President of the United States was under the impression that a movie camera was in use and that she must portray animation.

After her exit, the royal family were photographed in turn. The photographs primarily are for official purposes, and one must not take a chance on their not being technically perfect.

So, instead of taking informal pictures with ordinary lighting and candid camera, a barrage of enormous lights, with clumsy electrician attendants, is brought in. The lamps stand six feet from the ground and cannot, with safety, be raised more than nine feet. The blaze of ubiquitous light that they create is unlike life: it is the sort of glare you see only on an amateur stage. Not only must one try to regulate the lights in a bold and original way, but one must try to disassociate one's self from all those groups of royalty that have differed little since Queen Victoria's early days. To prevent these well-trained sitters from regimenting themselves into a rigid composition that is not merely a pastiche of the past, provokes a great challenge. I knew that today I was not meeting this challenge. In a desperate effort that some unexpected felicity would eventually arrive to save the situation, I exposed dozens of negatives that I knew would never be of interest. Quantity does not necessarily improve quality. The bolt from heaven never arrived.

The King was amenable, but I found myself completely uninspired. The lights would not do my bidding, although there in front of me were great possibilities, provided by the raw, bony, medieval aspects of that handsome face. I could only fall back in desperation on a Bond Street 'camera-portraitist' form of flattery!

'How potent cheap music is,' someone remarked in *Private Lives*. How contagious the prevailing forms of photographic flattery! Yet what a service it would have been to dare — to have the authority and originality of point of view — to show the King in a heightened reality.

While waiting for a brainwave, I played for time by scrutinizing an enormous Chinese vase covered with dragons. 'This is a strange object but it casts nice shadows.' 'Isn't it hideous!' remarked the King. 'Where did it come from, I wonder?' After we had surveyed it for some seconds in silence the King ventured, 'It's Chinese, I suppose.' The delay before continuing the photography could be no longer protracted.

The Queen was as sympathetic and full of charm as ever. Princess Elizabeth has developed her mother's smile. The two Princesses, posing together, reminded me of the beginning of my career when I used to photograph Nancy and Baba as school children.

I had no brainwave and felt desperate. Unless one has enormous vitality the conditions of taking photographs such as these are apt to overwhelm one. This evening I failed, and in my secret opinion the results were merely ordinary.

The session lasted longer than I had dared to hope: the voluntary woman driver from the Ministry of Information, waiting to take the films to be developed (a super-rush order), sent in a pencilled note to say she had waited twenty minutes and couldn't stay longer tonight.

AUGUSTUS JOHN'S LETTER

Augustus John showed me such a witty letter from the Queen. She had really enjoyed being laid up with a bad cold as it was the first time she had been able to relax since the beginning of the war. At last she had had time to think about lots of things including her John portrait. It had been such an agreeable experience, posing in her spangled dress, with music being played during the sitting, but, alas, the portrait had not come off, and now it would have to be abandoned. But the Queen had preserved a hat that John had once noticed flying by in a motor-car when the King and Queen went to inspect some troops in John's part of the country, and of which he had said he'd like to do a drawing. One day the Queen would come to his studio wearing the hat — as her own home was dirty and dark. A most delightful letter.

DAVID HERBERT'S ESCAPE

David Herbert, now in the Merchant Navy, has been torpedoed. He has returned from Oran safe though slightly unnerved. He was on night watch 9 o'clock to 3, sitting at his wireless set, or rather lying back in his chair, his legs on the table in front.

For the past three days, they had known that they were going through the danger zone and that chances of attack were high. Some of them had said they thought the Roman Catholic clergyman had been a bit too optimistic when, that very evening, he held a thanksgiving service for their safety. A tremendous bang — all lights out, and David, thrown backwards, could not find the safety light in the dark. His duty now was to go to his superior officer and report that the ship had been torpedoed. This was perhaps a little obvious as the ship had suddenly listed to an acute angle. The wireless chief was hale and bluff. 'So we've been pipped at last, have we? So we've been pipped after all.' There was very little panic considering, but a few men did jump overboard from quite a height, and their lifebelts jerked up and broke their necks. A few officers panicked, but the captain managed to regain order and told everyone that it would be some considerable time before the vessel would sink. An Indian managed to swim out of a room that was submerged within inches of the ceiling; some men trapped in the engine room could be heard tapping but could not be reached. Somehow most people managed to get into the boats; of the 5,000 troops aboard only 200 were drowned.

David was in charge of a motor-boat; a rope had wound itself around the propeller so that the engines were useless. The sea was choppy, they had only one pair of oars, and were afraid that they would get sucked under when their ship turned over. The bosun said, 'We'll sink now if we take one man more on board. We've capacity for sixty and there are ninety-nine of us already.'

At first they became strangely callous about having to ignore the people in the water moaning 'Help, help', but later the full horror asserted itself. Yet even among the appalling dramas there were comic instances: when at last a destroyer picked up the survivors and they watched the old ship burning, the chief engineer arrived with a fluttering hat; the captain laughed: 'What on earth's the matter with your cap?' 'I thought the canaries would be safer in my hat than in their cage.' The interest that was taken in saving the livestock was almost greater than in human beings. A bag was thrown on the deck, and out stepped three snarling cats. The destroyer backed under the burning ship to allow thirty cats to leap on board.

There were two instances of bad behaviour: an American doctor, out of sheer terror, had refused to help, and in the choppy dark night an RAF officer sitting on a raft shouted to a female hospital nurse swimming towards him, 'You can't come here. You know perfectly well you can't come on this raft. They're only made for one man. You must swim to the next,' and this nurse, swimming away, in a Cockney accent answered cheerfully, 'Okay — is it far?' A number of Red Cross nurses found their boat to be waterlogged, and they had to hold on tight to the seats not to be washed away with each wave that lashed over them. The matron, in veils, kept up a pep talk —

only interrupted by the swish of waves — 'We must all consider ourselves fortunate — (swish) — that we have been spared — (swish) — to carry out our tasks — (swish) and that we may be of help when we land — (swish) on Algerian soil.'

EMERALD CUNARD

Emerald Cunard has returned to bombed London from her native America with the feeling that she has now come back where she belongs.

In New York she was judged by her age in years — not admired for her ever youthful spirit. Her outspokenness made her many enemies, and few appreciated her wit.

'I know I should look after my affairs, but I don't. My house is burnt — and it wasn't insured; and it's all my own fault, and it's all terrible,' she chuckles with infectious gaiety.

Now she has made a life for herself at the Dorchester in two rooms that are overfilled with outsize Buhl and ormolu furniture left over from her more spacious existence. Here she shows complete disregard for the deafening guns firing below her in the park, and pooh-poohs the danger of bombs.

At first she was somewhat perturbed to discover the extent to which the war had encroached upon everyone's lives, and restrictions irked her a great deal: it was acutely embarrassing sometimes to hear her complaints about the inevitable frozen and ersatz foods to the harassed waiter in charge of her dinner party. Yet she soon acclimatized herself to the changed atmosphere, accepting the fact that the old world of society in which she had thrived had gone for ever. In fact, Emerald has few regrets, and is as interested as ever in new people, new plays, and all the latest manifestations of literature and art, as well as the political scene.

Since she is about the only woman attempting to entertain in London it is not difficult for her to ensnare Cabinet ministers and war leaders to drop in on their way home for a drink, or to sit at her dinner table, together with groups of writers, painters and decorative women, who are in transports of amusement at their hostess's sallies as she describes her attempts to keep attuned to the times. 'Now we've *all* got to learn to do things!' enjoins Emerald, with that warm, cosy chortle that sounds like mice in the wainscoting. 'I had the most interesting afternoon with the Princess! She told me how to cook! The Princess is a remarkable woman. I said, "Do you mean to say you can roast a chicken? And a duck or a partridge?" She said, "Yes," and, what's more, she explained all about it. Now, when you cook a bird you must let it sit on one side for ten minutes, and then on its other side. Then the juices don't run down and dry the breast. Never cover the chicken or duck or partridge with fat. Put everything *inside* the bird — butter or fat or stuffing. Everything *inside*! And mind you baste it well. Oh, and then the things you can do with spatch-cock!'

Emerald's delivery of her lines is brilliant; confiding and surprised, with the emphasis on the last word of a sentence.

'Oh, it's much better to eat plain, simple food,' she reminisces. 'I once had a cook who used to serve chickens in melon, and put all sorts of unexpected things inside a potato! The potato was scraped out, and all that was left was the uneatable outside! So I went to her one morning and said, "Now, we've got to stop all this nonsense!"'

Emerald's frivolities are so entertaining that her audience is apt to ignore the scholarly mind which is her *raison d'etre*, in effect, the play-acting with friends during the evenings is only a preliminary for her real life of the mind. After her last guest has gone Emerald will read for six or eight hours until long after dawn has lightened her taffeta curtains. Perhaps she will suddenly wish to absorb the whole of Martin Luther, and his sermons will have more meaning for her than anything written today. Emerald confides, 'My maid Gordon is such a snob. She never approves of any of my friends. Suddenly she started reciting Burns to me. I never knew she was fond of poetry. But she told me she always won the prize in class as a child and that she never forgets it. She reads nothing but poetry, except the *Daily Mirror* where she learns all the horrible things about my friends.'

Characters in Flaubert or Proust will have more reality for Emerald than her little 'Poppies' or 'Sheilas'. She will talk of some little 'golden hoof' — and you realize that she is living in mythology. This may be one reason why she is apt to judge contemporary mediocrity so severely. 'But he's not a cultured man,' she explodes about some successful playwright. 'I don't suppose he knows one word of an ode of Horace!' Returning from an American play that was enjoying enormous success, she whispers with disgust, 'It's for the servants! Really, we can't watch people trying to lift up a Scot's kilt to see what's underneath. We all know what's underneath: it can't be anything new! It isn't as if it were a sea anemone or a salamander.'

Emerald's lack of inhibition, together with her excess of enthusiasm, sometimes makes her an embarrassing companion in the theatre. In a loud aside she will punctuate the development of the plot with pointed comments. She once described her first visit to a theatre when, in San Francisco as a child, she was so appalled at the heroine falling for the machinations of the villain that she stood to her feet, pointed and, in her shrill pipe, shouted, 'Don't you believe him! He's a snake in the grass!' Her *sotto voces* today are almost as dramatic, while her curiosity about the performers is surprising. ('Isn't her hair lovely! Such a beautiful colour! It takes a little dye to make that effect!' 'Wasn't it *terrible* about that poor Miss Enid Stamp Taylor! She slipped on a cake of soap in the bath, and the fall killed her!')

However, Emerald is a genuine lover of 'Le Vrai Theatre', and there is no little drama movement, housed in no matter what basement, of which she is not a founder member or subscriber, and she essays forth from her ivory tower to see any new play of promise, however far away, in the outer purlieus of London.

In fact, she seldom goes out except to a play. A visit to the country to see Diana was a great exception. Diana, being unable to leave her farm and animals, must remain at Bognor. On arrival in the country Emerald tottered on her sparrow feet and said, 'The view makes me dizzy!' Her usual pastel-coloured feathers and veils had been discarded for a more rustic taste. Her simple country clothes comprised a leopard-skin coat, pearls, a *beret basque* and the usual exceedingly high-heeled shoes.

'Oh! Diana, this is very interesting! How do you do it? These are your pigs? Very interesting pigs! How can you milk that cow?'

Emerald's interest and curiosity were intense. 'Do let me help, Diana! Do let me carry the pail!'

Emerald teetered on her spindly little legs into Princess's byre. The pail was brimful of milk. Emerald patted Princess's nose, then leant over to pick up the pail. The ground was uneven and rough for Emerald, accustomed as she is to thick *Savonnerie* or *Parquet de Versailles*. As Emerald picked her way through the straw with the pail, Princess, interested in Emerald's leopard coat, slowly butted her. Emerald's legs, pearl earrings and milk pail, went flying. Diana kept a straight face and with stiff upper lip said, 'Pity you hadn't got your camera ready!' Emerald, unhurt, but bitterly ashamed of herself, did not mind the loss of an earring so much as the loss of milk.

Emerald has recently been telephoning to me a great deal. It was, at first, a shock to wake to answer the bedside bell at 4 o'clock in the morning. But Emerald is lonely, and after a moment's readjustment, I lie listening in the dark until I am so entertained by some of her remarks that I switch on the light and make a note of them.

Without her exquisite sense of timing her remarks lose much of their effect, but here are a few of her aphorisms:

'Only a brilliant man knows how to be ridiculous.'

'Oh, it was a most Lenten existence.'

'Life and art never overlap.'

'A witty woman can never keep a man. She can't afford to laugh at the wrong moment.'

'Never be sincere. The whole structure of society falls if you start to be sincere, and you can hardly ever afford to tell the truth. Very seldom can a wife tell the truth to her husband. It's much too dangerous. You must always live in a very rigid convention.'

Recently Emerald has fallen in love, and for hours she will talk in veiled terms of her unrequited romance. Tonight she held forth on the subject:

'The greatest men I have ever known have never been able to put up with love. Why? It's so distracting — and great men must never be disturbed at their work. George Moore used to sit all day in front of his papers, and if anyone called at his house he would tell them to go away. He couldn't see anyone before sundown. One afternoon Mary Hunter arrived in Ebury Street and saw him, through the open window, having his tea.

(He never had his tea in the drawing-room, but down in the dining-room.) She heard him saying to the maid who had announced her arrival, "I could not be more devoted to Mrs Hunter, but please tell her I don't want to see her." The poor woman never recovered.'

'I think it better to be feared than loved. I remember Sir Thomas Beecham used to say, "I pray that one day I may be sent to prison so that I may spend some weeks undisturbed." On many occasions he nearly got his wish, but he's resentful of people who love him. He's very grudging. He said, "I owe that woman a lot." "Why?" I asked. "She gave me my very first Bible." "When was that?" "At the time I must have been sixty-five. I owe her a lot, but I cannot love her."'

Discussing a well-known *amoureuse*, Emerald said, 'She knew all the arts of seduction. She would often display her tongue: she didn't put it out, but she'd let one have a tantalizing peep — just so that one should know she had a tongue. You forget that most people do have tongues because you never see them, but a tongue is a charming addition if you like a person.' 'And what about teeth?' I asked. 'Oh, teeth should never be a reality, only an indication.'

Emerald would then say, 'Now, when will you come to dinner? I'll read out to you those who are coming on different nights. Now, do you want to be impressed? Laura Corrigan and Chips always want to be impressed.'

After an hour and a half's conversation Emerald would suddenly say, in a sweet and formal voice, 'Well, I'll say good night to you, and send you much love.'

EMERALD'S DINNER FOR FIELD-MARSHAL WAVELL

Emerald has an unconventional way of introducing her guests to one another. Sometimes she explains: 'This is Poppy — everybody loves little Poppy.' 'This is our great poet from the Foreign Office.' Once she had nothing to say about one guest except that her mother had been killed on the Underground.

Tonight Lord Wavell, a newcomer to Emerald's circle, was the figurehead for whom the gathering was being celebrated. The Field-Marshal looked a little nonplussed when Emerald introduced a bald-headed man: 'This is Gerald Berners — he's a musician, and a saucy fellow.' 'This is Dr Stewart, a worldly prelate, the final authority on Pascal and a professional beauty.'

But the small party, under the aegis of such a brilliant *entrepreneuse*, soon acquired its own impetus, and before the synthetic ice-cream arrived we had recitations of Ronsard from Leslie Hore Belisha, followed by large slices of Browning and Dowson from the Field-Marshal himself. Gerald, perhaps determined to act up to his sobriquet, seemed intent on lowering the tone of the party and contributed a child's nonsense rhyme about Pussy Cat. When conversation turned to famous last lines ('Mehr Licht') Gerald croaked Schubert's last words. 'Don't let poor Tauber starve.' Emerald, really shocked, piped her foghorn, 'No! No! That's nonsense! Charles II said that of Nell Gwynn!'

Emerald talked with incredulity of her first years of marriage to Sir Bache Cunard. Arriving so young from America, England seemed extraordinary to her. Here she was, living in this huge house, Neville Holt, in Leicestershire, and 'all we thought about in winter was hunting! Do you know, we all hunted every day. The doctor, and even the clergyman, wouldn't think of anything else! But, by degrees, I used to ask musical people to the house. My husband didn't like that one bit. One August evening my husband was away; there was a huge, round, hot moon, the nightingales sang in the wood — Neville Wood. It was so stifling and airless that no one could sleep. Suddenly, across the court someone put his head out of the window and gave the Valkyrie cry, and this was answered by someone singing a call from *Gotterdammerung* — and so it went on. When my husband came back he noticed an atmosphere of love. He said, "I don't understand what's going on in this house, but I don't like it!"'

ROMMEL ON THE RUN

November 5th, 1942 (Ashcombe)

Mummie hurried into my room. She pulled the curtains earlier than usual. No nonsense about lying in bed — however late I'd been writing last night. This was worth waking up for: the most exciting event of the war — the turning point: 'Wonderful news! Rommel's army on the run — in full retreat!' The whole look of the war suddenly changed.

CHRISTMAS AND NEW YEAR'S CELEBRATION — 1943

January 1943

After the third year of war it is extraordinary how many of the population are able to find time to eat and drink and be merry during the holiday festivities. We had at Loelia's for Christmas a most wonderful succession of meals — always washed down with wine or even champagne. On New Year's night Anne O'Neill and Esmond (Lord Rothermere) gave their usual joint party. This year it was more amusing than ever. A circular table around which sat Brendan, Emerald, Duff, Diana, lots of Berrys, sister Laura and her fiancé, Eric Dudley, etc., etc. After coffee, conversation became general. Brendan, for whom I have a tremendous admiration, has become much less pompous, and held the table with his magnetism and razor voice. Yet he found rivalry in Emerald, who would throw out fantastic comments with such brilliance of timing and technique as to create an extraordinarily funny effect.

Brendan was attacked by other ministers for this morning's Cabinet changes. Why should old William Jowitt get £5,000 a year? Was it because he was Labour? Why had Duff only £2,000 a year? Didn't it pay to oppose? Why had Macmillan got sent to North Africa when he had rebelled against the Prime Minister a week ago, giving Oliver Stanley the Colonies? Why, it didn't pay to be a supporter! Emerald started her line about it being a good thing to get Macmillan out of the country. He's a dreadful man! Emerald tactlessly made her usual observation about Americans being uncivilized; when the presence of a young American soldier was pointed out across the table she smiled, 'Oh, hallo,' and gave him a charming wave. Brendan, violently attacked by Duff, took his blows well — answered 'my dear Child', and gave us most amusing snippets of his erudition. He also showed how well informed he was on more personal matters — about the Archbishop who was spending New Year's Eve quietly at home with his wife 'with whom he wished to endear himself'. (It can be imagined that this remark called for a great many ribaldries.)

That this was a collection of deeply responsible people with the fate directly or indirectly of many millions in their hands would have been impossible to gather from the light-hearted way they chaffed one another about getting paid. 'Oh, you've feathered your nest nicely, Regional Commissioner!' 'Duff, why don't you go off and be a spy!' 'Why, Child, you can say what you like about Master Churchill but he likes to make up his own mind!' The New Year came in (in the form of John Julius[31] wearing pyjamas) with hopscotch and 'Auld Lang Syne'.

DOWNFALL OF MUSSOLINI

July 26th, 1943, Bognor

We were just about to go to bed on Sunday night — standing up, lingering at the door, discussing morning trains, when the telephone bell rang. 'That's bad,' said Diana, the pessimist, pulling a face, as she went to answer the summons. It was Freda Casa Maury. Diana shouted, 'Mussolini's resigned.'

The bombshell has really churned us up in a way that no other piece of news has since the collapse of France! (Only this time the churning is of a different kind!) I felt weak, and slightly tearful, but the others were just gay, smiling like children, and being absolutely enchanting in their happiness. Duff opened a bottle of champagne, and we sat for half an hour while the clock ticked very slowly towards the BBC midnight news. Raimund[32] exclaimed, 'Oh, you British are so extraordinary! Here's this wonderful piece of news — and your radio wouldn't dream of interrupting a programme of gramophone records with it. In America the news will by now have been given over and over and over again.' Duff beamed. He did an imitation of Mussolini meeting Hitler for the thirteenth time and saying, 'I must have *una, due, tre ... divisioni!*' We roared with laughter. Diana was like a young girl. She said this was one of the greatest moments of her life. She looked

---

[31] J. J. Cooper, now Lord Norwich.
[32] Raimund von Hofmannsthal.

radiant. Duff said he thought the King would make Badoglio successor, then send for someone and surrender. He thought it 'all up' with Italy within the next week, that now we had the Mediterranean we could hammer Germany and the Balkans from Italy, and the effect on German morale would be immense. Bertram Kruger, beaming, said, 'It's all over.' Duff, still beaming, said, 'No — we mustn't go as far as that.'

The clock ticked, they played Debus, and an announcer made a boring commentary. At last midnight. We raised our glasses at the wonderful news. The beginning of the end! It was as Duff had anticipated — Badoglio was in Mussolini's place. 'The war goes on,' he said. Bertram Kruger said, 'Gesture!' No. It was 'all up'.

The war in its final phase, almost too good to be true! Everyone lingered before going to bed. We could hardly wait for further news, and the morning papers with their headlines and ridiculous photographs of the man who had rampaged from his balcony and made such a giant mistake in stabbing France in the back, the man who had asked for the 'privilege of bombing London', the first dictator to go. On the jubilant phrase 'the crack-up of fascism' we went to bed.

The others left for London by the earliest train. Duff had intended taking a morning off, but he would not delay here, he wanted to know all the gossip from London. Diana pulled back the blinds, and said, 'The newspapers are wonderful!' — a huge banner headline and a photograph of Mussolini looking just like one of the Chinese ducks that were at that moment quacking outside the window.

She drove me to the station, and everyone seemed to be smiling. The benign little ticket-collector, with a huge buttonhole, who is by way of being a great character, was grinning from ear to ear. Diana, unconscious of her extraordinary clothes, yelled at him, 'Isn't it wonderful?' The little man, who looked as if he couldn't hurt a fly, said, 'Yes, it's made all the difference. Now we just need to have him die slowly. I'd like to take on the job — cut off one finger to begin with.' He chuckled as he snipped another ticket.

EDITH EVANS

I was conscious of spending an afternoon that might have a certain historical interest, for it was passed in the company of Miss Edith Evans who will doubtless go down to posterity as one of England's greatest actresses. She deserves that eminence.

Edith had summoned me to discuss her appearance as Hesione Hushabye in the forthcoming *Heartbreak House* for which I am to do her costumes, wigs, etc.

My secretary had been warned that these talks might go on for a two- or three-hour period or more — and if more, Edith and I were to dine together. I was not altogether without qualms about the meeting, for rumour had it that Edith could be rather 'difficult': Already one or two points had cropped up on which we were not quite in agreement. I rang up Binkie[33] to find out if he had, for instance, broken the news to Edith that, contrary to Shaw's instructions about Hesione, we were all against her wearing a black wig. Yes, he had, Good! Then why did she want to see me at such length? Binkie laughed. 'Oh, "The Importance" came off last Saturday night, and when Edith heard we were not going to perform to the troops in Gibraltar for another three or four days, she said, "Oh, how lovely! Now we can have lots and lots of talks and discussions

---

[33] Hugh Beaumont, of H. M. Tennent, responsible for putting on the production.

about the new play!" Whereupon all the others concerned bolted.'

Luckily I was primed with fresh energy from a country weekend, and my afternoon was empty. I was even relishing the opportunity of listening to this fine actress discourse about her art and hearing her reasons for playing in certain moods and ways. It would surely be rewarding to watch her ferreting about for the real character behind the technical performance.

I had been a bit baffled when reading *Heartbreak House* (which, incidentally, reads less well than it acts), but Edith said that she now understood about three-quarters of the play although it had taken her three different productions in which to do so (originally she had played Hesione's younger sister, Lady Utterward). Sometimes the director had asked her 'What does this mean?' and she'd answer, 'Bosh! That's pure Shaw — it's nothing to do with the part — the character must say it — then gulp and get on with his characterization.' She said that when G.B.S. came to rehearsals of his plays he was intelligent and quiet, but when it came to giving directions for acting his ideas were old-fashioned.

Edith Evans lives in Albany, a suitable place for her with its collegiate dignity and somewhat dour feeling of repose. I arrived punctually at 4 o'clock. Edith answered the door and was apologetic — the fire hadn't been lit long — part of the furnishings had been blitzed — the flat was not as she wanted it to be — and yet she burst out laughing and in a sing-song voice continued, 'Why should I *apologize* for all these things — why should I be so *silly*?'

Her rooms are rather empty and impersonal with a few snapshots, no books, and with unadorned walls which I said were full of promise. 'Yes, that's always most interesting — promise and never fulfilment.' One wall, however, was fulfilled with a portrait of her by Sickert. Done from a photograph it was a huge head over life-size, in sepia, with a blue background. Beautiful! 'But my family said, "Your face isn't as crooked as that." But it's *me*! It's *me*!' and she felt an awful dog buying it! She told me of how, when she was in *Robert's Wife*, she had washed her own hair for the first time and many new red glints had appeared in it. Sickert had 'got' these glints. (But, in fact, Sickert was painting at Bath from a newspaper cutting and certainly would never have seen these new glints.)

Now we sat to discuss the play — its mood and atmosphere.

Binkie had told Edith he wanted to do something to lift the play, give it a height — even in the scenery. 'That's right, we must heighten everything!' Edith promised. 'The play's very long, and unless we can mesmerize audiences by the atmosphere they will become tired. Shaw has got such a mighty brain that he could talk or listen to discussions for eight hours on end, but if audiences are conscious of being indoors listening they soon need a sandwich. We must make them feel we're out in a garden, in the evening, sitting doing nothing. A garden gives you patience and repose; in the twilight you can sit and do nothing sometimes for an hour even! We must create that "evening in the garden" effect, then no one can be bored! No one is bored in a garden! And we must all concentrate hard. We must listen — and *think*! We mustn't just wait for our cues, we must live every moment of the play, and by that we can mesmerize the audience. If we all think hard enough it is easy to mesmerize an audience. When we are talking in this evening-garden the stillness will be suddenly stirred by a little breeze that blows this way and that; these breezes are the changes of conversation. We must remember these little breezes — they, and the out-of-door height and openness, will lighten the words.'

Talking about Hesione Hushabye, Edith said she felt she was not well-mannered or bad-mannered, but a complete 'original'. She saw her in flowing draperies but discarding their grandeur — screwing up her arms, and going to sleep in public lying back in a huddle with legs twisted. Edith shouted, 'She must gather up the sleeves of her lovely tea gowns, and wave!' It is by such touches that Edith brings her characters to life.

Edith now set about trying to convince me that H.H. *must* have black hair. 'These two sisters must really be something! They're just a little past their prime, but they must be stunning!' For Edith, with her pale skin and irregular features — for Edith, of all people, to face up to a black wig sounded hell to me, but I was determined to keep an open mind. 'Oh, of course if I wear a dark wig I alter my entire skin pigment. You'll never know I'm wearing a wig — the audience will think I've dyed my hair, for it will look so natural. It will, in fact, be made up of all colours and there will be very little extra hair. Always when I have wigs made I say, "Remember, only half the usual amount of hair!" and when I wear a wig in a play it isn't just something I put on like a hat: it becomes part of me. I do my own hair — dress it on myself. Sometimes in front of the audience a curl falls out of place, and it is very effective to do it up as part of my acting. No — I don't want to have my own coloured hair — it's mouse — mouse — mouse. Don't let the audience associate Mrs Hushabye with Edith Evans! Let me assume beauty with your lovely dresses and a dark wig. I'll not fail over that at any rate: if I feel satisfactory there is no limit to what I can seem to be!' Edith was not just arguing for argument's sake; this was the result of deep convictions.

We sat over a fire. The day became dark. Edith boiled a kettle in the kitchenette and we enjoyed excellent tea with strawberry jam from America. I asked her many questions.

Had she a good memory? Could she, like Randolph or Duff, recite poetry by the hour? No. To her poetry was generally part of her impersonation. She forgot Rosalind's speeches at the close of the run of *As You Like It*. To her, learning a part was frightfully difficult. She would put off the work as long as she could, but she knew eventually she would have to drum it into herself, going over and over again — la-di-da-di-da. She described her feelings with elaborate metaphors and descriptive gestures, her hands flayed out, her head cocked this way and that like a white cockatoo.

Her jargon is completely untouched by the usual theatrical clichés. She brought out of a drawer a book in which Agate had written about her. 'What's it like?' I asked. 'It's a bit praisey. It makes me very hot inside, but I like it. It makes me feel a bit galumphing!' She considered Gwen Frangcon-Davies, whose artistry she admired, needed a guy rope and that her central 'pin' had not found its joist.

Apropos Edith's performance of Millamant she said that others too often have the wrong conception of the eighteenth century. 'It wasn't just finicking daintinesses with little fingers raised, snuff-pinching and fluttering of fans. Why, the climate hasn't changed! Women nowadays are seldom hot enough to want to fan themselves! A fan should be used for poking the fire or, at best, making an aside behind, but it should never be used for fanning. A parasol, too, was useful for poking people.'

Edith talked about breathing spaces in plays: Shakespeare gave his actors plenty of breathing space before they went over their hurdles. 'Shaw makes you take your hurdles too quickly — one after another without interval.' She laughed at herself guiltily for using analogies about racing — 'As if I know anything about horses!' But nevertheless she felt that acting was like jogging along Paddy, Paddy, Paddy — and then whoop — over the hurdle — then Paddy, Paddy, Paddy again.

She had very likely said a lot of this before — but it was good for her to air her views for this was all part of the creation of her role. This was for her the most interesting aspect of acting: 'The mental processes that one goes through are the important things.'

Edith also talked of her private life. She owned a small farm in Kent which is 'ideal for an actress'. Edith is an actress in the sense of 'theatre artisan', but she remains untouched by the 'stagey' stigma that the word has come to acquire. 'Do you work on the farm?' I asked incredulously. 'I do a bit of haymaking, and chopping wood.' But as Edith said this she looked shamefacedly childish, for she knew one knew she was really no good as a country girl. But Edith did get a 'kick' out of being in the country and using rustic similes, e.g. (back to the wig) 'There's a type of hair that is silky and you can tie it up to become a walnut — a veritable *walnut*!' About her husband dying very suddenly when she was acting in America she mused, 'How did I go through the return trip? My husband had been there on the dock to say goodbye to me. Six weeks later, here I was coming back after his death; there was my father to greet me. I said to myself, "You've got to do this alone. You've got to accustom yourself to being alone!" These solitary experiences are the things that count in life. When I was here in this apartment during the *blitzkrieg* I was all alone; I knew, of course, I could go out with other people, but I wanted to face up to it by myself. Now I'm continuously setting myself disciplinary tasks — going on long tours with a cast that is not particularly congenial — and making myself take it calmly. Then I do ENSA tours — very rough and uncomfortable. But these things take one out of one's safety rut and give one confidence to stand alone. I always say to be an actor one must know how to stand naked, physically and spiritually. Growing old is merely a question of gaining experience. What one has gone through is the interesting part of life.' Edith told me that she was not going out anywhere tonight but would wallow in being alone and think about the forthcoming trip to Gibraltar and her next part.

I went off to work on costume designs — bearing in mind that Mrs Hushabye would probably wear a dark wig.

Working with Edith Evans will be an interesting experience. However tiresome and full of hot air she may become, one must give her the respect that is due to someone who has succeeded in maintaining her position on the pinnacle by dint of continually renewing her attitude towards her art.

I left Brighton, where I was recuperating from a stone in the gall bladder, for one day in London to fit dresses for *Heartbreak* and to see Edith Evans about her bloody black wig. I arrived for the first stage rehearsal. Edith was in a great state of subdued, pent-up thrill at being, at last, able to get going on this new production. In her excitement at jumping the next hurdle, Edith had forgotten all about Gibraltar, from whence she has just returned after appearing in a revue for the troops.

It was tremendously interesting to watch her looks of complete concentration when, wearing spectacles and appearing particularly plain, she listened to the director's instructions while keeping an eye on Isobel Jeans (who plays the sister) rehearsing by herself in a corner. (Isobel never relaxes — she is like a peahen, with the over-nervousness of a greyhound.)

John Burrell, the director, conducted the rehearsal for five hours on end. Burrell seems very sure of getting the effects he wishes, but today it seemed to me that the leading actors are such definite personalities that they were merely playing themselves. Maybe their characterizations will appear later. Only the minor actors seemed to become characters and not just personalities.

Edith said that a few of the things she was doing were right — that, by degrees, Hesione was appearing, but that she did not realize that she was going to be at all like this: the character was beginning to appear so strongly that Hesione already got up and did something for which Edith was not ready. 'Don't do that yet! I find Hesione doing all sorts of unexpected things — some are right, some are not.' Yet to me, a mere onlooker, it seemed as if Edith was just exploiting her own ego. Edith, as if reading my thoughts, said, 'We can't get rid of our own egos — they have to be dragged along with us wherever we go.'

By the end of the afternoon, the other actors were a bit dishevelled as, walking like sore bears in their solitary purgatories, they tried to memorize their lines. But Edith was as fresh as a dewdrop and eager, when the rehearsal was over, to go off to have her wig fitted. 'Aren't you tired, Edith?' 'Not a bit of it. If I'm interested I can continue for forty-eight hours without a nap!'

At Nathans, Edith's gluttony for acting asserted itself while waiting for samples of hair to be brought. She spied some 1840-60 fashion plates and sang mellifluously, 'I'd like to appear in a play in which I could wear a bonnet with plenty of ruchings.' Later, when Dolly, the wigmaker, fitted a *toile* on her head and she looked quite bald, Edith said, 'This is how I'd like to appear sometimes, looking like a Flemish Madonna. When I went to the Dutch exhibition my friends said, "These are all you — bald — with gooseberry eyes."'

At last a few wisps of black hair were produced. Edith held these up against her forehead and cheek. The effect of light on her was most harsh and unbecoming. Her eyes suddenly appeared like ping-pong balls covered with lids of chicken flesh, and one eye seemed so much lower in her face than the other. Even her complexion seemed to be coarse, with wide pores, and with alternately shiny or dry-flaked patches. Any other woman would have been horrified to see the effect in the mirror, but no — Edith was delighted. '*Ra-ther* nice!' she drawled. 'I can see that it's very becoming to my skin...!'

Edith absorbs herself entirely in her work. She could not have any other interest while rehearsing a part. To Dolly and Gus, she said, 'I'd like to fit this wig twenty times; call on me anytime you want me to come in. I'd love to work hard on it.' To me she said, 'How is it that you manage to keep your unbruised, shrewd point of view when you see so many people? You manage society so well — how is it? I'm scared of it. Those people all wanted to take me up — George Moore and the lot, but I couldn't say witty things, I couldn't compete. I became breathless and exhausted. I had to preserve myself. But you manage to see people as if for the first time. I can't do that — I can only do that with a part; I can recognize a part for the first time.'

With so much exuberance and warmth lavished on her acting, I wonder if Edith has affection for humanity or love for friends?

After an absence of a few days, I returned again to London to find that rehearsals had progressed at an astonishing pace. Already most of the characters had learnt their lines — not so Edith, who explained to the director, 'I don't want you to think I'm being behindhand in not giving up the book, I work like that — I always find I can develop my part more when I'm not fussing to find the words. I don't want you to think I don't pay any attention to this when I go home in the evenings. But I never give up my book for two weeks — it's the way I work. I'll know my part over the week-end.'

The cast, having been thrilled at the idea of playing with Edith, now began to realize the penalties of being with a great actress. Her avidity and egomania are certainly as pronounced as in most stage performers. At rehearsal she is businesslike, but selfish to the degree that even when it is reasonable to hold up proceedings to discuss her own problems for a certain length of time, she hammers on with such insistency that she succeeds in falling foul of the director. At one point she attempted to usurp a good position on a sofa stage centre. 'It's just to suggest the purely domestic thing of the married couple drifting together when anything unusual happens. Hector is sitting there — the burglar appears — wouldn't it be right that I should drift towards him and sit down holding him by the arm?' It takes a lot of strength for John Burrell to say, 'No, Edith,' in the way that he does. Edith counters: 'I stand very still for a great length of time. It doesn't look dead, does it?' When at the end of one scene Edith asked, 'Can't Ellie give me a look at that point?' John Burrell said, 'No, I don't think so, Edith.' A long discussion that was more in the nature of a war of attrition followed. Edith became very pink about the cheeks. She pursed her lips, put her tongue at one side of her mouth and held her arms akimbo with one heel dug into the ground. 'You must realize Hesione is a very difficult part — some of it almost as difficult as Shakespeare. Hesione moves from every emotion and, in many instances, with only one line to do it in. It helps me if Ellie looks at me. It makes it easier for me to weep.' 'No, Edith, it's the thought that makes you weep, not the look. Anyhow, try it again with the look.'

Edith, with a black mushroom on her head (a property wig) and a mink coat, fumed and emoted with added zest to show how much better she could act with Ellie's look. 'Well, Ellie, is that all right for you to give the look?' 'Yes,' said Deborah Kerr as Ellie. 'All right — keep it,' said John Burrell, and added, 'You're right, Edith — I'm sorry.' But that was not the end of it for Edith, who went on to the others in the cast in the same strain. 'I mean, I *know* what I can do! If they don't *like* what I do then they must get someone else. But I *do* know my job!' And, my God, she does!

The business-like way in which the rehearsals have been conducted is a great eye-opener to me. I feel, at this moment, though, that Edith is not yet the sensation she is meant to be and has not done anything remarkable in my hearing. Isobel Jeans, however, comes through with glittering colours. Isobel gives a brittle part tremendous sympathy. She transcends Lady Utterward's stupidity, her fecklessness, and sometimes touches the heart-strings. Edith takes her revenge on Isobel when she puts her down in a chair by practically manhandling her. Edith was told many times to do the scene more quietly — yet each time she threw gasping Isobel back with renewed venom.

For the past week I have spent a few hours each day watching the rehearsals. Sometimes the actors have been perfecting little scenes, in others just running through their parts with a parrotlike lack of emotion. Edith has succeeded with a dramatic last-minute sprint and comes in a good length in front of Isobel, who was winning all the earlier laps.

Isobel Jeans had a good training with the Phoenix Society in classical plays, but this is about the first time she has ever been in a modern play of first-class quality. Lady Utterward gives her a lift right out of the rather humdrum drawing-room comedies she has lately been associated with. When Edith heard her give an extraordinarily effective first reading Edith cocked an eye at her with intense curiosity and said, 'I think she's going to be admirable.' But Jeans suddenly discovered her part was unsympathetic and for several days went to pieces. Her distress reflected itself at the costume fittings. Although I know her clothes are going to be spiffing, Isobel became fretful and difficult. She looked in the glass with wrinkled face and said, 'What I mean is ...' but the inarticulate sounds that followed were unintelligible because Isobel is not pastmistress at completing sentences and cannot decide what specifically is distressing her.

When I asked her which costumes had pleased her during her stage career she seemed dissatisfied with the lot. 'But surely those remarkable Empire costumes designed by Aubrey Hammond in *The Man With a Load of Mischief*?' 'Nahir — nehir,' and biting her finger, and staring wildly at the floor, she threw away the remark, 'He could have done much better!'

The director remained calm and unruffled in the face of a nonstop barrage of requests from a lot of egomaniacs. Each member of the cast seems to be working only to his or her own end. One rather obscure actor, when ticked off for doing something wrong, had to put up an argument, palpable to the others for its lack of conviction, to prove why he thought he had done right in doing wrong. When asked why he seemed to interrupt continuously a speech of Isobel's, Isobel came forward whimpering and whining — 'Yairs, yairs, it's very difficult. I want a clear run on the lines — really. D'yer know — yairs — yairs.' She would like the entire play to be a clear run through on her lines. Later, she tried to explain, 'I think you'll find it all right when I've got the dresses, the dress on — there's a lot to it!'

Edith buttonholed me. 'Don't let anyone ruin my champagne satin. Remember, my champagne satin.'

I had bought a suitable dressing-gown from Austin Reed for Roberts, who takes the part of a poor little fellow. At the dress parade he held up the dressing-gown and shielding his eyes from the footlights called across to us, 'It's a bit meagre, isn't it?'

But to revert to Edith. She is a flirt and she is easily flattered; after a long rehearsal Robert Donat twitted her with a leer, 'Let's stay behind and rehearse alone together.' She ogled back with a coy wink, 'I'm too tired today!' But she was not too tired. She is never tired; as she said, 'No one rehearses enough for me!' During the lunch interval she remains on the stage with perhaps a thermos and a Marie biscuit to go over and over her scenes. She is never tired of acting: she acts all her living hours. She says, 'I would rehearse until I drop.'

It is fascinating to see her making little discoveries in her part and bringing the character to life, and she is astute at analysing her powers. She holds forth to the boredom of the rest of the cast about why she would like to do this and that. 'I can't falsify. My inside will become more flexible, and I'll be able to make my voice stronger later. I shan't strain. It wouldn't do to strain. You wouldn't like it, and I couldn't do it.'

I notice that she watches the director all the time he is giving the others their notes. She breathes in deep the foetid air of the theatre and it is balm to her; when others are exhausted and have aged ten years in a day, Edith, in the harsh overhead light, blossoms like a rose and begins to become a beauty.

It has been impossible to convince Edith that she should not wear black hair: yet black is too hardening to her contours. But she plonks on the thing as if it were a loaf or a hat. Then her eyebrows go up, her mouth stretches in a wide grin, 'Look, it's lovely. Look, I can wear it! I told you so — didn't I? Look, it's right with my skin!' What can one say?

Two days later I found Edith with a most extraordinary object on her head — a black, wiry mass of the stuff one finds in an Edwardian sofa. The following is the history of what had happened: Dolly and Gus had succeeded in approximating a beautiful Japanese lady's wig. It was composed of strands of silken hair set in a mould of shiny perfection. Edith was delighted with it but had wished 'to get intimate with the wig'. So she took it back to Albany, back-combed it, re-arranged it, had her dinner in it, rehearsed to herself in the glass in it, had slept in it, and quickly given it a little 'attention' before returning to the theatre in it.

Everyone but Edith was aghast: everyone agreed that another wig must forthwith be made. Admittedly not quite so black this time, but still giving the effect of darkness, not a Japanese wig either, but still not the interior of an old sofa! It was only when, after the dress rehearsal, Binkie told Edith that she looked sinister with dark hair and couldn't she envisage herself as a redhead, that she became upset. Edith looked tragically into the mirror and said, 'I have so many disadvantages to overcome — perhaps I'd better retire to my farm!' Nevertheless, next day her self-opinion was in no way dashed, and she was convinced again that another dark wig made of finer hair would be wonderful.

During the 'try-out' in the provinces I knew that certain alterations must still be made to Edith's appearance. I suffered at the thought of approaching her, for I must be firm yet must not be unkind to someone so vulnerable. Perhaps I was not as tactful as I should have been for Edith complained to each member of the cast, 'It's very difficult for me, you see — I'm quite happy about myself, and Johnnie (the director) is quite content.' But I knew that I must persist, and I knew how much these little details would make for improvement. Oh, dear! Edith had started to pout, fume, puff out her cheeks and blush down her neck. When eventually the alterations were made she said, 'Now I don't want to hear any more or I shall cry.'

Later. The play has been running for three weeks now. I have been away a lot and have had little news as to how it goes. However, Diana Cooper is not the only one who does not like it. Perhaps Diana is too logical. 'Is it a real air raid? If not, what's it symbolic of? If it *is*, why haven't they spoken of the war at all?' (I find it Shaw's only poetical play, and the last act is like a twilight painting by le Sidaner.) Many people do not like Edith in it. They loathe her black wig, and find her sing-song inflections exasperating, but to me she is beautiful, magnetic and utterly spell-binding.

I rang up Edith to hear how she was getting along; it seemed that a sixteen-year-old girl, very intelligent and gay, was speaking to me, someone with all the airs and graces of a beauty. 'Yaais — yais (tentatively). Yais, I'm very happy about it. No one knows anything, of course, but we *think* we may play for a nice long time. It's a lovely play.' 'Were the critics good about it?' I asked. 'Oh, I think so. Johnnie (Burrell) says the weeklies are good — but then I only see those papers that I get. I hate reading about myself. If they're unkind you suffer so terribly, and you can't alter your performance straight off like that. It's very unsettling.' 'But don't you have a Press clipping agency?' I asked. 'Oh no. What's the use? All these little green things arriving — I've not got room for them. No — no, I've given them up long ago, but if you could get the *Vogue* people to send me a copy with the pictures of me you took I'd like to see it — I'd give it back — but otherwise I don't like to see about myself in the papers.'

Edith has done what she knows is her best, and to her the rest — the lobbying, the gossip, the adulation, even the audience — is unimportant. She retains a remarkable purity of spirit and an innocence that is most impressive.

August, Ashcombe

For several days now I have been clearing out cupboards and boxes and drawers, thereby studying my past. There are so many albums, such an accumulation of papers, letters, and all the old oddments that for years I have refused to throw away: even the old cheque foils, income tax reports, and letters from my father to Miss Joseph[34] about my accounts when I was in America. Looking through this old rubbish I have a terrible feeling of despair. Most of my life, since I grew up and became independent, has been one long hectic rush. I have never put the date at the top of my scribbled letters, the writing is almost illegible — and it is typical that the years should have gone by in a dateless void of rush — people — acquaintances — parties — nonsenses. If the war has done anything it may have had a calming effect on me. Let's pray it has! so that when all this horror is over I may relish a certain leisure. T. S. Eliot said, 'A vacant mind is the greatest treasure of all.' Even this sorting and rummaging is part of a restlessness. I should be settling down to read a book.

'A NEAR THING'

---

[34] A former secretary and friend.

London — December

The M. of I. boys have at last decided that they want me to do the same job for them in the Far East as I did in the Near East. My first stop is to be India and they want me there quickly.

But I have discovered that to fly is not always the quickest means of travel. For the past arctic two weeks — the entire country under snow and ice — air activity in England has been at a complete standstill. The weather experts have watched anxiously the slow movement of a depression; but several times have, at the thirteenth hour, cancelled all departures. The order to 'go' came unexpectedly. 'They've got you on another route. You'll avoid Lagos and fly direct to Delhi on a Service transport plane.'

I had been having qualms about my trip, and become quite self-conscious when speaking to certain friends as if, perhaps, for the last time. Deborah Kerr, backstage at *Heartbreak House* had said, 'Cheerio,' and 'if I don't see you again'. I had felt embarrassed for her sake. The night before leaving I was not able to sleep, and for hours wondered about my possible early demise, and whether or not I should quickly make some sort of a will. I didn't.

Nancy was up at dawn to help me with last-minute packing, while I went upstairs to say good-bye to my mother who was in bed suffering from a bad cold. She was tearful and anxious. Somehow I could not even blurt out the words 'good-bye', and left the bedroom abruptly. I stood outside on the dark staircase with my head in my hands. It was some time before I could 'pull myself together' enough to join the others and make a robust adieu.

In the early morning Paddington Station was dark, misty and bitterly cold. A group of army officers, some with red tabs, and a posse of rather seedy-looking civilians waited at the barrier to be conducted to the 'reserved' compartment. Long lingering farewells are always lowering to the spirit and this morning's delays were exasperating. When, at last, the unpunctual train left I sank back with a great relief to sleep. There was no heating in the carriage and from now on I was almost perpetually cold.

At our secret destination we were met by RAF officers who doubted if the present North Pole conditions would make flying possible. We were taken to an anonymous mess and awaited further instructions. After hanging about all day in this frigid hut, we were told 'no flying tonight'.

Rather than congeal in the lodgings provided by the RAF, I had the idea of telephoning Gerald Berners to invite myself to spend the night at near-by Faringdon. Never has a welcome been more heart-warming. And never before had his house appeared more comfortable and luxurious. However, the war has changed Gerald into an old man. Admittedly he is happier now than he was, but the shock at first upset his nerves so badly that he had positive plans for suicide. Luckily, someone took him to live at Oxford at St Giles where he was successfully psycho-analysed. By degrees he recovered sufficiently to make new friends, Clarissa Churchill, the David Cecils, Maurice Bowra and the Harrods, and for therapy he has worked hard card-indexing for Blood Transfusion.

Clarissa was amazed when I told her of Gerald the erstwhile eccentric firebrand. He is now no longer interested in painting or greedy for good food or amused by the jokes that were once important to him. Here, at Faringdon, he has built himself an all-weatherproof, watertight, anti-worry tower, and forgets the war by working on his novels and autobiography. Sitting with legs wide apart, his bowed head encased in a scarlet knitted pixie cap, Gerald murmured, 'I don't feel a bit older than ever I was. I get tired, but I've been tired for a long time now and I like resting and sleeping. It's such a relief when sex is put aside, it makes one so unhappy in ratio to the happiness it affords. And it's so delightful to remember it all in retrospect. When I'm writing my memoirs I can remember everything of that nature so vividly that it gives me all the pleasure I had, without any of the awful tugging at the heart. When I see people going about tearing out their hair I feel, "Thank God I'm spared that anymore." I never feel I'm out of touch with younger people, or that they are younger than me. But I agree with Byron's Claire Clairmont who wrote, "There's one thing to be thankful for — I shall never be young again.'"

After dinner Gerald played classical music on his hand-made super gramophone, and on going up to my linen sheets I realized how fortunate I was to have had this night's escape, instead of...

It was a bright clear day when I left Faringdon early next morning. Excellent flying conditions. Later we climbed into a Dakota that was stripped of all but the minimum equipment. One side of the fuselage was piled with our luggage and miscellaneous cargo — huge rubber tyres for aeroplanes, crates, and 'secret' packages. The pilot of the aircraft was a young fair-haired Canadian of special beauty, with high cheekbones, lean, lithe figure and a stance like a gorilla. He had pale-almond eyes and a generous mouth continuously twisted in a smile. He piloted us to our takeoff point, and two hours later landed us at Land's End. Here on the icy snows, dozens of transport aircraft were lined up, having been stranded here for many days thanks to the worst weather for years.

We were all herded into an already overcrowded vast Nissen hut in which the temperature, in spite of two very small stove-fires at each end, was below freezing point. By now it was 4 o'clock in the afternoon. We were told that by midnight we would know if we were to 'take-off' or not. When I saw Smuts waiting amongst us I realized the seriousness of the delay. Smuts was savouring a mug of tea and looked out at the last rays of a watery winter sun. Some young Canadians maintained high spirits by ragging one another in rather coarse terms. One said to a lean and lily-like pilot, 'Phew! you are an anti-social louse. Why don't you take some Epsoms and clear yourself out or put a cork up your arse?' An elderly civilian, one of two tyre experts travelling for Firestone and Goodyear, described the night in the RAF lodgings, which I had missed, how his teeth had chattered all night long and that the sheets he slept in must previously have been used for wrapping ice.

Midnight. Our charming pilot came to doze by the edge of the weakly flickering fire. His friends continued to chaff him. He'd better fly off tonight, there was nowhere for him to sleep here, the mess was full up, there'd be no welcome for him in their room. 'Why, I know him — he shouts in his sleep and kicks and snores something awful.' The Canadian pilot smiled, 'I don't like to hear these things you're saying about me.'

At 1 o'clock in the morning we were given breakfast, a real egg and bacon too, and coffee, but the cold of the dining hut, on the edge of the cliffs, in the coldest night of the year, was even greater than in the Nissen hut mess. A pilot who was travelling with us as passenger said, 'You're cold now? You'll not know yourself when we've been flying a bit 20,000 feet up. Oh boy, you'll be conscious only of your extremities.' A grey-haired wing commander, deaf and rugged — Aubrey Smith would play his part in films — asked for some more bread. 'I want to toast it,' he explained to the numbed but still flirtatious WAAF waitress. 'I'll get you some done by electricity.' 'No, I'd

rather do it here over the stove — it'll make my fingers warm.'
'I wish someone'd toast me,' said the WAAF. Later she
brought some bits of bread, blackened with soot and smoke.

The news went round that Smuts had taken off. Every
chance of our leaving now — in a couple more hours.
Somehow or other the time passed. Zero hour: we were taken
out into the sharp blackness of the night and flare-lighted into
a lorry. First stop a farm building where, in flickering lamplight,
we were trussed up in boiler suits with zips — one of my zips
was missing — Mae Wests and harness. These clothes added
bulk without warmth and made one feel claustrophobic. When
we got back into the Black Maria for our last journey to the
attendant aircraft I noticed we all looked so grim and
frightened that I drew up the corners of my mouth into a
stylized smile.

Back in the Dakota that was to fly us through the night on
our first stop to Gibraltar, I found myself sitting almost at the
end of the fuselage, down by the door. As I leant against the
seat there was a loud crack and it fell back lopsidedly. The
sergeant steward and one of the tyre experts helped by flashing
his torch and they both tried to get the seat leg back into its
socket. No, no luck. 'Once we're airborne the seat will right
itself,' said the steward optimistically. The dim lights were put
out and we sat in Stygian blackness. It was the very positive
blackness of patent leather without the highlights.

The door was locked; we listened to the roar of the engines;
we trundled forward, bouncing along on the uneven icy
ground.

The agony of terror that followed, though it lasted only a few
minutes, seemed an eternity. Already, at the start of the run, I
bowed my head in my hands and prayed very hard because I
was so frightened. I prayed that if I survived this ordeal my life

might be simplified, that I should resist the distractions of so many unimportant things. We were racing furiously towards the sea, then the aircraft lurched lopsidedly into the air, and banged and rattled its occupants like dice in a box. I heard a man behind me say very quietly, 'Yes that's it — now we're for it.' My terror became intense. My eyes were shut and I tried not to take cognizance of anything outside my own head. For somehow I felt that these were my last seconds of this life, and I decided that I must spend them contemplating pleasant things.

All sorts of unexpected and forgotten pictures raced through my mind, like slides on a cinematograph sheet. I saw my family when I was a child. I sensed again the excitement of getting a present at Christmas of a picture postcard of Lily Elsie in a headdress she wore in *The Waltz Dream*. I saw a young preparatory schoolboy, Geoghegan, waiting for me to finish my school tea — as was his custom, under an arcade of chestnut trees outside the playground of my Heath Mount school. He wanted to give me a lift home on the step of his bicycle. I saw and savoured the pleasant tweedy aroma of Peter — chasing the dogs when our friendship was at its most halcyon. I had idyllic memories of the first time I fell in love, and of the soft welcoming look of Ashcombe, my house, in the height of a summer. I remembered the gaiety of certain New York winters and again could smell the hotel rooms I once occupied. I had visions of the silver-grey white trees against the blue skies of the Piero della Francesca frescoes at Arezzo. These appeared particularly Elysian and the sky such a heavenly blue that I tried to make myself visualize uglier things. This was all too pleasant; beauty doesn't consist only of pleasure. But I couldn't think of anything that was not ecstatic. My ideas worked up to a crescendo of clear, vivid thought. I was in a delirium of pleasure and terror when crash! Oh how I prayed, Oh God, oh God, oh God! I knew my worst fears had come true, that my nightmares had turned to reality. I found myself lying on a mound of parachute harness — half-way down the fuselage. I opened my eyes. Through the crack of the door leading into the cockpit I saw flashes of light. The engines were still roaring. Then the flames were everywhere. A huge tongue of blue darted down the length of the cabin. The cockpit was now an orange glow. Outside the night was lit by enormous different coloured fires. In the aircraft were patches of flame at odd places, and a bright incandescent fire centred in the extreme rear.

So this was the end. So this was Death. Any second now I should know the unknown. Meanwhile I analysed quite calmly the various stages through which I passed. No use fighting, there was nothing to be done about it. The flames approached. Everyone was very quiet in the aircraft; and even now they behaved with the polite reserve of Englishmen. I looked up to see the whole fuselage illuminated by dense, suffocating, orange smoke through which the silhouetted figures of the aircrew in their cumbersome divers' suits ran past me, groping in the fog of burning aluminium. Still no one spoke. I lay holding on to my head thinking that as soon as the flames reached us there would be panic and fighting and I should be trampled underfoot. And why not? This was it. I had accepted the worst. Suddenly someone shouted, 'Open that bloody door.' I could see various passengers hopefully and pathetically groping for an exit. The tyre expert had the presence of mind to turn his torch on the latch of the door. Its beam seemed very white in the glow of the fires. Then I understood, by some queer reflex, that the door was open. 'So they are jumping for it,' I thought, 'rather than be burnt. How high are we? Well, death is one stage farther away this way ... so here goes!' I was the last to leave the aircraft. I crawled along the floor backwards and tipped myself out head first into the cold, black night. A short drop and I was astonished to find myself, with a minor bump on the head, upside down in a grassy field covered with hoar frost and patched with snow. The air struck me as bitterly cold. Around and above me were flames.

'Get up and run,' someone shouted. 'The aircraft may explode.' In spite of a tremendous weakness in the knees, and the weight of my cumbrous harness, I ran, as we all ran, falling and getting up again and running, turning at last to watch the destruction of the plane from the vantage point of safety.

The broken monster lay spurting forth fire. Deep orange and black smoke coiled upwards in a great tower. The cockpit was diamond bright, the burning edges of the wings suggested flare paths on an aerodrome or gala illuminations on a pre-war pier. Our lungs filled with fumes, we coughed as we watched. It surprised us to find how little shocked we were. Someone said the shock would come later. It did. Meanwhile we gazed at the burning dragon as it vomited forth different coloured flames, and spat forth its distress signals of pink, mauve and golden rockets. We discussed our miraculous escape. We had crash-landed; another fifty yards and we would have plunged into the sea. But I couldn't feel proud of the negative way I had behaved: just to lie and accept death was of little help to the others, whereas the passenger pilot, who had known how to pull up an emergency level and to jettison the locked door, had saved all our lives. The tyre man with the torch had helped too.

'Are you all right?' 'Are we all here?' The airfield was dotted with theatrically-lit figures. 'The pilot didn't get away,' remarked the navigator. Fumes brought tears to our eyes as we looked at the funeral pyre of the charming young Canadian.

The night wind was icy and cut the scalp like a knife. Eventually the ambulance came up. And then, thank God, staggering out of the darkness, his neck and forehead bleeding, his face green, appeared the pilot. 'Good show,' the others congratulated him. 'No, no, it wasn't a good show,' he whimpered. He minded only about his responsibility to others. He was taken away in the ambulance suffering, we discovered later, from serious internal injuries: he had a broken arm and ribs; a kidney had to be removed — the stick had gone through his stomach.

Accepting the fact that we were safe, each of us now remembered his particular treasures as they burned before our eyes. 'There goes all I possess in the world.' 'I've nothing but what I stand up in,' the passenger pilot said. 'Most of all I mind losing the photographs of my child. They can't ever be replaced, they were taken of him at various stages ever since he was born.'

The tyre man said, 'All my papers have gone — the result of weeks of meetings.' Old Walsh, the RAF courier, added, 'But I've saved my bag all right.' While the others had been fighting to get the door open, he had been throwing baggage about to get at his precious burden. In the lorry, jogging on our way to hospital, someone congratulated him. 'What I want to know is, will they give us another breakfast. I'd go through that again any time so long as they allow us another egg.'

In the hospital we were given tea. Those with burnt hands were treated, and I saw the pilot lying like a corpse between blankets. Most of us looked grey and drawn: our clothes still smelt of the fumes. The navigator and second pilot (who turned out to be the boy who took me on my first night-flight when I was working on my RAF book) did all they could for our comfort. The atmosphere suddenly became very light, everyone making jokes.

Once more into a black hearse-lorry and, once more, back to the frigidaire of the Nissen mess. Once more a cup of sweet tea. Then bed.

I was lucky enough to be given a room to myself as I was very restless, writing notes and going continuously to the loo. I kept waking to horror pictures of what might have happened if I had fastened my faulty belt and hadn't been able to get out of it. If — if — After a few hours, we were called. I could either take a midday train back to London to re-equip, or there was a transport plane going in an hour. I knew if I didn't get into that aircraft I never would fly again.

At another breakfast I sat next to the controller who had watched our crash from his tower. He did not know what happened: maybe icing of one engine. He saw the Dakota give a swerve to the left, but he thought the effect might be caused by an irregularity in the glass window. By the time our aircraft was visible past the wooden strut of his window he could see there would be a crash, and he'd already telephoned to the MO before he had seen the flames. We had left the ground, and the undercarriage had been raised, when the trouble had started and we pancaked. Everyone in the mess took the whole matter excessively lightly, but, at moments, I found myself turning my head away to shake out a tear.

The flight up to London was no pleasure. Again I was terrified of the take-off, but slightly reassured by the sergeant who accompanied us. 'Oh, you were in that show last night? Well a thing like that doesn't happen once in a million times.' 'But why are we bumping about so much?' I asked. It helped to put my anxiety into words. The sergeant explained, 'We're very likely coming through some cross winds — and in any case it's pretty bumpy country we're passing over; on the other hand, it may be just that the pilots are having a friendly argument at the controls.'

When I got home Margaret, the maid, answered the door and raised her hands in horror at the refugee in flying kit who confronted her. My mother looked at me as if I were a ghost. Then I broke down. I blubbed and quivered, snivelled, and behaved in an uncontrollable way until my mother broke down too. This steadied me.

For the next days I was treated like an invalid and lay in bed with hot water-bottles and opiates. The effects of shock asserted themselves in some strange forms: I suffered from acute indigestion, a lassitude that went to the knees, and my temper was foul.

Francis of the Ministry of Information said that as soon as I had re-equipped myself I should set off again. On each buying expedition (for I had lost everything except my camera and films which had gone before me) I discovered that shopping among wartime merchandise was no pleasure. At Selfridge's I had a row with three officious people in the 'Men's Wear' department, and once, the general tone of regimentation being so rigid, I had a brainstorm on a bus. In my debilitated condition London at this dark time of the year looked greyer and drearier than ever.

When I set off again, in decent flying weather, it was with none of the qualms and anxieties that we had all subconsciously felt before.

Part X: India and Burma, 1943-4

December 25th, Delhi

The bearer, white-turbaned and bare-footed, pulls back the curtains to let in a blaze of sun. Outside, the fountains are playing, the birds are shrieking. Cascades of stocks, carnations and petunias hang over the edges of ornamental pools. Someone is practising on a bugle, and sentries clear their throats with resounding rasps to spit, then stamp their bulbous boots on the gravel. A bearer, in scarlet tunic, comes in, salaams and gives me a parcel tied with ribbon. Another servant, in an enormous cheese-cloth puggaree, brings in a necktie wrapped in coloured paper. It is Christmas Day in Viceroy's house...

After the black drabness of bomb-damaged South Kensington in the depths of the fifth war winter, the sun, glitter, colour and *bhari tamasha* (splendour) of imperial Delhi seem to belong altogether to another world.

These first days in Delhi have been spent wandering down the long corridors of the Secretariat. Arrangements are being made for me to go to the Burma front, to the North-West Frontier, to Madras, to Kochin. But each day brings some alteration of plans, some delay or disappointment. 'But, old boy, you can't expect anything to be done overnight. It all takes time. You should have warned us before. You see, *your* trouble is, old man, that you come under so many different headings! You see, there's HQ India Command (that's us): there's the Government of India, the Far Eastern Bureau, the Ministry of Broadcasting and Information — there's ... but I'll take you to Brigadier Oldfield of SEAC — he'll help you.'

It was difficult to hear quite what was happening in this crowded small office. On the telephone Major Arnold was giving someone hell for spelling air marshal with two l's, while from outside came a fearsome noise as of souls in torment — a dozen natives, hampered in their task by their draperies, were trying to lift a safe. Unperturbed, Brigadier Oldfield planned an itinerary for me on a map. 'Then you go to Cox's Bazaar — or Bawli Bazaar — get a plane at Ramu for Chittagong — on to Camilla. Let me explain,' he pointed, 'this is the front here — we're moving towards Maungdaw.'

I was allowed into the War Room of South East Asia Command. The chiefs of all departments, American and English, 'breezed in' for what is known as 'early morning prayers' (a study of the latest maps, the day's reports and a short lecture given by half a dozen specialists). The Supreme Commander, Admiral Lord Louis Mountbatten, who had arrived in this theatre not long before, seemed as yet unaffected by the climate. 'We mustn't let it be a damper on effort — we've got to galvanize everyone, got to teach 'em to hustle,' he said — and he appeared to have impregnated his immediate entourage with his own robust brand of enthusiasm. In spite of all the difficulties he had already encountered, no glaze of disappointment was yet visible in his pale-blue eyes. They twinkled with the delight of a boy who had just been given a Meccano for Christmas — which incidentally, I believe, was just about all he had been given. For was it not decided, at the Tehran conference, that the Eastern theatre could not be a scene of great activity until the European holocaust was over?

In the War Room, sitting among admirals, air marshals and generals, the Supreme Commander interrupts the lecturer to ask pertinent questions. Mountbatten's ebullient: his toy seems to be working well. It is early morning still; the droning voice of the lecturer, in the otherwise silent room, acts as a soporific, and some of the older men have gone to sleep again.

While awaiting further instructions I have spent many days sightseeing as far away from Headquarters as possible. I have had the excitement of glimpsing my first wild parrot, monkey and elephant, and been stimulated by the brilliant, poisonous colours and ceaseless movement of Old Delhi.

In the Chadni Chowk (the Street of Moonlight), at one time considered the richest street in the world, now an alleyway full of bargains and trash, a begging Sardhou, naked and daubed with dung, an 'exponent of destitution', extends a withered arm. Other holy men have whitened faces; and there are boys with heavily kohl-painted eyes, their teeth, tongue and lips scarlet with betel nut. In the thoroughfares, pedestrians, bicycles, carts and sacred animals are wedged together in an almost inextricable confusion. Women resemble human beehives, entirely covered with whitish cloth except for the small letter-box slot through which their painted eyes peer. The shops, no more than window-recesses, offer spangled tassels, glittering phials of perfume, filigree jewels and vivid foodstuffs. A stall of vile-coloured drinks, in bottles stopped with fans of magenta paper, has been built around a sprawling peepul tree; its bark, painted emerald green, adds to the general gaudiness.

I visited Hindu forts of the eleventh and twelfth centuries, early Mohammedan cities, relics of the old cities of Delhi, and admired the fort of Tughlakabad.

From the parapet of the Tomb of Humayan, in the precious moments of twilight, one sees India at her best. Beyond the domes of mosques lies the lilac-coloured jungle. A crescent moon appears, in silvery contrast to the few wisps of golden cloud that are hurrying to be away before the sky becomes completely dark: cranes and other large birds are flying home and their wings make a breathless flapping noise; while parrots, very small, but tightly clustered, give the impression, as they pass, of a flying carpet. Jackals come out and slink off again, horrible hang-tail scavengers. A shepherd, rather sadly, is playing on his flute; and from the distance comes the echoing call to evening prayer.

This afternoon, all the way from old Delhi to the Safdar Jung Tomb beyond the new capital, the highways are filled with a great concourse of Mohammedans, taking part in the yearly festival of the Mohorrun. The crowds on foot, or brimming over the sides of bullock carts, are in their best clothes. In the West, people seem to choose colours for no particular reason. Here each colour appears to indicate an uncompromising personal preference. One woman is a walking rainbow, in a small crinoline of apricot yellow that fades to pink and mauve. A ragamuffin has staked all on a surprising dark-red coat of the finest quality velvet. A delicate-looking little boy wears, very correct and straight across his brow, a gold embroidered cap of deep grape colour. Down the streets, enormous edifices of coloured paper and tinsel are carried on poles: each flimsy temple represents a very definite taste; one, of orange and silver, seems to be conscious of its loveliness; another, of white and pale pastel green, is timid and tentative. Each, as it sways or jogs along under the dark trees, has also its own variety of rhythmic movement.

On a piece of high ground, parched and pale yellow, with gnarled trees and rocks, the procession halts. The paper edifices are savagely pulled to bits, soused with water, then buried in a muddy grave of wet sand on which are placed bouquets of magenta and white paper roses.

I am constantly amazed by the beauty of the people. Women's faces peep from tinselled draperies and remind me of doves; their bodies as compact and firm as bronze statuettes. Some of the men seemed almost alarmingly arrogant while others, oblivious of their haunted, haunting beauty, cannot understand why a European should wish to stare at their eyes, admire their lank hair — like the foliage of water plants — or the extraordinarily aristocratic distinction of their limbs and features. The squatting positions they assume, knees drawn up to the chin, as they rest or meditate, remind me of the bird world.

All the aids to escapism are available in Delhi. Little chance of a flying bomb; European food is plentiful; no shortage of manpower, servants galore, countless boys to preserve the tennis court and pick up the balls for the players, masses of old men to water the garden. There is little noise and the lack of traffic, except for the tinkles of bicycles at luncheon time, gives an air of leisure and prosperity.

Servants of different categories in scarlet, white and gold liveries stand like poppies behind chairs and tables, or appear in the distance of vast halls and marble enfilades looking as small as figures in a landscape.

Viceroy's house possesses its own doctor, dispensary, barber and tailor. One hundred and fifty gardeners maintain the borders and the preserves. Altogether 300 servants are employed within these regal confines, but when considering this number you must realize that, due to the caste system, at least six servants are needed to do the work undertaken in England today by one hard-working and aged peeress. Any Englishman, living however quietly and simply in India, will have at least six servants: a cook, a butler, a laundryman, a sweeper, a groom, a gardener, and perhaps one other. Even so, he will be poorly attended, his bungalow dirty, food badly cooked; each servant, willing to do only one specific job, is inadequately trained and incompetent. If an Englishman is to work hard in this devitalizing climate he must preserve his energy and leave his servants to do some of the physical work he would readily undertake in England.

The pretentious buildings of the Viceroy's house and the Secretariat are of no known style. Made of tongue-coloured stone, which retains the dry heat of the day and throws it out angrily at dusk, they appear, at the far end of a processional drive, like a city built for an exhibition. They were designed for peacetime activities: few modern cities could be less practical or convenient for a war headquarters than the present capital. However, in an attempt to alleviate the overcrowding of Delhi, Lord Wavell has partitioned off the house to accommodate several large, separate households. One of the four wings now comprises the office of the Private Secretary to the Viceroy and his staff: another wing is occupied by the Commander-in-Chief, Eastern Fleet, with sixty naval officers; in another wing are army officers. The Comptroller's house is taken over by officers of GHQ, while the Military Secretary's house is coverted into a leave camp, as is most of the Viceroy's house at Simla. The Viceroy and his family insist on leading as simple a life as is possible in these awe-inspiring surroundings.

The general effect of new Delhi is of a complacent yet callous centre, without gaiety or the strength of cruelty; a heartless, bloodless display-city, without a past or the necessary roots to develop a future.

THE BUNGALOW LUNCH

In her shrill, baby voice, Jean McFarlane, my pretty, freckled and carrot-topped secretary at the Secretariat, said, 'You must come out to see us. Mummie longs to meet you. Lunch or dinner any day is OK.' I had been somewhat taken aback, for petite Miss Jean had given me no indication that my working with her had in any way impinged on her consciousness. She is, to me, an enigma: a Scottish seventeen-year-old brought up in India where her father has lived since 1913. She seems to take for granted the sudden excitement of war in her midst. Nothing ruffles her. She works because she has to — without complaint or interest.

However, my acceptance of her invitation had sounded so breathlessly enthusiastic that I am sure that, each day I postponed the *sortie*, she felt more and more sorry for me. Yet a whole week went by while I complained to her that, unfortunately, I had to go elsewhere for some awful VIP treatment of one sort or another. However, I knew, sooner or later, I must accept her invitation; besides, it would be interesting to see the way the Anglo-Indians live. Although I was suffering from an appalling case of 'Delhi tummy', I crawled into a very small motor-car, together with guileless Miss McFarlane, her good-looking, stolid father, a squadron leader, and a curly-headed boy friend of Jean's. In the heat of midday we motored, and in a haze of stomach pains I watched avenues of pepper trees, scarlet-flowering trees, and huge banyans, under which lay sleeping farmers and donkeys.

The small, freshly-painted bungalow villa which the Scot had built for his wife and two daughters was cool and unbelievably clean. The furnishing gave no indication of the occupants' taste. The mahogany was spindly: there were many calendars of herbaceous borders or mountain cattle: the net curtains were embroidered with iris; cape gooseberries, in an art pot, stood in a modernistic-tiled chimney piece, and on a Victorian sofa lay an orange and black futuristic cushion.

Out of the kitchen wreathed in smiles, came twittering Mrs McFarlane. Her ordinary, everyday voice had acquired a singsong tone, but when she wished to be particularly polite any sentence became an aria. She warbled to her husband, 'Now, will you show Mr Beaton where to wash his hands?' And ('Please excuse this domestic talk, Mr Beaton,' she said in recitative), 'Jock dear, please don't use first the fresh towel put out for the visitor.' My entrails were rumbling and bubbling to such an extent that no doubt Mrs McFarlane had intuited my condition. Even so I wondered if even now it was not too late to rush to the loo. Oh, the relief, to be by oneself behind a locked door! When I emerged, Mrs McFarlane set upon me with concentrated enthusiasm. 'A thimbleful of sherry — no? A dash of gin and orange Kiaora? Didn't I even smoke a Wills' cigarette? Wouldn't I prefer a more comfortable chair?' While the mother was indulging in a sort of 'Jewel Song' of banalities, her pretty daughter was reduced to silence, boy friend ignored, and father merely became redundant. A native servant, wearing a badly-tied turban appeared limply in a frosted glass door. Lunch was served. In the centre of the dining table, on a piece of mirror, a few china animals were placed together with bits of cactus and rock plants. Mrs McFarlane's whispered instructions to the servant were so contradictory and confusing that the poor man appeared haunted; sweat poured from his turban down his neck and came out in blotches through his cotton clothing. 'Put it here — no, let it alone — where are the plates?' Then suddenly Mrs McFarlane hit a high C as she discovered the servant had forgotten to give us big knives for the meat! Followed a long explanation of how she had come in to see the man laying the table and she noticed he had not laid out the big knives. Where were they? They had been taken to the kitchen for an extra polish, and lo and behold, even now he had forgotten to bring them back. 'Oh dear! The local servants are a fatuous lot! They still drug hopelessly, or leave you, without a "by your leave", after they have been trained for two years.'

I started to interrogate Jock about HQ but Mrs McFarlane interrupted operatically, 'What are you doing, Jock dear?' Crossly, Jock replied, 'I'm filling my fountain pen.' 'What are you doing now, Jock darling? Don't do the toast twice, dear!' Crossly the husband snapped back, 'I'm not doing it twice, I'm doing it for the first time!' Sarcastic-like, Mrs McFarlane sang in return, 'Oh, I *beg your pardon*, dear!' The recitative of pecking and bickering throughout lunch was interspersed with codas of 'Would you like some salt?' 'A little more butter?' 'You, Mr Beaton, you're an artist, and you should know — what do you think of our hollyhocks?'

Jean and her boy friend ate in silence until Jean was sent to show me her framed photograph. 'Mr Beaton is an artist; he'll appreciate your camera portrait — it's got such a good bit of lighting on the face.' Jean came back. 'I can't find it, Mummie.' 'I know where it is — it's in that drawer full of what I call your rubbish papers.' While the mother was foraging, the daughter aired her tremendous sensibilities of sensuous delight. 'I *hate* chicken skin!' she said, 'but I love smoking a cigarette when I'm wet after bathing, but it must be a cork tip or I won't have it!' Mrs McFarlane returned. 'Now, you're an artist, and I know...'

Determined to exclude India from her life, Mrs McFarlane gave us a typically English lunch, complete with roast potatoes, vegetable marrow under a heavy coating of stickphast, and beetroot in strong vinegar. The 'never say die' quality of these Britishers prevents them from even giving in to 'Delhi tummy'. 'We never have it here, that's all! My husband is a bit more delicate, but I always say that it is thanks to the way I run my kitchen that we are never ill. Not that we take any special precautions either: it is just a question of keeping the place clean. We don't wash the salads in anything special, and we eat everything — lettuce and strawberries. The servants work in the mornings, and then go off for their meals, as, of course, they never touch our food and they never eat here; they'd be making such a mess and a noise if they started cooking all the weird sorts of stuff they like, that my home would become a shambles.'

'May I have another cup of coffee?' asked Jock. 'Yes, of course.' 'And may I have it, this time, with sugar in?' Mrs McFarlane, with a wry smile, examined the bottom of the cup. 'No, you won't find a trace of it there — it's no use looking.' 'Then why did you wait until you'd finished the cup? You wanted to be a martyr, I suppose.'

After lunch I was given Mr McFarlane's bedroom, a hermetically-sealed, cold room, in which to take my siesta. The mattress was surprisingly springy. I woke with a headache, caused, no doubt, by too much anti-fly flit in the air, but the headache was a welcome change from the gut pains which now had subsided. 'Jean and her boy friend are still out at the club, but you must have tea before you get back to HQ.' The cantatrice and her lanky, lugubrious husband now began the ritual of plugging in electric kettles and toasters. I felt too weak even to offer to help with all the gadgets. Gloomily I watched the elderly couple going round opening shutters, never quiet for a minute. These two have no pleasure in one another's company, and their nerves are frayed. 'When will you be back from Agra? Tomorrow? By lunchtime?' 'How can I possibly be back by lunchtime?' 'I only wanted to know. By dinner-time?' 'Possibly.' 'By 7 o'clock?' 'Well, not to put too fine a point on it...' 'That's quite all right so long as I know.'

Suddenly, girlish laughter breaks in on the drab household as the pretty daughter, with wet carrot mop, returns from bathing. Now one sees why Jean, as a secretary, shows little initiative and shuts herself from her surroundings. Her twittering stupidity protects her from the depression that must set in if she looked around her. Her boy friend had come to life, but, in the family atmosphere of afternoon tea, he soon subsided back to silence. By the time we went off to work again, past the avenues of trees, we had nothing left to say to one another.

Back at the Secretariat Jean McFarlane became, once more, little more than a cipher. I dictated, for the fourth time, a wretched piece about the problems of leave in India. Jean said she was beginning to know it by heart. When the day's work was over and I thanked her for the expedition to her home, she said, 'That's quite all right. Come whenever you want to. Just propose yourself.'

VICEROY'S SPEECH

Thursday, February 17th

Went with the Viceregal party to hear the Viceroy's speech to the Legislative Assembly. No definite change of policy, but the same terms offered with such conviction that it must have impressed all there that heard it. (The voice was less sad than usual.) This speech was full of noble sentiments and fine phrases. ('Quick as a sword is drawn from its sheath.') Some of it extremely firm, and when he was at his firmest he said, 'My experience as a soldier prompts me to say this.' The comparisons of England's troubles with India and England's troubles with Scotland, with the French Canadians were good, and it seemed to me typical of Wavell's honesty that he should then have touched on our difficulties in Ireland — which are not yet settled. 'I firmly believe,' he said, 'it is every man's intention in Britain that India should thrive — be an independent country.' There was not a crowded house: nor much of a demonstration, though it was generally considered the speech went well. (Congress members forbidden the Hall: they are apt to be noisy.) The pomp and procession was impressive. The Viceroy looked an old man — white, not grey, haired. The various Cabinet members were pointed out; some of them wearing very exaggerated turbans and puggarees looked like strange fish or butterflies.

Friday, February 18th

It takes a great person not to become affected by this regal ceremonial and continuous sychophantic deference. Lord Wavell has this quality of greatness: at worst he becomes bad-tempered, but this is understandable.

After lunch I had a walk round the garden with Wavell. He said the Japs had suddenly attacked in Burma in great force. He couldn't imagine how such numbers hadn't been detected in spite of the fact that the Japs move at night, lie in wait all day, and need practically no communications. (They carry food for eight days on them.) Wavell thought it would take some considerable time before we were able to clear up the trouble in this part.

At last I feel fairly at ease with Wavell, and he seemed quite interested to hear of my itinerary and plan of campaign.

NORTH-WEST FRONTIER

Sitting in a eucalyptus grove planted by Lutyens, suddenly I found myself surrounded by servants. Word had come that I was to leave forthwith for the North-West Frontier. We ran in and did rough packing: within three minutes I was ready for departure. I started to give out largess to each servant but, with typically childish amusement, they ran out with a large box.

'Servants' box! Servants' box!' They all took up the cry and, before my eyes, pushed the rupee notes into the slot. Everyone was laughing, and I drove away to a cry of 'Servants' box! Servants' box!'

I was the only passenger in the aircraft to Peshawar. We ran into heavy rainstorms, and vast areas of wheat fields below were flooded. The Indian pilot beckoned me to sit in the co-pilot's seat by him in the nose of the aircraft. The rain lashed against the triplex nose of the aircraft and filtered inside. Clouds enveloped us — we were flying blind, and soon the pilot shouted: 'We're going back. There are hills near Peshawar.' We returned to Lahore. As we landed the pilot said, 'It's not what you expect. The engines cut out while we were in the clouds, but I didn't say anything as I didn't want to alarm you.' The one daily train to Peshawar had left two minutes ago and no aircraft was to leave for a few days. Later a Dakota arriving from and returning to Chaklala was prepared to lift me back there — from where I'd be only half an hour away from Peshawar. The Dakota appeared with a large crew, but only one passenger: a little Red Cross nurse, recently recovered from amoebic dysentery. We were told the weather was bad, and it was. After a few preliminary bumps and bangs the livid-faced nurse ran over to me saying, 'Do you mind? I'm not generally frightened, but perhaps since my illness ...?' I sat holding her hands and patting her shoulders. We were both scared stiff. We watched for an eternity as we flew at only a few hundred feet over the hills on which it would be impossible to crash-land. Once or twice the door of the cockpit was opened for a young man who ran to look from our windows into the haze of cloud that forced us to fly lower and lower. My hands sweated on the hospital nurse's: there was nothing to do but watch and pray.

Suddenly the salt hills, cedar coloured, and looking like jags of flake chocolate, swam by at a great rate, and very much too near our aircraft, yet we felt brow-beaten by the heavy ceiling which made it impossible for us to fly any higher. At last the captain came through with a map and a bright face. 'We're all right now,' he told us. 'We're in the plains — a straight run of twenty minutes and we shall be at Chaklala.'

No one knew of my arrival — yet, in a few seconds of landing, with that extraordinary generosity shown to outsiders by the RAF, I found myself whisked off for a drink in the mess, and forthwith taken to the home of an unknown young man, who made himself responsible for my needs. He turned out of his own room so that I should spend the night in the more comfortable bed, and he dosed me with his precious whisky before motoring me, as a preliminary to showing me all the glitter of this famous station now used as a training ground for India Command, to Rawalpindi. Here he introduced me to his friends at the club, who gave me the best dinner I had eaten since the war began. The steak was as thick as a dictionary.

The town of Peshawar has been sacked so many times that nothing of architectural interest remains. But the streets are crowded with interesting types — Asiatics, Pathans and many

Persians. The shops are a series of enlarged peep-shows. The fruit- seller kneels on his prettily built structure of oranges, melons, magenta aubergines. The hatter squats among the bead and tinsel headdresses, designed especially for a bridegroom. The florist is busy stringing garlands of white, peppermint-pink and orange flowers for a woman's wrist and ankles or for a horse's head. Most mysterious of all is the 'flour-sifter' on his white stage; he wears a white smock and a white dunce's cap, his face, beard and eyelashes are powdered white, his sieves and strings are covered with a frosty film, and he stares back amusedly as we gaze at him as if he were from some other world. The monochrome grain shops look like models of mountain ranges. Some spectacular shops display jewellery, bed-posts like toys, Ali Baba pots of brass for incense or warm, pungent perfumes and highly-coloured stolen goods.

'This is a tough corner of the earth,' my escort explained, 'where no value is given to a man's life. You notice everyone carries a gun; robbery, hold-ups, murder and rape are not uncommon.' If the police should turn its back for ten minutes, this quarter, filled with a fermenting mass of the world's most dangerous characters, would break out in chaos. 'You never know when it will be necessary to turn on the tear gas.'

Alexander the Great and Timur the Tartar had chosen the Khyber Pass for their invasions of India; I felt nevertheless today that the Khyber belonged rather to Kipling than to any earlier period of history.

In the officers' mess, polished silver cups stand in rows against the dark oak panelling. Another round is ordered: 'Yes, we get beer from the factory at Pindi — or how about a cherry brandy?' A young subaltern comes in and lays his revolver on the table, by the reading lamp with the crimson silk shade.

'Heard about old Claude's near shave? His lamp shot to blazes! Great stuff — maybe the beginning of something.'

Life on the North-West Frontier has changed very little since the Victorian age, when warfare was so well-conducted as to seem comparatively civilized.

The Wazirs, subnormal mountaineers, are still a restless gang and remain the inspiration of a thousand mess-room stories. But a hundred years ago, this frontier possessed a romantic quality, which it has largely lost since the invention of more modern forms of frightfulness — the flame-throwing tank and the flying bomb. The Fort Shagai, housing the Second Kashmir Infantry, combined for me all the least attractive features of a soldier's life: early calls for parades on the asphalt yard, draughty bare rooms, hard gritty ugliness.

A battalion of the Seventh Rajput Regiment was starting off down the bare, slate-coloured hills, towards Afghanistan, on a tactical exercise in frontier warfare. Everywhere one was watched by pickets looking down from camouflaged pillboxes on the mountain heights. 'You must understand what a poor life these tribesmen lead. They see, next to them, the most fertile plains of all India, yielding four crops a year; they cannot help coveting such richness, and they make continuous short, sharp sorties to grab a bit of someone else's wealth. The hostile tribal territory here is always a problem; and the rugged terrain makes it impossible to winkle them out of their caves without an enormous expeditionary force.'

I have seen *Carmen* and *The Maid of the Mountains* on tour, and can recognize a third-rate chorus of operetta brigands. Here they were again — the wild Wazirs who, though not a menace, are nevertheless of a nuisance value: toothless, squinting, stunted, with inane grins, unkempt beards and dirty undergarments swathed round their shaggy heads. One wore a long green tweed overcoat of loud check with emerald celluloid buttons; another sported an old tail-coat.

On the peaks of these gaunt hills, white sheets placed as indications to aircraft and guards signalled from slope to slope. Tochi scouts, with the agility of goats, scaled in thirty-nine minutes a height that would take a white man two and a half hours to achieve.

'TAKING THE STICK'

Flying away, the only passenger in a small aircraft, I noticed that the little Indian pilot was trying very hard to unwind a wheel — something to do with pumping down the undercarriage when the automatic release goes wrong. It proved too stiff; try as he might, he could not get it down. We were flying over nasty, tooth-like rocks, and into large lumps of dirty cotton-wool cloud. The Indian, sweating as he struggled with the levers, then beckoned me to join him in the cockpit. I shook my head and winked — No, I had had enough of the cockpit: I would remain with my novel! The pilot continued to beckon; it was only after a considerable time that I understood that the invitation had now become an order. The pilot was signalling for me to sit by him, to 'take the stick'.

Suddenly, flying an aeroplane for the first time, I felt like Harold Lloyd. I held on to the wheel rather gingerly, not knowing how much leeway I could allow before the aircraft reacted violently. Like a monkey, the sweating pilot crawled to and fro, among the hundred gadgets on the dashboard and the floor. The engine responded to my very tentative suggestion to climb a little higher, and I found this effort a relief.

Just as I was contemplating his having to climb out on the wings, to tie something together with string, the pilot put up his thumb with a jerk: he had mended the aeroplane.

'May I go back to my novel?'

Thumb up again. When we circled over Lahore Air Station, however, it seemed the thumb-jerk had been premature. As we came in to land, and were just about to touch down, we shot up again high into the air. The undercarriage was not lowered. We 'stooged' around the airfield, while the pilot tried to unwind the undercarriage. He kept re-adjusting fuses; we circled many times, looking down wistfully at the strip below. The pilot took control again. Perhaps he had decided to 'do a pancake' without the landing gear? Here goes. In which direction would I be thrown? I adopted several suitable poses in which to receive the shock. We skimmed low, bumped, and were relieved to find the undercarriage was in position. Only the wing-flaps were not working, so that our speed was greater than usual, and when we hit ground we bounced high like a rubber ball — but at last the land lay motionless beneath us.

ASSAM, BURMA AND THE ARAKAN FRONT

We landed in a bowl scooped from the mountains of Imphal. The year is at its best; sun all day; cold at night; the cherry-trees in blossom, rhododendrons ablaze. Soon the vast tropical trees will be sprouting with orchids and the troops will pick the parasite blossoms and put them in their large brimmed hats.

My first impression would have been less idyllic had I arrived during the monsoon period. This continues for nearly two-thirds of the year. The troops must exist soaked to the skin for weeks on end in an almost solid tropical rain. There is no chance of drying their clothes. In this fetid atmosphere, to wear a macintosh is to sweat so much that soon you are wet through. Boots are never dry, so that your toes begin to rot. Supplies suffer; the coarse flour breeds bugs. Mud reaches up to the thighs. Everything grows mouldy; even the bamboo poles grow internal fungus, and the smell of decay is everywhere.

Living in small holes dug in the mountainsides, supplied by a narrow mule track which zigzags up and down the mountains for over 300 miles from the nearest supply base, transport becomes impossible and essential supplies have to be dropped by air. Yet, strange as it may seem, water is often short — the mountains are so steep that the rain shoots off the sides before it can be cupped — and washing is permitted only once in three days. The enormous trees, garlanded with festoons of moss, drip heavily, ceaselessly, for months on end. Mosquitoes thrive in the elephant grass; millions of leeches appear, wagging their heads from side to side. They are small until they have feasted on human blood. Then their bodies swell to the size of your thumb. The soldiers have learnt that they will drop off if touched with a lighted cigarette; but, if you try to pull at their greasy black skin, the head remains embedded in your body and the wound becomes septic.

Jungle warfare, consisting as it does of lonely treks and skirmishes — at the most, men go out in twos and threes — demands the highest degree of courage on the part of each individual. Most men prefer desert warfare, although here there is shade, the roots and growths are a salutary substitute for fresh vegetables and a palatable addition to iron rations, and occasionally there is wild game. But the feeling of loneliness is greater; groups seldom trespass on one another's terrain. There is reassurance to be gained from fighting in numbers. Each man knows that, after a terrifying game of blindman's buff played through the coarse undergrowth, any encounter may end with a clash of knives. No quarter is asked or given. Every moment of the day each man must be on the alert; for the Jap sniper may be hidden behind that distant cliff, or in the nearest tree. There is the continual strain of listening for the sound of a footfall. Even during their sleep most men keep one ear open for the sounds of the night. They develop a sixth sense, so that they can distinguish every animal step, the calls of the birds, the laughter of hyenas, the yells of jackals, the creak of bamboo, the snapping of a twig and the Aristophanic chorus of frogs and crickets. After a time, even the most robust may show signs of nervous stress. One man, hearing steps coming closer to his *basha*, ran out in the dark and bayoneted a bear.

We were awakened in the dark; shaving in a small basin in a cold semi-outdoor was depressing. We started off for Tiddim in a fifteen-hundredweight lorry. The hearty onslaught of the captain of our party, so early in the morning, was the hardest cross to bear: he whistled through his teeth in imitation of a cockney tram conductor, and shouted abuse in four-letter English words and in Urdu to fellow-travellers.

By degrees the sun had warmed the icy cold air; one side of the mountain became brilliant, the other half remaining in dark shadow. Then the sun sank behind the hills where the Japs were in occupation, and everything became pitch black. Still we motored along the small ridges, past perpendicular drops of 400 feet; sometimes a passing lorry scraped our mudguards.

Our truck bounded about in a cloud of dust thrown up by the convoy of trucks ahead. Tropical vegetation through which we passed was coated with salmon-pink dust, churned by ceaseless traffic. The bamboos, their fronds of dead branches looking like fishing-rods, rose in a perfect pure arc.

Our trucks are the least suitable vehicles for negotiating narrow ridges cut into the precipices of the mountainsides; but there was no jeep available. For hours we were tossed from one side to the other, thrown high in the air to land painfully on the little iron seat, or on the sharp edges of our baggage. We continued in semicircles up or down a mountainside, over a surface of dust and potholes until, like Hitler's, our captain's patience was at an end. He had taken on the Herculean job of steering this heavy lorry around hundreds of hairpin bends throughout the day. We barged, crashed, thudded, ricocheted on into the night. The mountains were dotted with the small glowing fires of native encampments. After many dark vicissitudes, with distant lorries approaching like glow-worms, and passing us in a crescendo of noise and blinding light, we at last arrived, after 160 miles, on the top of a precipice covered with fir trees. We did some unpacking, sat over a fire, and waited while the sure, but very slow, black servant prepared tea and sardines and unrolled our beds.

Five thousand people live in rush-matted tents, in the encampment of Divisional Headquarters. Already by early morning the men are slick and polished as if for the paradeground; shoes shiny, everyone immaculately shaved.

The British gift of improvization is here, fully exploited, everywhere an ant-like activity. Typewriters are buzzing, and the most elaborate systems of telephone and wireless installed. The khaki *dhobi* (laundry) festoons the branches of the trees; the 'furniture' is made of the strangest objects, and the whole picture is reminiscent of Robert Louis Stevenson. Everyone, young clerks and grey-haired brigadiers alike, wear shorts and swashbuckling bush-hats.

But living conditions are tough and work almost unending. The men sleep in fox-holes dug into the peat-like earth. After working at highest pressure all day, often another batch of work appears that must be completed after the evening meal. The day's activity starts again before sunrise.

This pressure of work helps to maintain morale. At a place so remote — it is a ten days' journey to the nearest town — there is little else to do. Everyone is extraordinarily cheerful, though it is almost more than they can bear to ask for news of England.

'What's the blackout like?' — 'Do they have enough to eat?' — 'How's the bomb damage?' — they inquire rather shyly. When I tell them that only five weeks ago I was in England, they eye me as if I were from another planet. They touch my civilian jacket and remark: 'Can't remember how long it is since we've seen tweeds.'

Monday

After nightfall I sat in a cavern dug in the red earth, in front of a blazing fire, talking to Colonel Younger. My companion was one of the most charming and cultivated young men that one could ever hope to meet in a grey stone eighteenth-century house in the shires. Tall, good-looking, with clear complexion and brown silk hair, he was just the type to have inspired the romantic yearnings of a heroine in a Henry James novel. How strange to discover that this slightly sophisticated Adonis, with the well-tended fingernails, was one of the men who had built the mountain road over which we had travelled.

'It's a promenade now, compared to what it was a few weeks ago,' he said, 'since the bulldozers do each day as much work as fifty Chins, though it's difficult to aggregate Chin manpower with women and children included. I'll take you up to Kennedy

Peak tomorrow; I'd like to show you the flowering trees on the way.' He talked about the local wild flowers and orchids as if he were showing me around his estates. It was pleasant sitting drinking a liqueur in this caveman dwelling, but Younger suddenly flashed his wrist watch. 'We mustn't be late for the guns,' he said. We ran in the dark up the mountainside. The night air was bitter. When we arrived at the summit I was panting for breath in the unaccustomed altitude.

'Two minutes to go — one minute to go — half a minute — FIRE!' A twenty-five pounder gun let loose eight rounds. The noise hurt: it brought to the surface all the soft spots in one's body — the places where one's teeth had been filled — the nerve centres and the dormant fibrositis in the nape of the neck. The blackness of the night became vivid with the flashes.

I handed over a package of about 250 undeveloped rolls I had exposed during the past two weeks to be sent back by air for processing at HQ in Delhi. The aeroplane which took them did not crash; the package was merely 'mislaid'. Ceaseless, but nevertheless vain, attempts have been made to discover its whereabouts. The chances are small that I shall ever be able to send the promised pictures to the men living in jungle foxholes, firing the twenty-five-pound guns, the Howitzer teams, the Gurkhas of the 7th Regiment, the men of the Queen's Regiment and West Yorks who showed such enthusiasm and co-operation.

Friday

The Provost-Marshal misinformed us about the timing of the convoy's departure with the result that we found ourselves in a gigantic crocodile of trucks that were to accompany us throughout the mountainous journey home. A truck would get over-heated and stall, causing a halt for all others in the rear: an abortive start: another breakdown. Again the stream of traffic would remain at a standstill. It was impossible to pass on the narrow crags overhanging precipices. After six hours, we had travelled only thirty miles.

The captain's display of vile temper was in itself an incentive for me to remain calm; but one sympathized with him, knowing that the mere physical exertion of steering the wheel round the hairpin bends, apart from the shock of sudden stops and starts on the knife-edge precipices, with a drop of 1,000 feet over the side, was a terrible strain on nerves. We trickled along the passes at a rate of five miles an hour, if lucky. The heat increased: at each enforced stop we became obsessed with trying to gauge if a distant truck was on the move or not. Although we never gave up trying, we could never pass any vehicle.

I hated the captain bitterly at the outset of our trip, but I thawed towards him when one afternoon I found him poring over a map giving his moth-eaten Chin servant a lesson in geography. The old native had never seen a map before and had no idea which shapes signified India or Burma. He made hopeless gestures with his dark fingers.

During the next ten or twelve hours of the nightmare journey I learnt about the captain's life. He had been a Regular, wounded in an arm and leg by the Japs; had been towed across a river in a net kept afloat by empty bottles; had started to walk out of Burma on foot with a dozen others, most of whom died from exposure and starvation on the way. Now he wished to return to his regiment but was 'unfit'. Soldiering was the only profession he knew. Hence his bitterness.

Against the green surroundings of the jungle the face of the white man is easily spotted at a distance; so faces are 'made-up' with dappled dabs of blue and green grease. Corporal Mitchell, from Perthshire, looks like the original Bairnsfather 'Ole Bill'; in spite of his *maquillage*, he has carefully waxed the ends of his large moustache. Tin hats are worn with sprays of tropical leaves threaded through their netting cover. The white turbans of the Punjabis are veiled with layers of coarse camouflage net: Sikhs appear in turbans covered with huge woolly tufts of green and blue and Gurkhas, patrolling with mobile wireless sets, support tall branches like wings on their shoulders, as they lean forward to penetrate the undergrowth. A tropical Burnam Wood is on its way to Dunsinane.

We came unexpectedly upon a battle. A picnic lunch in a ruined temple was interrupted by gunfire. While we climbed a flight of stone steps to discover what was happening, two over-life-size black satin crows swooped down from the magnolia-trees and carried off the remainder of our meal. So we moved on, down a disused road, through an overgrown village, once bombed, now abandoned and looking like the precincts of the Sleeping Beauty: exotic creeping plants sprawled over the half-destroyed *bashas* and summer pavilions and over the gutted motor-car still parked in its neat, cement garage. At the deserted farm, provisions were dumped in a courtyard — tins of bully-beef and packages of biscuits lay among hundreds of small eggs, gourds and the exotic vegetation of the tropics.

A group of young officers, with serious expressions on their sunburnt faces, were discussing the situation. During the night some Japs had come down through a nearby jungle range and had taken up their former positions which, inadvertently, we had not filled in before advancing farther. Now this enemy group was dug into the earth as snug as moles, and with a two-pounder gun previously captured from us was doing considerable damage to our rearguard. Several men had been killed, and the wounded at this moment were being brought back under fire. The stretchers were placed in the Red Cross ambulances, which the drivers manipulated on the rough roads with dexterity and compassion.

A young major appeared, his khaki battledress stained with dark, dry splashes of blood. 'We thought you'd been killed,' the others greeted him. 'Better have your arm seen to, and if you can cross that bridge, do so quickly and on all fours.'

Meanwhile, in the fields of paddy, Indian men accompanied by their naked children were still working, unmindful of the bursts of shrapnel. Bombing by air alone will send them seeking shelter.

Old Dr Seagrave is accustomed to operating under fire. The old man's hand trembles until it touches the flesh of his patient, then he slices the body open as if he were taking the rind off a cheese, delves into the entrails, scoops out the shrapnel, and starts on the sewing up. That job finished, another begins. A young man, who had been shot through the eyes, is brought in. 'No, he has been unlucky! He's just one that lowers the average. Too bad.' The old doctor shakes his head with a terrible look of anguish. It is as if he had never before seen such tragedy. Then the next case: a young man shot through the groin — the shrapnel goes in small, comes out enormous — a huge hole in the left side of the thigh. 'Ah, this scrotum wound's not so serious after all! He's lucky! Here's one of the lucky ones!'

PRESS CAMP

Camilla

The Press camp is in process of being built. It will not survive a series of violent storms for it is made entirely of bamboo. But with its lofty pointed ceiling, elaborately contrasting textures of wattling and glowing honey-colour, it has a fantasy and charm. The PO of the RAF, Dickson, who says 'Tickety-boo' every sentence, is a Scot with staccato charm. He lent me his sergeant secretary, Jock, a swarthy good-looking fellow who worked on the *Glasgow Herald*, for help on a *Daily Mail* article I have contracted to do. Jock shook his sleek black head every time I started a sentence that had no connection with the former one. 'No, och! you caim't puett tuewh quhotes tergether.' 'How do you know?' 'Bay instinct. They are booth on diffurunt subbjecttes. To me that suntunce is just a nasty blott on the papair.' I had already rewritten pages of notes many times, and knew they made no sense. But in desperation I dictated a few jerky *non-sequiturs* in an attempt to get something down for correction. Jock winced visibly. Still he did his best to help me, and not only rewrote many fair copies before, together, we had evolved something good enough to send by wire, but then translated the article in 'cablese'. Jock worked at the typewriter until long past midnight, and I was touched by his generosity as this was a gratuitous gesture at the end of a full day's work.

Today there had been a great flap as the Press boys had naturally wanted to get off stories of the RAF's latest success in bringing down fifteen Jap fighters. But all communication with Delhi and Calcutta had been chaotic.

Dickson, undaunted, was now at the telephones and was shouting himself hoarse and using foul language in his determination to get a batch of troop newspapers down to the 'boys who are doing the job of bringing down the Japs'. He yelled and beat his fist, 'You arrange it, or I'll resign my commission and return to the Kemsley newspapers.'

By finding myself in the clutches of that pettifogging, narrowminded, bilious, razor-edged little martinet, Duncley, and having to go everywhere under his wing, I have really plumbed the depths. Imagine the relief when he put me on a plane for Chittagong and at my next port of call I was greeted by my new cicerone who turned out to be Anthony Beauchamp.

Beauchamp was a successful photographer of 'glamour girls' before the war, and said that he had gone into the business through my influence. He is dark and handsome in a rather flashy way with piercing leopard's eyes. I soon discovered he has a sense of fun and he proves that to be efficient in the army one need not be dull. Moreover, instead of making me feel at my worst, as Duncley did, he gave me zest and enthusiasm. His stories of life at Sandhurst were quite a revelation. I have always thought my idea of hell would be to find myself at Camberley under the irate eye of some fierce sergeant-major. 'No, it isn't serious enough to hate — it's just a lot of balls. I love sergeant-majors! You always bribe them — give 'em bottles of whisky and they'll make a special point of bawling hell out of you on parade, but you know it'll never go further. You'll get called early, but you needn't turn up to every parade, and the exercises are easy — childish. You're free in the evenings, and we all had our cars and went off to Great Fosters. Of course, after the week-ends everyone was swaying with dizziness on parade on Monday. It was bags of fun.'

While motoring along rough jungle roads we talked with zest about subjects completely unrelated to our surroundings.

Much of the time is spent being uncomfortable, dirty and tired and doing things that do not normally interest me; but I am without anxieties. I have discovered that, degrading as this remote and primitive existence can be, there are compensations: even warfare may bring peace of mind and a feeling of physical serenity. Now that the jeep races towards my aeroplane and a return to civilization, my former rut will envelop me. I am able to sympathize with the RAF officer who, on hearing that he was to be sent home, confided: 'It may be such an anti-climax to go back to England, after all these years of thinking about the place and building it up in my imagination. I have glorified it all this time, and now that I'm really going back I'm beginning to be frightened.'

BOMBAY — DINNER AT GOVERNMENT HOUSE

Less artificial than Delhi, less dirty than Calcutta, beautifully situated on the sea, Bombay cannot be considered an Asiatic city. It is the most cosmopolitan and emancipated city in India. In spite of its orchid-house climate, its inhabitants seem to possess unflagging initiative and make the town a throbbing Eastern metropolis that welcomes Western civilization. Sects, clubs, associations and newspapers are legion. Bombay is also a great town for gambling — particularly among the Parsees. Many of those present at the race meeting each Saturday have dreamt about doubles. 'Of course the favourite will win,' someone in the crowd is heard to say, 'or the stewards will want to know why...'

As the horses flash past, the crowd groans in a vast orgasm of excitement. Young women are extremely decorative in their clear coloured saris, but some of their menfolk, with tweed jackets worn over their muslin shirts, look messily indecent. The general effect, with the bright, coarse flowers set in stiff borders and a distant rainbow in the sky, has the period charm of a Manet painting.

Suddenly a violent downpour of dramatic rain disperses the crowds, not before they are soaked through. The drainage system does not allow for such a rainfall. Lawns are immediately flooded, cars are waterlogged: a few straggling Indians paddle with battered umbrellas held aloft in one hand, shoes in the other; and husky BORS, like children at play, proceed by slow degrees, climbing along with their stomachs pressed to the railings.

In the throne-room of Government House, an assortment of respectable English and Indian citizens is assembled. The inevitable Belgian Consul and his wife stand next to the huge retired colonel with high blood-pressure who must avoid the brandy. One of the Indians wears a dark green shade above his glasses, a most peculiar effect, as if he were wearing a Pullman-car reading-lamp. Some officers are in uniform; business tycoons, wearing baggy dinner-jackets of tropical weight, are accompanied by their scraggy wives.

Since there is no thought of arranging a formal dinner table such as this in any but the order of precedence, the same people find themselves, continuously and irrevocably, placed side by side. It is not to be wondered at that there is nothing much for them to say to each other and that the evening does not go with a swing.

'Will you kindly form a line along there?' suggests a rosy ADC, with only one arm and a cursory manner. 'Two rows please — come along now.' Some of the ADC's enjoy making the guests suffer. 'They don't come to Government House for nothing,' they snigger.

A long delay, long enough to make each guest fully realize what he is waiting for. At last a slight commotion is heard in the distance. 'Their Excellencies', shouts the obstreperous young ADC.

Dinner is served on an enormous strip of table decked with bougainvillaea. The inanimate faces of the heterogenous company are reflected in the row of silver cups.

Thirty servants, with scarlet turbans and bare feet, run around serving the inevitable banquet food. Each of the Governor's jokes is greeted with sycophantic laughter.

'Mercifully he seems in a good mood now,' says ADC2, sitting next to ADC3 in starvation corner. 'But I've seldom seen HE so rattled as he was this morning.'

Her Excellency personifies graciousness itself, though she, too, had a bad morning. Someone placed flower garlands round her neck at the opening of the agricultural exhibition, and they dripped down a new dress she had had copied by the *dzersi*.

The long ritual of the meal over, the company retires to the illuminated garden and sits out in arm-chairs and on sofas, placed on Turkish carpets. A police band plays 'Merrie Englande' and 'Poet and Peasant'. The bandsmen are in yellow and blue, with white spats.

At 10 o'clock more of the European colony are let in to the sacred precincts. A further display of Anglo-Indian fashions; some of the sailors of the RIN, in immaculate white uniforms, are almost throttled by their high collars — *beaux ideals* of all novelettes.

An intellectual lady, in a taffeta picture dress with a berthe of old lace, leans forward:

'Isn't it extraordinary that so great a country as India should have fallen so low? There is nothing of promise to be found anywhere here today. No writer, no painter. The only hope for the young Indian is to go into politics; and the only hope, if the country is to regain vitality and honesty, is revolution. If Congress were to take over, they'd make the inevitable mess of it; the dishonesty and craft of the Congress leaders would soon be discovered — bloodshed and anarchy would follow — but out of that some fresh life might spring.'

An elderly industrialist leans forward and says, 'India is a feminine country, all her faults are feminine ones,' and he raises his glass gallantly.

A beautiful Indian in a pink sari says, 'Whatever those faults may be, let *us* make them. Please allow us our own headaches. India for the Indians, please.'

The ADC's move everyone around, as if in a game of musical chairs.

Under a vast electric fan, like the propeller of an aeroplane, a lady in cornflower-blue lace welcomes a newcomer. 'We were just saying that the problems of India only begin to get really confusing after the first year here.'

A young subaltern says, 'Yes, I always say it takes a year to learn to hate India.'

Two ADC's are standing apart, eyeing the guests. One holds a small printed card up to his mouth.

'He's already had the sanitary specialist's wife three minutes. It's time we got the expert on humus heaps ready for him.'

'Oh no, Mrs Bumface gets seven minutes, she's on post-war reconstruction, but look, Her Excellency is getting a bit browned off with the Brigadier, hurry up and take that old chap over, he's the Commissioner of Police, what's his name?'

The obstreperous ADC is determined that the party shall end as soon as possible, as he has a clandestine appointment down in the hotel bar, which shuts at 11 o'clock.

Her Excellency is enjoying her talk about servants with the widow of the opium agent, Ghazipur, when the ADC interrupts.

'I think, your Excellency, that His Excellency is preparing to say good night.'

The guests are hurriedly thrown into line again. Their Excellencies smile with relief. It is the smile the dentist receives when his patient is freed.

'Good night — good night! — good night!'

The cars are churning up the gravel, especially imported from England. But in the first limousine, leaving a wake of dust and small stones, is the rubicund ADC, mopping his brow and telling the chauffeur to drive '*Jaldi*! *Jaldi*!'

Jaipur

The village of Purana Ghat, of colonnaded, pale yellow buildings, thrush-egg blue pagodas and massive archways painted with decorations of birds and flowers, leads to the coral-coloured town of Jaipur.

Laid out in the eighteenth century, the wide streets run parallel. With its open squares and pleasure gardens, the city is a pattern for well-planned spaciousness. Another overall felicity is the rule that every house must be painted pink. Some of these façades are embellished with designs of birds and bouquets of flowers painted in white. The general effect of Jaipur is of an almost dream-like beauty and serenity. The native populace seems to have an innate understanding of the use of colour, and they vie with each other in the beauty of their coats and turbans.

In the inner court of the Zenana Palace women in daffodil yellow, apricot and orange draperies, polish the white marble columns. A young man, wearing a pea-green turban and a lilac coat, spends his morning lolling against an archway and looking like a figure painted on enamel 500 years ago. Small carriages with hoods shaped like pagodas disgorge Rajputana ladies and their children, all dressed in varying reds, with heavily painted eyes and a mass of jewels. When the billowing, freshly-dyed lengths of vivid yellow or magenta muslin are brought out to dry in the sun even these robust colours produce a symphony that is refined, subtle and harmonious.

LEOPARD HUNT

Jaipur

The Maharajah had arranged a shoot for us. In my simplicity I had imagined a certain amount of personal risk was involved; but not on this occasion at any rate.

We drove into the mountains where the preparations had begun last night, when a tethered goat was provided for the dinner of a female leopard. She had been successfully shot while at her meal. A male leopard had subsequently finished off the goat *table d'hôte* and, it was surmised, would doubtless return tonight in the expectancy of a further banquet. Indeed, another goat was led out and staked. We sportsmen retired behind the foliage-covered windows of a small concrete building, strategically placed ten yards away, to watch the misery of the bait.

As the mountain landscape faded into darkness, plaintive bleats rang through the canyons. The lonely, chained animal strutted in circles around its stake. Suddenly in panic, its blunt, rock-like profile darted this way and that. Then its front legs collapsed, and the animal lay quite still. It whimpered to itself. Then, in abject terror at some noise, it was up in a flash; again its head pivoted in all directions — ears cocked the better to listen.

Why was I allowing myself to be party to something I considered so ignominious? It was awful to watch an animal suffering the mental torments that, mercifully, most of us leave behind in the night-nursery. Yet I must admit that I had worked up a certain blood-lust, as we watched and waited in deepest silence for the great moment when the lurking leopard would spring out of the blackness of the night and the loaded guns go off. Although there was little chance of the leopard escaping or attacking us in our concrete fastness, our eyes popped with excitement.

The goat continued to emit pathetic, grating croaks, like whimpers of despair, then, exhausted by misery, lay down to sleep.

After a one and a half-hour's wait no leopard came, and the colonel who was organizing the shoot said that it was useless to remain. The anticlimax was crushing, but the joy of the goat when we came out of hiding to unleash it was heavenly to see. The goat had, at any rate, one more day to live.

BENARES WITH HASHISH

Benares

I am staying with Raymond Burnier, a brilliant young Belgian photographer of early Hindu sculpture. The house is completely native, and since Raymond has adopted the Hindu religion one of the guest-rooms is occupied by a sacred cow. He asked me if I would care to take hashish. Willing to try anything once, I waited, full of anticipation, while he prepared a concoction of milk of almonds, rose-water, carminum nuts and eight other ingredients of which hashish, or *bhang*, the 'laughing drug', was the principal.

The drink was delicious. We sat on cushions on the floor of the *salon*, expecting the drug to alter our sense of space and time and to make everything seen incredibly humorous. Still no effect. So we had dinner.

Raymond started to giggle, but I was in no laughing mood. If other people's amusement is disproportionate, one feels suddenly sobered. After a while I noticed that my hands felt soft and boneless, the skin unusually silken; I could not quite feel the extremities of my body. But that was the only peculiarity in an otherwise disappointing evening — too bad!

We sat in the drawing-room prepared to spend a short while in conversation before retiring for the night. Suddenly my friend, as he sat regarding me with pink blotched face and pearly grin, appeared quite different from any former picture I had of him. Outside, a strange metallic clicking sound was heard. It struck me as comic that it should continue so long, and, imagining it to come from a woodpecker, I remarked upon the bird's insistence.

I realized that I was mistaken; but my friend's surprise, and his incredulity as he repeated 'a bird?' seemed to me so ludicrous that I laughed until I was unconscious.

The experience was not altogether pleasant; for when I reemerged into semi-consciousness I found I had laughed — and was still laughing — so much that I had a strange constriction in my chest. The sensation was so far beyond my control that I was somewhat apprehensive as to how the evening would end. My companion laughed at my merriment. I tried feebly to tell him that he seemed transformed and now looked like a school friend named Dudley Scholte, of the tailoring firm, but I was tongue-tied. The proportions of the room changed. The distance across the floor suddenly seemed as large as the Atlantic; one's eyes could scarcely travel to the far end of the music-room. The arches, under which my friend sat, assumed cathedral proportions, though, in fact, they were only a little over six feet high.

For the next two and a half hours we were violently drugged. The hallucination seemed to last an eternity. A reaction that would normally take only a fraction of a second seemed now to continue for ever. One wondered if the other person could read these long deliberations that were going on in one's mind.

So submerged in intoxication were we that the effort of speaking consecutively was too great: one gave up with a confidential look. Neither did one know if one had voiced a remark, or whether the thought had been so vivid that one merely imagined it to have been spoken. Somehow, one felt that speech would break the spell, and one did not wish to break it. Surely my friend's brain was acting better than mine? I was able to understand him to say that this drug gave a far greater degree of intoxication than any alcohol. I could not have managed such a sentence. He continued, 'Already we would have passed out or been sick, with an appalling hangover.'

With tears coursing down my cheeks I muttered, 'We are beyond speech.' Once more I was convulsed. Anxious not to forget this experience I kept asking, 'How much of this will we remember?'

Raymond and his friend Danielou, an authority on Hindu music, had a particularly beautiful and elaborate gramophone, with loudspeaker relayed from the ceiling: we decided to listen to a record. I have never appreciated or understood music so clearly as I did then: each instrument in a large orchestra was heard individually, with extraordinary distinctness. An Indian song was played — some Spanish music — a Russian march — and then some very hackneyed Debussy. I could not concentrate for the entire length of each piece but felt I could follow its construction as never before.

Most of the household had taken a few sips of the potion, and there was laughter behind every door. We watched two house-boys putting up the mosquito-nets over a bed, and they too giggled hysterically.

Even to move about the small sitting-room became a feat for not only was perspective altered, but the stereoscopic values were those of a faulty peepshow. There was a great distance between my host and the table, and another vast jump from the table to the curtain. Raymond's body appeared flat, as if pasted on cardboard. I noticed, too, that one's time-sense had broken down with extraordinary results — ten minutes would pass in a moment; a split-second would seem like many hours. One of the reasons for the popularity of this drug is that it gives the sensation of prolonging indefinitely the joys of sexual intercourse, and an orgasm seems to last for an eternity. The journey to my bed seemed to take an aeon and only an innate fear of being out of control of my senses cut short this extremely pleasant evening.

I do not know why I have not become a *bhang* addict, for the morrow brought no ill after-effects. In fact, my inclination to laugh was roused to the extent that even the sinister sights of the burning ghats along the Ganges struck me as vastly entertaining, and I was able to run up and down the highest towers for panoramic views of the city without the slightest feeling of breathlessness or strain.

The Indian climate can play havoc with the brain. I had telephoned to Natarajan[35] and said, 'I want you to do three things for me.' I enumerated the requests. Natarajan replied, 'I must put those down now before I forget — one, yes — two, yes — now what was the third thing you wanted?' Neither he nor I were able to remember.

HYDERABAD

Monday, March 13th

Although the heat is almost unbearable we are told to economize on electricity, so the use of the fan is frowned upon. Birds treat this house as an aviary: at night insects create a fog around the electric lights: bats rush around the matted ceiling. One gets accustomed to ants hurrying over everything, but this evening I was startled to find two frogs in the bath. Yet, all considered, this is a comfortable house.

This afternoon, while choosing, with my guide, material for an Indian dressing-gown, sirens went off shrilly and the air was rent with whistling. A few unknowing motorists continued on their way until the police cars caught up with them. With yells and curses the police cleared the road. A few seconds later the Nizam of Hyderabad sped past at high speed in a small motor-car. (He has been patriotic about saving petrol.) His appearance strikes one as oddly lacking in native character. Today, unshaven and untidy, he looked like one of the porters who hang about the orange crates in any market throughout the European world.

The main thoroughfare had not for long resumed its normal clamour when, again, whistles blew to pierce the eardrums.

---

[35] An agent at Government House.

Another motorcade came into sight, then halted. A huge yellow limousine was backing in curves from the centre of the street, and came at last to rest by the curb nearby, and I returned to the peaceful pressure of shopping. Within a few moments I heard an avalanche of oaths and curses. The shop assistant shot surreptitious but frightened glances into the street, but none would answer my inquiries as to the cause of the noise. The street was empty now but for a small crowd standing at a respectful distance opposite. 'What is all this?' I asked. My guide continued to look at silk for me as if nothing untoward had happened. From his desk a young cashier quietly answered me, 'It's Her Highness.'

Out of the elephant's breath limousine stepped an old hag. She wore her long, matted hair square at the ends, and the effect was as if she were wearing a string of loofahs. Her blue dress, with a muslin apron of pale green, was creased and messy. Her Highness stood in gold shoes with feet wide apart, hands on hips, then staggered backwards into the neighbouring shop where silver ornaments are sold. The shouting and screaming that followed was as terrifying as if knives were being drawn, and at least half a dozen fishwives were fighting to the death. But no one joined the fray. This was a solo performance by Her Highness.

Later, looking more dishevelled than ever, she reappeared and, arms akimbo, stood peering myopically into our shop. The aquiline nose, the pointed, pouting lips, the large, lean cheekbones and fierce bird-like eyes were enormously impressive in the manner of primitive sculpture. The wild appearance, though startling, even terrifying, was nevertheless on a grand scale. Magnificent, too, were the enormous drop pearl earrings and her many rows of large pearls. The grey-haired woman stood in the doorway of the shop and pointed at a blue scarf. Then she started shouting with renewed force. The young shop assistants in the tailor's shop behaved with extraordinary calm and politeness. A young boy produced the scarf for Her Highness's thorough inspection. Judging by the shrieks that followed, the young assistant's life was being threatened. Suddenly the wild woman pointed at me. I stood to attention. But the cashier whispered that I must go and talk to Her Highness, who became silent as I walked forward and bowed. As I went down the steps farther forward towards the royal lady, the screaming started again with renewed force. I had gone too near the presence. Everyone looked pained. After a scuffle the poor mad woman, for so I gathered her to be, returned to her limousine. Screaming at me from the windows, with the volume of forty dustmen, she was carried back home.

The reverence with which these shop people treated this pitiful lady demonstrated another proof of how highly civilized and dignified they are in so many ways. Everyone in the State knows that it gives Her Highness pleasure to go on elaborate shopping expeditions. Her requests are treated with tactful acquiescence. All the purchases she has ordered to be sent to the palace are delivered, but it is known that two days later they will be returned intact.

As for myself, I believe I had somewhat of an escape, for it seems Her Highness has quite an eye for young men, and she might have ordered me to be sent up to the palace where I might not have remained intact.

CALCUTTA

Its climate, perhaps the most unhealthy of any town in India, may be responsible for the weakness, indolence and apathy of so many of Calcutta's inhabitants, who seem resigned to the fact that they are doomed to disaster, famine or epidemic. The second largest city of the Empire, and the former capital of India, Calcutta is a city full of paradoxes of grandeur and poverty. There are many splendid parks, squares adorned with Edwardian statues, some elegant eighteenth-century buildings and florid commercial edifices; but only fifteen paces from the grand European hotels ragged groups on the pavement cluster around the fires, frying heavily-spiced food and bits of fish, while hordes of rats scurry about and scavenger dogs and enormous crows greedily explore the refuse bins.

European ladies in evening dress take themselves to the Philharmonic concerts on Sunday evenings. A few hundred yards away, at the Kalighat, the most primitive scenes of worship in all India take place.

But wartime Calcutta, recently recovered from famine, is thriving. Fortunes are being made. Directors of firms are 'reserved' from the army, and in the end, no doubt, receive knighthoods. (Calcutta is known as the city of 'dreadful knights'.) Moreover, it has become a sort of oriental Clapham Junction. Air commodores, generals and celebrities of every kind and race spend the night at one of the over-crowded hotels or at Government House. Men on leave from the Fourteenth Army, in their bush-hats and shorts, crowd out the hostels, canteens, air-conditioned cinemas, cafés, milk-bars and the sleazy 'attractions' along Chowringhee. They say it is wonderful, after years in jungle fox-holes, merely to walk along stone pavements, to gaze up at tall jostling buildings and to sleep all night in a solidly constructed edifice. After listening to the whispers of the jungle, the violent noises of the town come as a relief. Calcutta provides plenty of noise: the tick-ticking and thunder-rolling of the trams, the honking of taxis — for Sikhs always drive with the horn — the bells of the rickshaws and the incessant caw-cawing of the crows circling above.

Poles wander in search of distraction; American sailors, with cigars at an insolent angle, buy silk kimonos embroidered with dragons; at the bookstalls British Tommies rather clumsily finger the pages of *The Seven Pillars of Foolishness, Gone with the Monsoon*, or *Erotic Edna*.

In Bow Bazaar one shopkeeper advertises himself as 'Specialist in wet dreams'. All the oriental junk that Birmingham produces is here in the vast market: carved ivory by the ton, engraved metal and elaborate enamelling. Rare animals of the jungle are brought together under this glass roof: caged birds of all colours and sizes and, in crates, pathetic, black, long-haired monkeys with eyes like wallflowers and the dignity of saints. A young boy, holding a bird-cage, pauses a moment to rearrange his coloured girdle; another is sitting upon a trestle, sharing it with a goat and many vegetables; a young Hercules saunters by, balancing an enormous wardrobe on his turbaned head. One forgets how beautiful the human body can be until one sees it with the draperies so enticingly arranged.

Having given up all wordly possessions, the holy men, the Sadhus, satisfy their frugal wants by begging, and cover themselves with an ash that contains a sulphur which makes their naked bodies impervious to changes of heat or cold. They practise Yogi, and each morning go down to the Hooghly to bathe and do their muscular exercises, using the river water to irrigate their bowels. Under the influence of hemp and hashish, they laugh mischievously, peep and leer around corners, but their smoking does not affect their physique; the bodies of even the older men are remarkably lithe and energetic. The young men with their long bleached hair hanging below their shoulders, scarlet jockstrap and skin powdered half-elephant, half-circus performer, look more like devils than holy men. One naked young man, with his wild hair flowing behind him, comes charging down to the water astride a great bull. The head Sadhu, an old man with one eye and one tooth, reads from the Holy Book and tells us that twenty of his group have recently left for Nepal. They have gone begging their way on foot, and it will take a whole year to reach their destination. A nine-year-old boy, with grey powdered face and hair, in scarlet draperies, looks like an angel painted by Signorelli as he sits in the Lotus position, playing an enormous musical zither twice his size. The atmosphere is faintly vicious and sinister, though maybe it is only the rather uncanny laughter that gives one that impression.

An hour went by in a trance visiting the Jain temple, which could be described as of crystallized fruit, Turkish delight architecture. The wiry pagodas are painted white or pale blue, and a series of cone-topped pavilions are inlaid with coloured glass, semi precious stones or mirror. Glaring white European statues and monstrous garden chairs are dotted everywhere and so many surprising and preposterous objects are on display that the whole effect, while of an ingenuous lack of taste, is gay and like a setting for an *opéra bouffe*.

In the Science School of Calcutta University, the students seemed to be doing extremely exciting things: drawing coloured water into their mouths, giving pressure to liquids, making experiments that ended in explosions, etc.

Three surgeons and two matrons came for dinner. Old Sir Henry Holland is the only man in India who can perform the cataract operation, and during the year is said to bring back sight to 2,000 people. He is now training a fleet of Americans who will doubtless be able to continue the work.

The two matrons present were the 'salt of the earth': huge, over-size women who have been looking after Indians and teaching the women to nurse. In England there is one nurse for every 200 people: here one in every 30,000. They complained about the lack of funds the provincial governments allow for their work. They are here for a three-day conference to thrash out their difficulties and to try to get better conditions, not for themselves, but for the people for whom they have given up so unselfishly the best years of their lives. The more opulently proportioned of the two matrons told me how anti-British the Indians in the north are: in her hospital there is always an undercurrent of opposition, and she is continually finding notes on her chair or desk with the message 'Quit India'. Yet they are operating solely on Indians, are in charge of hundreds of Indians and their operation theatres are peopled with Indian anaesthetists, surgeons and nurses. The matrons sighed that existence is made so much harder, not only by lack of gratitude, but by sabotage. If a prize-giving has been arranged, she will doubtless find that another attraction has been fixed by the Indians for the same day. When a Christmas party is planned for the children, it is discovered, at the last minute, that their parents have taken them off on some other expedition. Whenever Matron challenges anyone, and suggests it would be easier if all play together in the compound, there is a slinking avoidance of the issue.

These noble nurses are paid only a pittance. One of them described her great pleasure in going to look at the Asia Crafts Shop. 'The painted bowls are so full of colour, and they don't mind at all if you don't buy — if you just look around. Occasionally I do buy something, but that is for wedding presents.' These two women, with their genteel manners and social giggles, are real heroines.

In a neighbourhood of cheap modernistic apartment-houses, of honeycomb tenement-buildings that seem so unsuitable for the climate of India, lives an Indian poet, in an atmosphere of an extraordinary sweetness and purity. Transparent *dhotis* and white saris, freshly laundered, are hanging from the landings and balcony, as emblems of cleanliness; the golden ewers sparkle in the washroom: the stark, almost empty bedroom, with the poet's children asleep, is innocent of all the unnecessary and stuffy impediments of a humble room in the Western world. Here are no cluttered drawers, here are the essentials alone; and yet, when I want, of all things, a tripod for my camera, the poet is able to produce it.

WITH THE ADC'S

John Erwin, nervous, miserable and anti-social, acted out of character by giving a cocktail party. Mrs Wilson, idly sipping, told me of a letter she had just received from her husband in the jungle. He had spent a night in a fox-hole playing 'deception' records (discs of people marching along, twigs being broken, etc.) when he realized he was encircled by the Japs. Nothing to do but remain silent, trusting for the best, but realizing there was little chance of escape. He listened at early dawn to the Punjabis going in to attack the Japs with bayonets and blood-curdling war-cries. During his greatest terror, when he felt convinced he was done for, his moments of waiting were spent graphically imagining himself going into all the best restaurants in London, and visualizing the meals he would order, course after course. His ordeal ended happily, for the Japs were unable to locate him, and the ground had been recovered by daylight.

I also enjoyed the company of pale, faded, romantic-looking Mrs Denham White, the sensitive wife of the doctor. She talked of the compensations of growing old: of watching others, and remembering rather than enduring and of being no longer wracked.

When his guests had left, John told me the only hope for me as a photographer after the war was to take pictures of the spirit of construction — the building-up of the new world. 'The war has been lucky for you — you dabble in *dégringolade*, your idiom includes the representation of broken tanks and ruined cities. But in future you must feel for the people, not for the individual. If you have photographed one society person you've photographed the lot, but have you never seen the eyes of the people? Crowds are what must be photographed.' In a cloud of mosquitoes he told me that for a person with my temperament I had rare powers of application: I had made my mark by using my feminine talents in an unfeminine way by doggedly applying myself. I was no genius, and my talents in another would have amounted to little, but my instinct and powers of adaptation were at the same time a weakness and strength.

My turn came to give advice. I told John that he should get another job if he was as miserable as he said he was among the flesh-pots of Calcutta. I told him that he should not mark time in an uncongenial atmosphere. He replied that life was hard; he had once been hungry, he still needed cash but, nevertheless, this environment was killing him; he suffered from appalling nightmares and was on a fair way to a nervous breakdown. Certainly his hands trembled like aspen, and his face resembled the underneath of something.

One of the ADC's has a great power of mimicry and a keen sense of the ludicrous and a talent for discovering secrets. Much of his private information, which he cannot resist passing on, is unsuitable for commitment to paper, but today he sent me a note informing me 'HE's stool was not so good this morning.' He told me, with mutual amusement, that on the return to the car from the picnic tea at Tuklabad Lady Wavell said to one of the ADC's as she passed through a scrum of beggars: 'Distribute the largess.'

Jaminy Roy, sitting in his studio wrapped in immaculate white muslin, looks like a long baked potato, nestling in a napkin; with many bowls of different colours on the floor in front of him, he paints as if he were making decorations on pottery. Once an academic portraitist, Jammy Roy became dissatisfied with the oily fulsome likenesses of rich people that he was able to produce with facility and technical skill, so retired to a small village. Here he studied Matisse and other modern painters, made his own water colours and started to paint in a brilliant and vital manner. After many years of poverty and hardship he is now considered India's best modern painter.

PARLIAMENT PROROGUED

The Governor has prorogued Parliament. There have been such disorderly scenes in the Legislative Assembly that it has been decided to curtail them. I went to hear the final flurry.

An *Alice in Wonderland* mad-house presented itself. Everyone at the same moment seemed to be shouting and beating the air. One man, with a voice like a siren, moaned above the others, demanding an opportunity to speak without interruptions. I noticed later that when others were taking the stand he was the first to heckle. The Speaker, like a Grandville drawing of an insect, had a hard time trying to keep some semblance of order. He cried into a microphone, banging with his mallet to no avail. A dignified man, in a tarboosh, kept shouting, 'Mr Speaker, may I go on? Oh, they won't listen!' he wailed. 'They don't want to hear truth and correct information — please Mr Speaker, oh please prevent us from becoming a laughing stock.'

A fat old man in a *dhoti* rose to his sandals and shouted in his metallic voice: 'This is most vexatious for the honourable minister!' Others took up the cry, 'Vexatious, most vexatious!' Finally the minister, who was supposedly so vexed, rose and remarked deprecatingly, 'I can assure you it is not vexatious. I am not easily vexed.'

The Speaker gave hopeless rulings. The document from Government House proroguing the Assembly was greeted with shouts of '*Ignorrit — ignorrrit*'. The bedlam of noise and confusion rose to a crescendo, to be ended abruptly by the Speaker adjourning the house for fifteen minutes of prayer.

I discovered from the finance department that I can draw in arrears 150 pounds allowance. I feel like Croesus, having been poor for the last weeks and carefully eking out my last rupees.

A beautiful 'authorized' beggar firmly refused to be photographed, but he did so with extraordinary dignity and amusement. 'Nothing doing,' his head wagglings indicated, and he flicked his hands in a feminine way.

At lunch a Canadian brigadier, hearing that I was about to go to China, expounded on the seamy side of Chungking: how the Chinese continue to trade with the enemy, with supplies coming in non-stop from Shanghai. He expatiated on the appalling prices we have to pay (7,000 pounds for an old car on the black market) and the smells and dirt. Immediately after lunch, Mrs Casey, on the spur of the moment, decided to visit Bengal Home Industries. David Clowes, one of the ADC's, and very punctilious about seeing that the new Governor and his wife do the social part of the job without a hitch, blew off steam. 'Things must be laid on properly in this house; she's got to have a flag on the car, and an outrider, and an OC.' In spite of his bellowing, Mrs Casey did what she wished, and together we all went to buy things for the house. On her return, Peel, the military secretary, gave Mrs Casey a few tips about how to succeed in Calcutta. 'You should encourage music: they would like it if you go to the concerts, and racing plays a large part in the life of the community. And HE should talk to some of the businessmen at the clubs here: they're very powerful, and they give a lot to the war.'

I suddenly felt rather ill and tired, with a strange tightness around the pelvis. I tried to listen with one ear to this amusing lesson while at the same time trying to follow John Erwin on Indian art.

I went up to my bedroom and have remained there now for a week, suffering from a severe attack of dengue fever.

My body aches in the most unexpected places — on the shoulders, in the small of the back and behind the knees. I feel most uncomfortable and try to find ways of being flatter and flatter. I have no appetite and eat because I'm told to. While trying to dispose of the evening meal Dickie Herbert comes in. He has recently suffered a nervous breakdown, and the doctor says his liver is in such a condition that he might die if he does not stop drinking.

Mrs C. says rather refreshingly that she is turning the house into a hospital. Her husband has now taken to bed with a temperature raging; she is amused to find mine had gone up to 102 degrees. Later this evening, as I lie in a pool of sweat, David Clowes, from behind the mosquito-net curtains, tells me the SEAC people are fed up with me: they don't see why the hell I should have preferential treatment over other journalists out here. He says it's bad luck on the House stenographer that I have given so much extra work by dictating articles to him. And so he continues until we have quite a row.

I am unable to sleep in spite of an opiate as my limbs are braced with pain. My pyjamas, soused with sweat, make the effort of turning over on the other side an unpleasant experience. This is my darkest hour. A filthy owl or bat breathes stertorously just outside my window, and I find the night a long agony.

Mrs Priestley, the Scotch housekeeper, comes in to commiserate. Her attitude to India is wonderfully typical. In a toneless, sad voice she drones, 'I don't like Calcutta. There's nothing to see here except their heathen temples and I wouldn't go near them. You feel there's evil abounding from them, because their religion is different, and they sacrifice wretched animals and do all sorts of things. No, there's nowhere to go in Calcutta. Why, if you walk into those back streets there's nothing but Indians — Indians — Indians — not a European to be seen anywhere. Yet the place must have colour or something, because when I went back home to Dumfries I was disappointed! You see, you never see a poor European in India, do you?'

Sunday

Awoke to feel seriously limp. No doubt about it — I am an invalid and have no fight left even to think of work.

Throughout the day I have quite a number of visitors: Mrs Priestley, the housekeeper, with her toneless, tragic voice, comes in to know if I'd like another eiderdown; the insincere Mr Bibbety, the under-controller of the House who, I'm sure, would like to receive a rake-off on my illness, salaams from the waist, purses his blue lips, and says that however high the thermometer shows, one's temperature is normal for Calcutta. Various ADC's come in occasionally; David is worried that Mrs C. doesn't do this or that, and afraid the prestige of Government House is going to be let down with a bang. John Erwin, very busy, starts on an intellectual talk. But his philosophizing is often interrupted. The Indian doctor smiles tragically and does not mind long silences. My bearer walks around silently, not understanding a word of English — nor I of Urdu — but he barks 'Wurrywell' and does just what I don't want.

Jimmy and Ed, two delightful dissolute Americans with biscuit complexions and knife-grinding voices, come in to inform me about the brothels of Calcutta. A native girl charges four annas; there are 1,500 girls in the biggest brothel (situated quite near this House). Fifteen per cent of the population have VD. The grand brothel for officers is run by Madame Carmen, a Polish Jewess with red hair, in the Karaya Road. She takes half the fees. One girl complained she had had a bad month (because of flu had been away for ten days); nevertheless she had earned 8,000 rupees, although her average was 22,000 a month. Her intentions are to save enough so that after the war she can retire and get respectably married.

Disaster once more as I woke to find my leg, which had at last recovered from last week's inoculations against plague, has now become inflamed and throbbed so painfully that I could not put it to the ground. Dr Mukergee was sent for, and he seemed alarmed when he took my temperature. Patting the heated portion of my thigh, he worked me up into a condition of alarm and despondency, as a knife-like pain increased and a raging fever took control. He would get Dr Denham White's advice. Meanwhile he suggested my going into a nursing home. I had visions of an amputation. Later, Denham White calmed us both by smiling, 'Oh, this is serum reaction. Nothing serious. Calcium will counteract that.' He gave me pastilles, but it was some time before the fires in my leg abated. My trip to China has had to be postponed.

I shall now be leaving on the day my late lamented brother Reggie was born — April 3rd. How long ago it seems since that night of his death, and yet how vivid still is his memory! One of the first pilots of the Flying Corps, he would have been in his element flying in this war. He would almost certainly have done great things.

Part XI: China, 1944

FLIGHT OVER THE HUMP

Saturday, April 8th

At Dum Dum Airport, a mere clearing among the palm-trees, a Douglas DC3 waited to take an RAF pilot, going to Kunming to fly back a Liberator tomorrow, a handful of Chinese passengers and myself on that famously dangerous journey over the 'Hump'. (These pilots are the highest paid of all with a salary of 200 dollars a month.)

To begin with, we flew low and bumped so violently and continually that all the Chinese were extremely sick. They made horrible noises into paper bags, and the smell was revolting. Then we climbed very high — mountains covered with icing sugar appeared on the right, their peaks soaring much higher than we were flying. The Gothic pinnacles were beautiful, but impossible to map-read and pilots get lost or caught in downward draughts. There are many Japanese fighters in the offing.

The second pilot came along with oxygen tubes which we were to share in turns. I found it a relief to breathe deeply into these masks, to fill my lungs with the warm, rather oniony, air. By degrees, the aircraft was getting very cold. I put on a scarf — I must reserve my overcoat for tonight's ordeal.

The late afternoon sun turned the mountain peaks pink. At the height of 19,000 feet I felt dizzy and uncomfortable — my head rolled from side to side. The light went out of the day: evening became night. We must now be flying lower for oxygen was needed no more. A few sparse twinkling lights below in irregular design — Kunming. We seemed to stop moving in the air, so slowly did the engines purr. The lights below slowly passed us by. We landed. The Chinese families all smiling. Here more Chinese came aboard for the last trip to Chungking. Babies, small children, women with no luggage but what they possessed wrapped up in a cloth or sack — poor, but smiling — in party spirits — flashes of white teeth — screwed-up eyes — guttural expectoration.

With what relief was I told by the pilot that the most dangerous part of the trip was now over. But had I seen the Japanese fighter? Fortunately, he had not bothered to come after us.

We took off again. My head ached intolerably. I finished the bromide drink supplied by Dr Mukergee: time ceased to exist.

Again we were motionless in the air. Twinkling lights in greater numbers this time — rivers reflecting lights — high mountains also covered with lights. We circled several times then eventually came down between two mountains, almost skimming a river. Brump — brrrump on terra firma.

A full moon — a colder night than any we have known in India. A great deal of throat clearing from the Chinese — perhaps their way of showing relief from fear?

CHUNGKING

Saturday, April 9th, Chungking

Dazed with drugs and exhaustion I looked about me in the darkness of the Chungking night for someone to tell me where to go from here. Eventually, among the orientals, a pink-moonface came forward. 'General Grimsdale[36] thought you would be more comfortable staying at the Embassy than at his

---

[36] General Grimsdale, GOC British Military Mission in China.

HQ, and Sir Horace and Lady Seymour are expecting you.' What benediction! 'Can you walk up 400 steps,' pink-moonface asked, 'or would you prefer to go in a chair?' I used my sore, stiff leg as an excuse to get into a light bamboo sedan, and be carried up a mountainside. Half-way, two Englishmen were heard approaching: one asked my name. Yes, it was Gordon Grimsdale come to greet me. Perhaps because of the bromides I reacted strangely unenthusiastically to his welcome, for I was really grateful that these two should have descended all these steps only to mount them again, on my behalf.

The full moon shone in an empty sky, and was reflected in a widely-curving river bordered by mountains. A few twinkling lights among black trees created an effect of mystery. Perhaps it was also my rather dazed condition that made everything seem slightly dreamlike and unreal. However, I was able to register the fact that Grimsdale informed me of a tour we are to make together to the front lines. We leave on Wednesday for ten or twelve weeks on a tour of British military missions. This is a piece of luck. We may be allowed within a few miles of the forward areas, though there is no possibility of visiting the Communist areas at Yenan or Shansi.

A small Chinese soldier with a rifle saluted. He was the sentry guarding a dwarf villa. We had arrived, by car, at the top of a mountain. This was the British Embassy.

A minute hall gave on to a tall, octagonal sitting-room. The Ambassador, a lanky, over-grown schoolboy with witty eyes and a tired, but benevolent, smile on his long, donkey face, wore grey flannels. He presented his wife. She had humorous eyes, dog-biscuit complexion, and a deep, dry voice. Surprisingly, she introduced me to an owl-like Brooks Atkinson, the *New York Times* drama critic. We sat talking, maybe for an hour, in a casual atmosphere about inflation, the

Generalissimo and Madame Chiang. 'We're just picnicking here: we get, through the king's messenger, per month one bottle of whisky, a pound of butter, and a pot of marmalade, but everything is prohibitive here — especially as the black market is in a panic that it may be officially closed down.'

In this stronghold against the Japs, Chungking, the makeshift capital of China, is thriving as never before. Even the coolies are rich, earning 3,000 dollars a month: to ferry a grand piano across the river would cost 40,000 dollars. Chungking, with its rich, red earth, yields two crops a year and is self-supporting, but aid is being flown over the 'Hump' to China at the rate of one plane every two and a half minutes.

Baffling were the prices they quoted: the official rate is eighty dollars to the pound, but on the black market the pound is worth 1,200 dollars. A candle costs twenty shillings, a pound of boiled sweets thirty shillings; or, in dollars, pork costs seventy dollars a pound, a bottle of ink 200 and a gallon of petrol 900 dollars.

Of Madame Chiang it was said that her reputation is much greater outside her own country. The local people are so little conscious of her that were she to go out to a cinema, or on the streets, she would not be recognized. It seems that she was much put out by being so closely guarded while in America for she had been unable to go out and indulge herself in serious shopping. However one may dislike the woman, one must feel sorry for her, suffering as she does from time to time from a scourge of boils, due to her blood being too thick.

Sunday, April 10th

By degrees, the heavy mist lifted and I could see that the place where I had spent the night was a small villa, built with centre dome and four little apses, its slate roof flowering with yellow weeds. From this vantage point a wonderful panorama stretched below: on one side the Yangtze river, and on the other the Kialing. The boats with dark-brown butterfly sails reminded me of cockleshells.

From lower down the mountainside one could watch, at the junction of the two rivers, the tremendous life on their banks. On the steep slopes leading up to the town there is no transport: everything must be carried by primitive labour. The weights that are borne are appalling — monoliths! Both men and women wear almost permanently an agonized expression of effort: head thrust sideways, an extraordinary wriggle of the body, a swelling muscle bulging from under the yoke holding their burden.

The colonies of rickety straw houses lean in every direction. One cannot believe they can survive a storm. Yet they are not built for permanence: the occupants know that if the Yangtze should rise to a height of thirty feet, then their home will be under water.

The women are sturdy, stocky, the men have tremendous muscles. They eat their rice ravenously, gluttonously, scooping it into their mouths with the joss sticks used as shovels. The earth is valued so highly for food that there is no space made available for growing flowers: no nonsense here about the perfect peony. This part of China is as unlike the fragrant concubine, and those elegant fantasies of China that we see on porcelain plates and lanterns, as a mining town in the midlands.

I wanted to remain here, watching the ant-like life, but a number of appointments had been set up at HQ to meet people who will figure largely in my life in the near future. Stanley Smith, the Australian head of the Ministry of Information, took charge of me and gave me words of comfort. 'Anything you say of China is true — it is so huge.' I was intrigued by the alert mind and distinguished leanness of aquiline Leo Handley-Derry who will come on the trip with us. With a long, bony finger he pointed to a map and showed me why it would take at least five weeks to reach the front lines. Then Gordon Grimsdale, in his office, did exactly the same thing.

Kunming

The jagged mountains of limestone, so weathered that the outline looks like the temperature chart of a consumptive invalid, are not only of great geological interest but prove that the backgrounds of Sung paintings are, in fact, true to nature.

The town is laid out with streets running in the four cardinal directions and is renowned for its gates, carved pagodas, gilded arches and old city wall (now being pulled down). Today the Chinese consider walled cities as part of an ignoble past. Instead, modern buildings, of no particular architecture, are put up hurriedly. Thus, everywhere we see bogus Spanish palaces and imitation Corbusier banks and cinemas. No rich merchant would dream of building himself a Chinese house.

The natives, until six years ago, had rarely seen a motor-car but now are accustomed to lorries and jeeps jamming the thoroughfares, and to the sound of aeroplanes, which day and night fill the air as they bring in supplies from the remote outside world. But after seven years of fighting, most people seem to have grown accustomed to war and have focussed their attention on rebuilding and the interests of their family. Only professional politicians are interested in politics.

The air-raid siren sounded; the sky vibrated with the roar of aircraft; but the enemy machines were flying too high to be seen. The crowds trekked to the caves in the mountains. These warrens extend along the entire range and form an impregnable underground fortress; the whole town can shelter here. Nobody showed any signs of anxiety; in fact, the occasion was treated as a picnic; kitchens were set up outside the caves, and children played organized games.

GENERAL CHENNAULT

General Chennault, looking like a footballer somewhat battered after a victorious match, sat at a table behind a sign on which his name, perhaps rather unnecessarily, was printed in large letters. His room had a collegiate atmosphere, with flags and trophies. We were given cups of coffee — a great luxury.

No other individual has done more for China in her fight against Japan. Before the attack on Pearl Harbour, Chennault's group of American volunteer pilots, the Flying Tigers, had written a wonderful little page of history. Now he is chief of the US Army Air Force in China: without his contribution, events in the Eastern theatre might have taken a very different course. His task has never been easy; he is always short of aircraft, supplies and co-operation; yet the personal effect he produces is one of wealth and magnanimity. Come what may, he maintains an unruffled calm and creates confidence in others. Formerly a renowned fighter pilot, the inventor of tactics that revolutionized aerial warfare, he knows every aspect of flying from personal experience. After the last war he organized commercial air-circuses that toured America. For five years he was chief instructor of the Chinese air force cadet school. At his desk he now deals simultaneously with Washington and Chungking, as he directs the manifold policies and tendencies of his vast organization.

With the passage of years, he has become a little deaf; his mouth is tight-bitten and turns down at the corners. His complexion, yellow, as if stained by walnut juice, is pitted with deep crevices, and the skin around the jaw and neck is as wrinkled as the leather of the poor quality windbreaker that he wears, with the Flying Tiger painted crudely on the pocket. His black shaggy hair is beginning to be peppered with grey. Yet there is much about him that refuses to grow up. His shyness and utter simplicity are boyish qualities; his Red Indian eyes have a schoolroom mischief in them; and it is only when members of his staff come in that one has a glimpse of the power that he wields so quietly.

He reads their suggestions. 'No — that leaves a loophole — phrase that sentence differently, more emphatically. No, you didn't quite get my thought there.' He starts to write. Much of his work is now largely a matter of literary composition. The free and easy side of American army life is here exemplified. Perhaps Americans take all generals as a sort of joke — a joke particularly enjoyed by generals — and doubtless are right in doing so. 'Hey, General,' says his secretary. 'Hadn't you better put your blouse on?'

'Where's your General's blouse?' inquires some other member of his staff. The cry is taken up — 'Where's the General's blouse? Anyone seen a general's blouse? The General's lost his blouse!' At last someone stretches out an arm.

'Here y'are, General!' And with a wry smile and a shake of his head, the General changes his tunic.

A CANTONESE PLAY

April 15th, Kweilin

Rickshaw coolies ran through mud and rain in large Ascot hats. With their wide-shouldered capes made of bark, which looks like monkey fur, they suggest smart women arrayed in the height of fashion.

At first it gave me a shock to see one human being being carried by another. But is riding in a rickshaw any worse than being rowed in a boat?

Through the ram in rickshaws to the theatre. A busy audience sits in the palely lit wooden auditorium or swarms on to the sides of the stage. Russian audiences smell of baked apples, English of mutton; the Chinese do not emanate body-odour, unlike the Indians, the negroes or the French. It is a remarkably youthful gathering. Everyone appears gay and pleased with life; all are busy fanning themselves, eating, talking; all seem amused by the play and even more amused by life in general.

The play, given in Cantonese, with women playing the female roles generally allotted to young men, is traditional, but modernized with the help of elaborate changes of scenery and the inclusion of a saxophone in the orchestra. Although I understand little of what is happening on stage, I enjoy the stylized movements of the actors and the cold precision of their performance, and the noise of gongs and cymbals, punctuating the actors' *bons mots*. Extraordinarily beautiful in colour and design, the details of embroidery on the elaborate costumes can be admired even by those sitting in the farthest seats. Female characters are resplendent in filigrees of gold and silver thread and different coloured sequins — the young men in scarlet and yellow and pale pistachio green.

The *coulisses* always possess a mystery for me. Here they are particularly surprising.

A sheet of paper, with rough design of each setting, is the only guide for the scene shifters when they change the acts.

The orchestra is placed in a wooden pen on the stage. The quality of stage lighting used is of the minimum, yet the effects are inspired. Here is theatre reduced to its essentials, independent of all the drawbacks of 1944. In a communal dressing-room the cast repair their mask-like maquillage, eat dinner or polish up their parts from the script. Ornate headdresses hang next to a large piece of dried fish; bowls of make-up paint stand on the same table as the actress's meal of eggs and onion shoots; someone is washing his hair in the basin next to the rice bowls. Unlike the reverential treatment accorded European stars, these actors have to fight their way through a stubborn dense throng each time they make an entrance on stage.

The Americans have a particular knack of making themselves at home wherever they may be. This is not just a question of money. Here, you would think it difficult for them to find anything they could enjoy, for few of the customary amusements are available. Nevertheless they chum up with all and sundry — thereby sometimes losing face — pick up local slang and yell from their jeeps in reply to the welcoming village children. They drink the local rice wine; they organize rickshaw races; for once they are carriers, not carried. Down the centre of the main street comes a stampede: terrified coolies sit back in the place of honour, until the climax is reached with a general upheaval of rickshaws. Dollar notes are brought out in thousands, to pay for the fun and damage.

The English are less adaptable. They maintain, in the face of all obstacles, a complete British atmosphere in whatever remote part of China they may happen to make their headquarters. At all costs their food must be cooked in the English style. Cooking at home is not always of a high standard: Chinese imitation English cooking is appalling. Most Englishmen in China today live contentedly in the acme of unnecessary discomfort. Field-Marshal Sir Henry Maitland-Wilson is said to have remarked, 'Any fool can make himself uncomfortable.'

The farther men are situated from any big town, the higher seems morale. Officers, living together in the mountains, who have not seen electric light or tasted liquor for two years, and who know that it may be many years before they see their homes again, are as free of rivalry, petty jealousy or personal ambition as sailors on a great ship at sea. The utmost magnanimity, tact and patience is shown under exasperating circumstances. Similarly, isolation and the sharing of difficulties have brought about harmonious and deeply sympathetic relationships between the English and Americans, whose lot has been cast in such a foreign and distant theatre of war.

Monday, April 17th

I was busy scraping the mud off my tripod with a nail file when, after a four-day delay, we were told that the weather was improving enough for us to leave by air tomorrow morning early, a 4.30 call...

Tuesday, April 18th

It was dark outside when the watchman tapped, but we could hear the rain still falling. It seemed to gather in momentum for our take-off, and there were bad-tempered flashes of lightning. Yet, in spite of mountain-tops boring through the clouds, the American pilot guided us safely to Kanhsien, where thousands of coolies in blue were making an air-station. From my position in the aircraft I could not see why it was we swooped so low over the grass and then shot up again to circle the fields, but I was informed this was the only means of clearing the runway of personnel. But the coolies rushed out again, the moment of landing, to release the wheels of our aircraft from becoming embedded in the soft mud.

From this point, there are no flying strips, and the journey is to be continued by truck. A young officer, George Dawson, welcomed us. He had been waiting for a week.

TOUR TO THE FORWARD AREAS

We have started off on our trip! We are a company of about a dozen, including drivers. I am coupled with quiet-voiced Leo Handley-Derry. We had hardly started when the first delay took place. A Chinese lorry in difficulties on the opposite side of a river burst into flames, and several hours passed before we could be ferried by eight coolies straining rhythmically against long bamboo sweeps. Arriving at the wartime capital of Kiangsi province, Grimsdale proceeded to call upon Chiang Ching Kuo, the son of the Generalissimo, the ruler of this town and of four other States. Learning that the great man was away, we set off again, but at the next ferry we waited another hour and a half while the coolies and a mixed crowd struggled unsuccessfully to push a heavy bus, filled with people, that was stuck between a ramp and an incline. The people inside the bus refused to help. They would wait days on end while someone else did the job, rather than leave their places. We decided to return to Kanhsien, but the hotel was full. However, the magistrate invited us to occupy the guest house of Chiang Ching Kuo, and it was a relief to find a clean lodging, even though the dwelling was built without benefit of bathroom or lavatory.

During a visit to some American Fathers in a former French mission, we listened to the radio news from Burma which has lately been disturbing. The bulletin, though very crackly, was more hopeful — the Japs driven from the Imphal plain and from Kohima... It was strange to hear a priest saying 'What a boy!' and using Broadway slang. One, half-shaven, resembled an oversize pugilist and was a native of Pittsburgh; another, dark and bright, came from Boston.

Dinner with a Chinese General (all smiles) and an ex-minister (rather gruff) was staged in one of the best and oldest restaurants in the most ancient and dirtiest part of the town. In a room which presented an appearance of tragic poverty, with rickety stairs, peeling walls, old newspapers pasted to the ceiling to prevent the dust falling through the cracks, threadbare red cloth on the table and old faded paper flowers, we had a banquet of exquisite subtlety and refinement. Of the dozen different courses, every dish was an event. It did not signify that conversation was difficult. We ate. Particularly delicious was a fish junket (hot) with two heads and tails offish to ornament the dish; lotus seeds hot and sweet; liver cut to look like under-the-sea plants; bean shoots, crisp and resilient; a big fleshy fish, unskinned, seasoned with fragrant herbs; and duck soup. Such a feast must have cost at least 30,000 dollars.

As we emerged, the night air was full of every sort of whiff, including opium; and a woman was buying one of the long straw tapers to light her way home into the country.

Wednesday, April 19th

Leaving Kanhsien we were thrown into the vast outdoors of China. Perched high on the truck, open to the air, sun, and the varying elements, we had a ringside view of how the peasant lives in the heart of this unspoilt country. It is springtime; and the scenery looks unbelievably fresh, of an infinite variety of greens, from the pale pristine shoots of the ricefields, banked up in a succession of swirling curves, to the dark viridian squares of the rice nurseries. From the air this neighbourhood reminded me of an abstract painting by Frances Hodgkins — cocoa colour, rose-pink and pea soup green. On the ground it seems entirely green — lucid and touching greens — except for the blue distances of mountains and blue-clad peasants.

The day produced a variety of impressions: of large mountains covered with acacias, and trees with aromatic perfumes; of forests that smelt of sperm, of the very juice of spring; of peasants ploughing with buffalo the waterlogged fields of rice, the mud stretching up to the calves of their muscular legs, their thighs powdery with dry flaky mud. Occasionally we saw an old man being carried under the canopy of a sedan chair. The villages were of smoked wood and dark matting. The farmhouses, with dragon roofs curving at the eave-ends, were built simply and with beautiful proportions. Bowls of rice were eaten under the shade of a straw-plaited awning; the children had exposed behinds, and their parents, as if emptying a pot, often turned them upside down.

After a picnic lunch of the usual bully beef, eaten on the outskirts of a small town, the others foraged for some oil for the truck while I went to sleep in the sun, a handkerchief over my already burnt face. But the search for oil was in vain. We turned back to a hostel to drink tea. Grimsdale suggested staying the night here, but Leo Handley-Derry warned us that all our plans would be upset if we did not reach Kanchen tonight. So we proceeded. As it turned out, the distance was too far for arrival before dark; and no one in their right senses would choose to drive by night in modern China. Bridges are broken, pot-holes become craters, and there is often the risk of bandits.

Rain clouds appeared, soon to deluge us, and we had to cower under the canvas coverings of the truck. The light went. We drove on in pitch darkness. Eventually we arrived at a hostel filled with a roaring mass of throat-clearing Chinese humanity. At dinner, our waiter with gusto spat out of the window — another spat heartily in the passage outside my room. All night long babies cried, the bare boards creaked under heavy footsteps, and throats were cleared with deep guttural rasps.

Thursday, April 20th

After the usual ritual of packing bed rolls and loading truck, we went off to the mission for a wonderful breakfast, with Irish Catholic priests, of home-cured bacon.

The Bishop, with amethyst ring, in purple and black, seemed pleased to see us. He described the months when the Japanese, who had taken this town, were installed in the mission compound:

'A number of people had come to me for safety,' he said. 'We were quite a large party for supper. Suddenly a little fellow with knife and gun, eyes blazing, rushed in and snatched the cloth off the table, with all the supper things on it! Heavens above! The clatter and crashing were enough to waken the dead! We all got a shock, for we hadn't been expecting the Japs just yet. We thought they would come in at the main entrance; but no, they came in by the back. Well, we didn't know if it was our turn next.' The Bishop laughed, and as he did so, his denture slipped. 'Oh, there's a holy uncertainty about my teeth,' he remarked in an aside before continuing his story. 'The little Jap fellow began to pick up every plate, cup and glass that wasn't broken, and proceeded to make amends. Some of the children started to cry. Just as suddenly as he had come in, the little creature rushed out. Later, when the Japanese field commander arrived, it was difficult to make him understand that I was Irish; but he must have given orders to leave us alone. But all the time the Japs were here we didn't know how they'd behave next. Some midget would point a gun at your chest, and you never knew whether it would go off — if it had, it wouldn't have cost him a thought. But they were so mean! They'd do such mean things! Anything valuable they'd destroy. One man came in with a hatchet and with three strokes wrecked my typewriter. Another came in with a gun, looked around, and shot the clock. They'd search you and take anything they had a fancy for. They lifted my watch, my fountain pen, and then before leaving the room, kicked me in the stomach. They're little men too, and they know it. We got on to some of their ways. They won't humiliate themselves in front of foreigners by standing on chairs or a table; so if you want to hide anything you put it on top of a cupboard.' The Bishop shook his head wisely, and then nodded as a grave afterthought. 'But I'm glad I could help by being here — worse things might have happened, I declare.'

'Did they loot the place before leaving?' I asked.

'They took everything they could lay their hands on. The village was bereft of everything — as if the locusts had come. On the last night here they ordered everyone out of the village and then set fire to it. Why, the blaze would have pleased the soul of Nero! He could have gone on fiddling all night. Unfortunately there was a wind and this carried the sparks and burning timbers hurtling through the air; and, although we fought the fires in this compound, the rafters caught in the chapel — one thing leads to another, and by morning all that remained was the little outhouse.'

FATHER MURPHY

How the others of our party always remain so optimistic about reaching our destination in these two rackety trucks is a continuous source of admiration to me. Some part of the mechanism seems always to be giving trouble; we often run out of petrol, and must remain sitting by some deserted mountain road until, miraculously, someone appears with a camphor-smelling tin of petrol-substitute. But yesterday our truck started showing signs of ill-health soon after our dawn departure. By the afternoon it was emitting the most appalling noises, and with the approach of evening it refused to make further effort and, 100 kilometres before arriving at Pihu, emitted a series of loud bangs before coming to an abrupt halt. 'The sump has gone,' we were told. Gordon Grimsdale laughed. Soon it would be dark: better walk on, he suggested to Leo Handley-Derry, and see if there's anywhere to unroll our bedding for the night. Leo, with Bill, a breezy young cockney corporal carrying a gun, and I set forth. With the mountains a deep indigo, and the sinking sun like an enormous ripe crab-apple, the mountainous scenery was a Hokusai print, but it gave no promise of habitation. Leo smiled wryly; Bill was in high spirits, enjoying the adventure, particularly when, after we had been trudging for half an hour, he let off his gun and bagged a pheasant.

My own spirits rose when we saw, half hidden by a forest of bamboos, the dragon-tongue eaves and tiled roof of a temple. This would be quite a romantic place in which to spend the night. The temple, on closer inspection, appeared to be abandoned but for a few small chickens pecking about.

We ventured inside. Oversize gilt idols phalanxed the walls, Christian religious pictures and pictorial calendars hung on pillars, in one corner stood a harmonium while in another was an improvised dispensary. More chickens pecked around among the planks, wood-shavings and carpenters' tools which lay around on the ground, but a broken-down brass bed, Victorian armchairs and packing cases around the room showed that the temple had been converted into a huge dining-room-bedroom and storehouse combined.

Leo picked up some books and read aloud the titles of some others: *The Beat of the Heart*, *The True Jesus* and *The Analysis of the Blood Stream*. The place, he conjectured, must belong to a medical missionary.

Suddenly we heard the familiar sound of someone rasping his throat prior to expectoration, and through a wicker doorway appeared an extremely aged and shabby Chinese man carrying a tray of medicine bottles and retorts.

Leo asked: 'Are you master here?'

'No, me Wang! Master itinerating!'

Leo asked if it would be possible for us to spend the night here as our truck had broken down. Wang was overcome with laughter. I have noticed that the Chinese do not merely laugh for amusement's sake. They are apt to laugh when they are embarrassed, when they do not understand a question, or merely when they know of no other way of remaining aloof.

'Everybody welcome,' was the curt reply, but the elderly man seemed more interested in his bottles than in us.

Leo then told Bill to go back for the others, and asked Wang if there was anyone to make tea.

'No, no servants,' replied Wang. 'Servants too expensive. Cook will provide.'

Leo was somewhat baffled. Wang explained, 'Cook no servant. Cook my young brother — but very difficult person. Cook, he heathen.'

Leo inquired, 'And you — are you a Christian?'

'I, pastor,' said Wang. 'I teach the gospel with Father, but my brother heathen.'

'Is he a good cook?'

'Yes, very good cook, but very bad man.'

A small Chinese boy appeared in rags, and carrying buckets of water on a yoke. He was given Leo's packet of tea, blew his nose in his fingers and left.

Leo asked, 'Who was that?'

'That's Li.'

'Isn't he a servant?' asked Leo doggedly.

'No, Li be orphan. No servants, but plenty orphans,' chortled the old man.

At last the well known sound of our truck horn was heard in the distance, and Leo asked if a few of Wang's orphans could help with the luggage and bedding before darkness fell.

Soon the boys came in excitedly, staggering under loads of bed rolls, basins filled with shoes and sealed bags. All the impedimenta was dumped down in the centre of the room as Gordon Grimsdale appeared, followed by Bill — with another pheasant.

Darkness was almost upon us and there was little in the way of lighting so, although our host was absent, the orderlies threw down our bedding in the various rooms at our disposal. My own room had a store of pomelo fruit in it, and it smelt the most appetizing. But 'arrangements' turned out to be next to the kitchen, as they usually are in the more primitive parts of China.

We were drinking tea, trying to dispose of a plate of sawdust cakes which Wang's brother had made for us, and discussing the missionary situation in China. It was a more or less recognized thing out here to put yourself up along the road with the missionaries, and they like it for they get very little opportunity of seeing people outside their flock. They are much respected, for they renounce everything in life, live only for others, are remarkably unselfish, and the medical ones do wonderfully useful work.

Someone was singing ecstatically in a high falsetto voice. Suddenly a small fat man with flashing eyes and pince-nez came in. He wore jodhpurs and a topi, and wheeled his bicycle in with him.

On seeing the company he reached a high 'C'. 'Why ho ho, you could knock me down with a feather! Why, for surely to goodness — can I be believing my eyes? Must I give my specs another rub? Oh, this is wonderful — company!'

Gordon trusted the little man would excuse this invasion.

'Why, my friends, I'm so delighted — so flabbergasted I can hardly put tongue to the words.'

Gordon explained our predicament and Leo formally introduced the party, while the little man explained, in an avalanche of words, that he was Father Murphy, 'a bloody neutral', and asked if we couldn't tell from his accent that he came from the west coast of Ireland. He confided, 'I was just saying to meself, "Why I can't be having visitors here for over two years!" — and goodness gracious, that was when Miss Armitage and Miss Wade from Puchang were going on furlough. God be with you — I'm surely glad to have you here under our roof for the night, though don't expect creature comforts! We live simply, mind you. We're so far away from everyone we can't get anything done for us — so we put our hands to anything, don't we, Wang?' Wang cackled. 'We make everything for ourselves. We make our own oil for the lamp: we dry the long grass for fuel: tobacco out of old tea, honey and treacle dried out — it's not the same, but it does. Prices are so terrific — why, if we had to buy *anything* we'd be destitute! We even make our own matches.'

He produced a long taper with which he tried to light a lamp. When he struck this improvised match a tremendous explosion took place.

'Our experiment has not been successful,' laughed Father Murphy as Leo lit the lamp with his own briquette.

'The great difficulty is to get drugs and medicines to carry on our work: we can't get the stuff even if we could afford it, so we have to rely on substitutes. But it's surprising what results you can get — why, we've even lanced an ulcer, haven't we, Wang?' Wang bellowed with laughter. 'You see, there's no one else in this part of the country. If they've anything wrong they come to me from miles around, and we have to do our best. It's only a mere scratching of the surface, but it all helps.'

Bill reappeared with a third pheasant. On seeing this, Father Murphy's enthusiasm almost reached the point of hysteria. 'Goodness gracious! You're just the man I want! We've got a leopard prowling around the neighbourhood. We've always wanted someone with a gun and ammunition. Several villagers have been eaten. Wang and I built all sorts of booby traps — but no success.'

Bill admitted he wouldn't like to tackle a leopard with this gun; the first shot might not kill the animal, and it was no use waiting for a second shot.

Then Father Murphy talked of another problem. 'You see that ladder? That's for Timothy O'Grady.' He pointed out a network of toy ladders and run-ways that ran up to the roof and along the rafters. 'Timothy O'Grady's a seven-year-old cat, but he's all we have to catch the rats.'

'Do you have many rats?' I asked.

'Oh, many rats!' said Father Murphy, whilst Wang broke into much laughter.

Leo asked if there were any cases of plague.

'Yes,' said Father Murphy. 'Oh, many plagues,' added Wang while he and the three Chinese boys were transported with mirth.

Father Murphy told of his life here. 'Of course my real work is spreading the gospel. The Chinese make such good Christians! They love "The Bibleman", as they call me. Oh, they love the ritual — they love to kneel — they can pray for hours on end without getting tired! When I go out to tend my flock in the country all the people come out — perhaps more to see the foreigner than to hear the gospel! But you get tremendous crowds! They lift up their babies on their heads. Sometimes I can't make them go away when I want to sleep. I always get them to take a door down off its hinges, and I sleep on that — there are apt to be less foreign bodies in it than in an ordinary bed board.'

Gordon asked if he bicycled all the way on his journeys.

'Sometimes you can't take the bike through the mountains — it's too much to push — and I walk — as much as fifty lee a day. But they do the same journeys when they visit here for the four big holidays of the year. Christmas is a great time for them.'

Gordon then asked if the Chinese sang English carols and hymns.

'Yes, we have a hymnal in Chinese, and they know all the tunes. Oh, they love to sing!'

I asked if they didn't have a completely different music of their own.

Father Murphy enthused with complete lack of self-consciousness. 'They have pentatonic music — only five notes in a scale — no half tones. "Doh, ray, me, fah, sol, lah, te, doh," we have ...' He sang in shrill falsetto. 'They just have ...' and he emitted in a squealing rasp the most tortured sounds.

Gordon admitted that he was surprised that Father Murphy had not taken down these huge gilded effigies. Heathen gods, weren't they? Surely it made it more difficult for him with these things around?

Father Murphy was shocked. 'Oh, the Chinese are most superstitious and would be terribly upset if I took these away. They'd think it very bad luck and wouldn't come here. So we simply ignore them, that's all. The Chinese pay no attention to them either. No, this isn't perhaps an ideal place to work in, but there's nothing else in the district. You see, we were burnt out of the compound when the whole village was set on fire. That happened over a year ago.'

Gordon, surprised, asked if the Japs came as far as this.

'I'll say they did, too!' Father Murphy whistled. 'They stayed for months before clearing out, and I'll never forget that for the rest of my days. They've behaved terribly — oh, it was terrible! Our whole village was destroyed. Only twelve families escaped, the mission compound was demolished, and we've had to come here. But I'm doing all the talking! I want your news — we haven't a wireless. Our aerial was blown away in a storm, and the condenser's long worn out. Wang and I have been working on one made out of an old burnt tin, but it isn't large enough; we're waiting until another tin turns up.'

At dinner tonight Father Murphy did not, for once, live off the land. His enjoyment of our tinned foods was good to see, and he partook with relish of the contents of our flasks. His enthusiasm was so great that we wondered how we could disappoint him by ever going to our beds. He would pay no attention to any wistful plaints of fatigue, and the earliness of tomorrow's departure.

Far into the night Father Murphy talked. He wove all sorts of elaborate theories about the way the war should be fought, and asked technical questions of its progress, but he never awaited the answer.

When, next morning, we bade Father Murphy farewell, he regretted that he had not asked us about things in the old world; he had not even inquired whether we thought all that much of Lord Louis Mountbatten. 'But, goodness gracious, I've had enough to keep me thinking for months on end!'

We were happy to give him more practical reasons for remembering our visit. We were able to fix him up with a condenser and put his radio to rights, and we left behind quite a large selection of canned delicacies. Wang watched our departure with his usual gales of laughter, but Father Murphy's pince-nez was clouded over as he waved good-bye.

CHINESE GENERALS AND TROOPS

Saturday, April 22nd

An early start again. Most of us were up by 4.30. By degrees I am getting accustomed to sleeping on a wooden board; but the pelvis is apt to become painful if one lies on the face too long; I find the skin is peeling off my left hip-bone; pity I am not fatter.

Our route today took us through the mountainous paths of Chekiang province. No country could be lovelier. Gigantic gorges and vast mountains in the distance. When seen close at hand, they are covered with every exotic and strange variety of tree; ilexes in new leaf, with pale stylized foliage as in medieval tapestry; bamboos growing like pipe-cleaners; cascades of blossom; azaleas, purple, shrimp, scarlet and yellow; a mauve tree covered with waxen trumpets; the flowers of the pomelo bursting from ivory nobs, are the apotheosis of all bridal blossoms, and their perfume is positively celestial. All day, the vistas before our eyes were varied and beautiful; winding rivers, bordered with white rambler-rose bushes and flecked with white shell-like sails; neat terraces filled with gold barley or pale-green bristles of rice.

The pathways, made through the mountainsides centuries ago, are still used as shortcuts by the coolies, who push their wheelbarrows, or small carts equipped with a bicycle wheel, throughout the hours of daylight. They look like souls in torment as they lumber past on their flat feet, sweating and flushed under the strain; their life is dedicated to this appalling labour. Someone said, 'It's easy for them to die, but their troubles start if they become ill.' It was a poignant and upsetting experience to watch this interminable procession of labouring humanity. Even midget children carry loads with an obvious sense of responsibility, and hop out of the way of our truck, terrified but agile. Now and then the groups of coolies in their pagoda hats and blue trousers look extremely gay and charming. But here is a ghoulish figure staggering along at a tortoise pace, his torso and arms covered with discoloured patches and spots; his yoke makes life a torture to him. It is comforting to think he may pity us strangers as mere foreign barbarians, while he is a privileged inhabitant of the Middle Kingdom, the Centre of the World.

Leo, unfortunately, pointed out to me the latrines in one village, and remarked how much the Chinese enjoy defecating in a public place while watching life pass by. After this, not only did I catch sight of hundreds of these primitive arrangements of barrels and planks trader a matting roof; but a horrible stink was seldom long out of my nostrils.

We lunched at a depot of the British Military Mission in Longchuan. Again I was struck by the pathetic plight of these English youths, planted so far from their homes, in a world of new wood, bamboo, mud and flies. Fortunately, their work keeps them extremely busy, but the visual aspect of their existence is extremely bleak...

The next stage of our journey, towards Wenchow, should not have taken us more than four hours to cover; but we are in China; our trucks are old; they have been evacuated down the Burma Road and are not meant to last more than a year without new engines; they have not been repaired because there are no spare parts. We broke down. George Dawson, covered with grease, was a most responsible and expert mechanic; but the valves were old; the maintenance people had not done their work properly.

Thus our arrival was behind schedule. Elaborate preparations had been made to welcome the GOC: a guard of honour and a band had been out waiting since early afternoon. (So often these military arrangements, made in such detail, end in chaos.) The remnant of daylight faded while we were still on the roadside being passed by energetic coolies on foot. We had over an hour's normal journeying ahead. At last the engine revived. We were greeted by varying outposts. Finally, under a bridge, a line of Chinese soldiers and Colonel Larcom of the British Military Mission, who hobbled on a stick, greeted the General.

A less military-looking assemblage than ourselves it would have been difficult to imagine. Ah sorts of bundles and oddly-dressed servants piled anyhow on the van; my face had a leprous appearance under a heavy coating of cold cream against sunburn. Our hosts were extremely business-like and kind. We were presented to a dozen Chinese generals, each with the unscathed looks of a twenty-year-old, then conducted into a pretty sampan, newly-built of strong-smelling wood. With Chinese lanterns to light our way, we were paddled down a river. The Chinese C-in-C, with a small fat rubber face, enormous nostrils and shaved head, and his staff welcomed us with the usual exchange of compliments. He might have been any age; one cannot tell the age of the Chinese between twenty and forty. In a dining-room decorated with Chinese and English plaques, bearing suitable inscriptions about Sino-British friendship, and photographs of the leaders of the four great powers, stood a huge table covered with oranges and every sort of cake. The scene had the look of a Christmas festivity in the village hall. Speeches interpreted; more speeches; compliments; tea; everyone started to tuck in with enthusiasm. Suddenly, in the next room, an enormous hidden band struck up the most appalling caterwauling. When everyone stood to attention, I realized this din was the local rendering of 'God Save the King'. The noise was so surprising that I could not keep a straight face and felt utterly ashamed of myself for shaking with convulsive laughter.

On each side of me sat a Chinese soldier who spoke no more English than I speak Chinese. Another stampede, when the hidden band embarked upon the Chinese national anthem. The noises were as if fifty cats had gone mad. I tried to think of all the most horrifying things that could happen — such as the invasion of the room by hundreds of Japanese who would proceed to slash us all with swords — but even this did not prevent my shoulders shaking at the incredible noises.

Tuesday, April 25th

A demonstration, involving over 1,000 picked troops, was staged for the benefit of Gordon Grimsdale. An inspection; physical exercises, with the Chinese troops falling twenty-five feet from the 'Heavenly Gate', performing all sorts of tough manoeuvres and firing from all makes of gun — the experts said they had never seen such guns before. We inspected the Staff school. We climbed mountainsides to watch five imitation Jap trucks ambushed in a gorge. The programme of events was lengthy. Although the average age of the troops was said to be twenty, most of them appeared to be boys. According to the standards of a crack European regiment, some of the drill did not appear particularly precise, their uniforms were of a poor material, and their sandals of straw. At the end of the long day, after crawling or running up and down mountains, igniting fuses, blowing up targets, firing guns, these youths seemed as fresh and enthusiastic as if they had just come on parade.

Wednesday, April 26th

Tropical rain all night. By early morning the compound was flooded. The river has risen six feet and the water leaked through the bamboo matting on to our papers and on to the bed. Woe is me! My stomach troubles are no better, and I have come to know the outdoor lavatory almost as well as my own room. It seems an eternity since I was internally stable; I can hardly remember what life was like when incessant visitations to an insanitary outhouse were not necessary. A Scottish doctor visited me and prescribed M and B. This had to come many miles; but since its arrival I've had more confidence.

Thursday, April 27th

Rain continues to pour. The mill-wheel is now submerged. We cannot leave tomorrow. Everyone in poor spirits, but for myself the extra day is a relief, as I feel far from well. I got up to go next door to make a drawing of the Chinese General, but by the end of the morning was thoroughly irritated by the nagging of his interpreter — 'General Li wants you to put his stars on this way — Madame Li thinks the neck is too full — Madame Li does not want you to put flowers on her dress.' — 'Why?' — 'She says it's too flowery — Will you do another one of Madame Li?'

The rain slashes down. I became rather unnerved as the day progressed, for I had apprehensions, though about nothing in particular; would I ever return to Western civilization? I visualized the possibility of being taken prison by the Japs and wondered how I would survive the mental ordeal. All these ruminations were founded on nothing more sensational than a telephone conversation with Leo, who rang me up from a neighbouring house to say he would discuss our plans later in the day when we met, but that it was unwise to do so now. I knew that the Jap advance was continuing and that in certain sectors the resistance was slight. However, in such a vast country there can be no precipitous invasion; progress must be slow. My qualms were the result of some form of nervous exhaustion.

RETURN JOURNEY WITH CASUALTIES

'You've got a weak tummy still; you'd better come with us.' I sat in the front of the second truck. I enjoyed, as a change, travelling with a new set of companions; nevertheless I had qualms lest our truck should break down and I should be unable to join the others at the lunch halt. We retraced our tracks of weeks ago. The azaleas were now over; double roses, *Rosa multiflora*, like ramblers, had superseded the big white rose, the *Rosa cathiensis*, of the voyage out. We caught up with the first truck at a ferry. Dr Young, the interpreter, like the shopkeeper out of *La Boutique Fantasque*, in a panama hat and white suit, was very gay, helping the coolies to row the truck across the swirling river. At this halt I had meant to get into the other truck; but at the crucial moment I was taking a snapshot. The first truck went ahead; we followed.

About half an hour later we were halted by an anxious looking Colonel Larcom, from the first truck, standing alone in the mountain highway with an arm raised. At one side of him, a high wall of rock; on the other, a fifty-foot drop to the river.

'We've had a serious accident,' he told us. 'The truck's gone over there. The General's broken his leg.'

Scattered about on the boulders shelving down to the river lay various members of our vanguard. Bits of luggage, suitcases, umbrellas and pieces of clothing were hanging on the branches of bamboos. Some Chinese boys walked about, their faces marbled with dark dried blood; one of them looked like a prune. A Chinese soldier and Leo, quite undamaged, propped up Gordon whose leg was giving him much pain. A few paces below him at the water's brink, on its side, lay the dead and battered truck. We were told that the truck had hit a large stone, had jerked over the precipice, before the driver was able to right the steering-wheel and had somersaulted several times as it crashed down the rocks below. With each somersault people and luggage were thrown clear. But for a very short snapshot exposure I would have been sitting next to the driver, inside the truck, in the place occupied by Dr Young, who now lay unconscious on a crag, his suit and hat gore-blotched, his huge boots looking as if they did not belong to his body.

Bleeding Chinese were sprawled on the roadside, being sick beneath parasols. It was fortunate that a Viennese doctor, who had a huge trunk of medical equipment, was travelling with us. Bandages were applied; a stretcher made for Gordon who was brave and smiling. How could he be dragged up the rocky slope? How to place him in a truck? How could he endure the three hours' journey back, bumping over the broken road? No, he must go by river. Someone walked miles to the nearest village to try to telephone for a boat, but returned, having found no telephone. Then someone discovered a boat to go back as far as the ferry. The wounded were piled in. At the ferry, the boatman refused to go farther. Some of our party went off to try to find other boats and boatmen. Mr Lee, the Chinese radio expert with us, managed to recruit six boatmen; but, although there happened to be fifteen sampans in the neighbourhood, no one would take the risk of allowing his boat to go on such a long journey. I was told that this refusal to help was typical of what might happen in a serious crisis.

We felt forlorn when, three hours later, the wounded were still awaiting removal from the ferry. At last everything was ready. A boat was launched. Gordon, in great pain and becoming weak and fretful, was badly bruised; he could not sit up. The Viennese doctor gave morphine tablets which did not help enough. Dr Young was still unconscious. A few minutes later the boat returned with a heavy leak. At last it was righted and sent off again.

The river was high after the rains, and was flowing fast. But it was a slow journey. When, hours later, we passed the mournful shipload in our truck and shouted from the mountainside, the replies were despairing. They doubted if they would be able to make the hospital tonight; there were rapids; the boatmen, afraid of the approaching dark, had begun to give trouble.

On arrival at the ferry, from which we had started this morning, I felt so weak I could hardly tell the story of our misfortunes. Meanwhile, night covered the unhappy boatload as it moved forward slowly among unknown dangers. We received continuous messages of its progress; it had passed such and such a village; only twenty more kilometres to go. Later, we heard shouts announcing its arrival as it passed a bend in the river, and at midnight it finally reached its destination. The recent floods had been helpful; if the river had been either higher or lower, the journey could not have been made in one day.

The local Chinese general ordered the electric light to be kept on until 3.30 am when the doctors finished work. Most of the casualties are not as serious as we had feared. Gordon will have to be flown back to India to have his leg X-rayed; but he cannot yet be moved. Some of the party will stay with him. The rest of us will continue on our return journey in a few days' time.

There were about eighteen people in our truck, when, at last, we set off this morning. Added to our usual number was a Chinese woman with her family of four small children, their nurse — a picture of gloom and despondency — their male companion, also four students who had not money enough to get to their university. The journey was uncomfortably crowded, dusty and hot; the sun gave us headaches. It was a relief when we dumped the large family at their destination, for the children had become dictatorial. The small boy aged seven had been furious when the miserable nurse drank out of the same water-bottle as himself. 'Don't you know rules and regulations?' he screamed.

Every small town and village we stay in is redolent of disease. I am bitten by fleas which, I can only trust, are not plague carrying. Each night I go to bed anticipating visitors from the insect world.

I think and dream of long baths in Calcutta. This morning the Viennese doctor diagnosed the symptoms of one of the orderlies as those of bubonic plague. Macabre jokes. 'The Plague Season is on! Have we got a Union Jack? Could we fire a volley with a machine-gun?'

My luggage has now become a pitiable mess. My bag, made for air travel, does not protect any of its contents. The vibration of the truck has caused all the tubes of cream (tooth, shaving and cold) to twist their caps and become perforated; paints have oozed on to cotton-wool, socks, ties and medicine bottles; my one pair of pyjamas is soused in petrol; no article of clothing remains undamaged.

The truck was crammed. Someone asked, 'Could we take three girl students to their school ten lee away?' 'Yes.' So ten girls turned up. Five were allowed on. Their destination, it transpired, was twenty lee away. Tomorrow, God willing, is our last day of truck travel after banging over 700 miles in this old crock, for we arrive at Laiyang, the railhead.

We ate frogs' legs and filleted eel; the bill came to 900 dollars.

Monday, May 8th
I was called at 4.15 am for the longest lap of our journey, to the railhead at Laiyang. We have been through a variety of

ordeals.

We have taken it in turns to sit, in comparative comfort, in the front of the truck; and, when in the back, we have sat on bedrolls, or stood up holding on to the cross bars while admiring the scenes that fly past so quickly. Ours has been an oddly assorted group. Leslie Shellam, responsible for our comfort and safety, organizing our itinerary, paying the bills and taking everything so seriously; Leo, always reserved and stoic; the smiling, happy Chinese driver, never tired, gleefully shouting 'Ohay' each time we set off after a halt or setback; Lee, the young wireless operator going to Laiyang on promotion; another driver being sent back in disgrace for having failed to report that he had venereal disease; and the four students, each with a toothbrush in his breast-pocket, who have spent most of the trip lying asleep on the luggage; somehow they have always managed to get even more dust-covered than the others, or maybe it is just because, being originally dressed in black, they show the dust more; their hair has now become dim-coloured. In addition to this company, there have been the hitch-hikers from each stopping point; we have taken on five or six at every run. It has been a rough and uncomfortable trip. For this experience, at the present rate of exchange, King George has had to pay out 1,000 pounds for petrol alone. It costs twenty shillings to travel each kilometre, and this does not include the oil and running expenses of the truck, or the salaries to be paid to those accompanying us. We have had only the simplest meals, have spent the night in squalid hostels; yet our expenses have worked out at ten pounds a head a day.

A storm broke unexpectedly. The tarpaulin leaked. Everything in the truck became soaked; but eventually we got through to fine weather. I enjoyed standing up as the avenue of trees sped by, and the scenery changed in character. Everything became flatter — patches of dried terracotta earth sprouted fir-trees and even a few palms. Then came the plumy tame scenery that I prefer, with smoky green trees perforated by sunlight. A great number of magpies and other birds, shrikes, jays, kingfishers and some huge black butterflies with fat bodies like bats. Everywhere labourers at work.

We passed a coal-patch where blackened infants were waddling along, laden with their yoke of heavily-filled baskets. We passed miserable looking files of recruits being taken to war, their guards carrying enormous cutlasses like weapons out of a medieval shadow-play. Some miles farther a fugitive was being chased by a guard with a gun. Both looked exhausted, but all my sympathies were with the fugitive and I prayed that he might escape.

The roads became smooth and our truck behaved well. We arrived in good time at Laiyang where the British Military Mission HQ consisted of a small Chinese farmhouse, which was in the process of being reconstructed. About a dozen workers were still sawing wood, planing more laths prior to fixing up walls. A temporary roof consisted of some bamboo matting. Chinese umbrellas, strategically placed, warded off a few rain spouts; the ground was a mess of wet shavings and mud. There were some upright bamboo chairs. Half a dozen Chinese clerks were at work in this confusion and some orderlies were carrying on among the carpenters in the half light. The ground was so wet that the wood shavings were mashed to a pulp; workmen covered the typewriters with sawdust. By the office-sitting-dining-room an open space gave on to the village lane, and children in various stages of nudity came to stare. The view of the river was blocked by a latrine, built eight feet away from the dining table.

To a stranger like myself, this house seemed quite unsuitable for a headquarters. It had been chosen because it was equidistant from, and comparatively close to, river, road and railway. But it will be cold, damp and dark in winter — in summer, a foetid fly and mosquito trap. The proximity of the village will certainly breed disease.

The glassless windows let in mosquitoes as well as the cold. Lee, the Chinese wireless operator, who has been so enthusiastic at the idea of being promoted here, said, 'I think it's a revolting place.'

WITH THE RED CROSS

Wednesday, May 10th

The rain bucketed down in angry torrents. By the light of a small lamp we packed our bed-rolls, and trekked through the mud and puddles to the truck, half a mile away. God willing, we were about to leave this dump for ever and ever, amen.

After waiting in the rain at the station the train was signalled to arrive an hour late. When, at last, it arrived we were soaked, and our belongings reduced to a poultice. Cold and miserable we slept sitting bolt upright. At Henyang we moved to 'first-class' compartments and could lay ourselves down.

Insistent rain can make life horribly squalid. Wherever I looked from the train windows unattractive sights assailed my eyes: women disembowelling animals or pulling the skins off eels, squatting to relieve themselves on the ricefields while they picked their noses or searched in their children's hair for vermin.

After seven hours we arrived at the rail-end where we ploughed through the mud to a ferry-boat on the river Chang, for a three-hour trip to Changsha. The river was so wide that its banks seemed very distant on this dull, grey day.

Leslie, our leader, was cheerful for he holds Changsa tender in his memories. It contains the Red Cross hostel where a few months ago he had met, and married, his wife. He had been walking for eight and a half days when he arrived back to spend the night here: he had been given a hot bath, tea out of a nice cup, bread and butter. His spirits had soared, for there was a lavatory with a plug that pulled. Someone had said, 'Let's go over and see the Red Cross people.'

'No, I'm sick of seeing Chinese officials.'

'Chinese officials! My eye! They're beautiful English nurses.' Leslie had fallen for romance there and then. His wife is now nursing in India, but this place for him is still full of the old magic.

The compound proved to be American. Some Bible society had built it ten years ago, at the cost of many millions of American dollars — a number of red brick buildings of no particular character, but comfortable, with all the latest amenities. Leslie's face was transformed, his eyes like stars, his teeth shining. He received a rapturous reception from the sisters and everyone else working here, including the Chinese gardener. The matron called him by his Christian name every second — it recurred like a hiccup.

We were fed scones and given tea by bespectacled nurses whose giggles mounted to gales of girlish laughter. To have a bath, wash one's hair, shave, put on a civilian suit, were great events. We had a good dinner in the suburban villa with the nurses.

Later a small Scots nurse came in with a lantern. 'I'm having an awful time with one of the relapsing fever cases; he's been out of bed three times, and has become violent. I can't find Dr Wong. Would you look at his papers, Doctor?' Dr Flowers, grey-haired, and grey-faced, prescribed some palliative; the night sister went back to her work. Suddenly one realized the *raison d'etre* of these women here — the background of serious work behind a façade of scones and cups of tea. The social trivialities occupy only a very small part of their existence. For the rest of the day they are empresses — rulers, with the responsibility of sickness or health, life or death, over large kingdoms. I was much impressed to hear them all speaking fluent Chinese, and treating their patients, not as strange objects to be stared at (which in a way, I confess, is still my attitude) but as fellow sufferers and fellow human beings. Some of the cases were terrible to look upon; but the nurses did not flinch.

The hospital, with its 180 beds, is filled to capacity; many cases cannot be admitted, and Chinese soldiers are apt to die of fever through lack of medicines. The doctors improvise or try to buy substitutes. Yet they meet with such opposition from the Chinese in control that often they earn more jealousy than gratitude.

Thursday, May 11th

Leo and Leslie took me into the town, but as an air raid alert was on most of the shops were boarded up. With the official rate of exchange, the prices are fifteen times more for us than for the Chinese; thus some gaudily embroidered satins were 100 pounds each length, and candles were twenty shillings each. Our craving for sweets led us to pay thirty shillings for a pound of rather ordinary caramels that would cost one and sixpence in England.

Saturday, May 13th

Our hosts, the American missionaries, were in fine spirits. One of the women had helped deliver twins during the night. Mrs Hekma had wrapped a great number of Bibles, while Mr Hekma addressed the packages in Chinese characters to be sent off by post. Here, in the remotest spot in China, we seemed to be living in any American old folks' home. A wizened Uncle Sam said grace before canned food meals, and a celery-coloured doctor, with a deep voice like a chisel, joined in the singing of hymns and old Southern folk songs, accompanied by a grey-haired lady in pince-nez and a foulard dress, who hit plenty of wrong notes on the upright.

They were a friendly, cheerful family and extremely hospitable, but we were too self-conscious to enjoy their parlour games, and since we have had no luck in hitch-hiking on a transport plane, we have decided to board the next train to Kweilin.

Monday, May 15th

'This train should arrive at 7pm,' someone said: others said, '9 o'clock'. Distance, 400 miles. Train travelled at snail's pace. Hot, thunderous weather turned to storm; rain poured down and came through ceiling of coach — and bugs came out. We killed some with the end of a spoon. Chinese in carriage yawned with the noise of bellowing cows, spat, gutturally grunted, broke wind, picked spots on their faces, excavated their nostrils, blew their noses in their fingers, then rubbed their fingers on chair-seats or wall. No one suffered from inhibitions or false modesty: men lay with barnacled feet out of windows, women fed babies at breast, everyone made their own personal addition to the general pandemonium. By degrees the energy stored up during the night seeped out of every pore of my body.

Leo has lived for many years in China. Before the war his firm planted 20,000 trees; a small proportion were eventually to be used as pit props. They were policed for protection; but of late, this had become impossible. Within a year all the trees had been cut down, stolen, sold or used for fuel. The people are so poor, know so well the horror of poverty, that if ever they can see a rare opportunity of rising above a degree of starvation-level they feel they would be foolish to miss it.

For sixteen hours we sat in the same bug-infested seats. Large bumps arose on wrists and arms. There was not sufficient light to read. At Kweilin North Station we started shunting backwards and forwards. After one hour and a quarter, we were back in the same station from which we had been painfully jolted. When eventually we arrived at Kweilin South, we had to wade through ankle-high mud to get into a truck. We came back to Hemming's house, a recently built, curiously suburban villa, which has been commandeered for the overflow of officers of the British Military Mission. Although it is almost unfurnished, and without a book or a fire, by comparison with our recent lodgings it now appeared comfortable and even luxurious.

Tuesday, May 16th

J. B. Priestley is said to have given a talk on the radio about a typical Chinese who spends all his money on some single object of beauty; how, when he walks along the street, he pauses to admire a tree, and a little farther, stops to listen to the note of a bird; how he will spend hours contemplating one perfect bloom. What utter bosh! He is much more likely to espy a particularly large cake of cow-dung, and rush to take it home before anyone else gets it!

A LITTLE ESCAPISM

Hemming's House

For many days now the skies have emptied themselves in a steady downpour. The mountains which surround this remote town and have the improbable contours of roller coaster railways have been hidden completely. Flying has been at a standstill so half a dozen of us have waited — with teeth chattering from the cold — for a break in the clouds so that we can fly back to the comparative civilization of Chungking.

The noise of heavily-shod feet stamping on the wooden floors, and raucous voices echoing in the empty rooms, prevents me from concentrating on a book, or even on the talk about the currency problem, the various forms of Chinese graft, or technicalities or statistics.

The first trapped minutes were the worst. Finding myself in this one-eyed dump, I began to know a little of what a prisoner of war must feel. By degrees, I became resigned to this Kafkaesque existence in this unfurnished Golders Green bungalow in a Chinese no-man's-land.

Yet it was a welcome escape when Akë Hartman, a Swedish-American, who has lived mostly in China and Japan (he recently escaped from Shanghai) arrived out of the blue mist and took Philip Smith and myself to have a Chinese-Turkish bath. This proved to be a unique interlude of sensuous delight — an astounding and welcome contrast to the austerity of the BAAGHQ mess.

Everything looked appetizing and unfamiliar: the honey-coloured wooden walls were bare except for a few notices in decorative calligraphy: discarded clothes were hung high around the ceilings — hoisted on long rods: everywhere hot water: a tireless bath-boy to soap and douche one, then to run with a relay of large hot towels. But more to follow: one boy massaged the feet while another banged one's legs and back in a manner that seemed to open the sluices and allow the blood to circulate in all sorts of long-forgotten regions of the body. Finally, another boy added a touch of nanny-like cosseting when, by the light of a small lamp, he started a lengthy and most meticulous *pedicure*. Not only was each nail treated as a jeweller might prepare a prize stone for setting, but the toes themselves were treated to a massage as if each had been a separate limb: one did not know how flexible each individual toe could become, or what a relaxing, delicious soothing of the nerves such concentration on these small extremities could produce. In fact, although this immaculate emporium was of the simplest sort, and catered for the ordinary poor man to whom such treatment is considered a necessity, for Westerners it was the apex of luxury and civilized subtlety.

Philip Smith became excessively British and, I fear, did not approve of such sybaritic *délicatesses*; he returned in the pouring rain for fried meatballs out of a tin at the mess. But I felt like the cat that had swallowed the Devonshire cream, and, deciding that Hartman was an ideal cicerone, hung on to him until he took me to the Vitamin Restaurant, which was curiously named in view of the exquisite refinement of the chicken dish which is said to be the best in China.

In our *chambre particulière* we ate every sort of local delicacy while Mr Wu, the manager, talked to us with an almost too determined erudition. Later, we were bidden to the upstairs room of the proprietor of the restaurant: looking like Jean Cocteau, he was a young Chinese who, having been wounded, was now free to run this rich restaurant, which he does with an imperious wave of his left hand. Everything seemed to him so easy. He gave me a cigar, and we talked on aesthetic subjects for a long while until he asked if we would excuse him while he went to his room for a smoke. Perhaps we would care to accompany him? We would. The bed was laid out with a clean spread, and coloured feathers hung in the window. The atmosphere brought me back to pre-war Paris: so did the scent of his opium. Would I like to try a pipe? I accepted. As before, the opium produced no effect whatsoever upon me, and I felt I had run the risk of getting into severe trouble for nothing but a pleasant evening's relaxation.

It became late, but still the rain poured. Yet it was useless to wait for the torrent to abate. So Hartman and I decided to walk back to the headquarters of the BAAG. But everyone there had gone to bed. So I must find my way back to my suburban villa. I knew it was quite a distance and was not too sure of the way. Luckily, Akë volunteered to accompany me. For quite a considerable time we walked in the dark, in mud that came over the ankles. We found ourselves close to some strange-looking hillocks that previously I had noticed in the far distance. No, this couldn't be right! We retraced our steps in the slush and rain. We were sweating now. We walked on a couple of miles or so — then luckily came across a little Chinese policeman. He could speak no English but pretended he understood Akë and convinced us that he knew the way to the British Military Mission. Discarding his bayonet, he would accompany us. Once more we retraced our steps. We staggered into potholes. The policeman's torch became fainter, but the rain poured ever harder. Suddenly, a row of houses: home at last! Oh, but no! We discovered we had been brought to the Free-French house of Major Vitel. A servant appeared from deep slumber — a squat Chinese girl with gold teeth who spoke English and giggled. Master was out at party. Home soon.

Since the Frenchman was such a long time in returning could we not, perhaps, telephone? Yes, there was a house farther down the mud track that possessed a telephone. By painful degrees we woke up more sentries. We cranked the telephone handle while servants, sleeping on the bare floors, woke enough to scrape their throats with appalling sounds before spitting great gobs around their fellow sleepers. No telephone operator at work. At length we decided to walk forth into the blackness again.

A feeling of appalling impotence overcame us. We were utterly lost. A young Chinese sentry explained that we were mad to wander through the night. Why not go to an hotel?

Because, said Akë, this master (pointing to me) was hoping to leave town early in the morning. But why not leave the next day?

We decided it was no use walking farther on: we were only exhausting ourselves needlessly. We must take the sentry's advice and try to find our way back into the town. On the outskirts of the town we recognized the turning that our lorry always takes off the main road. Surely *this* was the right way home!

The opium must have taken more effect than we realized, for we had completely misjudged our speed and distance. The poppy may not have given us dreams but it had endowed us with incredible physical strength. We had walked perhaps ten miles.

After a few minor mistakes we at last found Hemming's house again, and my troubles were over. However, the wretched Akë had still a long trek before him. He seemed quite confident after I had put him on the right track. Then, oh then, at last! I slowly peeled off my soaking, muddy clothes, and was able to unroll my bedding and sink luxuriously into a drugged sleep.

This expedition into the Chinese blue has thrown me back on to my own resources without even books or music. There have been days when I have had nothing but my own thoughts for company. Often my thoughts have been disturbing: my brain is a poor one, inadequately trained; I cannot take in more than a few facts or figures at a time. Perhaps insufficient interest causes me not to listen carefully to what is being said. My distracted thoughts are dissipated in many directions. Even when travelling for hours in a truck, I am incapable, hard as I try, of thinking along one particular line. I have always been unlike the majority of people. Since I have built up a life to suit my own interests, I have become more and more a specialist, remote from the world in general. Most people are interested in a greater variety of subjects, yet comparatively few make a study of the odd things that I find absorbing. This shaking-up has stirred me in a most wholesome way — even the unpleasant aspects of the trip have been beneficial: it does no one harm to get tired, to walk too much, to be either too hot or too cold, to go hungry for a few hours and use what Dr Carel called the 'adaptive functions'. If I have become painfully conscious of my mental weaknesses and limitations, it is heartening to see how well my constitution stands up to these tests.

In my companions, all the time, I have been most fortunate. I have learnt a deal about good behaviour. Although concessions are made all the while to me by Leo and the others, and instinctively I feel I am not really of their company, yet I am critical of them when I know they would be charitable towards me. The tolerance shown in the army is remarkable. A man is seldom judged, practically never condemned. There is little backbiting and malice; and every man is impelled to behave just as well as he can to the community of which he is an organic part. Selfishness is the exception. The only man who behaved unlike the others, who showed up poorly by contrast, was suffering from thyroid trouble, a hospital case of toxic poisoning which caused the mind to react in an unnatural way.

I have not flinched at some of the rough passages, and have enjoyed the idea of seeming to be 'a sport', yet secretly have clung to my selfish civilian interests. I have not renounced my home, and have known that soon, God willing, I shall be able to return to the life that suits me and to which I am accustomed. (Perhaps if I *had* given up my freedom, once and for all, it would have made some of the delays and setbacks easier for me.) There have been many times when I have wished that I could face possible disaster with the same cheerfulness as others. I have felt physically fitter than when I lived in the big cities; but, perhaps as a result of six months' hard travel, I have recently become rather morbid and introspective.

Chungking

Returning to the same house in Chungking I vacated aeons of time ago, everything looks so much more luxurious. My standards of comfort have changed. Attuned to such poverty, to find a few unexpected, forgotten treasures in my bag left behind — a half-filled cigarette tin, a pot of shaving cream and a fresh shirt — this is a Croesus hoard!

THE GENERALISSIMO AND SOME MINISTERS

I was awakened at dawn by the telephone. 'This is the last day of the session at which all the provincial governors and Cabinet ministers are meeting. Could you come to the Parliament building by 7 o'clock to take photographs of the great occasion?'

Tremendous heat: little Professor Chi, sweating from head to foot, was waiting by the roadside for me. The sun was already merciless but Dr Chi kept mopping himself, and like the rabbit in *Alice* muttered repeatedly, 'Oh dear, we're late. The ministers are arriving, the ministers are arriving.'

Armed with blue flashes, we went through the portals of the Parliament building, only to be stopped at the top of a flight of stairs by a young soldier who demanded to see our military permits. Dr Kung, the Finance Minister, arrived at this moment and said we could come in with him. But the soldier was adamant. An altercation ensued. Dr Kung threw his arms in the air. Professor Chi mopped himself anew, and invited me to 'Come and have a little rest'. I had learnt before that this means that somewhere there is a serious hitch. Dr Chi kept muttering under his breath, 'There's the Minister of the Interior — oh dear! there's the Minister of Education — Agriculture.'

The written permit arrived simultaneously with the ringing of a bell as everyone went into session. During the proceedings I prowled around clicking my camera, but it was during the morning's interval that I had my best opportunity to photograph the ministers and heads of Yunnan. It would be impossible to take an uninteresting picture of some of these old men with their long, straggling beards, fingers like cheese sticks and slenderly draped gowns.

Suddenly, the stamping of soldiers' feet and snapping of bayonets presaged the arrival of the Generalissimo. Wearing a topi and dark glasses, he walked slowly up the staircase. Off came the topi, off the dark glasses. He acknowledged the deferential nods of a few stragglers. He looked clean, well chiselled with high cheek bones and well pressed; perhaps most remarkable, he looked extremely cool. He is short of stature, with bright, furtive eyes, and his complexion is of a suety texture: his pate as carefully shaved as his chin. Unfortunately, he was followed by a rabble of tough-looking men in uniform. Some of these thugs gestured with wild flapping arms and impatient grimaces for the sentries, and others standing by, to move away. This menacing pantomime robbed the Generalissimo of much of his innate dignity.

Lady S. is extraordinarily frank and direct. She thought my drawing far too flattering. 'I know what I look like all right. My son has a friend who asked: "Can't you middle-aged women realize that when you look down with your head thrust in like that, you go all crumply under the chin?" But, my heavens,' she said, 'why regret lost youth? What a lot life teaches us all the time if we're living any sort of a life at all. All that must show itself in ourselves: we *must* be improving all the time!' Lady S. is a great companion to her husband. Last night there was a long discussion about whether a star keeps pace with the progress of the moon across the sky at night. 'Surely that star jiggles along in the same ratio to the moon?' asked Lady S. 'No, the moon jiggles along on its own.' 'Horace, do two pieces of ice last longer in a glass of water than one?' 'Yes, they keep each other cool.' Lady S. couldn't understand, but side-tracked the argument by admitting, 'I do see that one large lump lasts longer than two smaller ones.'

Monday, June 19th, Chungking

The Ministry of Information continues to send telegrams listing ever more subjects for me to cover before leaving China. I am somewhat resentful that so much trouble is taken in London to organize work for me which, once in the files, seems to remain ignored. It is, however, heartening to know that the whole outfit here are impressed with the amount of work I have done. Horace Seymour told me he will write to Brendan telling him that, under the present conditions of 'flap', I could not be expected to do more. It seems that the Japanese are advancing in the south, and there has been talk of giving up the British newspaper in Kweilin. The Ambassador said that it was right that we should abandon the hospital in Changsha, but the British must teach the Chinese a lesson in courage. It appears that Hollington Tong has said, 'The British are again a flying army.'

As a result of an attack of dysentery, added to a certain nervous exhaustion after the strain of the trip to Chengtu, I am a bit on edge. While I was doing a drawing of her, Lady Seymour remarked that I seemed depressed. Perhaps I am, but I thank heaven for her friendship, for her nice home, and its comparative comforts and peace. Her news from England was heartening: apparently the robot bombs are not doing much damage, and the advance continues satisfactorily in France. The Cherbourg peninsula is now cut off.

After the evening meal (tinned sausages and bacon) with Stanley Smith and his heterogeneous household, we discussed the wastage here of effort and money. Because the Treasury took five months to answer a request for 100,000 pounds, the money was worth only a quarter of the amount that it would have been had surety come through within six weeks, etc., etc. Stanley worked out that the petrol alone for sending me to

Chengtu would cost 300 pounds. He also remarked that I would never have been able to achieve so much work in Chungking had I not been staying with the Ambassador. If we had had to rely upon the Chinese Ministry of Information for making connections, I would still be waiting, cap and camera in hand.

Tuesday, June 20th

The pitiless rain continues — fog — mist. Early descent, with the Seymours, of the muddy mountainside only to discover, at the Press bureau, that Henry Wong, my cicerone, was unable to accompany me on a photographic outing today. A wait of two hours, reading torn magazines, before a Mr Lu appeared. In spite of leaden light and late start dozens of rolls were taken and gaps filled for the Ministry of Information visiting the Roman Catholic cathedral, all bombed but the spire, the principal fire station (the firemen wear huge Aladdin hats of black and gold straw), and a nursery school for the kids of Government officials, too badly off to afford nurses.

I had wanted, also, to photograph some war orphans but there was the usual hanky-panky and dishonesty. At first Mr Lu was told I had already photographed them. When I denied this, it transpired that they did not *wish* them to be photographed. This, it appears, was a punishment for the fact that I was alleged to have photographed the New Life building without permission. It seems everything has to be 'prepared' before being photographed, so the orphans' faces must be made up. Lady S. says there are about a dozen brats farmed out to be shown off in different places for official visits. When she went with Madame Cliiang to one hostel they recognized the same little 'orphans' serving them tea as at another centre they'd been to previously. At 2 o'clock, I returned to find Lady S.

eating a solitary meal, her husband having gone off to the airport to meet Vice-President Wallace.[37] She said, 'I hope you'll think of our life here as interesting, and as having a certain amount of charm.' But, frankly, I am amazed that she is able to think of it as charming.

PROFESSORS IN PENURY

Fuhtan University, evacuated from Shanghai, is now situated within 100 miles from Chungking. It was a shock to see the professors, who before the war were great figures in the world of culture and basked in an aura of esteem and luxury, now living in near-destitution. Professors' salaries have not been raised in proportion to the cost of living. Today our unappetizing roadside lunch for two cost 300 dollars. A professor is paid 1,000 dollars a month. He subsists on poor quality rice; he sleeps and works in a prison-like cell, with no one to tend him. He possesses no furniture except perhaps a board propped on two dictionaries as a bed, and a case with shelves for the volumes salvaged from his former life. In accordance with the 'oil thrift' movement, the lamp must be put out early at night. Living like peasants are the great specialists and experts on French literature or European philosophy; men who have been editors of scientific magazines, who have been the pivot of intellectual life and thought, are stranded here without money for cigarettes, some of them suffering from foot-rot so that they are unable to walk, and others from disease caused by undernourishment and lack of baths. Yet they remain astoundingly cheerful and full of verve.

---

[37] Many today consider that this visit was responsible for the unfortunate policy that the US adopted towards Formosa.

Dr Liang entertained us with fascinating anecdotes about Paul Valery and his other friends; and he gave us a glass of tiger-bone wine, a potent and invigorating drink.

Another professor talked of Dryden and Maugham with a combination of charm of manner, authority and humility. In the room next door his sister was working, but when called, she would not appear because she had not on her best dress and did not wish to be seen looking like a servant.

Dr Young is an authority on contemporary English poets, and quoted Empson and Auden. He is at the moment translating into English the poems of Dr Liu, not because he considered them good poems, but 'because he is a friend of mine'. He told us how Dr Liu is of the old school, is accepted by the Government and writes about poetic generals. Dr Liu publishes one book of poems per month. This is not considered excessive.

MADAME SUN YAT SEN

What greater tribute can one pay the widow of Dr Sun Yat Sen, than to say that in present-day China she is poor? She is the most popular woman in Chungking; kindly, sincere, courageous and known to have the welfare of China at heart. In a country where to be outspoken is sometimes dangerous, she does not hide her disappointment at the distance she believes the Government has travelled from the principles laid down by her husband, the Father of the Republic.

This gallant, rather tragic, little figure is continuously breaking into laughter. She screws up her face, like a baby about to cry, with a mirth that is alternately childlike and hearty. She laughs in answer to a compliment, laughs as a lament, laughs as a means of expressing agreement and when to be more precise would be unwise. She is almost peasant-like in her intuitive simplicity. She looks like Mrs Noah; her gestures are slightly masculine, her fingers fattish and pointed; her diminutive feet hang uselessly like a doll's, not long enough to touch the floor. She lives in a small gimcrack villa, immaculately swept and garnished, where the flowers, sent by faithful friends who possess small patches of garden, are plumped into metal shell-cases. Thence she sallies forth, and learns perhaps more of the public opinion in Chungking than any other member of her family.

Local news is bad; it seems probable that the Japs may cut China in two and capture all remaining Free China. They could even concentrate on stopping our supplies over the 'Hump'. No one is visibly panicky; the worst has been expected for so long; but everyone is secretly worried as to how the various armies will meet the three Jap thrusts.

CHINESE RETROSPECT

The west of China consists of the agricultural and more mountainous provinces in which transport has always been poor and existence hard. Life in these paddy fields and small dark villages can have changed little with the passing of the dynasties. From early childhood till oldest age, from dawn until dark, every day of his life, the labourer toils for the minimum reward. The carrier-coolie, his head bent sideways, minces, like Agag, under his appalling load. The farmer, almost naked, with legs as muscular as Nijinsky's and wide apart as a wrestler's, plants in the swamps, with zealous speed, the small aigrettes of rice shoots. The water-treaders at the wheels, covered with sweat, defy by the hour the laws of gravity and cause water to run uphill. Stolid young women weed in the mire, or thresh vigorously throughout the heat of the day; children, with a wisp of bamboo, drive the herds of goats and gaggles of geese; the old women pick the leaves off the tea-trees, or tie little bags, against the onslaught of birds, over the ripening plums. The river coolies, in the rain, wearing the short capes of palm-tree fibre that, although of a design thousands of years old, are distinctly fashionable, strain at every limb as they fight the unpredictable currents and the evil spirits beneath the water.

With infinite patience, everybody battles against discouragement and disintegration, and in the face of all disasters their spirit remains unbroken and unbreakable. When others would despair the Chinese smile with contentment, for they are of the celestial kingdom. Each farmer, coolie and soldier feels about his lot as did Shao Yung: 'I am happy,' he said, 'because I am human and not an animal; a male and not a female; a Chinese and not a barbarian; because I live in Loyang, the most wonderful city in the world.'

Smiles and laughter are never distant; they are the ever recurrent theme that runs through the overcrowded bamboo villages and newly-bombed towns, along the lines of coolies, human beasts of burden, in the curving mountain passes, down the river-banks where millions make their homes in flimsy, overcrowded sampans. Smiles appear at the misfortune of others, at moments of terror or anxiety; they are a means of 'saving face', are present at both birth and death (the two 'great happinesses'). The Chinese sense of humour, easy recognition of the comic and inveterate optimism combine with the national feeling of resignation to help them bear the misery — sometimes cruelly unnecessary — of present-day conditions.

In fact, the silent, inscrutable Chinese, who moves noiselessly and laconically through the pages of fiction, is an invention that bears no relation to the sturdy, boisterous people I saw fighting for existence. The Chinese are demonstrative and highly strung, easily roused to excitement or anger. They are apt to blush more often than the English, while a rapid change of expression adds much to the charm of these uninhibited extroverts. White teeth flash; eyes are tightly screwed up in an excess of convulsive mirth. I marvelled at the eloquence with which the Chinese physiognomy expresses different emotions, indicating in turn inquisitiveness, surprise, greed, terror or embarrassment. By the grimace he makes, we know how far a coolie has trudged, how rough the way has been, how heavy his load. As he toils up a precipitous slope, his contorted features resemble those of a martyred saint; yet when he reaches the summit to rest for a moment, the expression of relief is beatific. Every police-boy, perched high on a concrete rostrum at the crossroads, gives an heroic pantomime performance. Running the gamut of facial expression, he directs the traffic with the gestures of a great actor. With what scorn does he observe a driver whose engine has broken down; with what unabashed amusement does he witness some ridiculous mishap to a passer-by; with what popping of eyes and wild contortion of muscles does he control the ferocious rush of the approaching traffic!

The Chinese of fiction is always delicately proportioned with an ivory-coloured skin and eyes turned up at the corners. In reality, he is often husky, squat, with overdeveloped muscles and a thick bull-neck, and his skin is of a healthy apricot hue. Although the colouring of his hair is monotonous, his appearance otherwise varies to an astonishing extent. His mouth, being finely chiselled, is his best feature (just as it is an Englishman's worst), and his eyes, which seldom show any lids, turn down at the outer ends.

Pidgin English is scorned and seldom heard. If the Chinese speaks the English language, it is apt to be with grammatical perfection, a much wider vocabulary than the average Englishman employs, and possibly a strong Chicago accent.

Unlike the 'other worldly' Chinese of legend, the people I have met are shrewd and business-like realists. One has only to spend a night in a native hostel to discover just how 'soft-footed' the Chinese are! A traveller who wants to sleep must contest against the noise of furniture being lugged over the resilient floors of the rooms above, a Niagara of family gossip that continues outside his door all night, and the singing of a neighbour 'in good spirits'. The Chinese is no lover of silence — witness the noise in any restaurant, with cooks and waiters hulloaing, babies caterwauling, parties at neighbouring tables playing raucous gambling games, while cymbals are beaten and brass bands bray in the street outside.

During the last painful years China has struggled on, in spite of appalling shortages of equipment (including heavy weapons), transportation (including fuel) and all sorts of medicines. The Chinese genius for the makeshift has stood her in good stead. As the Japanese approach, the Chinese tear up the railway lines to make them into guns. The scarcity of petrol has led to the discovery that trucks and lorries can be run on camphor, alcohol, locally produced wines and spirits, and on crude oil made from the tung nuts that grow on the hillsides. Lorries, that might have been considered to have done good service after travelling these roads for twelve months, are, after four years, in spite of the non-existence of spare parts, seen hurtling along the mountain passes with seven separate pieces of outer tyre bolted on to their wheels; the driver hangs frantically on his door to warn pedestrians, for the horn and brakes are missing. As the truck vanishes round a hairpin bend the air is filled with a pungent reek of mothballs — anyone who has travelled in a camphor-run vehicle for a few hours is recognizable for many days to come.

Merchandise is floated down the rivers on improvised bamboo rafts. The winding roads to the forward areas are flanked by a chain of human carriers, whose strength and tenacity enable them to cover 100 miles of rough mountain path in four days. Young boys of the Transport Corps in pale, chutney-coloured uniforms, with straw-sandaled feet, stagger along under heavy yokes. Old coolies in huge hats, protection alike against sun and rain, push a small mountain of salt on their wheelbarrows, tiny Chinese tots become charcoal porters, cows carry coal.

The power and endurance of the Chinese is proverbial; troops live for days on end exposed to extremes of cold and heat, sustained by the minimum of rice. When a soldier falls ill, he is the most long-suffering of patients. I saw men, all but dead of relapsing fever one day, who three days later had given up their beds to more deserving cases.

The farmer has learnt the habit of complete frugality. In addition to his bowls of rice, he allows himself only a few dice of chopped pork every month. He makes his own oil for the lamp from rape seed, and for fuel, instead of using charcoal, he burns dried grass. Accustomed to disaster, the average Chinese does not worry about his future prospects. Used to suffering, he takes a fatalistic view of personal tragedies. No bad news can lower his spirits for long.

As soon as the floods, which have washed away his toil of years, have subsided, he starts to work afresh. The rebuilding of a bombed town is begun almost as soon as the 'raiders past' sirens have sounded. This stoic power of resistance constitutes a formidable threat to the Japanese invader. Such is the scale of the country that a regular army of 6,000,000 Chinese operates behind the enemy lines. The Japanese have learnt, to their chagrin, that the Frenchman spoke wisely when he said that China was not so much a country as a 'geographical expression'.

Throughout Free China, for thousands of square miles, the villages resemble one another in all the essentials. Houses are dark, smoky, with grey walls and black tiled roofs; the inhabitants, wearing the invariable indigo-dyed cloth that fades through so many varieties of blue to pale grey, move about their business in an inextricable confusion of scraggy chickens, pigs, pye-dogs and babies. The walls of old temples are somewhat unaesthetically decorated with stencilled heads of the Generalissimo. In tea-houses of bamboo matting, the tea-drinkers smoke pipes three feet long, while they listen to the itinerant professional story-teller — a precocious youth who accentuates his points with blood-curdling grimaces and a nerve-shattering clash of cymbals.

In contrast to the darkness and penetrating odours of the village streets, the natural scenery of the country is of an extraordinary grandeur and richness. Fantastic mountains, like upturned stalactites, half-veiled in mist; gigantic waterfalls; hillsides covered with fronds of bamboo or with wild azaleas; ascending pale green steps of ricefields, as eloquent as a flight of steps at Versailles; wild white roses rambling in bridal bouquets alongside a stream, or climbing over a tree sixty feet high; sweet-smelling camphor groves and jasmine — these are the natural luxuries of the poor, in a country vastly over-populated, little industrialized, essentially peace-loving, and seldom left in peace.

Part XII: Going West, 1944

Tuesday, June 20th, Chungking

So it seems that I am to leave tomorrow. But I must not be too certain, for any minute the telephone may ring with a message that Dr Kung's monetary advisor has decided to take all the seats in tomorrow's plane.

Wednesday, June 21st

Last night I bid a really deeply affectionate and grateful farewell to the Seymours, whom I have come to admire and love. It was dawn, and our highly-perched house — the dark, ugly little villa that had been my haven — was obliterated by a cloud — visibility zero — when Shu and Wong, the always funny, always smiling, Chinese servants waved me good-bye. Stanley Smith heroically got up to accompany me across the flooded canal to the airport. The daylight strengthened, but the mountains were still invisible as doggedly we waited for news of a 'take-off'. At length word came through that our aircraft was grounded at Chengtu, unable to leave until advised of better visibility. It was tough to have a six-hour wait before facing the perils of the 'Hump'. However, I enjoyed talking to Stanley. He is convinced we should not break with China, that we should trade with her, but that a different sociological attitude must be adopted. The slogans of praise for 'Brave Little China' have made every laundryman believe he is a hero. England and America have already given enormous aid, but the Chinese, instinctively greedy, always clamour for more. No Chinese knows when to stop his demands. But the moment has now come when we should give only for some specific purpose: the 'Aid to China' should provide aeroplanes to bring in medicine, clothes and other necessities, and should be distributed through honest sources instead of being squandered in graft. Stanley feels the only saving of this country after the war is to have a revolution. He considers that Chiang is in the grip of gangsters, that the Kung racket has been too strong for him, and that Madame Chiang is an opportunist adventuress without the real good of China at heart.

At last the crowd of fellow would-be passengers moved excitedly. The aeroplane had now left Chengtu, would be here in an hour. Meanwhile, the clouds were darker and lower as the rain fell like string. Soon we could hear, but not see, an aircraft as it circled above the cloud-enveloped mountains. The roar of engines became deafening as we watched one of the most spectacular landings ever attempted. A vast pale-grey shadow suddenly appeared through the mist between the mountain gorges and the wires stretching across the river. Within fifty feet of the landing strip the shadow turned to substance as, with a torrential splashing, the aircraft landed dead straight on the runway. The passengers and pilot came out bland and smiling, but I should have needed hospital aid if I had been *parti* to such a dangerous feat. As it was, the take-off was not going to be much fun, although informers said it would be less perilous than the arrival.

Grateful to Stanley for all his help, his patience and enthusiasm, I bid him good-bye. In the downpour about thirty of us made our way towards the aircraft. At the take-off my hands trembled. Soon our heads were bumped on the metal ceiling, then we were sprawling on the floor. A pink-faced American next to me said, 'Oh boy, I wish we'd bump some more. Oh boy, it's exciting.' The Chinese were immediately sick. I tried to take my mind off my terror by eating an egg sandwich, but this became sawdust in my mouth. I tried to read — couldn't: tried to sleep — couldn't.

As if a lantern slide were quickly changed outside the porthole, the blank of blind flying ceased, and we were over harsh, clear mountains. Then the lantern slide changed to a scene of gentian blue, yellow and silver clouds with a jagged mountain floor below. The 'Hump', treacherous and merciless as it was, has a grandiose, Wagnerian beauty.

Nevertheless, it was with a sense of relief that we arrived at Din Jan for refuelling and sandwiches. The Indian atmosphere, foetid and tropical, soothed one: the smells, so peppery, curry-flavoured and spiced, were enticing.

Evening had turned to night when the aircraft took off again. We flew for an unconscionable time. All the passengers were almost crying with exhaustion when, at longest last, we flew towards some distant lights, and we realized the pilot had located our goal. At last we were back in Calcutta: as we drove along familiar roads to my home from home, I felt I had come out of jail or was freed from the Gestapo. India! Civilization! Comfort!

CONVERSATIONS IN INDIA

Thursday, June 29th, Calcutta

At dinner Casey told us of a letter he'd had from General Ismay describing the suspense in England before 'D Day'. At the last moment they'd had to postpone the invasion on account of the weather. This was a terrible thing to have had to do. 'For Christ's sake,' said the men, all keyed up to go. But, even after the delay, the enemy had been taken by surprise, and the casualties were fifteen per cent less than expected. On the night before the great day everyone terribly strung up — some facetious — but 'one person — you can guess who!' — was particularly surly and difficult. I could visualize Churchill's mood.

Sunday, July 9th, Delhi

The great heat: everyone wringing out their handkerchiefs: everything dead-looking: the gardens dried up. The Viceroy's house was half-shut, and all Europeans who remained appeared pale and much thinner. The heat, it seems, has been like a plague. Sat next the Viceroy at dinner: this rather a strain as small talk comes to Wavell with difficulty. I feel sorry for the good man not being able to converse, for he is apt to be as awkward and floundering when with his son (than whom there is no one in the world he loves more) as he is with idiotic strangers. Wavell said he thought the invasion in Normandy had gone well in spite of appalling luck of having one month of foul weather since 'D Day'; that after a slow start there might be a run forward any time now. The flying bombs on London were causing minor havoc. One bomb fell on the Guards' chapel during a Sunday morning service and killed most of the congregation. One of the dead was Boy le Bas's sister. Gwen, an enchanting, flower-like girl, with periwinkle eyes, was a star of prettiness and sweetness during my Harrow and Cambridge days.

Was arranging to leave for Simla when a chit arrived saying the Viceroy wanted to see me to talk about China. Went to his almost freezing study with a few pencilled notes. Wavell asked me to show him our route on the map. After that he was not interested in my gabbling, for it all came under the same heading — hopelessness. He said, 'I've been under no delusion about China for the last three years, but couldn't say anything.' Wavell told me he was getting his staff to work out a comparison between the resources of India and China: he feels that India is much the better bet as a proposition. Had hoped for a long and illuminating discourse from HE: but he was busy and, after a slight reference to the Generalissimo's love affair (Wavell said a meeting was called at which it was decided that all mention of it must be censored, and that the two Chiangs agree on one point — they both deny the existence of a romance), I was out of the room and back in an atmosphere that, in comparison, felt like the orchid house.

Finished the day in an air-conditioned cinema where the temperature was too great a contrast to the appalling heat of the day. This was my first visit to the pictures since being away, and I was very moved by the newsreels of 'D Day' and overcome with nostalgia for home. The smiles of the men taken before the start of the invasion were charming, spontaneous and moving. One young man screwed up his nose as he smiled — one's heart missed a beat. Subsequently, the real horror of the undertaking was most graphically shown.

A telegram from home saying Pelham Place had been knocked about by a flying bomb.

Thursday, July 13th, Simla

When we woke there was a hurry to get out of the train which had arrived at the base of the mountains. Here we must change to the motor rail — a toy train that would chug its way in coils up the mountainside. First stop at 2,000 feet, another at 4,000 and, eventually, at 6,000 feet we were at the foot of the Viceregal Lodge and garden, and were welcomed by rickshaw attendants dressed in scarlet and indigo blue. How pleasant, after the drab dustiness of Delhi, to breathe in the crisp mountain air and the smell of healthy moss, ferns and palms. A brisk canter up steep asphalt drives and we were presented with the surprising spectacle of a huge, grey stone castle. It was, I believe, built by a former viceroy, Lord Minto, in the Scottish style by an Indian architect who had never left his country. The result is most bizarre. We were back among the faded snapshots of 1895: house-party groups on the porch steps and croquet on the lawn. Even the vegetation with Virginia creepers winding up stone pillars and iron staircases, and cascades of Dorothy Perkins' ramblers gambolling high among the tallest pine trees, seemed to belong to the past. The well-trimmed garden beds were planted with stiff, formal salvias in formations of military precision. Old-fashioned, starch-white wooden garden seats were set against vast hillocks of harsh pink hydrangeas. Everything was damp, lush and flourishing (the rain pours gently most nights of this month). Against this green the towering, blue Himalayas looked rather Scottish.

Inside the castle all styles were incorporated in a series of rooms that gave out of a vast baronial, balconied hall; each room was panelled and well appointed, but all the proportions were at fault, and so, too, the texture of furniture and furnishing. The eye was assailed by jaundice colours. This was a quaint monument to near-luxury that counted little in taste and charm.

Yet the comfort was almost unique in the war-torn world today: fires were crackling healthily in the grates, flowers stood stiffly arranged in ugly vases on occasional tables, and desks were well stocked with thick, crested writing paper. With as many servants and as much food and drink as we could contend with, no one, except the servants, was impressed.

Most of those enjoying the amenities of the viceregal hydro were recuperating from long ordeals in the jungle, or were recently discharged from hospital to start life again, minus a limb or a sound body. For Simla is not only a retreat from the heat of the plains but has become a great resuscitation and leave-centre, and most of its population is now wearing hospital clothes. Wandering about the garden with Peter Coats, the comptroller, he eulogized Wavell's campaign in North Africa; with totally inadequate forces and only a few tanks and small supplies at his disposal, the brilliance of his feat would be appreciated by historians.

We lamented Churchill's dislike of Wavell: this had started with Churchill's jealousy after the Sidi Barrani campaign. Churchill said Wavell was like the president of a seaside golf club, and criticized him harshly in front of President Roosevelt in Washington.

Unexpectedly, we came across George Abell, Wavell's Second Secretary. He said what a great man his master was. There was nothing small in his brain: he couldn't take in petty details, and only thought in broad terms: it was wonderful to work with someone like that. He said Wavell had a great gift for writing simple English, and that his letter, written to the King after he had been out here six months, was one of the most illuminating, informed, spontaneous and vital documents the monarch could ever have received.

Discussing Gandhi's latest proposals, Abell said they were just a further attempt to blackmail his enemies, and that Wavell considers his latest utterances are those of a dying man. Gandhi was only released from prison because they did not wish him to die in captivity, but the doctor's reports seem to have been unnecessarily pessimistic, and many people now said there was little chance of his dying soon. Yet his recent behaviour had been so pettifogging that even his supporters were slightly ashamed. Abell said that Gandhi with his people was like a clergyman with spinsters.

Returning to the front of the house we joined the Wavells playing golf-croquet. Lady Wavell full of smiles, sighs, tired, untidy, and wearing a pair of really bad shoes, was coy at successfully holing out with two long putts. Sycophantic laughter from the entourage. The Viceroy, gauche and clumsy, pivoted like a top when he missed a shot.

At dinner I got HE again. Drew him on to talk of the theatre, and for a while his enthusiasm was kindled. He laughed rather wryly about certain anachronisms in plays and films, and told me about an American movie of Mary, Queen of Scots, in which a warder entered, saying, 'You're for the block, Madam.' Praising Herbert Tree, he said that he was responsible for putting Shakespeare back on the stage. He liked Tree's wit. Returning an appallingly bad play submitted by some amateur, he wrote, 'My dear sir, I have only just now found time to read your play. My dear sir!' At a rehearsal Tree, directing, had said, 'Now, ladies — a little more virginity.' I remarked that it was sad that his brother, Max Beerbohm, had become recently such a querulous old man, complaining on the radio of today's vulgarity and the way the world was going. Wavell said, 'I expect in thirty or forty years you will be deploring the lowering of standards. I can hear you, as a man of seventy, regretting these old times when you sat having dinner here in a panelled room.'

The radio news told us of more flying bombs on London, and of deep shelters being opened; I felt how remote, and how horribly safe, we were here; yet, in spite of the Victorian comforts, this life is stifling and inhibiting except for the shortest of rest cures. I know that all of us are imagining the horrors that are taking place at home, and yet we can do nothing about it except to be busy on the job. Early bed (10 o'clock) a solace for the entire household.

AMERICAN STORM TROOPERS

Saturday, July 22nd

Four American storm troopers, Merrills Marauders, came to my sitting-room to be interviewed. Before the war one was a truck driver, another a pin-setter in a bowling alley, a third would have become a farmer only he was too young. They have just been flown out of Mytchima after four and a half months behind the lines. The battalion had fought sixteen engagements, but they had kept up the pace too long. They lost quite a lot of men, mostly through typhus: only those with a strong enough will to live had pulled through. Meanwhile, they were not fit to be sent back yet, were enjoying their leave — quietly — not overdoing things, preferring to talk leisurely 'like gentlemen', enjoying just a drink or two.

They were startlingly frank, without mental reservations or shyness, describing how frightened they had been. 'When a dog got loose behind the bushes I thought it was a Jap, and was much more scared then than, when crossing a river, a sniper was after me.' At night, if a bird whistled, a monkey screamed or the slightest sound was made, they were all wide awake. They never expected more than four hours of sleep; the first thing to do each morning, before eating, was to pack belongings, to be able to take off at a second's notice.

I asked if they felt apprehensive of getting ill and being a liability to their fellows. 'No, there's a lot of things that could happen you don't think about. But you think about killing Japs. It's important to kill them because, if you kill them, they can't kill you; and, incidentally, we fill them plenty full of bullets.' A cheery, apple-faced boy re-enacted, in graphic mime, an unexpected encounter with a Jap, who poked his head around a tree only five yards away. The Jap's rifle was hanging upside down under his raincoat. 'It would have taken him half an hour to get it into position, so he just smiled at me while I threw a grenade at him.'

They talked about the monotony of the rations, dropped with great precision. But sometimes they were too near the Japs for their positions to be given away by a dropping, and then they went three days on end without food. Occasionally their greatest delicacy, doughnuts, were dropped: generally they were as hard as grenades, even after being soaked a day in water. 'But they were good enough to eat!' These little-more-than-boys had outwalked their Missouri mules with sixty-five-pound packs on their back: the animals fell flat on their stomachs, with outstretched legs — 'Then we had to shoot 'em, and before leaving, we'd cut off a lump of flesh and cook it later. It was good enough until someone mentioned that we were eating horseflesh, then I'd have to spit it out, and later start over again.'

One, a pale, green-faced young man, seemed slightly jittery; he confided that the sight of some of his friends bayoneted by the Japs had left an indelible mark upon him. He had left his buddy in a trench for only a few moments; when he came back, 'he saw something he didn't like seeing'. 'My buddy had been bayoneted in the chest, and he hadn't a shirt on.' He seemed quite cynical about the people at home. 'They are not interested in us out here; they can't be bothered with the war in Burma — it's too remote — they are busy making fifteen dollars a day, and that's enough for them.'

The driver talked about prayer. 'I never believed in that stuff before — but I do now.' The pin-setter said he had prayed in every fox-hole, and that most of the guys he knew prayed for hours on end.

These chaps from the Middle West fitted into this Kiplingesque scene here with great ease of manner. They were extraordinarily easy to converse with, and much more communicative than the equivalent BORS. America can certainly produce a good brand of democracy.

I was greedily availing myself of the secretarial services of Mr Bannergee, and trying to finish some articles before leaving, when Peter Coats sent up a note saying word had come through that, as I had requested, it will be possible for me to go home via the United States: moreover, I can leave as soon as possible. The blood ran quicker in my veins: suddenly I became restless and excitable. Is it possible that, after all, I shall see my New York friends again?

GOOD-BYE TO WAVELL

Have just bid good-bye to Wavell. It was rather a moving little scene. This fine man is incapable of glib sentences. But somehow he wanted to show that, although we are so many poles apart, there is something in each of us that responds to the other. We have a mutual admiration for one another, and the fact that he approves of me makes me inordinately proud. I find Wavell has a genius for cutting through the façades, and seeing people as they really are, in spite of their shyness, their alibis, and their sometimes false presentation of themselves.

As for him, although his personality is not particularly vivid or spell-binding, he is deeply impressive. He never tries to charm or hypnotize, but cannot help emanating integrity of mind, directness of purpose and unaffected simplicity of style. Indians, who are always quick to note the dominant characteristics of Englishmen, are the first to appreciate the golden goodness of Wavell. They know that he is entirely devoid of malice, deceit or guile, that he is eminently fair, and, above all things, sincere.

To be complimented by him is a reward well worthwhile. For in his dry and somewhat melancholy voice, and talking quietly, without moving his lips, and in a tone that is deep and easy to listen to, he says nothing that is banal. His thoughts are never ready-made, and his conversation is carefully chosen. Literature and poetry mean much to him. At dinner at Emerald Cunard's one night he recited extemporaneously Browning and Dowson at great length.

He is a taciturn man, and can be as silent in the mess as on purely social occasions. But his silences are completely unself-conscious. He has extraordinary powers of concentration: when he is thinking it is a full-time, absorbing occupation, and he is oblivious of the world. I have sometimes tried to interrupt his thoughts, and only succeeded in realizing how foolish was the attempt. Occasionally the wife of some wretched official, sitting next to him at a meal, tries frantically, but in vain, to trap him into a conversation. The woman becomes distraught. Yet, if he is interested, he can become voluble.

Wavell has just given me, as a parting present, a dedicated copy of an anthology of all the poems he knows by heart. The Wavells have accepted me almost as one of their family, and my heart is full of gratitude and friendliness for each and all of the remarkable brood. But it is the father who is on a monumental scale: merely watching him be his simple, ordinary self has been an experience which I hope may have taught me a bit about greatness.

A Hungarian doctor got on to the bus with me. He had heard about my activities, knew I had been ill with dengue fever in Calcutta and had stayed so many weeks in Delhi. He said, 'No doubt you've realized how small a country India is. There are millions of Indians, but there is one set that knows everything about each other, and if you go to one city they know all about you in another.' While waiting for our aircraft he suggested we drink tea and asked the boy that it should be weak. The tea arrived very strong. 'Could we have extra hot water?' 'No, sir,' the boy laughed. 'It's nice and strong now, isn't it? If we keep it standing it will get weaker, won't it?' 'Yes,' the boy laughed, and started vigorously to stir the pot with a spoon. 'You're stirring it so that it gets weaker, are you?' 'Yes, Sahib,' laughed the boy. The doctor told me, 'You go into a shop and ask, "Are these chocolates old — nice old stale ones?" "Yes, Sahib." "Is this nice fresh port wine — quite new wine?" "Oh, yes, Sahib!"'

Thursday, July 27th, Karachi

Most of the air station was flooded out: scraggy Indians waded up to their knees, jeeps drove through waves of *café au lait*, the runway had become a lake, silver flying fish were marooned by the dozen on the dunes or floating on the sea and a whole area of tents was under water.

We were at an hour's call, and must not wander from the precincts. Boredom acute. At one point during the day we scrambled to be weighed in, filled in forms; but this activity proved a false alarm: floods had not subsided.

Next morning our chances were good, for other aircraft took off. Again we filled in forms, and were given a rather jolly briefing in case of ditching. 'Appoint a captain for each dinghy and do everything he says: don't be wasteful with your water ration for there's no knowing how long it might have to last! In fact, you must clean your teeth in it, swill it around the mouth for a long time, and eventually drink it! Never get despondent, for help will come eventually, and it's worth going to where you're all going (to the US) for there's a nice ice-cold drink there awaiting you. Now, about your Mae West. Put it on just like a halter, and you know which end of a horse that goes on. And another thing: leave plenty of room to spare under the arms and crotch, for when the thing inflates itself it becomes much tighter and may damage you. You don't want to take any risks: you don't want to go where you're going (to America) with anything wrong with the crotch!'

About a dozen of us trooped into a vast DC46: twin engines: backs to the wall bucket seats: as upholstered as a biscuit tin. Bisbee and myself the only English, all the others Americans; some Merrills Marauders — they were still yellow-complexioned as a result of the atapane they had taken against malaria. One rawboned chap from Alabama, with a tremendous drawl, was now going home having done the flight over the 'Hump' fifty times.

A blind take-off from the still water-logged runway. When, at last, the windows cleared of *café au lait* spray, we discovered we were in the air.

If lucky, it will take us a week to get to Miami. We are not doing the shorter northern route through Casablanca and the Azores, but across Africa from Aden to Ascension Island, then to Brazil, Trinidad and Miami. But time does not mean much when one is in this trance of unreality.

Yes! If lucky! But, it seemed we were not to be — to start off with. After flying over the sea for one and a half hours we were directed to return. The weather had closed in at Missouri. We flew back in this tin hades of a prison to arrive where, four hours ago, we had started.

The life on the air station has become a Kafkaish reiteration of doing once more what one had hoped to have done for the last time. Always more forms to be filled in, more cards for billeting, more tickets for meals.

AIRBORNE AT LAST

After two days of waiting to leave Karachi, we all looked a good deal older, dirtier, and more exhausted. I congratulated myself that my experiences in China had made me somewhat immune to further irritations; nevertheless, it wasn't enjoyable to be called at last into the plane, go back to our familiar buckets, backs to the wall, to be locked in, take position for the run, and then remain while the fuselage lights were merely switched on and off. Eventually, we taxied back to our starting point: 'Something wrong with the feathering of the air screws,' the pilot explained. We trooped out again, hung around, then got into the aircraft once more. Another false alarm. The pilot said, 'Missouri closed down.' After three false starts we were sent to our beds, and I, for one, was rather thankful not to have to spend that night in the aircraft. But ten minutes after undressing word came round that, after all, we were to take off at midnight.

The chill metal floor of the aircraft was covered with sleeping bodies sprawled out on most of the available space. After a couple of hours of reading sitting upright, I dossed down under my coat, my head on a familiar friend, my peacetime 'week-end' bag. It was pleasant to see daylight come through the windows when I turned over on the other painful hip to remain prone until told to fasten ourselves in. Missouri visibility was bad: rockets were sent up in the air for us. Three times we circled the field: we twice overshot the mark. Eventually we landed.

At Aden, 'the vestibule of the orient', we said good-bye to the chalky and sultry whiteness of India. Now below us was Africa, with palm trees, mud, marabouts and camels.

The noise of the aircraft makes one feel highly strung, and tears stream when one reads an emotional book. It is curious how, in spite of the volume of noise of the four engines, one hears every additional sound — the click of a playing-card slammed down, the metal ping as someone hits his head against the ceiling of the fuselage, the nasal voices of the passengers shouting to one another. I drifted into a sort of coma; no day had any particular beginning or end. We slept in the aircraft at all times of day and night. We landed at various anonymous-looking American airports scattered about Africa, to be bustled into lorries, to drink a gut-warming cup of coffee in the mess, and, in double quick time, be herded back into the aircraft.

After a day's flight in a sunny sky, evening clouds caused such 'disturbance' that even some of the huskies vomited, I contracted a cold, and everyone looked worse for wear. When a generator burst itself out a padre from Utah said the delay was a blessing as most of the boys could do with a night's sleep. It was a help to get the long growth of beard off one's face, and the coating off one's teeth.

We took off. Landed. Took off again: no idea of the time: once I calculated it would be about 4 o'clock in the afternoon, and discovered it was 10.30 in the morning. Sometimes we seemed to endure three nights in one. For instance, after an early dinner at Karno, I had gone into the deepest sleep, to be awakened five hours later. We took offin the darkness; and again I slept. After another four hours, we arrived in the dark at Accra.

Eventually we arrived at the great West African terminal for America. We had achieved half our journey. Here we were to change planes, but how long we might wait nobody knew.

I enjoyed watching the Americans on the station: they are without inhibitions, shyness or modesty; they walk about naked; their latrines are communal and are used as meccas for gossip; if there should be a door they will never shut it. They live in their shop window, letting all the world see their customs, their fears and their hustle. They are 'machine-made' in their mental neatness and physical precision. They shave and dress with such ease and nonchalance. They do not seem to contaminate the gum they chew. The clothes they wear never really become part of them and are perpetually being sent to the laundry; I enjoy their luxury; they are for ever buying new garments and presents and are all very bejewelled, with bracelets, shining watch straps, and enormous signet rings on both hands. Why is it that one always sees the American GI at the moment he takes his first puff at a cigarette — the British Tommy when he is sucking at a discoloured fag end?

Now for the last hop. We flew seven hours through the night, and then, in the early morning sunlight, saw Ascension Island below. The British gave up the idea of ever being able to make this into a landing base, but the American engineers, after dynamiting thousands of tons of rock, have succeeded in manufacturing a magnificent artificial runway. But I felt sorry for the lonely GIs who came out to gossip with us during our breakfast and refuelling interval and who are based on this forlorn island, where not a blade of grass grows. Cheerfully we embarked for another seven-hour hop; the sun moved from one side of the clouds to the other. After covering 2,500 miles we arrived at Natal; an enormous airport, again wonderfully engineered by the Americans, with white starched *décolleté* sailors and every sort of pilot, including RAF and Brazilians. Although the airport is 100 per cent American, a little of Brazil had infiltrated itself: the car driver wore a suit of ice-cream pink, the waiters spoke Portuguese, and the coffee was exceptionally good. We lined up for cafeteria meals, bought things from the PX. One pilot told me he had spent 300 dollars on trash gifts.

Belem, where the full moon shone on tropical trees and an airless night, consisted, for us, merely of a compound where Americans behaved typically, having shower baths, going to the movies and spending the minimum time over meals. Again we started off. Although my memory is hazy, I do not think we called anywhere after Puerto Rico. These names sound romantic, but the landings are impersonal: we merely circle a field, our ears buzz and hurt, and we 'b'rump' down. The aircraft becomes an oven of heat before we get out to queue for a sandwich, presently returning to the furnace for the next take-off.

BLACKPOOL OF FLORIDA

Miami

The last five hours of the trip before arriving at Miami were the slowest of all, and the bucket seat became intolerably hard. Too exhausted to read, I looked out of the window at the sea and skyscapes. The islands of rock, that one flies over before coming to Florida, were like a Leonardo background. The sea, so extraordinarily clear that one could see to the bottom, was of every different blue and pale green with yellow and apricot streaks reflected from the sky.

One hour and a half to go. Now the clouds, lit on one side by the evening sun, were like snow mountains: they looked quite solid, and indeed, as we flew through them, we felt they were.

The joy on my fellow passengers' faces as they landed was a pleasure to watch. 'Oh boy! I've not seen anything as good as that for years!'

But the freedom of arrival did not start immediately: many more queues, a series of vigorous investigations, and then a short lecture which impressed me: 'A good many of you chaps have seen extraordinary things, and your families will want to hear about them. Don't be unduly secretive. Tell them the names of the places that have appeared in the news; but if you've made an escape, and others are likely to try to get away by the same means, don't confide in your closest friend because, doubtless, he has a friend who writes radio scripts. And, men, don't criticize your Allies. It doesn't help any, and there's plenty of time for that after the war.'

The queries and examinations to which we now had to submit were lengthy and exasperating.

At 'Movements' a cheery, moon-faced official, whose sebaceous glands were working overtime, cracked his knuckles and said, 'You want to hop on to New York? I think we can get you on a plane tonight!' My fatigue left me instantly.

But it was not to be! Later, a gorgonzola-complexioned Jeremiah pronounced that my 'order' was not for an 'army' line. 'You'll have to get priority from Washington and go commercial.' I argued, and lied in my teeth. I pretended that I was the most I of Ps; but I didn't look very 'I', with five days' growth of beard. Eventually I saw it was no good: nothing to be done until tomorrow at any rate: disappointed, I must wait the night in Miami. 'Where are you staying?' 'I don't know.' 'Well, you'll never find a room at this hour of the night.'

The big hotels were all taken over by the Navy, and the lesser-known places to which the flea-bitten taxi-driver took me were not particularly inviting. Even so, with my unshaven chin and hobo clothes, I was seen as a delinquent, and not at all welcomed at the desk of several rooming houses. Yes, *I* knew my clothes stank; I was sick of every part of myself, and yet couldn't escape. I became desperate, highly critical, and somewhat hysterical. A negro, with grey stubble on his chin, taking me to a room in an evil-smelling hotel said, 'Are you French?' 'Why?' "Cos, Mister, there are some French people in dis hotel who want to talk to *anyone* who can speak French.'

Later I walked out from my furnace cell to buy an evening newspaper. The lights were blinding! Shop windows bursting with spot-lit attractions! Motor-cars had headlights! Pumps were filled with 'gasoline'! Everything appeared so affluent. An old woman selling so many shiny, fat magazines and such vast, pulpy newspapers, wore a flowered silk dress that an English countess would prize for a garden party.

The women on the 'sidewalks' wore their dyed, crimped-up hair piled on top of their heads, like Marie Antoinette, the whole edifice crowned with cotton flowers, but with a long page-boy mass hanging down their back. Their brilliantly-coloured skirts were as short as tutus; their lips, from which a cigarette hung, were monstrously enlarged (in imitation of Joan Crawford) like tattooed scarlet butterflies. This Constantin Guys parade had the air of an impromptu, horrific fancy-dress party. Old white trash sat on their porches delaying the torture of retiring to an airless bedroom. Yes, this was Miami all right

— the Blackpool of Florida! For me, Miami has always been the end of all hellholes, the final stronghold of vulgarity. But Miami, out of season and in wartime! Why had I come all this way?

To see New York again, of course. Early next morning I called at several offices about the 'priority'. I knew it was as well not to rely solely on getting action from the man in San Francisco to whom I had wired last night. At one office a sympathetic, faceless simpleton called me a 'victim of circumstances'. 'You should have been allowed to travel by army plane last night! But go to Colonel Letherbee's office. Surely you'll get on one tonight.' My heart jumped with expectation. Colonel Letherbee, deeply exasperated and looking like a piece of grey, chewed-up string, was doleful. He could give me priority to go by commercial airline only if the Office of Information wanted me in New York. He put a call through. It was dramatic. The man we wanted was in Washington — could be tracked there. When eventually reached, he told me it was impossible for him to give priority. 'But,' I said, 'this gentleman here can give it to me with your consent.' The receiver changed hands: my heart was now in my mouth. I obtained the priority, paid happily for the ticket, and was all set to leave at 8 o'clock tonight.

To enter a comfortable commercial aircraft with upholstered seats and walls padded against sound was like returning to the womb. The lack of noise was balm to the nerves. This was the first time for months that I was not frightened in the air. A wonderful night of full moon. A great number of stops, with Washington as the last of them. I was too keyed-up to sleep, and enjoyed reading dozens of magazines. As the sky turned pale, we came to New York.

FRIENDS AND MEMORIES IN NEW YORK

August 4th, New York

I was so pleased to arrive that even those pathetic wooden shacks that we passed in the bus from La Guardia field seemed to smile in welcome.

New York, bathed in a lightless, murky haze, was just beginning to wake. The news sellers were already at their kiosks, and radios were playing setting-up exercises in the honeycomb apartment blocks.

As the bus roared into the heart of the city, more memories, oddly in contrast to the experiences of the last five years, came creeping back again. I remembered much of my Manhattan past, from the earliest visit when I arrived, unknown, with sixty pounds and, by degrees, made my first New York friends, and pocketed my first cheque. I remembered those early plays, the popular tunes, the love affairs. Here were so many familiar milestones to remind me of forgotten frivolities and phases of work. Here was the studio where I'd taken my first advertising photographs, and here the art stores where I bought supplies. Here on 3rd Avenue my favourite florist, and here the cafeteria where, at one time, a group of English used to forgather for lunch; here again the dusty pigeons; the one-way streets, the seldom-green light, and then, at last, the Waldorf, where so many winters had been spent. Curiously, those early days seemed to be innocent of effort.

But an unfamiliar face regarded me from the reception desk. 'What was my name? What did I want? The hotel was booked solid.' Eventually I prevailed upon the clerk to allow me to have a bath and a shave.

I felt strangely self-conscious when I essayed out on to the streets and arrived at my favourite haunt of old times, the Colony, for lunch. Margaret Case, most loyal of friends, was standing erect waiting for me. She appeared thinner and older, but her voice had acquired a softness and a sympathy. Perhaps due to sudden exhaustion, or delayed reaction, I suddenly felt that so much had happened while I had been away — why, even the old-fashioned Colony had been re-decorated — that I could not compete with these self-assured men, so full of life and vigour, and the women wearing new clothes, and somehow looking so different in hats like platters strewn with flowers. (I noticed, too, that women exuded a delicious aroma of scent: since the war this luxury had been obsolete in England.) Margaret was following the bandwagon and, with her fragrance and rose-laden platter, was part of the scene. But I hung back as if, suddenly, I had become very old. Had the elderly Rip Van Winkle lost his touch?

Yet if I indulge in self-pity like this, how would they react — the prisoners of war, the men from the jungle or from a hundred isolated outposts? After years of separation from the life they knew, how could they hope to pick up, when they returned, a thread of continuity?

Margaret, quiet and sympathetic, helped me to sit up and take notice of the new world around me. I had that cold drink that we had all promised ourselves, and it encouraged me to talk of the years between. The war has given me a great jolt. It has pitchforked me out of my self-made rut into all sorts of different worlds. Some of the experiences have been a bit unpleasant, but, on the whole, I have been more than fortunate. Not only have I survived with no injury, but my work has taken me to all sorts of places that I would never have known. All sorts of people have appeared in my orbit, all sorts of new horizons have opened, and I have been given new interests. Will I go back into the same old rut?

REX WHISTLER

On Sunday, on my way to rest and swim at the Connecticut house of my friends, Natascha and Jack Wilson, the thoroughfares were filled with cars dashing so smoothly to the overpopulated countryside. Sexy, apricot-coloured husbands with their arrogant wives, their dyed hair blowing in the wind, paid no attention to the nest-full of children sucking goodies in the back of the car. Everyone seemed so independent and carefree, so self-assured in taking so much luxury for granted. The gargantuan Sunday joint we enjoyed would have used up a six months' ration ticket book at home.

But talk at lunch was not about the war, but of 'summer, theatre' and the various Broadway stars in circuit near by. Later with coffee, we were looking through Jack's remarkable collection of theatrical scrapbooks when we came across a photograph of Geoffrey Nares. Like so many other friends he would never return from the war. The pages were turned to reveal Rex Whistler's delightful designs for *Victoria Regina*. 'Oh yes,' remarked Jack, 'Rex — that's another one of our friends killed!' I let out a cry. 'It *cant* be true! When? How?' Jack looked aghast. 'I'm *sure* I saw it in the papers. Soon after the Normandy landings.' I did not need any further corroboration. I *knew* it was true! Somehow, instinct told me that Rex would be killed. There was something so indefinite and vague about him the last time he came on leave and stayed in my London house. He didn't know what he would do after the war: he didn't even know what to do with his leave. I feel somehow that people with a definite purpose are more apt to survive that awful haphazard shell ... 'Of course Rex is dead and I'm alive. It's so bloody unfair! I've been messing about doing a rotten, piddling little job that's only an alibi. I'm not capable of making any real effort as Rex has done.' I started to bellow. I was no longer in China among kindly strangers with whom one must behave with circumspection. I was with old friends. My nerves, long pent up, suddenly snapped. Here there was no necessity to keep a curb on my emotions. I blubbed. Jack and Natascha were naturally deeply upset by my tears, lamentations and hysterical cries of selfcondemnation.

I remembered the evening Rex and I had spent together just before war was declared. We were sitting on his balcony in Regent's Park: Rex had already enlisted, and said he knew he had the capabilities of being a soldier, and that to accept any other job would be impossible. He made, in fact, an extremely capable officer, much beloved by his men in the Welsh Guards. The timid little rabbit became a leader. All the time he was miserable, but he never complained.

Rex, a natural talent if ever there was one, would now never be able to develop the art of painting which, he said, he felt he was just beginning to learn. His work was, in fact, undergoing a great change, and he might have developed from being a decorative painter, a muralist and illustrator into another Turner. Now his potentials were cut, his lifework complete, and Rex, the person suffused with effortless charm, so romantic and youthful of appearance, with his bold, ram-like profile and pale tired eyes, would never grow old.

I wondered if Edith Olivier, nearing seventy, would survive the news. She loved him: he was everything to her — a son, a friend, her true love.

A little later in the evening Jack motored me, with Martin Manuelis and some other theatrical people, back to New York.

Jack had warned them that I was upset at hearing of the loss of a great friend; they were naturally surprised to find that almost all the way home I laughed almost as hysterically as, earlier, I had been wailing with equal lack of restraint.

However, back in my room, I again gave way. For the next few days I was utterly consumed by this sorrow.

Eventually this news from home caught up with me. After successfully landing in Normandy in his tank, Rex missed one of his men. He jumped from his tank to look for him, and was killed instantly. Rex's moonlit face now stared from an obituary notice.

A friend wrote me of how Edith's sister had broken the news. 'It was late in the evening when Edith drove back from her many duties as Mayor of Wilton to her little house in the park. She was quite fagged out after a particularly long meeting. "I'm too tired to put the car in the garage, but I'll do it later," Edith puffed. Her sister, meanwhile, had heard the news about Rex, but did not know how she could bring herself to tell poor Edith who, at this moment, looked already so white and drained of strength. "Now come and settle down in front of the fire and have some hot tea." Edith drank three cups of tea. And I put a lot of sugar in them to sustain her. Then I said how awful it was that some people received telegrams to say that their kith and kin had been killed, only later it would transpire that they were still alive — or prisoner of war — like the Colt boy. Then I told her that I'd had a wire that, alas, might be true. It was a terrible piece of news, but they had heard that Rex had been killed ...

'Edith remained as she was — staring in front of her with a glassy, glazed look. She seemed to be peering into another world. All the remaining colour went from her face. She continued to sit, wildeyed, staring and quite silent, utterly white. Then suddenly she started to become red around the neck. I thought I must move her, so I said, "Now we must go and put away the car." Edith whispered, "Yes, yes, we must put away the car." So we went to the garage, for I knew Edith could not go alone. Then I took her upstairs and laid her down on her bed. She lay, just gazing in front of her. I said, "I'm going to leave you alone for an hour." When I came back an hour later, it was only then that Edith started to cry.'

August 10th

My fatigue has entirely disappeared. A few nights of sleep were all that was needed. I am now avid to compete with New York — and start doing some work. Greedily I've taken the opportunity to make money, and have been inundated with requests for photographs and commissions to do drawings. In wartime London I reached the point where I wouldn't say 'no' to a job that would bring me in three guineas. Now, after a week in New York, I am making a small fortune. It is no hardship for me that the Ministry of Information has given me a respite and delayed my return home.

Monday, August 14th

Woken early with news of the Allied advance towards Paris. This is something that one has waited for with such longing for so long. Yet now, strangely enough, I feel ashamed that I was taking it almost for granted. Perhaps it is a question of distance, and one cannot criticize people here that have been fortunate enough to remain comparatively untouched by the maelstrom. New York restaurants, night clubs and theatres are flourishing, and people are determined to have a good time. Yet beneath the surface one sees to what an extent the war with such ruthless cruelty has spread tragedy through this vast continent. Everywhere one senses an undercurrent of anxiety if not of plain suffering; so many people whose sons are missing behave in a manner that cloaks their misery.

LIBERATION OF PARIS

Wednesday, August 23rd

Mercedes de Acosta, whose voice I have not heard for seven years, telephoned, as if the past had never existed, to tell me the news of the liberation of Paris. The Americans had surrounded the city which had then been taken from within by French patriots. Telephones buzzed all morning with more rumours — one said Pétain had been kidnapped — some were true, some false, but the fact remains that Paris has come alive!

From my hotel bedroom I could see paper flying like confetti from the tall buildings. At the Rockefeller Center ticker tape streamers were floating in the breeze like octopuses, while sheets torn from telephone books looked like doves or miniature aeroplanes.

In the sunken garden French troops were lined, tri-colours flying: speeches: songs: Lily Pons led the 'Marseillaise'. American sympathy and emotion for a country that had suffered under the Germans for these four years was shown in a spontaneous outpouring of emotion that is typical — and very moving.

Friends, new and old, want to know about the Far East, and being able to expatiate a little on this subject has given me a certain self-confidence. My fluke visit to New York has made me feel ten years younger. It has given me the assurance that, after the war, I can again earn my living.

Now the parcels are arriving from hospitable and generous people for me to take to family and friends in England. I was elated. However, Ben Thomas, my old Cambridge contemporary, and now a pillar of the British Information Service, administered an antidote when he came in to say good-bye. Ben, about seven foot tall, with 'blind-as-bat' eyes and a long, indecently pink nose, has the undiminished charm he possessed as an undergraduate, and the same gentle manner of handing out broadsides which, curiously enough, one cannot resent. 'You know you're the sort of a Britisher the BIS here wants to hide,' he said in his deep, plummy voice. 'You give the impression of being a *beau*, and the office wants to show that the British are really very like Americans.' He went on in his eighteenth-century mannered way: 'At Cambridge you told me that I knew the "right people". Well, at any rate, you seem to know them now. You are a snob.'

I replied, 'If it is snobbish to prefer people who are intelligent, amusing or beautiful, and who use their assets imaginatively, then I am a snob. But I don't like people only because they are well-born or rich, for they are often so dull and mediocre. Just imagine being closeted for three minutes straight with ...' and we simultaneously mentioned the name of an important mutual friend...

We laughed, and drank to the advent of peace. It cannot be far off now!

A NOTE TO THE READER

If you have enjoyed Cecil Beaton's Memoir enough to leave a review on **Amazon** and **Goodreads**, then we would be truly grateful.

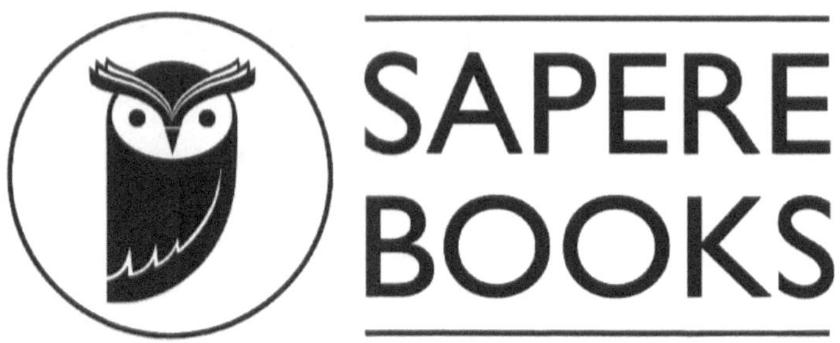